LITERARY CRITICISM
IN THE AGE OF JOHNSON

SAMUEL JOHNSON, LL.D.
AFTER THE PAINTING BY SIR JOSHUA REYNOLDS

LITERARY CRITICISM IN THE AGE OF JOHNSON

BY

A. BOSKER

SECOND EDITION, REVISED

GORDIAN PRESS
NEW YORK
1970

SECOND EDITION, REVISED, PUBLISHED 1953
REPRINTED 1970

PUBLISHED BY GORDIAN PRESS, INC.
BY ARRANGEMENT WITH
WOLTERS-NOORDHOFF NV
NETHERLANDS

Library of Congress Catalog Card Number 79-128185
SBN 87752-133-6

PREFACE

The literature of the Age of Johnson reflects the conflict between the two main factors in artistic creation, unimpassioned reason on the one side, emotion and imagination on the other. Reason had been the dominating force ever since the middle of the seventeenth century and under its powerful sway emotional and imaginative elements had been repressed, the old spontaneity of the Elizabethans had fled the domain of art, and the artistic expression of deep personal feelings had come to be looked upon with distrust. But the old romantic spirit, which had never become extinct, began to reassert itself and gradually restored the essential elements of poetic art to their proper places, so that the last decades of the eighteenth century saw the dawn of a new era, free from the restraints of common sense.

To this evolution in imaginative art the critical literature of the period offers a close parallel: in both the reaction is merely a phase of a far-reaching intellectual movement, a general revolt against the cold intellectualism of the Augustan Age. Reason and correctness, which had so long been considered by the critics as the sole arbiters of literary merit, had to yield up their authoritative position. A new conception of poetry was established, no longer based on purely rational principles, but recognizing that its primary appeal ought to be to the imagination.

It is only natural that many years were to pass before this opinion was firmly established. Rationalism in England was a strong and deep-rooted tendency, which did not at once give way when the forces that were ultimately to supplant it, began to make their influence felt. Till the very end of the century there were critics who continued to acknowledge the supremacy of common sense and tried to maintain the Augustan tradition. Thus the Age of Johnson witnessed the co-existence of two main types of criticism, one representing the old, the other illustrative of the new outlook. These two critical currents do not always move within definite bounds. Like every period of transition the time of Johnson is characterized by a good deal of vacillation and compromise, the two prevalent influences often overlap and interpenetrate.

The following essay is an attempt to trace the development of this complicated struggle. It does not pretend to give a complete survey of all the changes that the dissolution of the neo-classical creed involved. Some of them, mainly those connected with the stylistic and metrical sides of the question have scarcely been touched on. Nor has much attention been paid to philosophical writers on aesthetic theory like Shaftesbury, Hutcheson, Hume, Burke and others. Their treatises are for the greater part abstract speculations on art in general and are only indirectly related with the subject in hand.

Before embarking on my proper task I have thought it requisite to discuss the chief critical tendencies that prevailed in the latter half of the seventeenth century and the first decades of the eighteenth. Aesthetic theory during the Age of Johnson is to a large extent concerned with the same problems as confronted the preceding generations of writers. The leaders of the revolt against reason, the so-called 'romantic' critics, did not advocate an entirely new creed, but contented themselves in the main with expressing their dissatisfaction with the old. A short survey of the principal tenets of this doctrine has therefore been prefixed. For this part of the book I wish to record my special indebtedness to Professor Spingarn's introduction to his *Critical Essays of the Seventeenth Century*, Professor Paul's monograph on John Dennis, and some other works, to which due acknowledgement will be made for statements which are not the result of my own research.

It remains to express my sincere thanks to Professor P. N. U. Harting for the friendly advice he has given me during the progress of this study, and the valuable aid he has rendered me in seeing it through the press. I gratefully acknowledge the services of Mr. J. A. Falconer, M.A., reader in the University of Groningen, to whom I owe several useful suggestions for the revision of the text. Acknowledgement is also due to Mr. W. J. B. Crotch of Wembley Park (Middlesex) for looking through the MS and furnishing me with a number of corrections, to Mr. B. J. Timmer of Wageningen for doing some research for me in London and reading some of the proofs, and last of all to the staffs of the British Museum and the Library of the University of Groningen, of whom the names of Mr. Ellis of London and that of Mr. A. Nienhuis of Groningen, deserve special mention.

Groningen, January 1930. A. BOSKER.

PREFACE TO THE SECOND EDITION

The limited first edition of my *Literary Criticism in the Age of Johnson*, originally meant to serve as a doctorate thesis, was soon sold out. Owing to a continual demand for the book, especially in the United States, the publisher was requested about three years ago by Hafner Publishing Company, New York to reprint it, but as nearly all my attention was then taken up by professional duties, the preparation of a re-issue had to be put off till a more convenient time. More than twenty years have elapsed since the date of publication and much has been written on the subject ever since, chiefly by American scholars, so that the original idea of a mere reprint had to be rejected. Still, I have tried to revise the book without materially changing its construction. The division into two parts, one dealing with general critical tendencies in the Age of Johnson, the other discussing the various critics of the time separately, has therefore been retained. I am fully aware that this arrangement necessarily entails some overlapping, though I have done my best to keep it within proper bounds. In the second part, which is mainly meant to illustrate and elaborate the conclusions arrived at in the first, repetition of the same or similar dicta could not possibly be avoided. The critics of the period all harp on the same strings and do not shrink from reiterating the same statements over and over again. In many cases I might have restricted myself to a bare reference, but as several of the texts discussed are not available to the majority of students, or are at least difficult of access, I have thought it necessary to quote many illustrative passages in full. Considerations of space have often compelled me to reduce the length of others or to relegate them to the footnotes. A comparison between the two editions will show that some more attention has now been paid to writers on aesthetic theory like Burke, Hume, Hutcheson, Gerard and others, to whom there were only a few scattered references in the first edition. The discussion of Edward Young as a critic has been incorporated in a new chapter on imitation, genius and learning.

I am still as firmly convinced as I was twenty years ago that the work of the minor critics, some of whom cannot lay claim to great literary fame, must not be neglected in a book which is principally intended as a historical enquiry into the critical doctrines prevailing in the latter half of the eighteenth century and the genesis of a new critical outlook. On the other hand much of what is often of considerably more importance in itself, as for instance critical valuations of individual poets like Spenser, Milton, Pope and Thomson, and especially the many contributions to Shakespeare criticism, have been dealt with only in so far as they have direct bearing on the subject in hand. It need therefore hardly be said that no absolute estimate has been attempted of the critics that come under discussion and that an exhaustive treatment of any of them has not even been aimed at.

Neither my own further investigations in the field of eighteenth century criticism, nor the perusal of the many valuable contributions to its history that have appeared during the last twenty years, have led me to conclusions substantially different from those laid down in the concluding chapter of the first edition. The spirit of the period is mainly rationalistic, though there are distinct traces of a growing discontent with the old dogmas. It has not been my intention to stress these faint glimmerings of a romantic outlook too much, but it cannot be denied that they were there and that the critical verdicts of these 'precursors' of romanticism were not merely restatements in a milder form of the old conventional beliefs.

Obligations to earlier writers on the subject are very numerous and references to them will be found in the footnotes, where my indebtedness is duly acknowledged.

I should like to record my special gratitude to Professor T. A. Birrell of Nijmegen University, who was kind enough to look through the manuscript and who served me with many corrections and emendations, to Miss E. C. van der Gaaf of Amsterdam for the valuable help she gave me in seeing the book through the press, and to the staffs of the Bodleian Library at Oxford and the Groningen University Library.

Groningen, February 1953.   A. B.

CONTENTS

INTRODUCTION

The Chief Critical Tendencies of the Seventeenth and the Beginning of the Eighteenth Century

PART I

Some General Aspects of Literary Criticism during the Age of Johnson

PART II

The Believers in the Doctrine of Reason

PART III

The Champions of Taste

PART IV

The Revolt against the Supremacy of Reason

INTRODUCTION

The Chief Critical Tendencies of the Seventeenth
and the Beginning of the Eighteenth Century

NEO-CLASSICISM

In its main features the neo-classic creed of the Augustan Age
in England can be traced back to that of the Italian critics of the
Renaissance. The critical canons which they had evolved were
accepted as the basis of poetics in the different countries of
Western Europe. Though the national conditions of each particular
country could not but leave their own distinctive stamp, the body
of aesthetic theory was the same. There was a generally accepted
Renaissance doctrine, founded on the precepts and practice of the
ancients. The rules of Aristotle's *Poetics* and Horace's *Ars Poetica*
were its chief constituents, and together with these there was an
admixture of Platonic elements, which manifested themselves
especially in the discussions of the freedom of genius and the
imagination.

For the two main departments of poetry, the tragic and the epic
kind, Aristotle and Horace supplied a system of rules that came
to be considered as final tests of literary merit. In putting this
theory into practice the poet was to keep the Greek and Roman
models constantly before his eyes; the classic example became the
recognized standard of perfection, and the only thing that the
poet had to do was to study and imitate them.

'Immortal' Vida, whose *Ars Poetica* enjoyed such a high
reputation with both Dryden and Pope, and even with J. Warton,
one of the precursors of Romanticism in the eighteenth century,
carried this dogma to a dangerous extreme. As Professor Spingarn
observes: 'the highest originality becomes for Vida merely the
ingenious translation of passages from the classic poets' [1]. The
writer of epic poetry — to which throughout the Renaissance was
allotted the first rank among the different kinds of literary

---

[1] *History of Lit. Crit. in the Ren.*, p. 131.

1

achievement in spite of the universal reverence for Aristotle, who had considered tragedy as the highest form of the poet's art — had to follow the great masters of antiquity, Homer and Virgil. The influence of the former on the later Renaissance critics in Italy was less than that of the latter; Scaliger as well as Vida ranked the Latin poet above the Greek.

In England Aristotle's *Poetics* was first alluded to in Ascham's *Scholemaster*. In Sidney's *Apologie for Poetrie*, which was directly influenced by Italian critics, Aristotle is mentioned as an authority, at least upon the drama, though his name is mentioned in conjunction with 'common reason' [1]. First-hand knowledge of the *Poetics* was, however, not in proportion to the large number of references to it in Elizabethan critical essays [2]. Much of what was ascribed to the Greek had in reality been learned through Horatian mediation. The Roman critic was the chief master, the *Ars Poetica* the supreme guide of both critics and poets.

The reverence for classical precepts during the Elizabethan period did not act as a curb on the invention and imagination of its great writers, as it did in the hey-day of neo-classicism. On the contrary, there is in them a tendency to excess, an unbridled exuberance of fancy, which forms a striking contrast with the soberness and restraint for which the classics are noted.

The first symptoms of a neo-classic creed are to be found in Ben Jonson. Professor Spingarn calls him 'the first complete and consistent English classicist' and adds that 'his classicism differs from that of the succeeding age rather in degree than in kind' [3]. In his most important contribution to criticism, the *Discoveries*, which M. Castelain's investigations have shown to be a mere compilation of translations from various classical sources with occasional comments by himself, he advises the poet to consider Horace and Aristotle as his masters. 'Aristotle was the first accurate *Criticke* and truest Judge', he observes. At the same time, however, he deprecates a too strict following of the classics. 'Arts and Precepts availe nothing, except nature be beneficiall, and ayding' [4],

---

[1] G. Gregory Smith, *Eliz. Crit. Essays*, II, 197.
[2] *Ibid.*, (Index).
[3] *Lit. Crit. in the Ren.*, p. 306.
[4] Ben Jonson, *Discoveries*, ed. Castelain, p. 88.

he says, and calls it ridiculous to make an author a dictator, 'as the schools have done *Aristotle*' [1].

Italian poetic theory, which during the sixteenth century had exercised a dominant influence in England as well as on the continent, had lost its hold on European thought and had yielded the palm to France. Malherbe attacked the critical tenets of the Pléiade laid down in Du Bellay's *Défense et illustration de la langue française* and exemplified by Ronsard's poetry, the Academy was founded, two of its earliest members, Vaugelas and Chapelain began to exercise their restraining influence on style and criticism, and Corneille's *Cid* was condemned by the latter on the ground of its departure from Aristotle's rules.

During the latter part of the century the theories of these early reformers were further developed by the great neo-classical critics Rapin, Boileau, Dacier, Le Bossu, Bouhours, and others [2]. The Aristotelian and Horatian canons were carefully examined and explained, and elaborated into a body of rules which were no longer looked upon as guiding principles for the poet's art but rather as inexorable laws. Strict obedience to them was, in Boileau's opinion, the only means to attain the absolute standard of literary perfection in which he believed. This lack of historical sense, this inability to adapt their criterion of appreciation to the period and the circumstances in which a literary work was written, was characteristic of the neo-classic writers.

Rapin, Le Bossu, Dacier and Boileau became the new idols of English critics [3]. It was through their influence, especially that of Le Bossu, that they began to apply Aristotle's rules to the epic,

---

[1] *Ibid.*, p. 107.

[2] N. Boileau-Despréaux, *L'Art poétique*, 1674.
   R. Rapin, *Réflexions sur la Poétique d'Aristote et sur les ouvrages des poètes anciens et modernes*, 1674.
   R. Le Bossu, *Traité du poème épique*, 1675.
   D. Bouhours, *La manière de bien penser dans les ouvrages d'esprit*, 1687.
   A. Dacier, *La Poétique d'Aristote, traduite en français avec des remarques*, 1692.

[3] Very soon after its publication, Rapin's *Réflexions* was translated by Thomas Rymer (1674); the translation of Boileau's *L'Art poétique* by Sir William Soame appeared in 1680, and that of Le Bossu's *Traité du poème épique* in 1695. These three critical documents dominated English literary criticism in the days of Dryden and Pope and their influence continued to be felt throughout the eighteenth century.

for the Elizabethans had recognized their authority only for the drama [1]. Davenant's *Gondibert*, Blackmore's *Prince Arthur* and Dryden's *Annus Mirabilis* are deliberate attempts to follow classical tenets. Rapin's disciple, Rymer, who translated the *Réflexions* in the year of its appearance (1674), was even more rigid than his master. His attitude towards the rules is that of the extreme dogmatist. According to him Aristotle had reduced the practice of the Greek poets to principles, and the modern poet had to adopt them unconditionally for reasons 'convincing and clear as any demonstration in *Mathematicks*', as he says in the Preface to his translation [2]. Rymer thinks that the 'rudeness' of English poetry of what he calls 'the last Age' is mainly due to the fact that the poets were unacquainted with Aristotle's *Poetics*. Twenty years later (1695) Sir Richard Blackmore advises the reader to test an heroic poem by the commentaries on Aristotle and Horace, the critical opinions of Rapin, Dacier and Le Bossu, and the 'Judicious Remarks of our *excellent Critick, Mr. Rymer*' [3]. This veneration for the French critics continued throughout the first half of the eighteenth century, and even during the Age of Johnson their influence, though on the wane, had by no means died out [4].

Besides the rules of Aristotle as commented upon by the French exponents of neo-classicism, the Horatian precepts, either in their original or their translated form, were considered as laws for artistic creation. The first translation of the *Epistola ad Pisones* appeared as early as 1567. It was followed by Ben Jonson's in 1640. Two others belong to the Age of Dryden: Roscommon's (1680) and Oldham's, written about a year later. Dryden's prose as well as his poetry were strongly influenced by the Roman poet and in their turn helped to carry on the Horatian tradition. The effect of Horace on English poetry and criticism did not reach its acme until the first half of the eighteenth century. The terseness and elegance of his diction, his unrivalled clearness of statement,

---

[1] Sidney for instance ignores the epic theory of the Stagirite altogether, and adopts the Horatian maxim, when he warns the poet against telling a story from the very beginning (*ab ovo*).
[2] Spingarn, *Crit. Essays of the Seventeenth Cent.*, II, p. 165.
[3] *Ibid.*, III, p. 240.
[4] For the influence of the French critics see Clark, *Boileau and the French Classical Critics in England*, 1925, pp. 229 ff.

and his didactic tendency, appealed strongly to the writers of the Augustan Age, who made correctness and lucidity their aims. Pope's *Essay on Criticism*, the *Rape of the Lock*, the *Satires*, and *Moral Essays* all exemplify the Horatian ideal of precision, but it is especially in the *Imitations of Horace*, which the poet began in consequence of a suggestion by Bolingbroke, that the direct influence of the great critic is traceable. What Pope did in poetry, Addison did in prose; he, too, tried to emulate the pure style of the Roman Augustans, and to attain that '*curiosa felicitas*' which has been called the main characteristic of Horace's diction. Among the authors that are quoted in his works or those from whom passages are prefixed as mottos to the papers of the *Tatler*, *Spectator* and other periodicals, Horace takes up a prominent position [1]. Matthew Prior recognized him as his master, and was looked upon by his contemporaries as the Horace of the eighteenth century.

In France the critical verdicts contained in his *Ars Poetica*, his *Satires*, and *Epistles*, had been the object of careful study. Boileau, the most distinguished representative of French neo-classic criticism, embodied them in his *Art poétique* and adapted them to French conditions. In England it was eagerly read soon after its publication. 'If I would only cross the seas, I might find in France a living Horace and a Juvenal, in the person of the admirable Boileau', Dryden said in *A Discourse concerning the Original and Progress of Satire* [2]. English critics followed the path which Horace and Boileau had pointed out to them, and it is often impossible to decide whether the maxims of their treatises spring directly from the Roman source or have found their way to England through the French imitator. Both Roscommon's *Essay on Translated Verse* and Pope's *Essay on Criticism* offer many instances in point.

The study and imitation of the classics had become a generally accepted doctrine among the writers of the Popean Age. In Pope's *Essay on Criticism* the poet is advised to study Homer by day and night, to use Virgil for a commentary, and to hold the rules of

---

1 See C. Goad, *Horace in the English Lit. of the 18th cent.*, 1918, pp. 298, 99.
   A. M. Ellis, *Horace's Influence on Dryden* (PQ, IV, 1925).
2 Ker, II, p. 26.

the Stagirite in high esteem. The superiority of the ancients over
the later writers was so self-evident that the best chance of success
was to imitate them. Boileau and Pope were so convinced of the
impossibility for a modern author to say anything that had
not been anticipated by the Greeks and Romans, that originality
was in their eyes restricted to expression. 'All that is left us is to
recommend our productions by the imitation of the ancients', Pope
wrote in the Preface to the edition of his works (1717). Addison,
when reviewing Pope's *Essay*, expresses his agreement with
Boileau's statement: 'Wit and fine writing doth not consist so much
in advancing things that are new, as giving things that are known
an agreeable turn' [1].

But, however great might be the veneration professed by critics
like Rymer and Pope for classical precepts, it must not be forgotten
that there was a general tendency in the latter part of the seventeenth century, and also in Pope's time, to regard the rules in their
strictest form as un-English. Temple, after having observed that
the *'French* Wits' have refined their own language and that with
success, adds that 'The same Vein has been likewise much
Cultivated in our modern *English* Poetry', and he doubts if this
influence has been to the good when he compares 'the former
Heights and the present Declines both of Power and of Honour' [2].
In the preface to *All for Love* Dryden says that he has endeavoured
'to follow the practice of the Ancients, who, as Mr. Rymer has
judiciously observed, are and ought to be our masters'. But, after
quoting Horace [3], he gives his own opinion: 'though their models
are regular, they are too little for English tragedy, which requires
to be built in a larger compass' [4]. He regrets that 'our *Chedreux*
critics' form their judgments wholly by the French poets and then
goes on to say: 'But for my part, I desire to be tried by the laws
of my own country; for it seems unjust to me, that the French
should prescribe here, till they have conquered' [5]. The great critical
problem for Dryden and Pope, and for their contemporaries was

---

1   Addison cites Boileau's opinion, *Spectator*, 253.
2   Spingarn, *Temple's Essays*, p. 73.
3   *AP*, 268, 269.
4   Ker, *Essays of John Dryden*, I, p. 200.
5   *Ibid.*, p. 195.

how to reconcile with Aristotelian and Horatian formalism the practice of the great Elizabethans, especially the 'divine Shakespeare', whose works were the products of genius, not of rules. Addison thought there was more beauty in the work of a great genius who is ignorant of the rules than in those of a little genius who observes them, and he added: 'Our inimitable Shakespeare is a stumbling-block to the whole tribe of these rigid critics' [1]. In Pope's time there was perhaps a more general reverence for the French neo-classic postulates, but even then dissident voices were heard [2].

It has become a commonplace to say that the imitation of the ancients which the French and English poets advocated and practised was merely a pseudo-imitation. The veneration which the Elizabethans felt for them had been due to their richness of material, their wealth of thought and imagery, as well as to their lucidity and perfect expression. The fear of extravagance and irrelevancies, which is characteristic of the classical writers, could not but have an influence for the good in that age of metaphysical poetry. After the Restoration, however, correctness and propriety of diction threatened to become the be-all and end-all of literary art, and classicism became a mere veil for the rationalistic and matter-of-fact cast of thought of the time. Of this more will be said in the following chapters.

RATIONALISM

The other important critical tendency of the seventeenth century, which gained a much firmer foothold in England than the dogmatic belief in the rules ever did, was that of making reason the final criterion of literary merit. Though the revival of learning and the progress of humanism had fostered an unalloyed veneration for classical precepts, the emancipation of the human mind from the bondage of mediaeval dogma, which was one of the chief results of the Renaissance, had led to an absolute trust in the

---

1 *Spectator,* 592.
2 See J. W. H. Atkins, *English Literary Criticism: 17th and 18th Centuries.* London, 1951.

dictates of human reason and a consequent disbelief in any kind
of external laws.

The rationalistic spirit in criticism may be traced back to the
beginning of the sixteenth century. Vida's *Ars Poetica* (1527)
had already emphasized the authority of reason and Scaliger had
set up his standards for the different species of literature on a
rational basis [1]. By the Italian critics *individual* reason and classical
canons were considered as independent authorities; they were two
guides that the critic was to follow [2]. But when the French form
of aesthetics gained the supreme position in Europe, the relation
between the two arbiters of poetic excellence changed. Reason now
became the ultimate standard, to which even classical precepts
were subservient. This change in attitude did not immediately take
the form of antagonism to Aristotelian and Horatian canons, they
continued to be regarded as authoritative laws, because it was
believed that they conformed with reason. They were not merely
the invention of the critics, but were based on experience and the
unvarying elements in human nature. Thus the Abbé d'Aubignac
holds that the classical rules for the drama are not founded on
authority, but on reason [3]. Boileau bases his well-known dictum
about the necessity of observing the unities on rational deduction [4],
as does Rymer in his *Tragedies of the Last Age* [5]. Dennis thinks
the canons of Le Bossu and Aristotle incontrovertible, because they
are consistent with reason [6]. Pope's *Essay on Criticism* voices the
conviction that good sense, nature, and the precepts and practice
of the ancients are identical. Rymer had even gone so far as to
recognize reason as his only guide; the rules are to him nothing
but mechanical beauties, not indispensable requirements, but even
he does not consider the two standards as necessarily conflicting.

It has been observed before by Professor Spingarn and others

---

[1] Spingarn, *Lit. Crit. in the Ren.*, p. 149.
[2] Sidney, whose views were greatly influenced by Minturno and Scaliger,
      founds his belief in the unities of place and time on '*Aristotles* precept and
      common reason' (G. Gregory Smith, *Eliz. Crit. Essays*, II, 197).
[3] *Pratique du théâtre*, liv. I, ch. IV.
[4] *Art poétique*, ch. III, ll. 43—46.
[5] Spingarn, *Crit. Essays*, I, p. LXX.
[6] E. N. Hooker, *The Critical Works of John Dennis*. Baltimore, 1939—1943,
      I, pp. 55, 59.

that the 'reason' of the earlier critics was individualistic in nature
and corresponded to Horace's 'good sense', but in Boileau and
his contemporaries 'la raison' and 'le bon sens' became an abstract
and undifferentiated notion. Its dictates were no longer the result
of personal observation and experience but infallible universal
precepts from which there was no appeal.

This rationalistic outlook on literature was, to a large extent at
least, due to the influence of contemporary philosophy [1]. In France
the Cartesian doctrine became the basis of literary aesthetics, in
England it is the materialistic philosophy of Thomas Hobbes, in
which the movement is generally believed to have found its origin.
Hobbes was a literary critic as well as a philosopher. In his *Answer
to Davenant* (1650), and the *Preface to Homer's Odysses* (1675)
he deals with the relation between judgment and fancy, and like
his French contemporaries inveighs against obscurity and conceits.
Still, the terms 'reason' and its correlatives 'nature' and 'truth' did
not obtain their great vogue till twenty-five years later. It manifested itself clearly in that admirable satire on heroic plays, *The
Rehearsal* (1671), with which, according to Professor Spingarn, the
school of common sense in English criticism was born [2]. The sudden
popularity of these terms little more than a decade after the
Restoration can hardly be explained without the influence of the
French rationalists. The relation between the two countries was
very intimate and tended to facilitate the interchange of critical

---

[1] Krantz in his *Essai sur l'Esthétique de Descartes* (1882) explains the whole
rationalistic movement in France, as exemplified in Boileau's *Art poétique,*
as the result of the application of the Cartesian method to the domain of
poetics. Brunetière (*Études critiques,* 1899, sixième série, pp. 152 ff.) opposes
this view and observes that Boileau is more a disciple of the classics than of
Descartes, and that his most important critical tenets had already been
foreshadowed by earlier critics, especially Vauquelin de la Fresnaye, who
wrote before the appearance of the *Discours de la méthode.* Among these the
French critic mentions the doctrine of reason and that of imitation. Apart
from the question whether 'la raison' and 'le bon sens' meant the same in
Boileau and Bouhours as in their predecessors, their insistence on the importance of universal truth, their abhorrence of anything extravagant and
irregular, last of all their restriction of originality to form, are unmistakable
Cartesian traits. Moreover in his 'Conclusion' M. Krantz admits that he is
content to have shown 'les traits communs à l'un et à l'autre'. (p. 361).
Descartes's contempt for the past and his aversion to dogmatism are certainly
non-classical.

[2] Spingarn, *Crit. Essays,* I, p. LXIX.

views. The French critics became the lawgivers of taste, their
works were translated, their superior insight in literary questions
was acknowledged [1].

Something must be said about the meaning of the two words
that were often found in conjunction with 'reason', and continued
to be used as a kind of catchwords throughout the period of pseudo-
classicism: nature and truth. The term 'nature' had been taken in
a rather loose sense by the critics of the Renaissance [2]; with the
neo-classic writers it assumed a definite connotation under the
influence of contemporary thought. Professor Spingarn remarks
that it was more and more restricted 'to the specific interests of
the age, — to that social order which seemed the best safeguard
against individual whim, and to the regulated life of cities' [3]. To
Hobbes the law of nature was identical with 'the dictate of right
reason', the breach of it due to false reasoning, the neglect of the
duties man has to perform for his own benefit [4]. By him and
Davenant the word was introduced into the field of criticism to
express the same harmony and order as the new scientific
movement had found in the mechanical universe. The writers
of the Age of Enlightenment, both in England and in
France, implicitly believed in this cosmic order, and in their
opinion, art was to aim at the same harmonizing regularity and
unity of design. In his *Answer to Davenant* Hobbes assigns to
judgment the leading function in poetic creation: She 'busieth
her self in a grave and rigid examination of all the parts of
Nature, and in registring by Letters their order, causes, uses,
differences, and resemblances; ....', whereas its associate Fancy
is to act in strict subordination to the precepts of philosophy [5].
Under the influence of Hobbes's mechanical system the old

---

1   For references and illustrative comments see Clark, *op. cit.*, pp. 229 ff.
2   Spingarn, *Lit. Crit. in the Ren.*, p. 133 (Vida), 134 (Scaliger).
3   Spingarn, *Crit. Essays*, I, p. LXVII.
4   Hobbes, *English Works*, ed. Molesworth, II, p. 16 and passim.
5   Spingarn, *Crit. Essays*, II, pp. 59, 60. Cf. especially the passage from Dennis's
    Epistle Dedicatory to the Advancement and Reformation of Modern Poetry
    (1701), quoted by Cowl (p. 70), and Clark (p. 380): 'Now Nature, taken in
    a stricter sense, is nothing but that rule and order and harmony which we
    find in the visible Creation', etc.

Aristotelian maxim that the poet was to imitate nature received an altogeteher realistic interpretation. Instead of implying the expression of the universal element in nature, far transcending the world of reality, it began to mean that the poet was to give a picture of everyday manners, especially those of polite society, and that he was to avoid any form of extravagance, anything that was not consistent with a rationalistic conception of the subject. What was either too silly or too bombastic was pronounced to be unnatural. Dennis's remark on Addison's criticism of *Chevy Chase* leaves no doubt as to the conception of the thoroughgoing rationalist. The critic distinguishes three ways of deviating from nature: by 'bombast or tumour', by 'affectation' and by 'imbecility'. This statement is quoted and endorsed by Johnson [1].

This attachment to order, balance, simplicity and self-restraint [2] tended to increase the veneration for the rules; they were considered as an infallible means to arrive at the rational reproduction of reality which the pseudo-classicists considered as their ideal. Rapin was the first to state that the rules were merely methodized nature, and Dennis and Pope were to repeat it after him.

In Pope and the other Augustans the term was mostly used in the limited sense of *human* nature. This restriction was probably due to the influence of the philosophy of the Enlightenment, which made man, his religious and moral knowledge, and the solution of his ethical problems the central object of interest. The poet's aim was to be, to give a philosophical view of human nature, the description of lifeless things was considered to fall outside his pale [3].

---

1   *Lives,* II, p. 147. Cf. Rymer, who contrasted 'Romance' and 'Nature' (Spingarn, *Crit. Essays,* II, p. 199) and in his discussion of Shakespeare's Othello exclaims: 'If this be Nature, it is a *lascheté* below what the English Language can express (*ibid.,* II, p. 251). Compare also Walsh's letter to Pope, dated Sept. 9, 1706: 'For you are certainly in the right that in all writings whatsoever (not poetry only) nature is to be followed; and we should be jealous of ourselves for being fond of similes, conceits and what they call saying fine things.' (*Pope's works,* ed. Elwin and Courthope, VI, p. 54).

2   Cf. A. O. Lovejoy, *On the Discrimination of Romanticisms* (PMLA, XXXIX, 1934): 'No two words were more fixedly associated in the mind of the sixteenth, seventeenth and early eighteenth centuries than "Nature" and "simple".

3   Cf. Warburton's commentary on l. 653 of Pope's *Essay on Crit.*: 'For the poet not only uses the word *Nature* for *human nature* throughout the poem; but also, where in the beginning of it, he lays down the principles of the acts he

Universal nature, independent of place and time, and universal
reason which, as Dryden said, 'underlies the order of nature' and
'is the only faculty granted to all men', were to direct him. For
the critic these two criteria were at the same time the only reliable
tests by which the merits of a work of art could be determined [1].
Rules could only be accepted if they had proved to be principles
of universal validity. The poet's task was to deal with the essential
and permanent attributes of the human mind and man's invariable
ethical principles, which had existed at all times and could be
understood by everyone. He had to portray the general and the
uniform and to eliminate the particular and the abnormal. Personal
idiosyncrasies, individual traits and the mere vagaries of fancy,
which would only please a limited few, for that very reason lay
outside his scope.

When the neo-classic critics, like their predecessors of the
Renaissance, stressed the universal element in art, they followed
the precepts of the great masters of antiquity and their French
interpreters. Aristotle had called poetry 'more philosophical and
a higher thing than history: for poetry tends to express the
universal, history the particular' [2]. Longinus had considered 'those

treats of, he makes the knowledge of *human nature* the foundation of all
Criticism and *Poetry*'. Cf. what Brunetière says of Boileau: 'Croirons nous
qu'effectivement "le naturalisme" de Boileau s'étende à l'imitation de la nature
entière? .... Non, assurément, Boileau ne veut pas qu'on imite la nature
tout entière, mais seulement la nature humaine; ....' (*Etudes critiques,*
sixième série, 1899, pp. 152 ff).

1 'Nature is still the same in all ages and can never be contrary to herself',
said Dryden (Ker II, p. 134), a statement re-echoed by Pope and several
other 18th century critics. Cf. Pope's *Essay on Criticism*, ll. 70—74:
      Unerring NATURE, still divinely bright,
      One clear, unchang'd, and universal light,
      Life, force, and beauty, must to all impart,
      At once the source, and end, and test of Art. (Italics are mine.)
Cf. A. O. Lovejoy, *The Parallel of Deism and Classicism.* (MP, 29, 1931-32).
For the various meanings of 'nature' in neo-classic criticism of the 17th and
18th centuries, see the valuable survey by the same writer: *'Nature' as
Aesthetic Form.* (MLN, XLII, 1927.) Professor Lovejoy calls the term
"nature" 'the most sacred and the most protean word in the vocabulary of
these periods'. For the idea of 'nature' in religion, ethics, philosophy, etc. see
Basil Willey, *The Eighteenth Century Background.* New York, 1941.

2 *Poetics*, IX. S. H. Butcher, *Aristotle's Theory of Poetry and Fine Art.* London,
1923, p. 65.

examples of sublimity to be fine and genuine which please all and always' [1]. And Boileau had been of opinion that a work of art cannot be called 'un bon ouvrage', 's'il n'est plain d'un certain agrément et d'un certain sel propre à piquer le goust général des hommes' [2]. The neo-classic critics appreciated objective beauty, based on the moral and aesthetic experiences of all men, which were fundamentally alike. It could be recognized by all whose natural taste was not corrupted.

Closely connected with the view of nature is that of truth, which similarly bears the impress of the rationalistic movement.

Aristotle's poetic truth, which did not mean a faithful reproduction of actual life, but a transmutation of reality into an ideal world of the poet's own creating, had not been sufficiently understood by the critics of the Renaissance. For this imaginative truth they had substituted the truth of fact. Imitation of nature meant for them the invention of something which, though not actually existing, was in strict accordance with the laws of universal nature and reason. This conception of the *verisimile,* the *vraisemblable,* measured by purely rational standards, came to be one of the tenets of the pseudo-classic creed. Instead of applying the Aristotelian test of probability, which did not reject things incredible if made acceptable by artistic treatment, the critics accepted only what was credibly true. Conformity to the laws of experience became the final criterion. In France the insistence on truth as a test to measure the value of poetry was furthered by Descartes, who made the search for truth his principal aim. His influence may be traced in Bouhours, when he makes Eudoxe say that 'la vérité est la première qualité et comme le fondement des pensées' [3]. He carefully distinguishes between 'la fiction et la fausseté' [4] and observes that 'la raison est d'elle-mesme ennemie du faux' [5]. The best-known expression of the pseudo-classic ideal is Boileau's

---

1 Longinus, *On the Sublime,* ed. by W. Rhys Roberts. Cambridge, 1907, p. 57.
2 *Préface pour l'édition de ses oeuvres,* 1701.
3 *La Manière de bien penser dans les ouvrages d'esprit,* Paris, 1687, p. 6.
4 *Ibid.,* p. 10.
5 *Ibid.,* p. 70.

Rien n'est beau que le vrai: le vrai seul est aimable;
Il doit régner partout, et même dans la fable [1].

In England the realistic movement which has been discussed in
connection with 'nature' also made its influence felt in the use of
the word 'truth'. The poet was required to give a picture of reality
itself or that which resembled reality. It is again Hobbes who
clearly defines the length to which poetic fiction may go. 'As
truth is the bound of Historical, so the Resemblance of truth is
the utmost limit of Poeticall Liberty.... Beyond the actual works
of nature a Poet may now go; but beyond the conceived possibility
of nature, never'[2]. This statement condemns anything irrational
and shuts the poet out from the higher regions of imaginative
art. His contemporary Davenant contrasts 'Truth narrative' of the
historian with 'truth operative', which he calls the 'Mistris of
Poets, *who hath not her existence in matter but in reason*' [3]. The
italicized words leave no doubt as to the limited sphere that
Davenant wants to allow the poet. He, too, expects mere logical
correspondence to the facts of life. This strict 'verisimilitude' in
fiction remained the slogan of the rationalistic critics down to the
end of the eighteenth century; even the detractors from reason's
supremacy are not entirely free from its fascinating power [4]. Dryden
expects 'a likeness of truth, something that is more than barely
possible' in the action of a tragedy [5]. Edward Phillips calls it the
business of the poet 'to deliver feign'd things as like to truth as
may be, that is to say, not too much exceeding apprehension or
the belief of what is possible or likely, or positively contradictory
to the truth of History' [6]. No less emphatic is the Earl of
Shaftesbury. In his *Letter concerning Enthusiasm* he postulates that

---

1 *Epître* IX.
2 Spingarn, *Crit. Essays*, II, p. 62. It is a curious fact that T. Warton, R. Hurd
   and T. Twining, three of the leaders of the revolt against the tyranny of
   reason, quote this passage from Hobbes as an illustration of their view of
   poetic truth.
3 Spingarn, *Crit. Essays*, II, p. 11. Italics are mine. Davenant's 'Truth operative'
   has of course nothing in common with Wordsworth's truth 'general and
   operative; not standing upon external testimony, but carried alive into the
   heart by passion'. (*Wordsworth's Lit. Crit.* London 1905, p. 25).
4 Cf. the chapters on the Wartons.
5 *Preface to Troilus and Cressida*, Ker, I, p. 209.
6 Spingarn, *Crit. Essays*, II, p. 268.

'*Truth is the most powerful thing in the World,* since even Fiction itself must be govern'd by it, and can only please by its resemblance' [1]. And Blackwell, the writer of the interesting *Enquiry into the Life and Writings of Homer* (1735), ascribes the great merit of the Greek poems to their faithful reproduction of nature. Fiction is regarded with suspicious eyes. 'Tis the Traces of *Truth* that are only irresistible .... [2]. The Fiction every now and then discovers its cloven foot, betrays its Dissimilitude to Truth and tho' never so willing, we *cannot* believe....' [3].

The term 'truth' is repeatedly used with reference to stylistic questions and is then synonymous with the word 'nature'. It implies a simple and unadorned diction, the absence of any extravagances, of conceits, and far-fetched allusions. In this application of the word, the influence of Boileau and Bouhours is distinctly discernible. George Granville, Lord Lansdowne, is indebted to the latter critic in his *Essay upon Unnatural Flights in Poetry* (1701), where the poet is advised not to explore forbidden regions and to take care 'That every line the test of Truth endure' [4]. In the first of the 'Explanatory Annotations' he observes that only what is invented 'according to Nature' shall be reputed as Truth. 'But what so ever shall diminish from, or exceed, the just proportions of Nature, shall be rejected as False, and pass for extravagance, as Dwarfs and Gyants for Monsters' [5]. Byssche professes that a strict regard for Truth has guided him in selecting his illustrative passages from various English authors, that he has considered it necessary that they should show 'a Probability or Semblance of Truth'. Boileau's well-known dictum is quoted in support [6].

As Byssche quotes Boileau, so Addison cites Bouhours, whom he looks upon as 'the most penetrating of all the French critics'. Truth is to him the basis of all wit, good sense the groundwork of every thought [7].

In the dedication prefixed to his translation of Bouhours's

---

1 *Characteristicks,* ed. 1733, I, p. 4.
2 *An Enquiry into the Life and Writings of Homer,* London, 1735, p. 285.
3 *Ibid.,* p. 290.
4 Spingarn, *Crit. Essays,* III, p. 295.
5 *Ibid.,* p. 295.
6 *The Art of English Poetry,* 1702.
7 *Spectator,* 62.

Manière de bien penser (1728), Oldmixon quotes Lord Lansdowne's above-mentioned lines and expresses the view that 'many great Genius's have miscarry'd by not thinking rightly on Subjects they were otherwise well able to handle and adorn and for want of considering that Truth, in all the Productions of the Mind, is what only renders them agreeable and useful and that the false Brilliant of Thoughts is like the Glare of Lightening . . . .' [1]. Last of all, John Brown, the author of the '*Estimate*', thinks it necessary to cultivate 'that maxim in poetical composition which the two best of *French* critics, *Boileau* and *Bouhours*, have so much insisted on; "that all poetical beauty must be founded in Truth" ' [2].

This rigid adherence to rational truth, this testing of fiction by the laws of experience, meant the rejection of anything that lay beyond the bounds of empirical fact. In the preface to Davenant's *Gondibert*, Tasso is taken to task for his description of supernatural events, for 'his Councell assembled in Heaven, his Witches Expeditions through the Air, and enchanted Woods inhabited with Ghosts' [3]. In the same way Rymer censures Spenser's neglect of probability: 'All is fanciful and chimerical, without any uniformity, without any foundation in truth; his Poem is perfect *Fairy-land*' [4].

Aristotle had considered 'the marvellous' as a necessary constituent of epic poetry and also of tragedy, though in a less degree. The genius of the poet ought to make these irrational elements acceptable to the reader, it is his creative talent and not 'reason' that determines their truth: 'probable impossibilities' are therefore preferable to 'improbable possibilities' [5]. This doctrine of the 'wonderful', the 'marvellous' (le merveilleux) was accepted by the critics of England as well as France. Here the rule of 'le vraisemblable selon la raison' [6] could not be rigidly applied, consequently the critics attempted to reconcile this Aristotelian precept with their rationalistic creed. Le Bossu, whose *Traité du poëme épique* was translated into English in 1695, and enjoyed a higher re-

---

1   *The Arts of Logick and Rhetorick, Illustrated by examples taken out of the best Authors etc. . . . .*, London, 1728, p. VI.
2   *Essays on the Characteristics* (1751), p. 17.
3   Spingarn, *Crit. Essays*, II, p. 5.
4   *Ibid.*, p. 168.
5   Butcher, *op. cit.*, pp. XXIV, 95.
6   Le Bossu, *Traité du poëme épique*, 6ième ed., 1714, p. 248.

putation in England than almost any other work of the French pseudo-classicists, interpreted the fable with its supernatural admixture merely as an allegorical disguise of the moral truth which the ancient poets wanted to inculcate; the human as well as the divine characters were mere allegorical personages [1]. Moreover the meaning of the word 'vraisemblable' included that which, though not consistent with the laws of reason, was founded on popular belief [2]. But the thoroughgoing neo-classicists drew the line at the extravagant fictions of romance, though the same excuse of popular tradition might be urged here. Saint-Évremond draws a parallel between 'le merveilleux' in the ancients and that of the books of chivalry. In itself the two are often equally absurd, but in the poems of classical writers these absurdities are made up for by 'l'esprit et la science qu'on y trouve', whereas in the books of chivalry they are mere imbecilities [3].

Long before the appearance of Le Bossu's treatise Hobbes had expressed the same lenient view. 'The conceived possibility of nature' is to him, as 'le vraisemblable' was to the French critics, something relative, dependent on the current conceptions of the age. 'In old time amongst the Heathen such strange fictions and Metamorphoses were not so remote from the Articles of their Faith as they are now from ours, and therefore were not so unpleasant' [4]. In accordance with Aristotle's opinion that the irrational must be accepted if the poet succeeds in 'telling lies skilfully' [5], Dryden defends Shakespeare's use of fairies, pygmies and the effects of magic in *A Midsummer Night's Dream* and *The Tempest* and Jonson's in the *Masque of Witches*. 'Things which really exist not', may be admitted into poetry, 'if they are founded on popular belief' [6]. The character of Caliban is acceptable for the same reason. He is represented as an unnatural monster, as a person 'not in Nature', ... 'begotten by an incubus on a witch', but, though this 'at first sight would be intolerable', it is not wholly beyond the

---

[1] Le Bossu, *Traité,* liv. III, ch. v.
[2] *Ibid.*, liv. III, ch. VII.
[3] *Oeuvres mêlées de Saint-Évremond.* Paris 1865, II, 503.
[4] Spingarn, *Crit. Essays,* II. p. 62.
[5] Butcher, *op. cit.*, p. 95.
[6] Ker, I, p. 187.

bounds of credibility, 'at least the vulgar still believe it' [1].

It was on the same grounds that Addison defended *the fairy way of writing* [2]. His paper is directed against 'the men of cold fancies and philosophical dispositions', who think that the introduction of supernatural elements leaves no sufficient probability to affect the imagination. He refutes their objection, however, by observing that many people believe in the existence of these beings, while others, preferring to be kept in a delusion, do not care to see through the falsehood. After Addison the theory of popular belief remained one of the canons of the critical code, as later references will show. Though the use of the supernatural was therefore restricted, it was not necessary to exclude it altogether, provided it was based on fundamental concepts that were universally agreed on.

The reverence for the great writers of antiquity, and for Homer in particular, had engendered the conviction among the pseudo-classicists that the use of pagan mythology was an indispensable element of epic poetry.

When, in the time of the Reformation, religious sentiment received a fresh impulse, attempts were made to substitute for the heathen deities objects of Christian belief. Christian themes were chosen by Tasso in Italy, by Du Bartas in France, by Spenser, Milton, Davenant and Cowley in England. Critics like Vauquelin de la Fresnaye, Godeau and Desmarets recommended the use of them, the author of *Gondibert* defended the introduction of 'such persons as profess'd Christian Religion' on the ground that they conduce more to virtue than the pagan gods and Cowley wrote in a similar strain in the preface to his poems. Then came Boileau's rejection of Christian machinery [3] and the potent influence of the French critic was felt in Engeland as well as on the continent. Both Dryden and Temple show distinct traces of

---

1   Ker, I, p. 219.

2   *Spectator,* 419. Addison's term was probably taken from Dryden, who had spoken of 'that fairy *kind* of writing' in the dedication to *King Arthur* (*Works,* ed. Scott-Saintsbury, Vol. VIII, p. 136). In *The Rehearsal* (Act V, Scene I) there is a hit at the poet in Bayes's remark that spirits must not be confined to speak plain.

3   *Art poétique,* III, 193—208.

it [1]. Sir Richard Blackmore refuted Boileau's arguments in the *Preface to Prince Arthur;* Dennis on the other hand, though he advocated the cause of religious poetry, agreed with the author of the *Art poétique* that Christian machines were out of place in an epic [2].

Thus paganism maintained undisturbed sway over epic poetry throughout the period of neo-classicism. Though the heathen gods had lost their vitality for the modern poet, the introduction of them was considered as a convenient adornment, a means to invest the poet's fiction with an air of importance and dignity. Pope praised Homer for bringing them into a system of machinery and asserted that in spite of the disparity between his own time and that of the great Greek, they still continued to be the gods of poetry. What the neo-classical critics disliked particularly was the mixing of paganism and Christianity. Milton's practice in *Lycidas* and Dryden's in *Astraea Redux* struck the champions of common sense as highly incongruous and elicited the censure of various eighteenth century critics.

THE SCHOOL OF TASTE

Another characteristic tendency of seventeenth century criticism calls for a short discussion, as it made its influence felt in the Age of Johnson, namely that which is generally known by the term *The School of Taste.* It was not an entirely independent critical current, as the word 'school' might lead us to expect. It was intimately connected with the two already mentioned, but recognized other standards than those either of neo-classicism or rationalism. It represents the individualistic element in its struggle against external authority. Its members all had this much in common, that they did not believe in the infallibility of the rules; they were convinced that there was something in poetic art, certain effects in literature, that fell beyond their pale and could be explained only by what they vaguely designated *taste.* Within the

---

[1] Dryden: *Original and Progress of Satire* (Ker, II, pp. 15 ff).
   Temple: *Of Poetry,* Spingarn, *Crit. Essays,* III, p. 99.
[2] *Remarks on Prince Arthur.* See Hooker, I, pp. 105 ff., 461 ff.

school were unqualified admirers of the ancients, but none of them
went so far as to recommend a strict observance of classical precepts
to the modern poet. They accepted reason as an important guide
for both the poet and the critic, but realized that certain elements
in poetry were of too elusive a nature to be examined on purely
rational lines. To them the ultimate appeal of art was not to the
rational faculty but rather to sentiment or the heart. The antithesis
between *heart* and *head*, which became almost a platitude among
later critics, owed its origin to the adherents of the School of Taste.
The origin of the term *taste* to denote this critical concept is
attributed to the Spanish prose-writer Gracián, whose *El Oraculo
manual y arte de prudencia* (1641) was translated into various
languages [1], into English in the year 1685. Both in England and
France it obtained its vogue about the latter half of the seventeenth century. In France it found its chief advocates in Méré,
Bouhours, La Bruyère and Saint-Évremond. 'Cette divine grâce . . . .
qui se rend maîtresse de la volonté en la laissant maîtresse d'elle-
même, cette grâce, dis je, qu'est ce autre chose qu'un je ne sais
quoi surnaturel qu'on ne peut ni expliquer ni comprendre', Bouhours says in one of his *Entretiens d'Ariste et d'Eugène,* where he
deals with this indefinable something in art [2]. And Saint-Évremond,
the link between the English and the French advocates of taste,
observes that 'La poésie demande un génie particulier, qui ne
s'accommode pas trop avec le bon sens . . . .' In this critic we find
the conflict between reason and neo-classic dogmatism clearly
illustrated. He owns that certain rules have their foundation in
'un bon sens' but thinks that there are only few 'qui portent le
caractère de cette raison incorruptible'. He therefore calls it
ridiculous to measure modern works by too strict laws [3].

In England this concept of taste did not at once obtain the
popularity that it was to enjoy later on. Hobbes and Sir Robert
Howard used the word in a strictly individual sense. The former

---

[1]   Addison refers to him in the *Spectator,* 419.

[2]   The term *je ne sais quoi* had been used long before Bouhours in Italy, Spain
and France (Cf. Spingarn, *Lit. Crit. in the Ren.,* p. 328, note 1). Eugène says
it was common among the Italians, who used their term *non sò che* 'en toutes
rencontres'. He also observes that 'le je ne sais quoi a beaucoup de vogue
parmi nous et que nous sommes en cela aussi mystérieux que nos voisins'.

[3]   *Oeuvres mêlées,* II, pp. 501, 502.

denied that there was a fixed standard of taste [1], the latter asserted that the difference between tragedy, comedy and farce could not be determined by rules, but only by taste [2]. It was probably against this statement that the staunch devotee of common sense, Rymer, levelled his censure in *The Tragedies of the Last Age,* where he called those who make 'what will please' the test of literary merit *'Stage-quacks* and *Empericks* in Poetry' [3]. The same passage elicited Dryden's animadversions in *A Defence of an Essay of Dramatic Poesy* [4], where he defends 'reason' and 'the rules' against his brother-in-law's dictum. It was especially among the so-called 'virtuosi', of whom Sir William Temple was the chief representative, that the term 'taste' came into vogue and was considered the true touchstone of poetry. As their interests were not restricted to the study of fine art but extended to scientific and antiquarian research as well [5], criticism became pervaded by a new spirit which greatly conduced to the recognition of the relative character of classical standards. It fostered the opinion that literature is intimately connected with the social and climatic conditions under which it is produced. This makes Temple's *Essay upon the Ancient and Modern Learning* an important contribution to the progress of the historical point of view in criticism.

Gradually however, the encroachment of rationalism on the individualism of the School of Taste began; instead of an essentially personal instinct, an intuitive feeling, taste came to be looked upon as an absolute standard, just as fixed and immutable as reason itself [6]). But even in the days of its perfect rationalization,

---

1   *Letter to Edw. Howard,* Molesworth, IV, p. 458.
2   Spingarn, *Crit. Essays,* II, p. 106.
3   *Ibid.,* p. 183.
4   Ker, I, p. 120.
5   Cf. Shaftesbury's definition of the 'VIRTUOSI or refin'd *Wits* of the Age. In this latter general Denomination we include the real *fine Gentlemen,* the Lovers of *Art* and *Ingenuity;* such as have seen *the World,* and inform'd themselves of the *Manners* and *Customs* of the several Nations of EUROPE, search'd into their *Antiquitys,* and *Records;* consider'd their *Police, Laws* and *Constitutions;* observ'd the Situation, Strength, and Ornaments of their *Citys,* their principal *Arts,* Studys and Amusements; their *Architecture, Sculpture, Painting, Musick,* and their Taste in *Poetry, Learning, Language,* and *Conversation'. (Characteristicks,* III, p. 156).
6   Cf. Spingarn, *Crit. Essays,* I, p. XCVIII, where La Bruyère's opinion is quoted.

it continued to imply a certain independence of authoritative precepts. Addison believes in this standard, and considers the appreciation of the great ancients and the approved moderns the best proof that a critic has attained it [1]. No less firm a believer in it is the Earl of Shaftesbury. He warns critics against judging of what is beautiful by 'their humour only': philosophers, critics and authors should all endeavour to frame their own taste by the 'just standard of Nature'. But he used the term '*je-ne-sçay-quoy*' — which through his influence was introduced into English criticism — to denote a 'kind of *Charm*, or *Inchantment*, of which the Artist himself can give no account' [2]. The same idea was expressed by Pope when he spoke of 'a grace beyond the reach of art',

> Which without passing thro' the judgment, gains
> The heart, and all its end at once attains [3].

The advocates of taste insisted that it was the critic's duty to point out the beauties of a work of art rather than the faults, a view that we find frequently restated in the critical literature of the eighteenth century. Though it may have been suggested to the pseudo-classic critics by Horace's *Ars Poetica* [4], the development of this new conception was largely due to the influence of Longinus, which, apart from a few occasional references, may be said to have begun in the year 1674 after the appearance of Boileau's translation. The French critic rather than the Greek is responsible for the instances of this beauty-blemish cant in Dryden, Dennis and others [5], and even a long time afterwards the translation continued to take the place of the original [6]. Longinus had contrasted the poet of sublime genius who will sometimes violate the rules, with the writer of moderate talents who avoids all errors but never rises to the height of true sublimity, and he had unhesitatingly professed his preference for the first. In the works of several English critics,

---

1   *Spectator,* 409.
2   *Op. cit.,* I, 332.
3   *Essay on Crit.* 154, 155.
4   ll. 351 ff.
5   Cf. Ker, I, pp. 179, 80; Hooker, *op. cit.,* I, pp. 13, 49. Cf. Paul, *Dennis,* p. 157.
6   For editions of Longinus and English translations, see A. Rosenberg, *Longinus in England bis zum Ende des 18. Jahrhunderts,* Diss. Berlin, 1917.

most of all in those of Dryden and Addison, his statements are cited and endorsed [1].

Thus the belief in the infallibility of the rules had been greatly shaken, even in the hey-day of neo-classicism.

THE LITERARY KINDS

One of the tenets of the neo-classical school was the rigid distinction between the various departments of literary art or rather the different types of poetic composition, for the critics were almost exclusively concerned with poetry and neglected any other form of literature. Both Aristotle and Horace had laid great stress on this separation; in their critical treatises it was the types that were the subjects of discussion, not the individual works. The Renaissance critics followed in their wake, they classified the writers according to the different *genres* that they had made their own [2]. The French authorities of the seventeenth century and their English disciples naturally insisted on a strict conformity to the rules that their classical masters, whom they pretended to follow, had laid down for each particular species, and when they advocated imitation of the ancients, it was taken for granted that these rules should be carefully observed. The extreme devotees of the 'kinds' even went so far as to deny any merit to a literary work that had not constantly kept these precepts in view [3].

Rapin, whose influence on English aesthetic thought was scarcely less marked than that of Boileau, divided his *Réflexions sur la Poétique* into two parts, one dealing with the question in general, the other containing a systematic discussion of each kind of poetry in particular [4]. The greater part of Boileau's *Art poétique* is taken

---

1 Cf. *The Author's Apology for Heroic Poetry,* Ker, I, p. 180; *Spectator,* 291.
2 Cf. the enumeration in the *Arte of English Poesie,* 1589, Bk I, ch. 10 (ascribed to Puttenham, but cf. *Rev. of Engl. Stud.,* I, 284). Sidney comments upon the different kinds of poetry, but before doing so, he says that they have been intermingled by some authors. He does not denounce this method, 'for, if seuered they be good, the coniunction cannot be hurtfull'. (Gregory Smith, *Eliz. Crit. Essays,* I, 175).
3 Hooker, *op. cit.,* II, pp. LXXXVI and LXXXVII. Cf. Paul, *John Dennis,* p. 113.
4 *Oeuvres.* La Haye, 1725, II, pp. 139 ff.

up with precepts for the various forms of poetic art. His English
disciple, John Sheffield, Earl of Mulgrave, closely follows Horace
in his *Essay upon Poetry*. In the *Answer to Davenant's Preface to
Gondibert* Hobbes speaks about the 'Nature and differences of
Poesy' and mentions three sorts: '*Heroique, Scommatique* (= satire),
and *Pastorall*'. Each of these he subdivides according to 'the
manner of *Representation,* which sometimes is *Narrative,* .... sometimes *Dramatique*', so that altogether he distinguishes six kinds [1].

The neo-classicists were very severe in their strictures on tragi-
comedy. The two dramatic forms were to be rigidly kept apart.
The intermixture of comic and tragic elements in the drama was
felt as a transgression of the laws of propriety. Sir Robert Howard
denounced it on the ground that the audience should be kept in
'one entire disposition both of Concern and Attention' [2], Edward
Phillips repudiated the '*Linsie-woolsie* intermixture of *Comic* mirth
with *Tragic* seriousness' [3], and Addison spoke very disparagingly
of it in the *Spectator*. It was only natural, however, that this
popular form of composition, which had attained its greatest vogue
in the reign of Elizabeth and the first decades of the seventeenth
century, should find its advocates even in the hey-day of classicism.
The best-known defence is that of Dryden in his *Essay of Dramatic
Poesy* (1668), where Neander — who stands for the poet himself —
refutes the objections raised by Lisideius, and praises it as a more
pleasant way of writing than ancient or modern writers of any
nation have ever known [4]. In the preface to *Cleomenes,*
however, he himself seems to be conscious of its impropriety. He
says he has written the play 'unmixed with comedy; which, though
it be the natural and true way, yet is not the genius of the nation' [5].
But to please the barbarous part of the audience he has put in a
short rabble scene. In *A Parallel of Poetry and Painting* he admits
that tragi-comedy must be confessed to be 'wholly Gothic' in spite
of its popularity [6].

---

1   Spingarn, *Crit. Essays,* II, p. 55.
2   *Ibid.,* p. 100.
3   *Ibid.,* p. 270.
4   Ker, I, p. 70.
5   *Works,* ed. Scott-Saintsbury, VIII, p. 220.
6   Ker, II, p. 146.

CORRECTNESS. ATTITUDE TOWARDS THE OLDER WRITERS

The study of Greek and Roman writers had fostered an un-qualified reverence for their formal excellences: the perfect lucidity and simplicity of their style, the elegance and polish of their diction. It was especially on these qualities of the ancients that the doctrine of imitation was founded. The poet was to try to attain the same consummation of external form that these writers in general, and the Roman poets of the Augustan Age in particular, had manifested. He' was to be on his guard against extravagance, irrelevance, far-fetched images and laboured diction. Poetic expression as well as poetic subject matter was to be in strict accordance with the laws of common sense.

Malherbe was the first to advocate this classical ideal in France; he set about reforming the French language and freeing it from the mannerisms that the Pléiade had introduced. Both Bouhours and Boileau acknowledged the important services he had rendered to poetry [1]. His critical principles were fully developed by the latter critic in his *Art poétique* [2], where the neo-classic doctrine of clarity and correctness found its most explicit expression. In the preface to his translation of Longinus he called simplicity of language and diction the essential characteristics of true sublimity.

In the beginning the tendency was a gain rather than a loss. In France it meant a wholesome reaction against the extravagant caprices of the *Précieuses,* in England it acted as a beneficial antidote against the unreserved luxuriance of the Elizabethans and the eccentricities of the metaphysicals [3]. Before the influence of the French school made itself felt in England, Ben Jonson had already recommended classical order and restraint [4].

Rapin, La Bruyère and other French critics had condemned the false eloquence and affectation of the pulpit and had recommended simplicity, naturalness and good taste. In England John Wilkins,

---

[1] Bouhours: *Le bel Esprit,* ed. cit., p. 161.
   Boileau: *Art poétique,* I, ll. 131 ff.
[2] Canto I, ll. 101, 102; ll. 165 ff.
[3] Cf. A. H. Nethercot, *The Reputation of the 'Metaphysical Poets' during the Age of Pope* (PQ, IV, pp. 161 ff).
[4] *Discoveries,* ed. cit., pp. 100, 101.

bishop of Chester [1], John Eachard [2] and especially Joseph Glanvill in his *Essay concerning Preaching* (1670) directed their strictures against the false rhetoric, 'a bastard kind of eloquence' of the 'Metaphysical School' of preachers. Hobbes praised 'perspicuity, property, and decency' in poetry and he warned against inflated expressions, like 'the windy blisters of a troubled water', which, 'though of magnifique sound', have no meaning [3]. Sprat's plea for a plain, unadorned prose style and his condemnation of carelessness and extravagance, found response far beyond his own circle [4]. The rationalistic spirit of the seventeenth century and its interest in science awoke a general desire to reform and regulate the language. For this purpose Sprat urged the establishment of an English Academy.

It was, however, not till after the Restoration that correctness came to be looked upon as the highest quality of poetic achievement, though even then the veneration for the older English writers prevented the doctrine from being carried to an extreme [5]. As has often been pointed out, the inconsistencies in Dryden's critical opinions are due to his wavering between two opposite forces: his admiration of the Elizabethans, and the general reverence of his day for French maxims. Dryden certainly warns the poet against too strict regard to verbal expression. In his view 'a work may be overwrought, as well as under-wrought; too much labour often takes away the spirit by adding to the polishing, so that there remains nothing but a dull correctness, a piece without any considerable faults, but with few beauties; . . . .' [6]. Pope and his contemporaries, however, appreciated nothing so much as thorough polish; their ideal was a concise, terse style, free from any sort of verbal redundancy. When fifteen years of age the leader of the

---

1 *Ecclesiastes, or a Discourse concerning the Gift of Preaching as it falls under the Rules of Art,* 1646.
2 *Grounds and Occasions of the Contempt of the Clergy enquired into in a letter to R.L.,* 1670.
3 Spingarn, *Crit. Essays,* II, p. 63.
4 *History of the Royal Society,* 1667.
5 Cf. E. Phillips, *Preface to Theatrum Poetarum,* Spingarn, *Crit. Essays,* II, p. 271: Wit, Ingenuity, and Learning in Verse, even Elegancy it self, though that comes neerest, are one thing, true Native *Poetry* is another; . . . .
6 Ker, II, p. 152.

English Augustans was advised by 'knowing Walsh' to make correctness his special aim and study [1], and many statements in his works go to prove that it continued to be the chief canon of his critical creed.

Addison was no less profuse in his praise of the simplicity of the Greek and Roman writers, and he severely denounced 'the Goths in poetry', who, unable to attain the standard of classical propriety, tried to make up for their want of genius by 'foreign ornaments'. In his paper on *true and false wit* [2] he follows Bouhours and endorses the French critic's opinion that no thought can be called beautiful which is not just and 'has not its foundation in the nature of things'. 'The basis of all wit is truth' he continues, 'and no thought can be valuable, of which good sense is not the ground-work' [3].

The prevailing taste of the Age for correctness naturally involved a depreciation of the great but irregular earlier writers. Though their genius was beyond doubt, the monstrous absurdities in which their works abounded were considered as blemishes too serious for them to be put on the same level with the poets of the age of refinement. It became the general belief that poetic diction had been in a state of pristine rudeness, from which Waller had saved it, and that the later generation of poets had raised it to perfection. Even Dryden believed that 'the excellence and dignity' of rhyme had never been fully known in England before Waller taught it [4], and ranked the variety and harmony of his verses higher than those of Spenser [5]. What Malherbe had done for poetry in France,

---

[1]   Spence, *Anecdotes*. London, 1858, p. 212. Spence adds: 'This, I suppose, first led Mr. P. to turn his lines over and over again so often, which he continued to do till the last; and did it with surprising facility.'

[2]   *Spectator*, 62.

[3]   Of the many passages that might be quoted as illustrations of Bouhours's views the following one from *La Manière de bien penser*, p. 219, may be subjoined: 'Qu'entendez vous donc, dît Philanthe, par ce que vous appellez naturel en matière de pensée? J'entends, repartit Eudoxe, quelque chose qui n'est point recherché, ni tiré de loin; que la nature du sujet présente et qui naist pour ainsi dire du sujet mesme. J'entends je ne sçay quelle beauté simple sans fard et sans artifice, telle qu'un Ancien dépeint la vraye éloquence....'

[4]   *Epistle Dedicatory of the Rival Ladies*, Ker, I, p. 7.

[5]   *A Discourse concerning the Original and Progress of Satire*, Ker, II, p. 29.

Waller was believed to have accomplished in English. In the translation of the *Art poétique* by Sir William Soame, written with the
collaboration of Dryden, his name is substituted for that of the
French critic [1], and to him is ascribed the honourable achievement
of having 'changed hard discord to soft harmony'. Atterbury
praised Waller's versification and observed that English came
into Waller's hands like 'a rough diamond', which he polished
first [2].

Shakespeare's incorrectness was regarded as an established fact;
it was taken for granted by his admirers as well as by his most
violent detractors [3]. His ignorance of art was admitted on all
sides, his glaring transgressions of the laws of order and regularity
were looked upon as serious faults, though the strength of his
genius was universally felt. Some critics there were, however, who
realized that a rigid attention to the precepts of art would have
been detrimental to his poetical powers. In the *Life of Shakespeare*
prefixed to his edition of the plays, Rowe expressed the view that
it might have made him a correct writer but that it would probably
have had a restraining influence on his 'furor poeticus' [4].

The appreciation of Spenser never sank to such a low ebb as
has often been thought, though it was but natural that he, too,
should incur the censure of poets and critics who made correctness
their aim. Ben Jonson had already observed that Spenser, 'in
affecting the Ancients writ no Language', but that he should be
read for his matter [5]. Davenant, though ranking him among the
great poets and placing him next to Homer and Virgil, found fault
with the language as well as the subject of the *Faerie Queene* [6].
The rigid Aristotelian formalist Rymer allowed the poet 'a large
spirit' and 'a sharp judgment' but thought that, owing to his

---

[1]   Waller came last, but was the first whose art
      Just weight and measure did to verse impart,
      That of a well-placed word could teach the force,
      And showed for poetry a nobler course.
             (Translation of the *Art poétique*, I, ll. 131 ff.).

[2]   Preface to Waller's *Posthumous Poems* (1690).

[3]   Lounsbury, *Shakespeare as a Dramatic Artist*, 1911, p. 365.

[4]   *Ibid.*, p. 358.

[5]   *Discoveries*, ed. cit., p. 90.

[6]   Spingarn, *Crit. Essays*, II, p. 6.

ignorance or wilful neglect of classical canons, his epic was wanting in unity and probability [1]. But Denham, Dryden and the two principal exponents of Augustanism, Addison and Pope, spoke of him with a certain amount of enthusiasm. As H. E. Cory has made clear [2], the critics of the Age of Reason reconciled Spenser's manner of writing with their own ideals. Though there are occasional references to the sweetness of his poetry and his power of invention, there were in the main only two qualities for which they felt a warm esteem, because they fell in with their own poetic creed: his moralizing and his fondness for allegory [3]. But they all liked him in spite of his imperfections, of which in their eyes there were many, the two most notable being the exuberance of his fancy, which was apt to skip the bounds of reason, and the extravagance of the fable, which was flagrantly at variance with the rules of the classical epic and with the precepts of Le Bossu. Dryden's objection to the structure of the *Faerie Queene* became a stock remark with the later critics [4].

The view that Milton was neglected by the Augustans, 'till he was claimed by the Romanticists as one of their own' [5], has long since been given up as erroneous. Attention has been drawn to the number of editions of his poetical works in the seventeenth and the first decades of the eighteenth century, and to the many laudatory remarks on his epic which can be culled from various sources, in spite of Rymer's condemnatory verdict [6]. Much more important evidence has been supplied by Professor R. M. Havens in his thorough investigation of Milton's influence on the subject-matter, diction and prosody of eighteenth century poetry [7]. Another aspect of the Milton vogue, the development of commentary on the poet's works, may be considered one more proof of the deep admiration which Milton's poetry inspired, even in the early years

---

1   *Ibid.*, p. 168. Cf. p. 16, supra.
2   H. E. Cory: *The Critics of Edmund Spenser*. [University of California Publications in Mod. Phil., vol. 2].
3   *Ibid.*, pp. 116, 129, 130, 158.
4   Cf. infra, p. 225.
5   W. L. Phelps, *The Beginning of the English Romantic Movement*. Boston, 1893, p. 87.
6   Spingarn, *Crit. Essays*, II, p. 208.
7   *The Influence of Milton on English Poetry*. Cambridge (Mass.), 1922.

of the century [1]. There is no doubt that it was considerably stimulated by Addison's *Spectator* papers, though earlier and contemporary critics like Edward Phillips, Dryden, and Gildon had expressed their warm appreciation. At the time when *Paradise Lost* was highly praised, (much more so than Spenser's epic, because it was considered to be far less irregular), Milton's minor poems were still generally ignored. Their popularity was to come at a later date.

EMOTION AND IMAGINATION

The domination of reason necessarily entailed the repression of the higher qualities of poetry: emotion and imagination. They are the two elements of poetic art which have, at all times, been considered its indispensable requisites. However, as they were both individual and subject to change, the rationalistic critics of the seventeenth and eighteenth centuries, who weighed everything in the balance of universal reason, looked upon them with suspicion. If allowed to have free play, they were likely to disturb the balance and harmony in which the Augustan critics so firmly believed. To the extreme neo-classicists a poem was not the result of an imaginative experience in the poet's mind, but of an intellectual process, in which emotion and imagination were kept under the sway of common sense. The violent impulses of the human heart were not considered fit for literary treatment before they had been properly calmed down by reflection. The reasoning faculty of the writer ought to hold his feelings continually in check to prevent them from overstepping the limits of moderation.

The critical literature of pseudo-classicism in England as well as France offers plenty of illustrations of the distrust with which excessive indulgence of emotion was regarded. The devotees of reason did not deny that the poet was divinely inspired [2] — their reverence for Plato, Longinus, and most of all for Horace made it necessary to accept this classical conception, — but they did not do it without reserve. Rapin, for instance, believed in inspiration,

---

[1] Cf. Ants Oras, *Milton's Editors and Commentators from Patrick Hume to Henry John Todd* (1695—1801) [University of Tartu, Estonia, 1931].

[2] Cf. Boileau, *Art poétique,* opening lines.

but he thought it necessary to insist on keeping the mind serene and restraining the poetic fury [1], and Saint-Évremond thinks 'le bons sens' the only safeguard against 'l'ardeur d'une imagination allumée' [2]. The same warning note is sounded by the French rationalists of the beginning of the next century. La Motte observes that enthusiasm, which often means nothing else but inspiration, may become a dangerous element in poetry if it is not guided by reason [3].

In England the necessity of restraining emotion is acknowledged as early as Davenant, who defends 'painfull Poets' like Virgil and Statius against the charge that they were wanting in 'extemporary fury' or 'inspiration', which he calls a dangerous word [4]. Rymer speaks contemptuously of those who say that 'Poetry .... is *blind* inspiration, is pure *enthusiasm*, is *rapture* and *rage* all over' and dubs them the '*Fanaticks* in Poetry' [5]. Very characteristic of the half-hearted attitude of the pseudo-classic critics towards the 'furor poeticus' are the following lines from the Earl of Roscommon's *Essay on Translated Verse:*

> But tho we *must obey when heaven Commands,*
> And man in vain the *Sacred Call withstands,*
> Beware *what Spirit* rages in your breast;
> *For ten inspir'd ten thousand are Possest.*
> Thus make the *proper use* of each Extream
> And *write* with *fury,* but *correct* with *Phleam* [6];

---

[1] 'Car quoy qu'en effet le discours du Poëte doive en quelque façon ressembler au discours d'un homme inspiré: il est bon toutefois d'avoir l'esprit fort serein, pour sçavoir s'emporter quand il le faut, et pour regler ses emportemens: & cette serenité d'esprit, qui fait le sang-froid & le jugement, est une des parties des plus essentielles du genie de la Poësie, c'est par là qu'on se possède'. (*Oeuvres du P. Rapin,* nouvelle ed., 1725, II, p. 98).

[2] *Op. cit.,* p. 387.

[3] La Motte: *Discours sur la poésie en général et sur l'ode en particulier:* 'On sait que *enthousiasme* ne signifie autre chose que inspiration; et c'est un terme qu'on applique aux poètes, par comparaison de leur imagination échauffée avec la fureur des prêtres lorsque le dieu les agitait et qu'ils prononçaient les oracles .... Mais c'est le plus souvent un beau nom qu'on donne à ce qui est le moins raisonnable .... Enthousiasme tant qu'on voudra, il faut qu'il soit toujours guidé par la raison'. (Vial et Denise, *Idées et doctrines littéraires du XVIIIe siècle,* p. 97).

[4] Spingarn, *Crit. Essays,* II, 25.

[5] *Ibid.,* p. 185.

[6] *Ibid.,* p. 306.

It must not be forgotten, however, that there were critics in both countries who allowed to emotion a much more important function in poetic creation. The members of the *School of Taste* recognized the necessity of the appeal to the reader's sentiment. As has already been said, it is to them that we owe the antithesis between 'head' and 'heart' which was commonly used in the days of Bouhours and Méré in France and by English critics up to the time of Joseph Warton. Sir William Temple observes that 'a certain Noble and Vital Heat of Temper, but especially of the Brain' is the true source of poetry and music [1], and William Wotton considers 'true Enthusiastick Rage' the first requisite for poetic creation, though he again thinks it necessary that 'Sedate Judgment' should keep a restraining hand upon it [2].

The Miltonic conception of the poet as a divinely inspired interpreter [3], 'soaring in the high region of his fancies, with his garland and singing robes about him' [4], found a restatement in Edward Phillips's *Preface to Theatrum Poetarum* [5].

In England there was a much stronger substratum of genuine emotionalism than in France, owing to the powerful influence of her essentially romantic older literature. Elizabethan tradition was an important factor in the time of Dryden and Pope and was constantly at war with the predominating rationalistic trend. In no writer of critical essays is the conflict between the latter and a strong, romantic temperament better illustrated than in Dryden. This clash between his own 'inborn vehemence and force of spirit', to which he refers in the *Preface to Troilus and Cressida,* and his reverence for the French school of critics and English common-sense standards, is the main cause of the many inconsistencies in his statements. It is this lack of any definite guiding principles that has puzzled his critics to such a degree [6].

---

[1] Spingarn, *Crit. Essays,* III, p. 80.
[2] *Ibid.,* pp. 211, 212.
[3] Cf. Miss Ida Langdon: *Milton's Theory of Poetry and Fine Art,* 1924, p. 154.
[4] Spingarn, *Crit. Essays,* I. p. 194.
[5] *Ibid.,* II, p. 259. T. Warton thinks that 'this book contains criticisms far above the taste of that period'. (*Edition of Milton's Minor Poems,* 1785, p. 60).
[6] Cf. Hamelius, *Die Kritik in der englischen Literatur des* 17. *und* 18. *Jahrhunderts,* pp. 63 ff., and Bohn, *John Dryden's Lit. Crit.,* PMLA, vol. XXII, pp. 56—139.

Another beneficial influence was that of Longinus, whose demand for emotional appeal had found response in France and even more in England. According to this Greek critic, the two most important 'innate' components of the sublime were 'the power of forming great conceptions' and 'a vehement and inspired passion' [1]. Though Longinus did not consider emotion as an absolutely indispensable element of sublimity, he again and again stressed its emotive effects. Boileau himself had looked upon the sublime as something that inspired the reader with noble sentiments, awoke strong emotions and transported the soul by its overwhelming power [2]. In Dryden's opinion Longinus, whom he considered the greatest critic among the Greeks after Aristotle, had rightly observed that 'to write pathetically .... cannot proceed but from a lofty genius'. Like the Greek rhetorician Dryden is convinced that the pathetic and the sublime are closely connected and that a good poet is born with the power to evoke violent emotions naturally [3]. Addison, too, thinks that following mechanical rules is not enough to make a good poet; something else is more essential, 'something that elevates and astonishes the fancy, and gives a greatness of mind to the reader, which few of the critics besides Longinus have considered' [4].

In France Longinus' *Peri Hupsous* [5] had enjoyed a high reputation ever since the appearance of Boileau's translation in 1674, and had played an important part in the Ancients and Moderns Controversy. In England various translations appeared. The first, 'rendred out of the originall' was that by John Hall (1652). J. Pulteney's (1680) was based on Boileau's, an anonymous one from the Greek was published in 1698, L. Welsted's followed in 1711, but the most important of all was that by William Smith (1739), who added copious notes and observations, together with illustrative passages from Shakespeare and Milton, as Longinus had done from the ancient writers. In the Saturday papers in the *Spectator* Addison observed that Milton 'had raised and ennobled his conceptions by such an imitation as that which Longinus had recommended',

---

1   W. Rhys Roberts, *Longinus on the Sublime,* 2nd ed. (1907), Sect. VIII.
2   As a good example of true sublimity both he and Bouhours quote the passage from *Genesis*: Let there be light; and there was light.
3   Ker, I, pp. 220 ff.
4   *Spectator,* 409.
5   For its authorship see the Introduction to Professor Rhys Roberts's edition.

that he had excelled both in the pathetic and the grand and had
served the reader with the best illustrations of Longinus' dicta [1].
Addison particularly stressed the sublimity of *Paradise Lost* and
this quality continued to be intimately associated with the epic
of the Puritan poet. Critics like A. Blackwell [2] and R. Lowth [3] drew
attention to the sublimity of Hebrew poetry and their statements
were repeated by later critics.

The great advocate of emotion during the Augustan period was
John Dennis. His insistence on ecstasy and mental exaltation as
the fundamental element of poetry gave him the name of 'Sir
Longinus' among his contemporaries and excited the ridicule of
Pope [4]. 'Passion is the characteristic mark of poetry and consequently
must be everywhere', he observed in his *Grounds of Criticism in
Poetry* (1704). For him, too, poetic fury was not incompatible with
strong sense. He was no less convinced than his contemporaries
that 'enthusiasm' in the poet ought to be guided by judgment, but
he broke away from the conventional creed by making emotion
and not reason the basis of poetry, by insisting that passion must
have the upper hand in all poetic creation.

Another champion of emotion, whose work has been too much
neglected, is Thomas Blackwell, the author of *An Enquiry into
the Life and Writings of Homer* (1735). Though he lived in a
somewhat later period than Dennis, his essay appeared before
Pope's powerful sway had ceased to dominate poetic theory. It is
all the more important, because the treatise was probably not
without influence on some of the leaders of the reaction in the
second half of the century, as references to and quotations from the
book lead me to suppose. It is pervaded by the same spirit of
enthusiasm as is so characteristic of the Wartons and Richard Hurd.
The domain of the poet is in Blackwell's eyes enchanted ground.
His art raises a 'commotion' in the soul; a rational analysis of the
effects it produces would be irreverent and moreover would prove

---

1 *Spectator,* 339.
2 A. Blackwell, *The Sacred Classics Defended and Illustrated,* 1725.
3 R. Lowth, *Praelectiones Academicae de Sacra Poesi Hebraeorum,* translated
by G. Gregory as *Lectures on the Sacred Poetry of the Hebrews,* 1787.
See S. H. Monk, *The Sublime, A Study of Critical Theories in XVIII-Century
England* [Modern Language Association of America]. New York, 1935.
4 Hooker, *op. cit.,* p. 215. Cf. Paul, *Dennis,* p. 204.

futile: 'It would be like prying into the Author of Fairy-Favours which deprives the curious Enquirer of his present Enjoyment'. The emotions are often of too subtle a nature to be examined by the light of reason: 'They cannot bear to be stared at and far less to be criticized and taken to pieces' [1].

When common sense and correctness were set up as ideals, when extravagance and irrelevant allusions were treated with contempt, the imagination began to be considered as a dangerous quality, which should always act under the control of reason. Bacon had called it one of the three faculties of the human understanding. The three great departments of human learning, history, philosophy and poetry all have, according to the Elizabethan philosopher, their own basis of appeal. History directs itself to the memory, philosophy to the reason, and poetry to the imagination. The last faculty, 'beeing not tyed to the Laws of Matter, may at pleasure ioyne that which Nature hath seuered and seuer that which Nature hath ioyned' [2]. Poetry is therefore only restrained 'in measure of words', but in all other respects it is 'extreamely licensed'. Instead of the Aristotelian conception of an idealistic mimetic art, Bacon substituted that of a creative process. Poetry is to him nothing but feigned history, a means of escape from the actual world. Whereas reason binds the human mind to the limited sphere of reality, the imagination raises and erects it, 'by submitting the shewes of things to the desires of the Mind' [3].

But under the influence of the rationalistic tendency of the seventeenth century the imagination, though still considered to be indispensable, was only allowed to act in subordination to reason. Far from being any longer the basis of poetic art, as it had been in the Baconian philosophy, it merely served to supply the adornments. The origin of this new conception is to be found in the works of Thomas Hobbes, which were to leave a very distinctive impress on English aesthetic theory. He was the first philosopher to apply his psychological method to literary composition, by which he influenced, not only the critics of his time but also those of the following generations. According to his psychological views

---

1   *Op. cit.*, p. 154.
2   Spingarn, *Crit. Essays,* I, p. 5.
3   *Ibid.*, p. 6.

all human ideas, or 'phantasms', as he calls them, are the result of internal motions, caused by the contact of an object with one of the organs of sense. The 'phantasm' remaining after the object is removed, is called *'imagination'*. It is therefore defined as *'conception remaining, and by little and little decaying from and after the act of sense'* [1]. When he means the 'decaying sense' itself, Hobbes speaks of *imagination,* if he wants to express at the same time that the sense is past, it is called *memory* [2]. Between these two faculties there is therefore no essential difference. The two words *imagination* and *fancy* are used in the same meaning. Hobbes prefers the latter term: its original meaning of *appearance* makes it applicable to conceptions which are the offspring of any of the senses, whereas imagination can, properly speaking, only be applied to those whose parent is sight: 'an *image* in the most strict signification of the word, is the resemblance of something visible' [3].

Great importance is attached in Hobbes's psychology to the sequence of these conceptions. The phantasms bring other phantasms to the mind, which are sometimes like themselves and sometimes entirely different. This theory foreshadows the doctrine which was later on to play such an important part in the development of English psychology and for which John Locke chose the name of *Association of Ideas* [4]. He who quickly sees the resemblances between things of different natures, has, according to Hobbes, a good *fancy,* whereas he who finds out the differences between things that apparently resemble each other, has a good *judgment* [5]. Both qualities may be possessed by the same man, it depends only upon the aim that is in the person's mind, which quality is predominant. But though fancy without the help of judgment is not considered as an intellectual virtue, judgment is commended for itself even without the help of fancy.

Applying this theory to poetic art, Hobbes makes the important

---

1 Hobbes, *Works,* ed. Molesworth, IV, p. 9.
2 *Ibid.,* III, p. 6.
3 *Ibid.,* p. 648.
4 It is the title of a supplementary chapter incorporated with the fourth ed. of the *Essay concerning Human Understanding.* Cf. M. Kallich, *The Association of Ideas and Critical Theory in XVIII-century England.* Baltimore, 1945. (reprinted in ELH, XII.)
5 Hobbes, *Works,* I, p. 399.

statement that for all departments of poetry, for the epic and the dramatic kinds as well as for sonnets and epigrams, both judgment and fancy are required. Fancy must, however, preponderate: poetry must 'please for the extravagancy; *but ought not to displease by indiscretion*' [1]. This is the earliest example of the distrust with which the imagination was generally treated during the latter half of the seventeenth century and the greater part of the next. It is one of the first intimations that the encroachment of judgment on the domain of the imaginative faculty had begun. But Hobbes's view is not that of the extreme rationalist: he at all events allows the imagination the most important function and only objects to excessive indulgence. Fancy must take the lead, but must not overstep the bounds of reason.

To Hobbes the imagination is, however, no longer a creative faculty but merely a means of adornment. This becomes evident when he says that from fancy 'proceed those grateful similes, metaphors and other tropes, by which both *poets* and *orators* have it in their power to make things please or displease'. In his *Answer to Davenant's Preface to Gondibert*, where we find so many traces of incipient neo-classicism, he is even more explicit: 'Judgment begets the strength and structure, and Fancy begets the ornaments of a Poem' [2].

The conception that fancy traces the resemblances between things of different natures, whereas judgment finds out the differences between things resembling each other, was a generally recognized doctrine during the century and a half that followed. The word fancy began to be used in the same sense as the term *wit*, which changed its meaning in Hobbes's time. The philosopher himself uses *wit* in the more comprehensive sense of the mental faculties, comprising both fancy and judgment. He defines it as 'a tenuity and agility of spirits, contrary to that restiness of the spirits supposed in those that are dull' [3]. He grants, however, that in his time many use it in the restricted sense of fancy.

---

1 *Works*, III, p. 58. Italics are mine. Cf. his *Preface to Homer's Odysses:* 'A fourth (virtue) is in the Elevation of Fancie, which is generally taken for the greatest praise of Heroique Poetry; and is so, when governed by discretion'. (Spingarn, *Crit. Essays*, II, p. 70).
2 Spingarn, *Crit. Essays*, II, p. 59.
3 *Works*, IV, p. 56.

When rationalism began to grow in strength in the latter half of the seventeenth century, there was a tendency among the critics to give reason a higher place in literature than imagination. In spite of this important deviation, the influence of Hobbes's philosophy on the interpretations of the two terms is distinctly traceable [1].

Distrust of imagination is one of the characteristic features of the neo-classic period [2]. The moralists of the seventeenth and of the earlier part of the eighteenth century appealed to reason as the chief guide in human life, and, as so many moral reformers had been before them, were suspicious of the faculty of the imagination, which was apt to run riot and must therefore be kept in check. Shaftesbury warned his readers against giving free course to one's fancies. A too free indulgence would, in his opinion, inevitably lead to madness; reason was therefore to act as their '*Controuler and Corrector*' [3]. Theologians, too, like Eachard, Glanvill and Isaac Barrow, were disposed to suspect unbridled imagination. Human reason, the noblest gift bestowed by God on man, was to keep it within its proper bounds, for truth required no outward adornment. To the seventeenth century advocates of a simple, unadorned prose style, fancy was the cause of extravagance and ornateness, which were not consistent with scientific truth. Thomas Sprat called a 'vicious abundance of Phrase', 'the volubility of Tongue', and all other excesses that the members of the Royal Society condemned, the offspring of fancy. They are 'in open defiance against *Reason,*

---

1   Milton refers to the operations of fancy in the fifth book of *P. L.* He too
    makes fancy subservient to reason:
> . . . . But know that in the soul
> Are many lesser faculties that serve
> Reason as chief; among these Fancy next
> Her office holds; of all external things,
> Which the five watchful senses represent,
> She forms imaginations, airy shapes,
> Which Reason joining or disjoining, frames
> All what we affirm or what deny, and call
> Our knowledge or opinion; . . . .

2   Cf. D. F. Bond, *"Distrust" of Imagination in English Neo-classicism.*
    (PQ, XIV, 1935).

3   *Op. cit.*, I, p. 322.

professing not to hold much correspondence with that, but with
the Slaves, the Passions; they give the mind a motion too changeable
and bewitching to consist with *right practice*' [1].

The literary critics of the time all agree in considering both
imagination and reason as indispensable elements in poetic
creation. Only a harmonious co-operation of the two could result
in literary excellence. 'Fancy and Reason go hand in hand; the
first cannot leave the last behind; . . . .' says Dryden in the *Defence
of an Essay of Dramatic Poesy* (1668) [2]. John Sheffield, Earl of
Mulgrave, expresses the same opinion in his *Essay upon Poetry*:

> As all is dullness, when the Fancy's bad,
> So without Judgment, Fancy is but mad;

and he follows it up with the traditional remark that judgment
'gains the Head, while 't other wins the Heart' [3]. Temple, one of
the chief exponents of the doctrine of taste, considers 'a spritely
Imagination or Fancy' and 'soundness of Judgment' two essential
things: 'without the Forces of Wit all Poetry is flat and
languishing; without the succors of Judgment 'tis wild and extravagant' [4].

It was only natural that in the latter half of the seventeenth
century the literary critics, who thought probability of fiction 'the
soul of poetry', should sound the same warning note as their
contemporaries, the moralists, divines and men of science. Thomas
Rymer denounces the opinion of those critics who think that poetry
is 'the child of Fancy' and then remarks: '*Reason* must consent
and ratify what-ever by *fancy* is attempted in its absence, or else
't is all *null* and void in law' [5]. His statement was probably suggested
by Rapin, whose *Réflexions sur la poétique d'Aristote et sur les
ouvrages des poëtes anciens et modernes* he translated [6].

---

1   Spingarn, *Crit. Essays*, II, pp. 116, 117.
2   Ker, I, p. 128.
3   Spingarn, *op. cit.*, II, p. 287.
4   *Ibid.*, III, p. 81.
5   *Ibid.*, II, p. 185.
6   'Car quoy que la Poësie soit un ouvrage de genie, toutefois si ce genie n'est
    reglé, ce n'est qu'un pur caprice, qui n'est capable de produire rien de
    raisonnable'. (Rapin, *op. cit.*, II, p. 105). The passage is translated by Dryden
    at the end of his *Preface to Troilus and Cressida* (Ker, I, p. 229).

Dryden also thinks that excessive indulgence of fancy leads to improbability, and 'in resemblance of fiction to truth consists the excellence of the play' [1]. He compares fancy to 'an high-ranging spaniel', which 'must have clogs tied to it, lest it outrun the judgment' [2]. He endorses Rapin's view that 'ridiculous mistakes and gross absurdities have been made by those poets who have taken their fancy only for their guide, that if this fancy be not regulated, it is a mere caprice, and utterly incapable to produce a reasonable and judicious poem' [3].

Sir William Temple considers 'Invention and liveliness of Wit' indispensable for the poet but at the same time he recognizes the necessity of 'the coldness of good Sense and soundness of Judgment' [4]. Dennis goes even further. He, too, believes in the restraining influence of reason. Wit is according to him 'a just mixture of reason and extravagance'. The poet should be careful that reason predominates, he must 'make its mortal Enemy subservient to its grand design of discovering and illustrating sacred truth' [5]. Reason and fancy are no longer represented as confederates but as conflicting forces, constantly fighting for supremacy.

The terms 'fancy' and 'imagination' are generally used interchangeably in the seventeenth century. Dryden is the only critic who discriminates between them and uses 'imagination' (also called 'wit') in a wider meaning, comprising 'invention, or finding of the thought', 'fancy, or the variation, deriving, or moulding of that thought', and 'elocution or the act of clothing and adorning that thought' .... 'The quickness of the imagination is seen in the invention, the fertility in the fancy and the accuracy in the expression' [6]. This would seem to mean that fancy is only one element in poetic creation and that the term imagination comprises the whole process [7], a view which would mean a considerable

---

1   Ker, I, p. 128.
2   *Ibid.*, p. 8.
3   *Ibid.*, p. 229.
4   Spingarn, *Crit. Essays,* II, p. 81.
5   Hooker, *op. cit.,* I, p. 6. For Dennis's critical views see Introd. to vol. II.
6   *Preface to Annus Mirabilis.* Ker, I, p. 15.
7   Cf. T. S. Eliot, *The Use of Poetry and the Use of Criticism.* London, 1933, pp. 55 ff.

advance in the direction of the nineteenth century conception. From the context it is clear, however, that Dryden, just like his contemporaries, limits the domain of operation to sense-perceptions stored in the memory, from which the imagination selects the material it requires, and varies and moulds it so that the absent object can be represented in an idealized form [1].

The neo-classic critics closely followed Hobbes. The sphere of the imaginative faculty continued to be restricted to impressions received through the senses, chiefly even to those received through sight. These views received additional support from the doctrines of John Locke, the philosopher of the English *Aufklärung*. He uses the word *wit* [2] instead of fancy and its function is the

---

[1] Ker, I, p. 14.

[2] The word *wit* is used in a great variety of meanings by the critics of the seventeenth and eighteenth centuries. It has already been said that the Elizabethans used it for the mental faculty and that in Hobbes's time it came to be used for the fancy. It has the same sense in Dryden's *Preface to Annus Mirabilis,* but in the *Apology for Heroic Poetry* (Ker, I, p. 190) he defines it as 'a propriety of thoughts and words'. This definition was accepted by some other critics (Spingarn, *Crit. Essays,* I, p. XXXI), but rejected by Addison in the 62nd number of the *Spectator.* In Pope's *Essay on Criticism* the term is used in various senses: the intellect, genius, fancy, judgment (See Elwin and Courthope, *Pope's Works,* V, p. 51). It was especially owing to the extravagancies of the metaphysical poets that wit began to be looked upon with disfavour. In ll. 289—293 of the *Essay* Pope speaks of critics who judge poetry by the number of glittering thoughts and are pleased with a work which is 'One glaring Chaos and wild heap of wit'. Here wit is equivalent to *conceit.* A few lines further on the poet warns against excessive use of ornament: 'For works may have more Wit than does 'em good, | As bodies perish thro' excess of blood'.
In Locke wit is synonymous with fancy. Warburton follows Locke, when he says that 'wit consists in chusing out, and setting together, such ideas from whose likenesses pleasant pictures are made in the fancy'. In his commentary on Pope's line: 'In search of wit these lose their common sense', (l. 28) he explains the poet's words as follows: 'the *Judgment,* thro' an *habitual* search of Wit, loses by degrees its faculty of seeing the true relations of things; in which consists the exercise of *common sense*' (*The Works of A. Pope,* 1751, I, p. 142). It became an established belief that 'men who have a great deal of wit and prompt memories, have not always the clearest judgment, or deepest reason', as Locke puts it.
In Johnson's *Dictionary* eight meanings of the word wit are mentioned. The first two are: 1. the mental faculties, 2. imagination, quickness of fancy. The critic deals with the use of the word again in his *Life of Cowley.* The wit of the metaphysical poets is explained as a kind of *discordia concors,* 'a

assemblage of ideas; it puts together those which resemble each other, whereas judgment carefully separates them, lest one thing should be taken for another. Addison quotes Locke's definitions and uses them as the starting-point for his discussion of *true and false wit* in the *Spectator* [1]. He adds that not every resemblance of ideas should be called wit, but only that which gives delight and surprise to the reader.

Addison distinguishes wit from imagination and fancy, though between the latter two terms he does not discriminate. In the papers on the *Pleasures of the Imagination* he deals with the operations of this faculty and the manifestations of its powers in poetic art. These essays have been represented as marking quite a new era in the history of aesthetic theory, as being the first enunciation of the true principles of poetic art [2]. Undoubtedly Addison is the only writer of the neo-classic period who clearly and unreservedly represents the appeal to the imagination as the chief test of merit. 'It sets off all writings in general, but is the very life and highest perfection of poetry', he observes. According to him its principal function is that of creating an ideal world, far superior to that of reality: 'It has something in it like creation, as it draws up to the reader's view several objects which are not to be found in being'. The reason why the poet indulges it is a dissatisfaction of the human mind with what it finds in nature. The imagination is always sensible of some defect in that which the eyes have seen and tries to perfect it. It is evident that this view of the poet's task bears a close resemblance to that of Bacon. The passage from the *Advancement of Learning* that may have suggested Addison's

---

combination of dissimilar images, or discovery of occult resemblances in things apparently unlike'. A similar interpretation of the term had been given much earlier in one of the *Ramblers* (no. 194). Johnson disagrees with Pope's conception of wit (*Essay on Crit.* 297) which would reduce it 'from strength of thought to happiness of language'. He thinks there is a much nobler and more adequate conception and defines it as that 'which is at once natural and new, that which though not obvious is, upon its first production, acknowledged to be just; .... that, which he that never found it, wonders how he missed; ....' (*Lives*, I, p. 20).

[1] No. 62.

[2] Cf. W. Basil Worsfold, *Principles of Criticism*, 1897; 3rd ed. 1923, pp. 82 ff.

statement is quoted below, side by side with the words of the Augustan critic [1].

It must not be forgotten, however, that Addison does not allow the imagination the same unlimited freedom as the Elizabethan philosopher did. Like Hobbes and Locke he makes sight the only source of the ideas on which it can operate [2]. It is incapable of creating anything new but has the power of 'retaining, altering and compounding' the images that have entered the mind. As Addison himself explains [3], this is done according to the Cartesian laws of association. The distinction between *primary* and *secondary* pleasures, of which the former proceed from objects before the eyes and the latter 'flow from the ideas of visible Objects, when the Objects are not actually before the Eye' can be traced back to Locke's *Essay concerning Human Understanding*. Neither Addison,

---

[1] 'The vse of this FAINED HISTO-RIE (= poetry) hath beene to giue some shadowe of satisfaction to the minde of Man in those points wherein the Nature of things doth denie it, the world being in proportion inferiour to the soule; by reason whereof there is agreeable to the spirit of Man, a more ample Greatnesse, a more exact Goodnesse, and a more absolute varietie, then can bee found in the Nature of things .... And therefore it was euer thought to have some participation of diuinenesse, because it doth raise and erect the Minde, by submitting the shewes of things to the desires of the Mind; whereas reason doth buckle and bowe the Mind vnto the Nature of things'.
F. Bacon, *Advancement of Learning*, (Spingarn, *Crit. Essays*, I, p. 6).

'But because the Mind of Man requires something more perfect in Matter than what it finds there, and can never meet with any sight in Nature which sufficiently answers its highest ideas of Pleasantness; or, in other words, because the Imagination can fancy to itself Things more Great, Strange, or Beautiful, than the Eye ever saw, and is still sensible of some defect in what it has seen; on this account it is the part of a Poet to humour the Imagination in its own Notions, by mending and perfecting Nature where he describes a Reality, and by adding greater Beauties than are put together in Nature, where he describes a Fiction'.
(*Spectator*, 418).

[2] 'It is this Sense which furnishes the Imagination with its Ideas; so that by the Pleasures of the Imagination or Fancy, (which I shall use promiscuously) I here mean such as arise from visible Objects, either when we have them actually in our View, or when we call up their Ideas in our Minds by Paintings, Statues, Descriptions, or any the like Occasion. We cannot indeed have a single Image in the Fancy that did not make its first entrance through the Sight; . . . .'. (*Spectator*, 411).

[3] *Spectator*, 417.

nor any other neo-classical writer of the period is of opinion that the imagination can transcend nature and can create a world of its own instead of adorning and recombining the impressions retained in the memory. In this the neo-classicists followed Aristotle, who allows the imagination the same narrow sphere of passive reproduction, and combination of material supplied by the senses [1]. But, like Aristotle, they must have been aware of a higher creative power, for which they did not find a foundation in contemporary philosophy. How else could they have admired older writers like Shakespeare, Spenser and Milton, whose imagination went far beyond the bounds of the empirical world and whose poetry was so diametrically different from that of the Augustans? Though their fear of exuberance and extravagance prevented the critics from bestowing unalloyed praise on the Elizabethans, their strictures are chiefly directed against fanciful imagery, stylistic irregularities and fantastic idiosyncracies, against all that was unnatural and incredible. But Milton's lofty flights of imagination in the sixth book of *Paradise Lost*, far from being censured, were highly praised by the Earl of Roscommon [2] and Charles Gildon [3]. Both Dennis and Addison eulogized the majesty of his descriptions, which in the latter critic's opinion compared favourably with those of the Latin and Greek poets. Shakespeare ranked far higher than any other poet in spite of his 'unfiled expressions, his rambling and indigested Fancys' [4]. But the Metaphysicals were strongly disliked for their eccentricities, which were thought to be due to their unrestrained wit and lack of judgment.

---

[1] Butcher, *op. cit.*, p. 126.
[2] Spingarn, *Crit. Essays*, II, p. 308.
[3] *Ibid.*, p. 200.
[4] *Ibid.*, p. 271.

PART I

Some General Aspects of Literary Criticism during the Age of Johnson

CHAPTER I

RATIONALISM

Rationalism remained the prevailing tendency during the greater part of the eighteenth century. Both philosophy and theology regarded reason as the chief source of knowledge. Locke, the typical representative of the English Age of Enlightenment, made it his one guiding principle: only what could be rationally proved was accepted as truth. No one interpreted the general trend of contemporary thought better than he; his creed fell in with the current beliefs of the educated classes and for a long time he was looked upon as an authority both by theologians and politicians. Though he was by no means a sceptic like Hume, but a firm believer in Christianity, he considered that religious faith was subservient to reason, and must submit to its tests. Locke's principles were taken up by his many disciples and continued to influence English religious thought. However much difference in opinion there might be between churchmen and deists, all looked upon rational evidence as the highest authority and discarded doctrines not conformable to the laws of reason. Religion was no longer regarded as the expression of man's deepest emotions, but as a practical guide for the solution of life's ethical problems. The belief in the inner light, in divine inspiration, fell into disrepute, and 'enthusiasm' became the general object of contempt. Hobbes had censured it in his *Leviathan* as early as the year 1651 [1]. Locke discussed it in a special chapter of his *Essay concerning Human Understanding* [2], Shaftesbury wrote his *Letter concerning Enthusiasm* and mentioned

---

[1] *Works,* ed. Molesworth, III, p. 102.
[2] Chapter XIX, Book IV.

reason and ridicule as the proper remedies. Hume, who dominated English thought in the middle of the century, as Locke did in the early part, dealt with it in his essay on *Superstition and Enthusiasm* and maintained that its chief sources were a warm imagination and ignorance [1].

But though this distaste for the spontaneous flow of devotional feeling and fear of strong emotional effects in poetry were the outcome of the same rationalistic cast of thought, it would be wrong to suppose that these two ran parallel and existed to the same degree. Religious fanaticism was generally decried, whereas a certain amount of poetic fervour was not only tolerated, but even considered indispensable. The critics of the period themselves offer sufficient illustrative material. John Brown, the author of the *Essays on the Characteristics,* in which he opposes Shaftesbury's views, discusses the relative degrees of enthusiasm in his own country and France: 'although in *France,* the applauded Pulpit Eloquence is of the *Enthusiastic,* in England of the severe and *rational* Species; yet the Taste of these two Nations in Tragedy or *Theatrical Eloquence,* is mutually *reversed:* the *English* are Enthusiastic, the *French* severe and rational', and he believes that in England the intense strain of poetic fury and the 'unrestrained Warmth of Imagination' are largely due to the great reverence for Shakespeare, whereas in France the severe strictures of the Academy quenched the flow of true poetic feeling [2]. To mention one more opinion, the reviewer of Beattie's *Minstrel* [3] makes a contrast between the influence of enthusiasm upon poetry and upon religion and calls it 'poison to the latter' and 'nutriment to the former' [4].

---

[1] *Essays Moral, Political and Literary.* London 1875, I, pp. 144 ff.
[2] *Essays on the Characteristics,* pp. 33, 34.
[3] *Monthly Review,* 44, 1771.
[4] John Byrom in his Preface to '*Enthusiasm*', *A Poetical Essay in a Letter to a Friend in Town* complains that 'enthusiasm' has grown into a fashionable term of reproach, and in the poem itself calls it absurd that it should be restricted in its use to religious matters. Critics, poets, the virtuosi, connoisseurs, and philosophers,
> .... in one absurdity they chime
> To make religious entheasm a crime.
This poem, inspired by William Law, just as his *Thoughts upon Human Reason,* were written to defend religious enthusiasm against the extreme

The constantly growing popularity of Longinus tended to stress the necessity of emotional appeal. This popularity continued throughout the Age of Johnson, though its direct influence lessened as the century advanced [1]. The dictum that 'sublimity is the echo of a great soul', and that 'the truly eloquent must be free from low and ignoble thoughts' [2], could not but find a sympathetic response among the Augustan writers and critics, as well as among those of the first decades after Pope's death, who were characterized by the same strongly moralistic outlook. Moreover, as Professor W. Rhys Roberts says in the introduction to his edition of Longinus: 'No modern critic formulated more precisely, in relation to literature, the *quod semper, quod ubique* principle' [3]. On the other hand his dictum that the effect of the sublime should be to transport the audience out of themselves was not in keeping with the spirit of urbanity and restraint of the Augustan period. Had not Hobbes warned that fancy, in which consists the Sublimity of a Poet, 'which is that Poetical Fury which the Readers for the most part call for', should be discreetly used and should operate under the guidance of reason and judgment? Nor could Longinus' conceptions of a sublime style be said to tally with those commonly held by the neo-classical critics. But Boileau had already adapted them to his own views and had called simplicity of style and diction the essential qualities of sublimity. Under his influence these views were commonly accepted and propagated.

An abundance of passages might be quoted to demonstrate that the critical literature of the Johnsonian Age manifests the same rationalistic outlook on literary art as that of the Age of Queen Anne. Not only was good sense considered as the chief arbiter of poetic merit, it was also looked upon as the primary factor in artistic creation, to which emotion and imagination were to

---

worshippers of reason. In his *Contrast between Human Reason and Divine Illumination, exemplified in three different Characters,* he emphasizes the limitations of human reason and the necessity of 'belief in a heav'nly light'. Yet in his earlier *An Epistle to a Friend,* dealing with the art of poetry, we find nothing but the ordinary neo-classic postulates. (Chalmers, 15, p. 212).

[1] See Rosenberg, *op. cit.*

[2] *Op. cit.,* IX, 3.

[3] The reference is to a passage in Section VII, 4: 'In general, consider those examples of sublimity to be fine and genuine which please all and always.'

act in strict subordination. Excessive indulgence of either of these
two was incompatible with the laws that reason imposed. In his
Life of Congreve Johnson lauds this poet for curing poetry of
the 'Pindarick madness'. 'He has shewn us that enthusiasm has
its rules and that in mere confusion there is neither grace nor
greatness' [1], he says, and in this statement is struck the keynote
of Johnson's conception of art, his love of order and regularity, his
fear of extravagance. 'Notwithstanding its apparent licentiousness
true Poetry is a thing perfectly rational' [2], observes the author of
The Minstrel, who is also of opinion that emotion should be kept
within the bounds that reason sets to it, and that everything not
conformable to rational tests should be discarded. Stockdale's *Inquiry
into the Nature and Genuine Laws of Poetry* (1778), intended as a
defence of Pope against Warton's attack in the *Essay*, illustrates
the same dread of excess; 'the fire of the poet, if he would reach
his aim . . . . must be modelled and directed by deliberation and
choice' [3].

Sir Joshua Reynolds recommends a little more enthusiasm to
the painters of his age [4], but at the same time cautions them against
the other extreme. 'It is very difficult to determine the exact
degree of enthusiasm that the arts of painting and poetry may
admit' [5], sounds like a warning to those who give free rein to
their emotion and imagination. It is repeated in the second of his
Discourses, where he advises the young painter to consider that
'mere enthusiasm will carry you but a little way', and that only
careful attention to models of great masters will ensure lasting
success.

But it is obvious that these warnings are directed only against
excessive demonstration of emotional feeling, against affectation
and false sentiments. The rationalistic critics by no means denied
that it was the poet's duty to move the heart of his audience or
readers. Johnson, though a thoroughgoing rationalist, was also a

---

[1] *Lives*, II, 234.
[2] *An Essay on Poetry and Music as they affect the Mind* (J. Beattie, *Essays*,
     Edinburgh, 1776, p. 350).
[3] *Op. cit.*, p. 4.
[4] *Idler*, 79.
[5] *Ibid.*

man of a strong temperament: his *Prayers and Meditations* are the expression of a strongly emotional nature, and we know from Boswell that in conversation he was often carried away by his feelings. But he was of opinion, and this opinion was shared by most of his contemporaries, that the poet, who wrote for the reading public, should give no expression to his emotions before they had been properly toned down by reflection. He should keep his personal sentiments to himself [1]. Though Johnson's love of truth drove him into violent opposition to any false display of passion and to morbid sentimentalism, it would be wrong to say that he could not appreciate artistic expression of genuine emotion. Of the several instances that his critical writings afford in support of this statement, I need only mention his strictures on Addison's *Cato,* in which he sees merely a 'splendid exhibition of artificial and fictitious manners'. He admires its 'just and noble sentiments' .... but 'its hopes and fears communicate no vibration to the heart' [2]. Human sentiments and human feelings are absent in Addison's tragedy, whereas Shakespeare's characters all 'act upon principles arising from genuine passion'.

What has been said of Johnson is true even to a higher degree of some of his contemporaries. Kames severely inveighs against florid declamation and cool descriptions which often take the place of truthful delineations of the human heart. He attacks the pompous tragedies of his time, 'showing only the mere outline of passion', and contrasts Shakespeare's sentiments, which are 'the legitimate offspring of passion', with those of Corneille, who describes in the style of a spectator instead of expressing emotion like one who feels it [3].

Vicesimus Knox denies that Addison has the right to be called an eminent poet. He possessed 'a dispassionate temperature', which made him fit for the cool disquisitions of criticism and morality, but he was deficient in 'that animated spirit which is the soul of poetry' [4]. And James Beattie, whose rationalistic conception of

---

[1] Cf. J. Sutherland, *A Preface to Eighteenth Century Poetry.* Oxford, 1948, pp. 66 ff.
[2] Raleigh, *Johnson on Shakespeare.* Oxford, 1925, p. 34.
[3] *Elements of Criticism,* 6th ed., 1785, I, p. 459 note.
[4] *Essays, Moral and Literary.* London, 1824, I, pp. 561, 62.

4

poetry has already been quoted, thinks it the first requisite of
poetry that it should appeal to the emotion: 'Poetry is little
esteemed, unless it touch the heart.... In a word, everything in
poetry ought to be pathetick.... the true poet touches the heart,
whatever be the subject' [1].

But no one of these writers made the emotional appeal the *conditio
sine qua non* of literary excellence. With the majority of the critics
reason remained the supreme guide. The suspicion with which
an unrestrained play of the fancy had been treated by the earlier
critics, is expressed time after time in the critical treatises of the
Age of Johnson. The literary dictator himself repeatedly states
that a constant guard should be kept over its operations. In one
of his *Ramblers* he calls it 'a vagrant faculty, unsusceptible of
limitations and impatient of restraint', which is always trying 'to
baffle the logician' [2]. Here, as well as in one of the chapters of
Rasselas, Johnson warns against excessive indulgence of the
imagination in the domain of ethics [3]. And in a letter to Boswell
he expresses his conviction that in religious thinking fancy ought
to act in subordination to reason [4]. In artistic creation the relation
between the two was to be the same. In his *Life of Milton* he
calls poetry 'the art of uniting pleasure with truth, by calling
imagination to the help of reason' [5]. But he rejected the narrow
neo-classic conception that there is a natural antagonism between
judgment and imagination [6]. The sphere of action that he attributes
to the imaginative faculty is in perfect accordance with the
sensualistic philosophy of Hobbes and that of Locke: 'it selects
ideas from the treasures of remembrance and produces novelty
only by varied combinations' [7]. The same may be said of John
Brown, the author of the *Estimate* and the *Essays on the
Characteristics* (1751). The senses are to him the fountains
from which we derive our ideas, the imagination combines and

---

1   *Dissertations Moral and Critical.* London, 1783, p. 181.
2   *Rambler,* 125.
3   Ch. XLIV.
4   Boswell, *Life of Johnson,* ed. G. Birkbeck Hill, II, p. 277.
5   *Lives,* I, p. 170.
6   *Ibid.,* p. 235.
7   *Idler,* 44.

associates, reason compares, distinguishes and separates them [1].

Another writer's opinion may be cited to illustrate that the psychology of Hobbes looms behind many of the critical utterances on this problem of aesthetic theory. In one of the introductory chapters of *Tom Jones,* Fielding enumerates the qualifications that the writer of a fictitious history [2] should possess. The most important is *invention,* which he defines as 'a quick and sagacious penetration into the true essence of all the objects of our contemplation'. The other is *judgment,* without whose 'concomitancy' the first cannot exist, because the true essence of two things can never be discovered before their points of difference have been traced, and this is the undisputed province of judgment. Like Johnson he opposes the view that these two qualities cannot be united in the same person [3].

In his psychological analysis of aesthetic impressions, Kames follows Locke. His description of the play of the imagination is based on the doctrine of *association,* which played such an important part in eighteenth century experimental philosophy, and was accepted by nearly all the writers on aesthetic theory. Hobbes was, as we saw, the first thinker in England to deal with the phenomena of mental succession; but the eighteenth century critics generally did not trace it further back than Locke's *Essay* [4], though Hobbes's explanation was much clearer and more accurate. The doctrine implied that ideas based on sensation which have often occurred simultaneously or in sequence and are consequently intimately connected in the human mind, will recall each other mechanically. The principles on which these mental associations were founded were of various kinds: similarity, contrast, cause and

---

1 *Essays on the Characteristics,* p. 12.
2 Fielding classes himself among 'the historical writers who do not draw their materials from records'.
3 Book IX, Ch. I.
4 The reviewer of Beattie's *Dissertations Moral and Critical (Monthly Review,* 69, 1783) observes that the doctrine of the A. of I. serves as the basis of many modern theories and then adds: 'It is but justice to the memory of a great philosopher and very original thinker of the last age, to observe that this doctrine, which is commonly considered as having been first proposed by Mr. Locke, is to be found illustrated with great ingenuity in the philosophical writings of Hobbes'.

effect and others. After Addison and Dennis, Locke's disciples of
the early part of the century, the Scottish theologian and philosopher
Francis Hutcheson was one of the first to resort to associatism for
his explanation of aesthetic problems. Besides the ordinary
'external' senses, generally recognized, he distinguishes various
others. In his discussion of the 'moral sense', by which he discriminates virtues and vices and traces the relation between beauty
and virtue, he closely follows Shaftesbury [1], in his aesthetic theory
he is indebted to Addison. In his *Inquiry into the Original of our
Ideas of Beauty and Virtue* (1725) [2], he calls the powers of the
imagination *internal* or *reflex senses,* in his later works he
substituted the word *subsequent* for *internal,* because the powers
of imagination cannot operate without some previous perception
of the objects on which they are employed. They are therefore
considered as holding a middle rank between the bodily senses,
and the rational and moral faculties. Memory exhibits its ideas
in the same form and order in which they were perceived; as soon
as remembrance loses its hold on them, and the natural connection
of their parts is dissolved, the associating power of imagination
combines them again. In these operations it observes some general
rules, based on *resemblance, contrariety* or *vicinity* [3].

Hutcheson's term 'internal senses' is also adopted by Mark
Akenside in the preface to his long, frigid poem *The Pleasures of
Imagination* (1744) and by Alexander Gerard in his *Essay on Taste*
and *Essay on Genius.* Akenside calls the Association of Ideas
the source of many pleasures in life, and allows it a great share

---

1   See Ch. XIII, infra.
2   First Treatise, Section I, Art. 10 (pag. 7): 'It is of no consequence whether
    we call these Ideas of Beauty and Harmony, Perceptions of the External
    Senses of Seeing and Hearing, or not. I should rather chuse to call our Power
    of perceiving these Ideas, an *Internal Sense,* were it only for the Convenience
    of distinguishing them from other Sensations of Seeing and Hearing, which
    men may have without Perception of Beauty and Harmony'.
    Cf. Art. 11 (pag. 8): 'There will appear another Reason perhaps afterwards,
    for calling this Power of perceiving the Ideas of Beauty an *Internal Sense,*
    from this, that in some other Affairs, where our External Senses are not
    much concern'd, we discern a sort of Beauty, very like, in many respects,
    to that observ'd in sensible Objects, and accompany'd with like pleasure:
    Such is that Beauty perceiv'd in Theorems, or universal Truths, in general
    Causes, and in some extensive Principles of Action'.
3   Cf. A. Gerard, *Essay on Taste,* 2nd ed., 1764, p. 168.

'in the influence of poetry and other arts' [1]. The poem, at least part of it, is founded on Addison's essays, from which the title was also taken. Like Addison, Akenside distinguishes primary and secondary pleasures, and thinks the first kind the result of the perception of greatness, novelty and beauty.

Gerard calls imagination a creative power in so far as it can transpose, vary and compound perceptions. He thinks that judgment ought to regulate and direct it, but he condemns servile submission to its authority, which is apt to check the efforts of genius and to result in insipid correctness [2]. Hume distinguishes three principles of association: *resemblance, contiguity* in time and place, and *cause* and *effect* [3]. It was especially through David Hartley's *Observations on Man* (1749) that the theory won a wide recognition. Hartley, a physician and the founder of the 'Associationist School of Psychologists', based his explanation of all psychical processes on association and drew a parallel between mental and physiological facts. His views were warmly supported and propagated by Joseph Priestley [4] and Archibald Alison [5], who both explained the importance of the principle of association in investigating and interpreting aesthetic experiences [6].

Earlier critical essays, like Burke's *Philosophical Inquiry into the Origin of our Ideas of the Sublime and Beautiful* (1757), Gerard's *Essay on Taste* (1756) and *Essay on Genius* (1774), Kames's *Elements of Criticism* (1762), and Beattie's *Dissertations Moral and Critical* (1783), take for granted that the imagination acts in strict accordance with the laws of association. Though they all appeared after Hartley's book had been published, they do not show any traces of his direct influence, but follow Hobbes and Locke. The mind is the mere passive recipient of sense-impressions which recall each other mechanically. Burke states emphatically that the

---

1 The Design, prefixed to the poem.
2 *Essay on Genius,* Part II.
3 *The Philosophical Works.* Boston, 1854, I, p. 26.
4 *A Course of Lectures on Oratory and Criticism.* London, 1777.
5 *Essays on the Nature and Principles of Taste.* Edinburgh, 1790. See S. H. Monk, *op. cit.,* pp. 117 ff.
6 Cf. Coleridge's opinion: 'Association in philosophy is like the term stimulus in medicine; explaining every thing, it explains nothing; and above all, leaves itself unexplained'. (Shawcross, *op. cit.,* II, p. 222).

imaginative faculty is incapable of producing anything absolutely
new; it can only represent the images in the order and manner in
which they entered the mind, or can combine them in a new way [1].

Sir Joshua Reynolds's ideas about the range of the imagination
are those of the Associationists. Architecture has some principles
in common with poetry and among them is 'that of affecting the
imagination by means of association of ideas', as he said in his
address to the Royal Academy in the year 1786. Twelve years
earlier he had observed that the imagination is 'incapable of
producing anything originally of itself, and can only vary and
combine those ideas with which it is furnished by means of the
senses', so that 'there will be necessarily an agreement in the
imaginations, as in the senses of men' [2]. This is the ordinary neo-
classic conception as Hobbes had taught it. In the fifth *Discourse*,
however, Reynolds compares the two great Italian painters whom
he admires above all others, and about whose relative merits he
constantly wavers in opinion. Raphael has, in his opinion, more
taste and fancy, whereas Michelangelo excels in genius and
imagination. It would appear from this passage that the painter
considers imagination and emotion indispensable to attain to
sublimity, and that a lively fancy is necessary to produce beauty.
'Michel Angelo's works .... seem to proceed from his own mind
entirely, and that mind so rich and abundant, that he never needed,
or seemed to disclaim, to look abroad for foreign help. Raffaelle's
materials are generally borrowed, though the noble structure is his
own' [3]. The difference between the two concepts is not elaborated,
but Reynolds apparently considers the operations of the imagination
to be of a higher order, for the 'effect of sublimity is greater than
that of beauty'.

As I shall have occasion to point out, when dealing with Reynolds
in a separate chapter, we find indications in the later *Discourses*
that the painter no longer considered 'reason' in the neo-classic
sense as an adequate guide in solving aesthetic problems. He
distinguishes a kind of super-rational, intuitive faculty, by which
the artist draws his conclusions, before reason can have made its

---

1   *The Works of E. Burke.* London, 1826, I, p. 105.
2   *Discourses,* p. 107.
3   *Ibid.,* p. 61.

deductions [1]. The belief that the sphere of reason was too limited and that its operations were too slow to make purely rational inferences reliable became more and more common. As the authority of reason declined, that of imagination grew and its range widened. It came to be considered as the primary force in man's mental activities [2]. At the close of the century Alison, following Hartley's psychological way of approach, inquires into 'the NATURE of those QUALITIES that produce Emotions of Taste', and 'the NATURE of that Faculty, by which these Emotions are received'. He considers the imagination the most important factor in producing aesthetic emotions. The object itself only serves to awaken the imagination, the association of ideas suggested by the object produces the aesthetic effects. These associations may be closely related to the object perceived, but they awaken any analogous idea in the memory. Alison's views were discussed and accepted by Jeffrey in the *Edinburgh Review* [3]. Coleridge, though acknowledging that 'much has been said well and truly', thought the principle of association that Alison propounded 'too vague for practical guidance' [4].

When this important step in the direction of the romantic conception of art had been made, and Imagination began to be looked upon as 'the living Power and prime Agent of all human Perception' [5], as Coleridge said, the aestheticians who inquired into the nature of its operations must have felt the need of another term to denote the faculty which receives 'all its materials ready made from the law of association' [6]. There is hardly any reference in the eighteenth century writers on the subject which foreshadows Coleridge's distinction between 'the imagination or shaping and modifying power' and the fancy or the 'aggregating and associative power', a distinction he defended against Wordsworth's assertion

---

1 *Discourses,* XIII.
2 Cf. W. Jackson Bate, *From Classic to Romantic.* Harvard Univ. Press, 1946, pp. 114 ff.
3 May 1811, no. 38.
4 See S. H. Monk, *op. cit.,* pp. 148 ff.
5 Shawcross, *op. cit.,* I, p. 202.
6 *Ibid.*

in the preface to the edition of the *Lyrical Ballads and other Poems*, in 1815 [1].

Reynolds's tentative attempt to keep the two apart has already been discussed. A clearer distinction is made by James Beattie, though he admits that they are two names for the same faculty and grants that they are often used as synonymous terms. The word imagination, however, is used by him for the more solemn, and fancy for the more trivial manifestations of it. A witty author is a man of lively fancy, but a sublime poet is said to possess a vast imagination. He does not agree with Addison that all images in the fancy have made their first entrance through the sight, from which would follow that a person born blind could have no imagination. Beattie's own conception of the operations of the faculty is much wider. The imagination has two important functions: first, that of conceiving ideas simply as they are in themselves, without any view to their reality, and secondly that of combining into new forms the ideas or notions derived from experience or information. It would appear from these words that the Scottish critic differs from his contemporaries in allowing the imagination a wider sphere of action, not restricted to the aggregation of sense-impressions [2].

---

[1] Cf. Cl. D. Thorpe, *The Imagination: Coleridge versus Wordsworth* (PQ, XVIII, 1939).

[2] Cf. John Bullitt and W. Jackson Bate, *Distinctions between Fancy and Imagination in Eighteenth Century English Criticism* (MLN, LX, 1945), and E. R. Wasserman, *Another Eighteenth-Century Distinction between Fancy and Imagination* (MLN, LXIV, 1949).

CHAPTER II

DISBELIEF IN AUTHORITY. INFLUENCE OF SCIENCE

The neo-classic code in its most rigorous form was such that it could not possibly enjoy a long life. In its very nature lay the germs of inevitable decay. Its extreme devotees did not realize that there was something irrational in accepting Aristotelian canons, which were exclusively founded on the practice of some Greek poets, and of which some were merely the result of the particular character of the Greek stage, as immutable standards for modern poets living under entirely different circumstances. They completely overlooked that it was their duty to adapt their standard to the works of art with which they were dealing. This lack of historical perspective and historical tolerance, the strict adherence to the schedule of the 'kinds', and last of all the view that only imitation of classic patterns could lead to satisfactory results, tended to reduce literary production to a state of sterility and petrifaction. It ignored the fact that the one supreme principle of art is that of originality and that instead of being something static, literature as well as any other art, is essentially dynamic. Inexorable laws, blind obedience to established precepts, can only hinder its growth and condemn it to stagnation and death. It has been pointed out that this rigid doctrine was repeatedly challenged in the days of Dryden and Pope, and the causes that opened a wider outlook have been discussed.

Dogmatic criticism was never entirely given up during the Johnsonian Age; traces of it may be found even in the last decades of the century, as I shall have occasion to point out. But the critical literature, of which the last fifty years before the appearance of the *Lyrical Ballads* were so extremely productive, clearly illustrates that the belief in *a priori* rules, which had always been far from general, had had its day, and had made way for a broader historical rationalism. The deference for rational criteria is accompanied by a strong tendency to break away from the restraints of authority. A disbelief in the accepted postulates of earlier generations of critics is the main distinguishing trait of the

Johnsonian Age. Only those rules are   accepted which are the
result of a renewed analysis on rationalistic lines.

This phase of critical thought, which rejected all *a priori* rules,
was strongly influenced by the scientific spirit dominating the
intellectual movement known as the English 'Aufklärung'. The
rapid strides that physical science had made during the latter part
of the seventeenth century had led to a great reverence for the
experimental methods which it followed. Its successful investigations
had established the belief that the whole universe was subject to
permanent and inflexible laws, which might be discovered by the
continual application of human reason to the observation of facts.
The restless spirit of inquiry which characterized this period, left
its impress on all branches of human knowledge, on ethics, religion,
politics, and at last also pervaded the domain of literary criticism.
The methods of physical science were transferred to them, an
empiric process of research came to be considered as the only
adequate means to acquire a thorough knowledge of the human
mind. Man was the principal object of interest, human reason the
one supreme source of knowledge, the ultimate criterion by which
the validity of all laws and systems was to be tried [1].

The typical philosopher of the Age of Enlightenment, John
Locke, applied the experimental methods of physical science to
mental problems. No one gave evidence of a stronger repugnance
to believing anything on arbitrary authority than he. In the first
book of his *Essay concerning Human Understanding* (1690) he
rejected the doctrine of innate ideas, and accepted experience as the
only source of human knowledge. Dogmatic theology was a thing
of the past. Traditions of all sorts which had long been venerated,
became the objects of painstaking investigations. The general
disbelief in authority in the first part of the eighteenth century

---

[1] In his *Gray's Inn Journal* Arthur Murphy voices the opinion of the day,
when he recommends the study of the human mind, 'the most rational and
pleasing Employment we are capable of!' He ranks it much higher than that
of mathematical problems: 'In trying to solve the latter we may mistake
one Figure, and then all our ingenious Labour evaporates into air, whereas
in the Pursuit of self-knowledge our Reasonings are from Feeling, and all
our Discoveries, besides the advantage of being as surprising as in any other
Science, carry with them a further accession of Pleasure, as we are ourselves
more immediately concerned in them'.

cannot be better illustrated than by David Hume's words in one of his *Essays, Moral, Political, and Literary:* 'Now, there has been a sudden and sensible change in the opinions of men within these last fifty years, by the progress of learning and of liberty. Most people, in this island, have divested themselves of all superstitious reverence to names and authority: The clergy have much lost their credit: Their pretensions and doctrines have been ridiculed; and even religion can scarcely support itself in the world. The mere name of *king* commands little respect; and to talk of a king as God's viceregent on earth, or to give him any of those magnificent titles, which formerly dazzled mankind, would but excite laughter in every one' [1]. It is only natural that the strong insistence on individual judgment, the general tendency to reject the validity of anything that could not be rationally demonstrated, proved detrimental to the belief in established critical canons.

Of the influence of science on the critical opinions of the Johnsonian Age more will be said in Chapter IV. Before discussing this aspect of the change more fully, it is advisable, however, to deal with the most important factor in the reaction against classical dogma: the revival of the interest in the past and more in particular the resurrection of Elizabethan tradition.

---

[1]   Seventh essay: *Whether the British Government inclines more to Absolute Monarchy, or to a Republic.*

CHAPTER III

THE GROWTH OF THE SENSE OF HISTORICAL RELATIVITY

Just as the rediscovery of the world of chivalry and romance was the most potent factor in the liberation of poetry from reason and correctness, it was also the chief motive force in the attack on the stronghold of static criticism. Only an intimate knowledge of older vernacular literature could remove the mistaken notion that imitation of the classics was the only safe road to the temple of fame, and foster the conviction that it was illogical to apply Horace's and Aristotle's canons to works composed under the most varied circumstances. Some of the mediaeval forms of literary art, like the ballads and romances, were not even represented in classical literature, while others, like Spenser's epic and the romantic Elizabethan drama, displayed a flagrant violation of classical maxims, and a marked deviation from the models of antiquity. If any merit was to be allowed them, it was obvious that a different standard of appreciation must be applied. They were not to be judged by a system of pre-ordained laws, but by the laws of their own being; the critic was to follow the poet, not conversely.

The prevailing taste for older literature was only one of the aspects of the wide-spread interest in the past which is one of the most striking features of the latter half of the eighteenth century. Historical inquiry enjoyed an almost unparalleled vogue which grew in strength as the century advanced. At no time of English history were books on historical subjects so much in demand as in the Age of Johnson. 'History is the most popular species of writing', says the author of the *Decline and Fall of the Roman Empire* in his *Autobiography* [1], and another famous authority, David Hume, observes in one of his letters: 'I believe this to be the historical age and this the historical nation' [2].

Hume, Robertson and Gibbon are the three most illustrious

---

[1] *The Memoirs of the Life of Edward Gibbon,* ed. G. Birkbeck Hill, 1900, p. 194.
[2] Hume, *Letters to Strahan,* ed. G. Birkbeck Hill, 1888, p. 155.

exponents of historical writing that this period can boast of, but besides these there were many others, endowed with less brilliant acquirements, whose very names have long since passed into oblivion.

No less great was the popularity of antiquarian and archaeological studies. Antiquarian research, which had been common in England ever since the days of Queen Elizabeth, was treated with contempt by the leading Augustan critics, to whom any kind of minute investigation was distasteful. Pope ridiculed it in his *Dunciad*, where the Oxford scholar and antiquarian Thomas Hearne became the butt of his satire [1]. Even Johnson and some of his contemporaries looked down on this sort of historical inquiry, and thought it beneath the notice of literary men. In the Doctor's own eyes, a mere antiquarian was 'a rugged being' [2], and Warburton asserted that antiquarianism was to true letters 'what specious funguses are to the oak' [3]. Other equally inappreciative views might be quoted, but on the other hand there was a numerous group of scholars and critics who held different opinions. Antiquarian pursuits were intimately connected with the literary interest in the past. Thomas Warton, Tyrwhitt, Malone and Steevens were literary scholars as well as antiquarians. Like Percy they were all members of the *Society of Antiquaries*, which was incorporated in 1751, and issued publications regularly from the year 1770 onward. The *Society of Antiquaries of Scotland* included among its members critics like Kames and Blair [4].

The rapid progress of historical studies in the eighteenth century was again largely the result of the general advance of science. The processes of induction which had been so successfully applied to its different departments, were extended to the field of historical research [5]. The belief in these processes received additional strength from contemporary philosophy, which employed the same

---

[1] Book III, ll. 185 ff.
[2] Boswell, *Life of Johnson, etc.*, ed. by Birckbeck Hill. Oxford 1887, III, p. 278.
[3] *Letters from a Late Eminent Prelate*, p. 265.
[4] The antiquarian interest in ballads is best of all illustrated by Vicesimus Knox's remark in one of his *Essays, Moral and Literary:* 'Books printed in the black letter are sought for by the English antiquary with the same avidity with which he peruses a monumental inscription or treasures up a Saxon piece of money'.
[5] Cf. R. Flint, *History of the Philosophy of History*, p. 16.

empirical methods in its search for truth. It gradually began to be realized that the historian is not only concerned with a bare statement of facts, but that an important part of his task is to connect them with the general tendencies of the age with which he has to deal. More and more it became a recognized fact that the various aspects of human development, its political, social, religious, and literary issues, are all intimately interrelated, and that the study of one of them entails a careful examination of the others.

The investigation of the past was not at once carried on in the spirit that an unprejudiced interpretation of its records requires. The historical outlook of a certain age is always determined by its general cast of thought. The conception of history cannot be studied apart from the contemporary intellectual tendencies of which it is a product. No time offers a better illustration of the important truth that the past is always more or less contemplated in the light of the present, than the Age of Enlightenment. The consciousness of the great progress that civilization had made, had given rise to a spirit of self-sufficiency. There was a general dogmatic belief that by the sustained efforts of the last few generations, civilization had made tremendous strides, so that the final stage of development had almost been reached and a further advance was scarcely to be expected. This feeling of complacency was at first an insuperable barrier to a strictly objective course of research. No wonder that the old contempt for the past, and the want of historical perspective which was so common among the writers of Augustan England, did not at once disappear, when the tendency to historical inquiry arose. Voltaire's disgust at the barbaric ages strongly affected his account of mediaeval history, and Hume, the principal representative of 'the school of Voltaire in England' considered this period hardly worthy of any serious attention [1].

The critical literature of the Johnsonian Age is pervaded by the same spirit of self-confidence. It is especially in the essays of the minor critics that we meet with a firmly-rooted conviction of superiority, a conviction that they are living in an enlightened age which has shaken off the bondage of the past. But even Thomas

---

[1]   Cf. J. B. Black, *The Art of History*. London, 1926, pp. 87, 88.

Warton, who did more than anyone else to further the interest in earlier writers, is not free from the prejudices of his time. In the Preface to his *History of English Poetry* he says: 'We look back on the savage condition of our ancestors with the *triumph of superiority*; we are pleased to mark the steps by which we have been raised from rudeness to elegance, and our reflections on the subject are accompanied with the *conscious pride* arising, in a great measure, from a tacit comparison of the *infinite disproportion between the feeble efforts of remote ages and our present superiority in knowledge*' [1]. It was this very belief in the advanced state of civilization that prompted the critics of the eighteenth century to examine the earlier stages of development. In the same Preface Warton refers to the pleasure that the literary historian feels in pursuing the progress of poetry from its rude beginnings to its perfection in a polished age. And E. Watkinson observes in one of his *Essays on Criticism,* contributed to the *Critical Review:* 'These faint glimmerings we view with a secret, though sensible satisfaction . . . . One would not be totally ignorant of the manners and transactions of past ages; though the scene is dark and gloomy, yet to a mind of taste and sensibility, it is pleasing to trace the gradual progression of the human understanding' [2]. These are only two of the many illustrations that the student of eighteenth century criticism is sure to come across. He who takes the trouble to look through the many volumes of the *Monthly Review* and its rival the

---

[1] As Professor D. N. Smith observes in his *Warton's History of English Poetry.* (Warton Lecture, 1929), p. 28: 'For a real lover of the Middle Ages, Warton is surprisingly fond of the word "barbarous" '. Cf. what Johnson says in the *Preface to Shakespeare:* 'This fault (= sacrificing virtue to convenience) the barbarity of his age could not extenuate' (*op. cit.,* p. 21). Cf. also Percy's preface, in which he called the *Reliques* 'the barbarous productions of unpolished ages'. (Ch. XXIV, infra.)

[2] *Critical Review,* XVIII. Cf. also the review of Percy's *Reliques* in the *Monthly Review,* 32: 'Next to the pleasing prospect of living in the minds and memories of posterity, — a prospect in which only a few privileged names can indulge themselves, — is the more certain gratification of taking a retrospect of past ages, and tracing back our distant claims to the honours, or virtues, of our progenitors. Such a Review is attended, indeed, with uncommon satisfaction to people of a polished and enlightened age; who, seeing themselves elevated so much above the rude simplicity of their ancestors, are proud to think the heroes and bards of former ages as much honoured by their descendants, as the latter by any hereditary title to the distinctions of the former'.

Critical will be struck by the number of treatises dealing with the origin of some branch of learning that are discussed there. Percy's *Essay on the Ancient English Minstrels,* and his *Observations on the Origin of the English Stage and on the Conduct of our first Dramatic Poets,* Hurd's remarks on the origin of poetry, and Thomas Warton's *Two Dissertations* prefixed to his *History* [1] are the best-known attempts in the literary field. Though most of them teem with baseless conjectures and fanciful explanations, they illustrate at least the general belief that things cannot be rightly judged if we do not know how they have come to be what they are. Continuity of development began to be recognized, and this was the one thing necessary to arrive at a sounder conception of history. The more the records of the past were studied, the more the interest in the earlier ages grew, and the more the investigators began to realize that their age was greatly indebted to the achievements of former generations of mankind. The contempt with which they had at first been approached made way for a feeling of grateful recognition of the important heritage their predecessors had left them to enjoy. 'He must have formed a very inadequate idea of the powers and the energy of the human intellect, who imagines that nothing was produced, even in the dark ages, by the efforts of native ingenuity, worthy the adoption of a more refined period', Vicesimus Knox says in one of his essays, and he points out that many principles in English laws and many political institutions have their foundations in feudal times [2].

Mediaeval studies were of course principally concerned with moral and social conditions. Mediaeval literature was at first only read as an interesting record of life and manners, and ballads and romances were considered as instructive social documents. Percy himself recommended his 'barbarous productions of unpolished ages' to the reading public merely as illustrations of the manners of antiquity. The reviewer of the *Critical* praised them for the same reason and called them an ethical history of the dark ages. Thomas Warton did the same with the romances. He thought they merited more attention than had been paid to them, because

---

1   *On the Origin of Romantic Fiction in Europe.*
     On the Introduction of Learning into England.
2   *Works.* London, 1824, I, pp. 358, 359.

they are 'the pictures of antient usages and customs; and represent the manners, genius and character of our ancestors' [1]. He called the writing of a history of poetry an entertaining and useful task, because the object of the poet's art is human society and poetical compositions give a faithful representation of the features of the times [2].

The study of historical development fostered the conviction that a work of art is at least partly the result of the social and mental conditions of its era, and that these underlying forces should be studied by the critic. What had been stigmatized by the critics of the preceding age as extravagant and grotesque, was seen in quite a different light when due allowance was made for the difference in manners between modern times and those in which the poet lived. The affectations, conceits, and fopperies of chivalry, which had so often been ridiculed in the days of the Augustans, were pronounced by Hurd and the Wartons to be imitations of real life. Thus the defence of 'Gothic' poetry necessarily conduced to the rejection of the judicial method in criticism and to the acceptance of the historical point of view. The following pages will show that most of the critics of the Johnsonian period recognized that it was the only method to arrive at a just estimation, though they did not always apply it consistently and often reverted to the old dictatorial ways. Even the 'Great Cham' was by no means so insensible to the new way of approach as is often supposed. It was not only accepted and advocated by the detractors from reason like the Wartons, Hurd and a few minor figures, but even the rationalists defended it in the name of reason and nature. This should be borne in mind to prevent the erroneous view that only the precursors of the romantic conception of poetry believed in it.

When the literary forms were traced to their earliest stages, it

---

1   *Observations on the Faerie Queene,* II, p. 268.
2   Preface to Warton's *History of Poetry.* Cf. II, p. 264: '. . . . the chief source of entertainment which we seek in antient poetry, the representation of antient manners'. Cf. also J. Warton, *An Essay on Pope,* II, pp. 1, 2, where the tracing of the origin and progress of poetry is called a subject of no small utility: 'For the manners and customs, the different ways of thinking and of living . . . . appear in no writings so strongly marked, as in the works of the poets in their respective ages'.

5

became evident that they were the result of a natural growth and not the outcome of an artificial process.

The idea of *progress* in art can be traced back to the controversy between the Ancients and Moderns in France. It was started by the latter in their attempts to prove the superiority of the writers of their own time to those of antiquity. Perrault, the champion of the moderns, expressed the view that nature had had the same productive power in all ages [1], and that it would consequently be wrong to ascribe to that of Homer a higher degree of genius than to any other period. On the other hand he maintained that the modern writers, having the advantage of living much later, had profited by the continual progress of sciences and art; their greater knowledge of the rules, invented in the course of this development, gave them the same advantage over the ancients as Virgil had over Homer [2]. It was on these grounds that Perrault in that memorable meeting of the French Academy of the 27th of January 1687 [3] asserted the superiority of the Age of Lewis the Fourteenth.

Fontenelle, his supporter on the side of the moderns, endorsed Perrault's assertion about the unchanging power of nature: the dough of which mankind, animals and plants are kneaded has been the same in all periods of history. Plato, Demosthenes and Homer are therefore not made of a finer clay than the modern philosophers and poets [4]. Like the author of the *Parallèles* he grounded the superiority of the authors of his own time on the fact that they could profit by the harvest of the preceding generations [5]. But he at least was aware that the progress of science could not be identified with that of the arts, that the first is due to experience, whereas the other principally depends upon vivacity of the

---

1 A former les esprits comme à former les corps
   La Nature en tout temps fait les mesmes efforts,
   Son estre est immuable, et cette force aisée
   Dont elle produit tout ne s'est point épuisée.
                        Perrault, *Siècle de Louis le Grand.*
2 Vial et Denise, *Idées et doctrines littéraires du XVIIe siècle,* p. 279.
3 Rigault, *Histoire de la querelle des anciens et des modernes* (1856), p. 141.
4 Vial et Denise, *op. cit.,* p. 267. (Fontenelle: *Digression sur les anciens et les modernes,* 1688).
5 *Ibid.,* p. 269: 'Un bon esprit cultivé est, pour ainsi dire, composé de tous les esprits des siècles précédens'.

imagination [1]. He defended the moderns, however, in the name of reason, and asserted that they surpass the ancients in rational power. In Fontenelle's opinion no age could boast of more 'raisonnement' than that of Descartes.

In England the question of literary progress was amply discussed by the 'virtuosi' [2]. They were already convinced that the evolution of the arts and sciences was not an uninterrupted process but that it was necessary to distinguish periods of growth and decay. But they failed to see that there was some difference in this respect between science and arts. The author of *An Essay upon the Ancient and Modern Learning* expresses himself as follows: 'Science and Arts have run their circles, and had their periods in the several Parts of the World. They are generally agreed to have held their course from *East* to *West* . . . .' [3].

Dryden, too, believed in cycles of progress for science as well as for art. The degree of perfection which they attain, depends, according to him, on 'a kind of universal genius', which every age possesses [4]. In *A Discourse concerning the Origin and Progress of Satire* he refers to it again: 'It is manifest', he says, 'that some particular ages have been more happy than others in the production of great men' [5].

Temple's superficial essay elicited an elaborate discussion of the subject by William Wotton, called *Reflections upon Ancient*

---

1 Prof. Spingarn observes that Pascal was probably the first to make this distinction. (*Crit. Essays*, I, p. LXXXIX).

2 For the earlier attempts to disprove the superiority of the ancients, like those of G. Hakewill, whose *An Apologie or Declaration of the Power and Providence of God in the Government of the World, etc.* (1627) was a protest against the current opinion about the world's decay, I. Glanvill (*Plus ultra, or the Progress and Advancement of Knowledge since the days of Aristotle*, 1668, a defence of the Royal Society), T. Sprat, and others, see J. B. Bury, *The Idea of Progress*. London 1920, and R. F. Jones, *Ancients and Moderns, A Study of the Background of the Battle of the Books*. St. Louis, 1936. [Washington University Studies — New Series (Language and Literature — No. 6).]

3 Spingarn, *Crit. Essays*, III, p. 50.

4 *An Essay on Dramatic Poesy*, Ker, I, p. 36.

5 Ker, II, p. 25. Cf. also his *Defence of the Epilogue,* where Dryden examines the poetry 'of the last age' in the self-confident spirit of his own day: '. . . . I profess to have no other ambition in this *Essay,* than that poetry may not go backward, when all other arts and sciences are advancing'. (Ker, I, p. 163).

and Modern Learning (1694), to the second edition of which Bentley, prompted by Temple's praise of the *Letters of Phalaris*, added his learned disquisition, followed two years later by his masterly *Dissertation* (1699). Wotton is the only one of his contemporaries who makes a sharp distinction between an art which owes its origin to a certain invention and whose further improvements he compares to 'Superstructures raised by other Men upon that first Ground-work', and arts, founded in nature, which are independent of time. The ancients could therefore have as much knowledge of the human mind as the moderns [1]. Wotton was one of the English critics who influenced the Abbé du Bos. The author of the *Réflexions critiques sur la poésie et sur la peinture* carefully distinguishes between scientific development and evolution in art. The latter is not an uninterrupted advance to the goal of perfection, keeping pace with the accumulation of knowledge, but a complicated process of rises and falls; a period of great creative genius may be followed by one of sterility, or even by a relapse into barbarism. This evolution is, in Du Bos's opinion, determined by climatic influences; social and moral changes are insufficient to account for it.

There is no doubt that this theory of the French critic was known to many of the eighteenth century critics. References to his *Réflexions critiques sur la poésie et sur la peinture* (1719) are numerous. It was translated into English by T. Nugent in 1748, after it had gone through many editions in France [2], and seems to have enjoyed a high reputation. It is, however, difficult to make out whether we can speak of a direct influence, for some of his views had already been expressed by critics like Temple and Wotton [3].

In eighteenth century critical essays, the idea of evolution in art is repeatedly stated. Blackwell, speaking of the progression of manners, which are dependent upon the social conditions of the country, says: 'For the manners of a People seldom stand still, but are either polishing or spoiling'. As the epic poet has to give

---

1   William Wotton, *Reflections upon Ancient and Modern Learning*, 2nd ed., 1697, p. 51.
2   *Critical Reflections on Poetry, Painting and Music*, 1748.
3   See the discussion of climatic influences, below.

a true picture of what he sees about him, his art is subject to the same changes [1]. It is therefore necessary for the critic to adapt his standard to the circumstances under which Homer wrote, and to put himself in the place of the audience for whom his poetry was intended.

In the discussion of Spenser's *Faerie Queene,* contributed to the *Critical Review* (Febr. 1759), Goldsmith observes: 'Learning and language are ever fluctuating, either rising to perfection or retiring into primeval barbarity', and adds, with the self-sufficiency proper to the rationalistic critics of the time, that 'perhaps the point of English perfection is already passed, and every intended improvement may be now only deviation' [2].

The tenth chapter of Johnson's *Rasselas* contains that memorable dissertation on poetry, where Imlac tells of his adventures in the different countries he has seen. It has struck him that in almost all of them the most ancient poets are considered as the best, and he suggests as one of the explanations that 'every other kind of knowledge is an acquisition gradually obtained, and poetry is a gift conferred at once'. In these few words Johnson draws a parallel between the gradual accumulation of facts on which scientific progress depends, and the manner in which art progresses. Du Bos had called this 'un progrès subit', which he had contrasted with 'le progrès lent' of science.

Reference has already been made to the theory of climatic influences on literary production, which is one of the aspects of the historical doctrine of the 'milieu' championed by the great critics of the nineteenth century and carried to an extreme by Taine. This doctrine has of course a much wider scope, and includes besides the influences of climate those of race, morals, and political and social conditions.

The effect of *climate* on the human mind had been recognized long before the period in discussion [3]. In the sixteenth century Bodin in his *République* had dealt with its influence on social life;

---

1   *An Enquiry into the Life and Writings of Homer* (1735), p. 13.
2   *The Works of Oliver Goldsmith,* ed. by J. W. M. Gibbs, IV, p. 335.
3   See Spingarn, *Crit. Essays,* I, p. CII ; Lombard, *L'Abbé du Bos, un initiateur de la pensée moderne,* 1913, pp. 243 ff.

he had investigated the relation between climatic and geographical conditions, and the morals, manners and customs of the people living under them [1]. His book is generally mentioned as one of the sources from which Montesquieu may have drawn many of the propositions laid down in his famous *Esprit des Lois* (1748).

The theory did not find recognition in the domain of aesthetics till the end of the seventeenth century. It appealed strongly to the adherents of the school of taste, and in their works we find many allusions to it. Bouhours, in one of his *Entretiens,* namely that on *Le Bel Esprit,* makes Ariste suggest that the scarcity of 'les beaux esprits' in the cold countries of the north may be due to the difference in climate, and that the peculiar nature of the French genius may be ascribed to the same cause [2]. Fénelon, though agreeing in the main with Perrault's statement that 'the trees of to-day have the same form, and bear the same fruit as two thousand years ago and that men produce the same thoughts', yet thinks that some allowance should be made for the difference in climate, as one climate conduces much more to the production of genius than another [3]. Madame Dacier observes that some nations are so much favoured by the sun that they can imagine and invent for themselves, whereas others can only by means of imitation keep out of rudeness and barbarism [4]. Fontenelle, like Fénelon admits the justice of Perrault's remark that the human mind is the same in all ages, but it differs, according to him, in different countries owing to climatic influences. It was especially through the critical writings of the Abbé du Bos that the theory received a wider recognition. He thought there was an intimate relationship between genius and climate, and, as has already been observed, founded his idea of progress on this premise: climatic changes were to him the causes of the alternate periods of growth and decadence

---

1   Cf. R. Flint, *History of the Philosophy of History,* p. 198.

2   'J'avoue, interrompit Ariste, que les beaux esprits sont un peu plus rares dans les pays froids, parce que la nature y est plus languissante et plus morne, pour parler ainsi . . . . Ce n'est pas que je veuille dire, ajouta-t-il que tous les Septentrionaux soient bêtes. Il y a de l'esprit et de la science en Allemagne, comme ailleurs, mais enfin on n'y connaît point notre bel esprit'. (*Op. cit.,* p. 181).

3   Rigault, p. 383.

4   Vial et Denise, *Idées et doctrines littéraires du XVIIIe siècle,* p. 13.

of literary production. As Lombard has already suggested, Du Bos drew from English sources, especially from Temple and Addison [1].

In English critical literature references to climatic influences on art are to be found as early as the second half of the seventeenth century. The new scientific movement would naturally lead to the study of climate, and owing to the intimate relation between the scientists and the 'virtuosi', it soon entered the field of literary criticism. Cowley, in the preface to his poems, has the following remark which demonstrates his belief in the influence of atmospheric and social conditions on literary production: 'if *wit* be such a *Plant* that it scarce receives heat enough to preserve it alive even in the *Summer* of our cold *Clymate,* how can it choose but wither in a long and a sharp *winter?* — a warlike, various, and a tragical age is best to *write of,* but worst to *write in*' [2]. A few lines further on he attributes the coolness of Ovid's verses to 'the *cold* of the Contrey' [3]. After discussing the salutary influence that the Royal Society had had on the English language 'by rejecting all amplification, digression, and swellings of style', and returning to 'the primitive purity and shortness', Sprat lavishly praises his countrymen for their unaffected sincerity and sound simplicity. These qualities, proper to the soil, he attributes to 'the climate, the air, the influence of the heaven, the composition of the English blood, as well as the embraces of the Ocean', and it is due to these influences that nature will reveal more mysteries to the English than to other nations [4]. A strong impetus to the development of the historical conception and the study of social environment was given by the greatest of the 'virtuosi', Sir William Temple. Entering the lists on the side of the ancients, he suggests that various happy circumstances: 'exact Temperance in their Races, great pureness of Air, and equality of Clymate, long Tranquility of Empire or Government' may have been conducive to the advancement of learning in Greece and Rome [5]. 'May there not many circumstances concur to one production that do not to any other in one or many

---

[1] Cf. *Réflexions sur la poésie et sur la peinture,* II, p. 592.
[2] Spingarn, *Crit. Essays,* II, p. 80.
[3] *Ibid.,* p. 81.
[4] Spingarn, *Crit. Essays,* II, pp. 118, 119.
[5] *Ibid.,* III, p. 45.

Ages?', he asks [1]. In his other essay: *Of Poetry* he ranks the English drama higher than that of any other nation, as it possesses a 'Vein Natural perhaps to our Country, and which with us is called Humour ....' These superior qualities are attributed by Temple to the fertile soil, the unsettled climate and the liberty the English nation enjoys [2].

In his *Heads of an Answer to Rymer,* directed against this critic's *Tragedies of the Last Age* but not intended for publication, Dryden suggests that climate and the spirit of the age determine taste: 'the climate, the age, the disposition of the people to whom a poet writes, may be so different, that what pleased the Greeks would not satisfy an English audience' [3]. Dennis looks upon the difference of climate and customs as the main reason why dramatic scenes that moved the Greeks, appear contemptible to modern eyes. On the same ground he believes that the frequent appearance of love upon the modern stage would have found little appreciation with the ancients [4]. Blackwell, the author of *An Enquiry into the Life and Writings of Homer* (1735), enumerates the various conditions that favoured the development of the Greek poet's genius [5]. Among them he mentions 'the happy climate' of his country. Blackwell's words are quoted later on by J. Warton in the fourth volume of his edition of Pope [6].

It is difficult to say whether the critics of the Age of Johnson adopted their ideas on climatic influence from their English predecessors of the seventeenth century or from France. To the present writer it seems highly probable that in many cases Fontenelle, but especially the Abbé du Bos suggested them. There are various references to the *Réflexions sur la poésie et sur la peinture* in the critical literature of the period. Johnson implies that he considers it as an example of good criticism and mentions Du Bos's name in conjunction with those of Burke and Bouhours [7],

---

1 Spingarn, *Crit. Essays,* III, p. 49.
2 *Ibid.,* p. 103. The classical idea that art can only flourish in a country enjoying political freedom, is repeatedly expressed in 18th century criticism.
3 Dryden, *Works,* ed. by Scott-Saintsbury, vol. XV, p. 385.
4 Spingarn, *Crit. Essays,* III, pp. 150, 151; Hooker, I, pp. 436, 437.
5 P. 334.
6 P. 379.
7 Boswell, II, p. 90.

Thomas Warton quotes his opinion on allegory [1], just as Kames does in his *Elements of Criticism*, Bishop Hurd refers to his theory of the influence of climate in the notes to Horace's *Art of Poetry* [2] and adduces a passage from the *Réflexions* in his *Discourse on Poetic Imitation* [3].

As I shall have occasion to illustrate later on, Johnson himself was firmly convinced that it was the poet's principal task to depict the passions of the human heart, which were the same in all ages, and that those elements which were subject to change, were of minor importance to him [4]. Yet, as appears from the tenth chapter of his *Rasselas*, he did not consider the study of these accidental elements as altogether worthless. He thought a knowledge of nature indispensable to the poet but believed that he should at the same time be acquainted with all the modes of life. Johnson named it as the poet's duty to 'trace the changes of the human mind, as they are modified by various institutions and accidental influences of climate or custom, from the sprightliness of infancy to the despondence of decrepitude' [5]. In the *Life of Dryden* he observes that 'to judge rightly of an author we must transport ourselves to his time, and examine what were the wants of his contemporaries, and what were his means of supplying them' [6]. The same view is expressed by Hume: 'every work of art, in order to produce its due effect on the mind, must be surveyed in a certain point of view, ... A critic of different age or nation, who should peruse this discourse, must .... place himself in the same situation as the audience, in order to form a true judgment of the oration' [7].

In the second chapter of *An Inquiry into the Present State of Polite Learning* Goldsmith discusses the factors which contribute to its

---

1   *Observations on the F. Q.*, II, p. 112.
2   Q. Horatii Flacci, *Epistolae ad Pisones et Augustum,* etc. London, 5th ed., 1776, I, p. 263.
3   *Ibid.,* III, p. 126.
     For other references to Du Bos see A. F. B. Clark, *Boileau and the French Classical Critics in England*, 1925, p. 300.
4   Cf. *Rambler,* 36 and various other passages from Johnson's Works. See *Imitation of Nature,* Chapter VI, infra.
5   *Rasselas,* ed. W. Raleigh. Oxford 1898, p. 63.
6   *Lives*, I, 411.
7   *Essays Moral, Political, and Literary,* ed. by T. H. Green and T. H. Grose. London, 1889, vol. I, p. 276.

perfection: permanently peaceful conditions and political freedom; but besides these there are physical causes. 'To attain literary excellence also, it is requisite that the soil and climate should, as much as possible, conduce to happiness. The earth must supply man with the necessaries of life, before he has leisure or inclination to pursue more refined enjoyments. The climate, also, must be equally indulgent; for, in too warm a region, the mind is relaxed into languor, and, by the opposite excess, is chilled into torpid inactivity'. All these advantages were, in the writer's opinion, united in Greece and Rome, during their periods of highest literary achievement.

Similar views are enunciated by J. Warton in his *Essay on the Writings and Genius of Pope* (1756). He thinks that Theocritus wrote his pastorals under very favourable circumstances: the delicious climate of Sicily was extremely beneficial to their production: 'The poet described what he saw and felt, and had no need to have recourse to those artificial assemblages of pleasing objects, which are not to be found in nature' [1]. A little further on Warton emphasizes the importance of the critic's task to study the historical environment of a work of art. The passage is one of the best-known of the whole *Essay:* 'We can never completely relish, or adequately understand any author, especially any ancient, except we constantly keep in our eye his climate, his country and his age' [2]. In his comment on Pope's lines:

> Know well each ANCIENT'S proper character;
> His fable, subject, scope in ev'ry page;
> Religion, Country, genius of his Age: [3]

he censures those critics of Homer and the Greek tragedians who neglected the poet's advice. 'There is no author', he observes, 'whose capital excellence suffers more from the reader's not regarding his climate and country, than the incomparable Cervantes'. In Warton's edition of Pope's works (1797) there is another remark in which the superior merit of the classics in general, and Homer in particular, is attributed to 'the *united* influence of the happiest

---

[1] *Op. cit.,* pp. 3, 4.
[2] *Ibid.,* p. 5. The reviewer of the *Monthly* calls this 'a sensible observation . . . . which has a foundation in nature'.
[3] *Essay on Crit.,* ll. 119—121.

climate, the most natural *manners* to paint, the boldest *language* to use; the most expressive *religion*, and the richest *subject* to work upon' [1]. This passage was probably suggested by Blackwell's *Enquiry* where we find a statement in nearly the same words.

P. Stockdale, whose *Inquiry into the Nature, and Genuine Laws of Poetry including a particular Defence of the Writings and Genius of Mr. Pope* (1778) was prompted by Warton's *Essay*, and was meant to show this critic's vitiated taste, is at least in so far at one with his antagonist that he believes in the close relation between the literary activity in a certain country, and its physical conditions. He thinks that climate has either a restraining or a dilating influence, 'limiting, or enlarging the endowments of reason and fancy', and that 'the English climate is of a temperature extremely favourable to freedom and the Muses' [2].

No writer of the period shows a keener sense of historical relativity than Thomas Warton. In the *Observations on the Faerie Queene* he deprecates the too common practice of his day of looking at the customs and manners of a remote age with modern eyes, and calls it the first duty of the critic to place himself in the writer's situation and circumstances. In his *History of English Poetry* he suggests that the great violence of the Scottish satirists is at least partly due to the sternness of the national character, and attributes the disparity between English and Scottish poetry to racial and climatic differences [3].

Blair's observations on the subject were evidently inspired by Du Bos. Blair calls it a remarkable phenomenon that famous writers and artists have lived in great numbers in certain periods of history, while other ages have been curiously unproductive of genius. He then mentions the causes to which this fact has been attributed: moral causes, such as favourable circumstances of government, encouragement from great men, and emulation among men of genius: 'But as these have been thought inadequate to the whole effect, physical causes have been also assigned: and the Abbé du Bos, in his Reflections on Poetry and Painting, has collected a great many observations on the influence which the air, the

---

1   *Op. cit.*, IV, p. 379.
2   *An Inquiry into the Nature and Genuine Laws of Poetry*, p. 60.
3   *History of Poetry*, II, p. 321.

climate, and other such natural causes, may be supposed to have upon genius'[1]. Blair does not give us his own opinion on Du Bos's explanation, but proceeds to enumerate the four great ages of literary history, and the exponents of each in particular.

His thirty-eighth lecture deals with the origin and progress of poetry, and is one of the many fanciful critical essays dealing with the genetic side of literary art, in which the eighteenth century was extremely rich. Here he compares the nature of Gothic poetry with that of Peruvian and Chinese songs and the Celtic poetry of Ossian. The great difference in spirit that has struck him is, in his opinion, the result of 'diversity of climate, and of manner of living', which is bound to occasion 'some diversity in the strain of the first poetry of nations; chiefly, according as those nations are of a more ferocious, or of a more gentle spirit; and according as they advance faster or slower in the arts of civilization'. This is the reason why Gothic poetry is fierce, and the Peruvian and Chinese songs breathe a much milder spirit. The Celtic productions show a more advanced stage of civilization, 'in consequence of the long cultivation of poetry among the Celtae'[2].

It is evident from the enumeration of these various references that the pseudo-classical belief in absolute standards had been greatly shaken in the second half of the eighteenth century. It began to be realized that literature is to a large extent the outcome of social conditions, the reflection therefore of constantly changing circumstances. It followed naturally from this conviction that the standard by which literary art is to be judged should be adapted to the customs and manners that prevailed in the author's time. The eighteenth century saw the dawn of the sociological method, which in the next was to find so many fervid adherents. The separate articles in the second part of this essay will show to what extent the historical way of approach was adopted by each of the critics in particular.

---

1   H. Blair, *Lectures on Rhetoric and Belles Lettres*. London, 1833, pp. 469, 70.
2   *Ibid.*, p. 515.

CHAPTER IV

THE PERMANENT ELEMENT IN ART.
SCIENTIFIC CRITICISM

Though most critics of the period were conscious of the intimate relationship between the literary production of a certain age, and its social, moral, and physical conditions, and consequently realized the necessity of using relative aesthetic standards, they were by no means blind to the fact that there was an element of permanence in art, something independent of place and time. It was on this essentially immutable something in the poet's works that his fame would rest, when the elements which vary with the shifting conditions of human life, had lost their interest for the reader. The historical conception in criticism did not lead to an undervaluation of the ancient writers. On the contrary, it was looked upon as an unmistakable sign of their genius that their writings had found admirers in all periods of literary history; the experience of the many centuries that had elapsed since they were written was the best proof of their superior merit. Longinus' *quod semper, quod ubique* principle was therefore as generally accepted in the Age of Johnson as it had been in Pope's time. 'Boileau justly remarks', Johnson says, 'that the books which have stood the test of time .... have a better claim to our regard than any modern can boast, because the long continuance of their reputation proves that they are adequate to our faculties, and agreeable to nature' [1]. 'Human works are not easily found without a perishable part', he observes in his *Life of Butler*, where he distinguishes between the accidental qualities of a work of art, and

---

[1] *Rambler,* 92 .... Cf. Hume, *Essays Moral, Political and Literary,* I, p. 271: 'The same HOMER, who pleased at ATHENS and ROME two thousand years ago, is still admired at PARIS and at LONDON. All the changes of climate, government, religion, and language, have not been able to obscure his glory. Authority or prejudice may give a temporary vogue to a bad poet or orator; but his reputation will never be durable or general .... On the contrary, a real genius, the longer his works endure, and the more wide they are spread, the more sincere is the admiration which he meets with'.

those which will always appeal to the human mind, because they depend on the natural and invariable constitution of things: 'Such manners as depend upon standing relations and general passions are co-extended with the race of man; but those modifications of life and peculiarities of practice which are the progeny of error and perverseness, or at best of some accidental influence or transient persuasion, must perish with their parents' [1].

In the dissertation on poetry in *Rasselas*, Johnson advises the poet to divest himself of the prejudices of his age and country and 'consider right and wrong in their abstracted and invariable state; he must disregard present laws and opinions, and rise to general and transcendental truths, which will always be the same' [2]. In the *Preface to Shakespeare* (1765) he once again states emphatically that only just representations of general nature can be of any lasting merit, and his admiration of the great dramatist is founded on the fact that his characters 'are not modified by the customs of particular places, unpractised by the rest of the world . . . . they are the genuine progeny of common humanity, such as the world will always supply, and observation will always find'. To works 'not raised upon principles demonstrative and scientifick, but appealing wholly to observation and experience, no other test can be applied than length of duration and continuance of esteem'. Homer's reputation is therefore firmly founded and so is that of Shakespeare. All temporary advantages and disadvantages are at an end. 'He has long outlived his century, the term commonly fixed as the test of literary merit'. Johnson rejects the verdicts of critics like Dennis and Rymer, who 'think his *Romans* not sufficiently *Roman* . . . .'; 'But *Shakespeare* always makes nature predominate over accident; and if he preserves the essential character, is not very careful of distinctions superinduced and adventitious' [3].

Johnson's friend, Sir Joshua Reynolds calls the art of painting neither 'a divine *gift*', nor 'a mechanical *trade*'. Its foundations are laid in solid science; and practice, though essential to perfection, can never attain that at which it aims, unless it works under the

---

[1]   *Lives*, I, pp. 213, 14.
[2]   *Rasselas*, p. 63.
[3]   *Johnson on Shakespeare*, ed. W. Raleigh. Oxford 1925, p. 12 ff.

direction of principle [1]. Reynolds distinguishes two sorts of truths, those founded on the unchanging laws of nature, and others, 'proceeding from local and temporary prejudices, fancies, fashions or accidental connexion of ideas' [2]. He, too, considers it as the poet's as well as the painter's task to depict the universal and immutable and to eliminate as much as possible all that is of a transitory nature. Not the approbation of the poet's contemporaries, who will judge him mainly by his skill in describing their own modes of life, but that of later generations, who will only appreciate his general delineations of human nature, is to be considered as the true touchstone of his merits.

The rationalistic critics of the Age of Johnson were firmly convinced that by a careful investigation of the permanent elements in art, exempt from the shifting conditions of human life, it would be possible to fix an immutable standard. They thought that criticism had at last reached such a high degree of perfection that it might be called scientific. By a new analysis on scientific lines it would be possible to arrive at the establishment of the principles by which literary art was governed, and in obedience to which the artist was to act. In this inductive process no other guides were to be accepted than reason and human nature, both invariable criteria. The empiric methods of science, which had been so destructive of all arbitrary authority and abstract theory, left their distinctive mark on literary criticism as well and favoured the disbelief in external laws. Conformity to Aristotelian and Horatian precepts was no longer considered as a sufficient guarantee for artistic merit. Classical rules had been deduced from the practice of the ancient writers and could therefore not be binding precepts for the modern poet. They were not all to be discarded as worthless; some of them, being founded on universal humanity, which does not conform to changing fashions and tastes, were excepted from this condemnatory verdict [3].

---

1   *Discourses*, World's Classics ed., p. 91.
2   *Ibid.*, p. 117.
3   Cf. A. Murphy, *Gray's Inn Journal*, no. 87, June 15: 'Those rules only which are founded upon the inward frame and constitution of man, can be regarded as permanent and unalterable. All the others are merely observations upon

This new mode of procedure was not restricted to England. In Italy Gravina and Muratori had enunciated views that showed a marked deviation from the Cartesian doctrine. Though, like Descartes, they had looked upon reason as the final test and had laid great stress on expression of truth as the aim of art, their empiric methods were completely at war with the abstract rationalizing of the French philosopher [1]. In France the Cartesian influence on pseudo-classic criticism was much stronger, and it was not before the appearance of the *Réflexions sur la poésie et sur la peinture* (1719) that a reaction against its powerful sway began to set in. Du Bos was one of the first eighteenth century critics to state that essential rules ought to be the result of experimental methods of procedure. All that the dogmatic critics had laid down ought to be reconsidered and verified by the laws of experience [2].

Nowhere was the effect of empiric philosophy on aesthetic theory stronger than in England during the Age of Johnson. The great dictator himself considered it as the critic's task to establish such principles as were based on 'unalterable and evident truth' and therefore of universal application. By following this method, he thought, it would be possible to bring literature under the dominion of science, and to establish order and regularity where up till then either anarchy or the tyranny of rules had prevailed. In the *Preface* to Shakespeare's works Johnson allows the dramatist great merit as a delineator of human nature, and admires him all the more because in Shakespeare's time no systematic study of man had yet begun: 'Speculation had not yet attempted to analyse the mind, to trace the passions to their sources, to unfold the seminal principles of vice and virtue, or sound the depths of the heart for the motives of action' [3]. This passage clearly illustrates how much importance the critic attached to this scientific analysis and what a beneficial influence he expected it to have on literary art. Johnson thought that in this respect his own time showed a con-

---

the practice of great writers. The critics have reduced these examples into laws, which are therefore arbitrary'.

[1]   Cf. J. G. Robertson, *Studies in the Genesis of Romantic Theory in the Eighteenth Century*, 1923.

[2]   Cf. Lombard, *L'Abbé du Bos, un initiateur de la pensée moderne*, p. 232.

[3]   *Op. cit.*, p. 38.

siderable advance upon the Augustan period. We learn from him that in his day Addison's reputation as a critic was no longer what it had been among the immediately preceding generations, because it was 'tentative or experimental' rather than 'scientifick', and he decided by taste rather than principles. This was due, in Johnson's opinion, to the fact that general knowledge — the privilege of his own time — was rare in Addison's days and that he therefore 'presented knowledge in the most alluring form, not lofty and austere, but accessible and familiar'. The method followed in the Milton papers of the *Spectator* is defended on practical grounds: 'Had he presented *Paradise Lost* to the publick with all the pomp of system and severity of science, the criticism would perhaps have been admired, and the poem still have been neglected' [1]. Johnson believed that the reading public of the Age of Queen Anne still had to learn the rudiments of critical theory, which came natural to that of his own day. Nevertheless he deemed it necessary to warn the critic of his time not 'to repose too securely on the consciousness of their superiority to Addison', for in various other *Spectator* papers, as for instance in those on *The Pleasures of the Imagination*, his method was subtle and refined: 'he founds art on the base of nature, and draws the principles of invention from dispositions inherent in the mind of man' [2].

Lord Kames, the Scottish critic, goes even much further than Johnson. He no longer considers criticism as an art but calls it a regular science. The avowed purpose of his interesting and original treatise is 'to examine the sensitive branch of human nature, to trace the objects that are naturally agreeable, as well as those that are naturally disagreeable; and by these means to discover, if we can, what are the genuine principles of the fine arts' [3]. Kames thinks that if once these principles have been discovered by a sustained course of experience, criticism will have reached a high degree of refinement. Both Johnson and he carefully distinguish between *rules,* which are merely the dictates of authority, and *principles,* which are the outcome of renewed investigations.

---

1   *Lives,* II, pp. 146, 147.
2   *Ibid.,* p. 148.
3   *Elements of Criticism,* 6th ed., 1785, I, p. 6.

We find similar distinctions made by other critics. James Beattie in his *Essay on Memory and Imagination* speaks of *essential* and *ornamental* rules, of which the first are founded on the permanent qualities of human nature, the latter on the examples of some previous writers. In the same way Joseph Warton contrasts *fundamental and indispensable rules,* which are dictated by nature and necessity, with *frivolous and unimportant laws.*

The reviewer of Kames's treatise in the *Monthly* strongly emphasizes the difference between the old and the new outlook. 'Former writers', the critic observes, 'have considered Criticism merely as an art and have prescribed slavish rules for the regulation of taste, as if a Critic were to be formed by directions purely mechanical'. It is curious to see him make a distinction between an *art*, which is to be learned by rules, and *science,* which only accepts principles. Criticism, 'in its enlarged signification', must in his opinion be ranked among the sciences: it follows no rules but those which, as Kames had remarked, 'are derived from the human heart' [1].

At the end of two essays, contributed to the *Critical Review* by a certain Ed. Watkinson and entitled: *An Enquiry into the Nature and Tendency of Criticism with regard to the Progress of Literature,* there is a short summary, in which the author draws a parallel between the dogmatic methods of the older critics, and the method adopted by the new workers in the field. It was probably J. Warton's observation in the *Essay on Pope* on the natural antithesis between criticism and creative literature that prompted the following defence: 'The present age is a convincing proof that critical skill and literary perfection may be united; that the extraordinary acumen of the one is not derogatory to the interests of the other'. Watkinson thinks that criticism has in his days attained its acme of perfection, and that its spirit is no longer hostile to literary art: 'It doth not blast the bloom of genius, so as to preclude the fruit of maturity; but it regulates taste by an invariable standard' [2]. This standard is, as appears from what follows, rational to a degree: the pruning of the exuberance of fancy, the checking

---

[1]   *Monthly Review,* vol. 26 (1762), p. 413.
[2]   *Critical Review,* vol. 15 (1763), p. 161.

of the impetuosity of the imagination are among the critic's principal aims.

George Campbell, the author of the scholarly treatise *The Philosophy of Rhetoric* (1776), holds similar views to those of Johnson and Kames. He thinks that the Greeks and Romans have devised many useful rules of composition, but that the moderns have not advanced the art of criticism far beyond what the ancients had already established. The task of the modern critic is to explore a new country, he should try to 'canvass those principles in our nature, to which the various attempts (modes of arguing or forms of speech used for the purposes of explaining, pleasing, moving) are adapted, and by which their success or want of success may be accounted for' [1]. The only important step in this direction has, according to Campbell, been taken by Kames, but he regrets that the author of the *Elements* has treated rhetoric or eloquence — by which Campbell means very much the same as criticism — as 'a *fine* art', without paying attention to the effect its principles may have on artistic creation. He himself considers it as 'a *useful* art': 'From observing similar but different attempts and experiments, and from comparing their effects, general remarks may be made which serve as so many rules for directing future practice; and from comparing such general remarks together, others still more general are deduced.... the artist and the critic are reciprocally subservient' [2]. As is apparent from this quotation, Campbell, too, expected to arrive at fundamental, unvarying principles by following the experimental methods of scientific research.

The painter Sir Joshua Reynolds advocated the same forms of procedure in his *Discourses*. Though they are principally concerned with painting, the author constantly keeps the other arts in view. As they all have the same ultimate purpose, namely that of pleasing, and address themselves to the same faculties, it follows, according to him, that their rules and principles must have great affinity. He is convinced that *taste* is regulated by certain causes, and that 'the knowledge of these causes is acquired by a laborious

---

[1]   *The Philosophy of Rhetoric,* ed. 1816, p. 16.
[2]   *Ibid.,* p. 19.

and diligent investigation of nature, and by the same slow process as wisdom or knowledge of every kind' [1]. As appears from this passage and others, Reynolds, like his contemporaries, wants to transfer the empiric methods of science to the domain of art. 'The application of science gives dignity and compass to any art', he says in the thirteenth Discourse [2]. He protests against the mistaken conception that a scientific basis will cramp its sphere and restrain the flights of the imagination by a too rigid adherence to the dictates of reason. Every art is subject to two kinds of principles: they are either *fluctuating* or *fixed*. Only a sustained application of empiric methods will enable the critic to ascertain which are founded on the customs and habits of a certain age and have therefore a temporary character and which 'are fixed in the nature of things' [3].

David Hume was the great exponent of empiric philosophy in England after Locke. His early *Treatise of Human Nature*, of which the first two books appeared in 1739, sufficiently indicates the author's manner of thinking. In the introduction to it Hume expresses his intention to deal with 'the science of man', on which all the other sciences depend. The knowledge of the powers and qualities of the human mind can, according to him, only be acquired by careful and exact experiments, and he warns his readers against conclusions that are not based on experience. These empiric methods are necessary for all kinds of scientific research and it appears from Hume's *Essays Moral, Political and Literary* (1741—42) that he thinks they ought to be followed by the literary critic as well. In one of these essays, entitled *On the Standard of Taste*, he rejects all rules of composition which are the result of abstract reasoning. 'Their foundation is the same with that of all the practical sciences, experience; nor are they anything but general observations, concerning what has been universally found to please in all countries and in all ages', he observes. He grants that a writer may enjoy a temporary vogue, in spite of flagrant transgressions of the essential rules, but such a reputation will not last long. Like

---

[1] *Discourses,* p. 109. Cf. also pp. 106, 107.
[2] *Ibid.,* p. 197.
[3] *Ibid.,* p. 110.

Johnson, he holds that posterity will soon arrive at a juster estimate of the merits and demerits of his works [1].

Last of all, some attention must be paid to Edmund Burke's *Philosophical Enquiry into the Origin of our Ideas of the Sublime and Beautiful. With an Introductory Discourse concerning Taste* (1757). The first part of the essay contains an investigation of the leading human passions and is meant as a preparation for the enquiry proper contained in the last two parts. Following the methods of empiric philosophy, Burke discusses the characteristics that all sublime and beautiful objects have in common and which must therefore be considered as essential to affect the imagination. The true standard of art is *human nature*. A careful observation of all its qualities will throw light on the fundamental principles by which all artistic creation must be governed. In the concluding 'section' of the first part the author contrasts his own method with that of the critics who look for the rules of art in the wrong place. They seek them 'among poems, pictures, engravings, statues, and buildings' and neglect the only true source of knowledge. Artists in general and poets in particular who follow the precepts of these false guides, become imitators of each other rather than of nature. Burke realizes that his own essay is only a weak attempt to settle the question. He was prompted to publish it, however, because he felt convinced that 'nothing tends more to the corruption of science than to suffer it to stagnate. These waters must be troubled, before they can exert their virtues. A man who works beyond the surface of things, though he may be wrong himself, yet he clears the way for others, and may chance to make even his errours subservient to the cause of truth' [2].

Enough has been said to prove how widely criticism in the Age of Johnson had diverged from that of the preceding generations. When the sense of the relative in art awoke, the rules were felt to be no more than observations on the practice of great writers. On this ground the new investigators discarded the old artificial

---

[1] *Essays Moral, Political, and Literary,* ed. T. H. Green and T. H. Grose. London, 1889, vol. I, p. 269.
[2] *The Works of Edmund Burke.* London, 1826, I. p. 155.

code and cast about for a new basis, exempt from the flux and change to which literary art is subject. They accepted one authority only and appealed to one standard: human nature. 'Art can never give the rules that make an art', Burke observes, and his words are the key-note of the prevailing critical trend [1]. A constant study of this supreme source of knowledge was to supply the principles of universal application. No one of these writers understood, however, that their tendency to stereotype these principles would be as detrimental to the free play of genius as the pseudo-classical insistence on conformity to classical examples and French precepts. Art is something essentially individualistic, and even the most scientific system of rules must prove to be an inadequate guide. The number of forms in which poetic genius appears, the number of ways in which it manifests itself, is unlimited, and every new work of art may show an aspect of human nature that has hitherto remained unnoticed. An immutable standard is therefore an impossibility. As Wordsworth said: 'Every great and original writer, in proportion as he is great or original, must himself create the taste by which he is to be relished; he must teach the art by which he is to be seen' [2].

We shall see that some contemporary critics at least were convinced that the attempts of the scientific critics to establish fixed canons were bound to fail. Reynolds himself was aware that an account of first principles would for ever elude the search, and Pinkerton and Belsham (q.v.) expressed the view that there was something in art that could not be reduced to laws. What made their investigations all the more fruitless was that they erected their doctrine on a purely rationalistic basis. The great exponents of romantic critical theory, Coleridge, Hazlitt, and Carlyle, also insisted that an artistic production should be judged according to its power to express universal human thoughts and emotions. But their principles of universal beauty were not founded on the perverted deductions of reason, they were written 'in the hearts and imaginations of all men'.

---

1   Cf. A. Murphy, supra, p. 79 n. 3.
2   *Wordsworth's Literary Criticism.* Oxford, 1905, p. 54.

In transferring the empiric methods of scientific research to the field of art the critics of the Johnsonian Age forgot that between science and poetry there is an impassable gulf. 'Poetry is the breath and finer spirit of all knowledge; it is the impassioned expression which is in the countenance of all Science', Wordsworth wrote in the Preface to the *Lyrical Ballads* [1]. 'Could a rule be given from without', said Coleridge, 'poetry would cease to be poetry, and sink into a mechanical art'. He did not consider genius as lawless but he realized that the laws which the poet obeys are those of its own creation.

---

[1]   Cf. Leigh Hunt: 'Poetry begins where matter of fact or of science ceases to be merely such, and to exhibit a further truth'; (*Imagination and Fancy*. London, 1910, p. 3).

CHAPTER V

TEXTUAL CRITICISM. THE NEW WAY OF EDITING

The influence of science on literary criticism manifested itself in another way. It also affected the manner of dealing with poetical texts.

The great classical scholar Bentley was the first to apply its methods to literature in his controversy with Boyle on the *Letters of Phalaris*. His *Dissertation* marks an epoch in the history of classical scholarship and inaugurated a new way of approach. Historical research was here for the first time combined with accurate philological inquiry: Bentley was the first great philologist in the modern sense of the word. Textual criticism, which had been almost ignored by the French as well as the Italian scholars, received a great impetus from his publications. Both his *Dissertation* and his edition of *Horace* laid great stress on this part of the critic's task and it was owing to Bentley's example that its value began to be recognized in the course of the eighteenth century. Its vogue even became so great that the term criticism was for a time almost exclusively used in the limited meaning of verbal criticism.

It was Theobald, who first adapted Bentley's method to his own particular field of investigation. His edition of Shakespeare is the earliest example of the application of sound scholarship to English letters. His extensive knowledge of the Elizabethan stage, his intimate acquaintance with the history and manners of the Shakespearean Age, — the result of wide and careful reading — enabled him to carry out his task with consummate skill. He made use of Shakespeare's sources to show how much the dramatist was indebted to them, he carefully compared the editions and had recourse to emendation only if collation failed to give a satisfactory solution [1].

In the Preface we find the important statement that the first

---

[1] Cf. R. F. Jones, *Lewis Theobald, A Contribution to English Scholarship. With some unpublished Letters*. Columbia Univ. Press, 1919.

duty of the critic is to 'be well vers'd in the History and Manners of his Author's Age, if he aims at doing him a service'. The explanatory notes that Theobald added to the text bear out how punctiliously he carried out his plan. His method in editing meant a tremendous advance on that which had been followed before him. Neither Rowe nor Pope had been sufficiently qualified to embark on such a difficult and comprehensive task. As Professor D. Nichol Smith remarks, the former had 'approached his task as a dramatist', the latter as a literary executor rather than as a scholar [1].

Bentley and Theobald are the forerunners of the many eminent editors that the eighteenth century produced. In spite of the contempt with which the two scholars were regarded by their contemporaries, who considered their minute investigations as a mere waste of time and held that all problems could be solved by common sense [2], the demand for critical editions of classical as well as English writers constantly increased in the course of the century. However much verbal criticism was abused by its enemies, it began to be recognized that it was the only means to establish an accurate reading of the text. Johnson gave utterance to this conviction in his *Proposals for Printing the Dramatick Works of William Shakespeare* (1756). He realized that the corruptness of Shakespeare's text could only be remedied by a careful collation of the oldest copies, and promised that his own edition should exhibit all the variants that could be found. He comments on the various duties of a Shakespeare critic and commentator who wants to arrive at a sound understanding and proper appreciation of the plays: he has to read the books which the author read and trace his knowledge to its source, he has to make a careful study of the language of the period and last of all compare his work with that of his contemporaries. All this will help him 'to ascertain his ambiguities, disentangle his intricacies, and recover the meaning of words now lost in the darkness of antiquity' [3].

No editor before him had taken so much trouble as he did to arrive at a correct reading of the text. He carefully collated the

---

[1] *Shakespeare in the Eighteenth Century.* Oxford, 1928, pp. 31, 38.
[2] See Appendix, infra, pp. 317 ff.
[3] Raleigh, *op. cit.*, p. 6.

folio editions with the quartos and was the first to recognize the superiority of the first folio over the two others. Unlike his predecessor Warburton, he seldom resorted to conjecture. Those of his notes which required nothing but shrewd common sense and wide knowledge of human nature are still considered to be of supreme merit. His successors surpassed him only in one thing, in historical research. His knowledge of Elizabethan English was not extensive and his acquaintance with Shakespeare's fellow-dramatists far too superficial [1].

The work of scholars like George Steevens, Edmund Malone, Edward Capell, Isaac Reed and above all that of the greatest philologist of the period, Thomas Tyrwhitt, bears ample evidence of the tremendous strides that the historical, scientific method of dealing with a poet's text had made. Steevens's first edition of Shakespeare, a revision of Johnson's, appeared in 1773. The editor's great antiquarian learning, his thorough knowledge of Elizabethan literature in general, gave him a considerable advantage over his friend the Doctor. Reed prepared a new edition of Dodsley's *Old Plays* (1780), and at Steevens's request re-edited his edition of Shakespeare's works (1785). E. Malone made the first scholarly attempt to ascertain the order in which the plays of the great dramatist had appeared (1778), and two years later published a supplement in two volumes to Johnson's and Steevens's editions. Capell's, which appeared in 1768, was the result of indefatigable research, and careful collation of texts. His commentary, published separately in 1783, was an important contribution to Shakespeare scholarship.

Thomas Tyrwhitt published his *Observations and Conjectures upon some Passages of Shakespeare* (1766), and contributed some critical passages to Malone's *Supplement,* of which his refutation of Warburton's fanciful theory about the origin of romance has already been referred to. His fame as a critic and editor is especially due to his edition of *The Canterbury Tales* (1775) and that of the *Rowley Poems* (1777). He was the first to give an accurate text of Chaucer's poems, while his *Essay on the Language and Versific-*

---

1   These statements are based on Professor D. Nichol Smith's *Shakespeare in the Eighteenth Century.*

ation of Chaucer, which preceded it, tended largely to remove the erroneous views that had so long been prevalent. Tyrwhitt's extensive knowledge of fourteenth and fifteenth century English enabled him to expose Chatterton's forgery. The 'Appendix' to the Rowley poems was, according to Professor Skeat, the only contribution to the controversy between the Rowleians and the anti-Rowleians that showed any real critical knowledge of the subject.

It came to be looked upon as one of the first requirements of an editor that he should be thoroughly acquainted with the manners of the poet's time and with the poet's learning as the result of his reading. The value of explanatory notes, illustrating passages from the writer's works, began more and more to be recognized. Jortin's *Remarks on Spenser's Poems and Milton's Paradise Lost* (1734), Newton's edition of Milton's epic (1749), Thomas Warton's *Observations on the Faerie Queene of Spenser* (1754), the edition of Milton's minor poems by the same critic (1785), that of Spenser by the great classical scholar John Upton (1758), were all more or less influenced by Theobald's example. This new way of editing was one of the great factors in the revival of the interest for the older writers and as such conduced greatly to the delivery of literature from the bondage of neo-classicism.

CHAPTER VI

NATURE AND TRUTH. THE MAXIM THAT THE POET IS TO IMITATE NATURE

In the new analysis by which the rationalistic critics expected to establish the underlying principles of literary art, *reason, nature,* and *truth* remained the three undifferentiated tests. They had the same magic charm for the new investigators as they had had for the Augustans, though the days were past when authoritative rules and the laws of nature were considered as equivalent forces. In their conception of the poet's task and in their interpretation of the two terms 'nature' and 'truth', the critics of the Johnsonian Age followed Augustan tradition. We meet with the same tendency to reject anything for which they could not find a rational foundation, the same fear of extravagance, excess or affectation, the same insistence on reality and veracity as in the days of Addison and Pope. In the Prologue to his *Irene* Johnson enumerates the three idols to which he remained true all his life:

> In Reason, Nature, Truth he dares to trust,
> Ye Fops be silent, and ye Wits be just!

He censures the *Vicar of Wakefield* for its faulty construction and its want of reality. 'There is nothing of real life in it and very little of nature. It is mere fanciful performance', he is reported to have answered to Mrs. Thrale's question whether he liked the book [1]. Reason, nature and truth, the leading principles of his creed, prevented him from appreciating Gray's somewhat laboured odes: 'He has a kind of strutting dignity.... His art and his struggle are too visible, and there is too little appearance of ease and nature' [2]. In his *Life of Cowley* he denied the 'metaphysicals' the right to the name of poets, because they could not be said to imitate anything: 'they neither copied nature nor life' [3]. In

---

[1] Frances Burney (Madame d'Arblay), *Diary and Letters,* ed. Austin Dobson, 1904, I, p. 77.

[2] *Lives,* III, p. 440.

[3] *Lives,* I, p. 19. Cf. Johnson's definition of *nature* in his *Dictionary:* 'sentiments or images adapted to nature, or conformable to truth and reality'.

his discussion of Milton's *Lycidas* he used the two catch-words as equivalent terms: 'there is no nature, for there is no truth' [1].

Somewhat earlier, Blackwell had blamed Tasso and Ariosto, because 'quitting life, they betook themselves to aerial beings and Utopian characters, and filled their works with Charms and Visions.... whereas the best poets copy Nature and describe it as they find it'. Both he and Wood, the author of *An Essay on the Original Genius and Writings of Homer* (1775), praised Homer for following nature by describing real scenes instead of having recourse to fiction. "'T is in this as in other things; no Imagination can supply the want of *Truth:* Flowery Meads and horrid Rocks, dismal Dungeons and enchanted Palaces.... can be easily imagined. But they take only with young raw Fancies.... 'T is the Traces of *Truth* that are only irresistible', Blackwell postulates, thus drawing a line of demarcation between nature and the fantastic [2]. Even Joseph Warton uses the word in the Popean sense when he contrasts Grecian and Gothic architecture: the latter is called fantastical and is pronounced to be founded 'neither in nature nor reason, in necessity nor use; the appearance of which accounts for all the beauties, graces and ornaments of the other' [3]. Warton's critic Ruffhead, whose edition of Pope's works was mainly directed against the first volume of the *Essay,* attaches the same meaning to the term. He expresses the neo-classic dread of extremes when he observes that in 'the sublime and the pathetic', which Warton had called the chief nerves of poetry, 'nature is generally represented in the *outré*' [4].

The meaning of the other catchword, 'truth', so commonly used by the rationalistic critics of the Age of Johnson, is closely related to that of 'nature'. Credibility and correspondence with the facts of life are its criteria. Horace's influence is often beyond a doubt; his *incredulus odi* [5] was one of the doctor's favourite maxims,

---

1   *Lives,* I, p. 163.
2   *Op. cit.,* p. 285. This passage is quoted by T. Warton in the third volume of his *History of English Poetry.*
3   *Essay on Pope,* II, p. 21.
4   Ruffhead, *The Works of Alexander Pope* (1769), V, p. 340.
5   *A P,* 188.

and both Fielding [1] and Shenstone [2] use it to support their view
that nothing is truly poetic if it passes the bounds of the credible.
'Poets indeed profess fiction, but the legitimate end of fiction is
the conveyance of truth', Johnson says in his *Life of Waller* [3].
He mentions Bouhours among the writers of true criticism, because
he showed that all beauty depends on truth [4]. Like some of the
Augustan critics, he makes allowance for popular belief. Gray's
Bard, an imitation of the prophecy of Nereus in one of Horace's
Odes, finds no favour in his eyes, because 'the copy has been
unhappily produced at a wrong time. The fiction of Horace was
to the Romans credible; but its revival disgusts us with apparent
and unconquerable falsehood. "Incredulus odi" ' [5].

It has already been observed that the word nature was mostly
used in the limited sense of *human* nature by the critics of the
English *Aufklärung.* Human life and all its circumstances, its social
and ethical problems were the things in which the age took an
interest; they were considered the only fit subjects for literary
treatment. External nature was hardly considered worthy of any
serious attention. The knowledge of rural scenery was held in so
little esteem by the poet that a first-hand acquaintance with it was
not even thought necessary. 'The Study of the human Mind is . . . .
the most rational and pleasing Employment we are capable of',
says Arthur Murphy in the *Gray's Inn Journal* [6]. He grants that
the contemplation of natural scenery may conduce to the pleasures
of the imagination, 'but a Man will certainly feel more lively
sensations when riding upon Land belonging to himself'.

'The great object of remark is human life', Johnson observed to
Boswell [7], and his biographer has left us several trenchant dicta,
all illustrative of his preference for the intellectual pleasures of the
town and his low estimate of life in the country, 'where a man's
body might be feasted, but his mind was starved'.

---

1   *Tom Jones,* Bk. VIII, Ch. I.
2   *Essays on Men and Manners, (On Writing and Books).*
3   Perhaps this statement refers rather to *moral* truth than *poetical* truth.
4   Boswell, *Life of Johnson,* II, p. 90.
5   *Lives,* III, p. 438.
6   Vol. II, p. 57.
7   Boswell, III, 301.

Johnson was pre-eminently a moralist; morality was the chief motive power of all his writings, ethical problems were his chief object of interest. In one of the best-known passages in his Life *of Milton* he calls the religious and moral knowledge of right and wrong 'the first requisite of any rational being'; he speaks with contempt of those among his contemporaries who devote their attention to the descriptions of external nature and forget that life is their chief business. 'They seem to think that we are placed here to watch the growth of plants and the motions of the stars', are the memorable words in which he has a fling at the romantic 'innovators'. The poet's chief concern is man, the universal principles of human life [1].

That the strong ethical bent made man the central object of imitation in art is also illustrated by the views which the age held about painting. Historical painting was ranked much higher than any other kind because of its greater capacity to instruct, then followed portrait-painting, and last of all came the representation of rural scenery and still life. Reynolds, though a great admirer of Claude Lorrain, the favourite landscape-painter in England at that time, shared the opinion of his age [2]. Vicesimus Knox, dealing with painting and sculpture in one of his *Essays Moral and Literary* observes that landscape-painting pleases the imagination, but 'To touch the heart with sympathy, to excite the nobler affections . . . . man must be the object of imitation . . . . the sentiments and passion of the human bosom must speak in the features and attitudes of the canvass or the marble' [3].

It naturally follows from this that in the eyes of the neo-classic critics descriptive poetry ranked much lower than the departments of poetic literature which deal with the human mind: the epic and tragedy. In this respect the Age of Johnson followed their example. John Brown thinks it merits only the lowest place with regard to the secondary end of poetry, namely that of instruction. He calls it *pure Poetry;* nothing else is expected of it than that it should please the imagination and not offend reason, whereas the tragic, comic

---

[1] *Lives,* I, p. 100.
[2] For further details see E. Wheeler Manwaring, *Italian Landscape in Eighteenth Century England,* 1925.
[3] Vol. I, Essay LXVII.

and satiric kinds as well as the elegy ought to depict the passions
of the human heart [1]. As the century advanced, feeling for nature,
which had so long been dormant, gradually revived and the interest
in descriptive poetry naturally kept pace with it. Commendatory
remarks on Thomson, who had been the first great poet to do
away with the conventionalities of the Augustans, and to give
descriptions of external nature based on actual observation, are
numerous in the critical writings of the period. But the old prejudice
was never entirely removed. Curiously half-hearted is J. Warton's
defence of it in the *Essay;* he opposes Pope's dictum that descriptive
poetry is 'as absurd as a feast made up of sands', but at the same
time agrees with his contemporaries that it is not equal 'either in
dignity or utility, to those compositions that lay open the internal
constitution of man' [2].

Aristotle's term μίμησις had been translated as 'imitation' by
the French and English commentators. This was a very inadequate
equivalent [3], as appears from a passage in the *Poetics*, where the
Greek critic observes that the poet, like the painter or any other
artist, 'must of necessity imitate one of three objects, — things
as they were or are, things as they are said or thought to be,
or things as they ought to be'. Aristotle did not expect a work of
art to be a mere reflection of the actual, he wanted the artist to
produce something entirely new, a higher reality surpassing the
world of primary sense-perceptions. Nature is considered as a
creative energy, pervading the whole universe and aiming at an
ideal form, often representing a higher degree of perfection than
the artist can ever attain, but sometimes striving in vain. The
artist's task is to remove the imperfections and correct nature
where she has failed to carry out her artistic intentions. Imitation,
as Aristotle understood the term, is therefore a creative art.
Art in general and poetry, 'the highest form of imitative

---

[1] *Essay on the Characteristics*, p. 18.

[2] Vol. I, p. 49. In Ruffhead we find an illustration of the old contempt. To
Warton's stricture that 'Descriptive poetry was by no means the shining
talent of Pope' he answers that 'the studious cultivation of *descriptive poetry*
was far below the poet's comprehensive and sublime genius'. (*The Works of
Alexander Pope*, V, p. 44).

[3] See Butcher. *op. cit.*, p. 97. *Poetics*, XXV.

art' [1], in particular, is to aim at giving an idealized picture of the original and that original is human life. The poet is to express the essence of the human mind and to eliminate anything contingent.

Something has been said about the realistic interpretation which the Aristotelian precept that the poet is to imitate nature, received at the hands of the Augustan critics who were under the influence of contemporary philosophy and science. But though they insisted that a poem should give a picture of every-day life, that it should adhere to apparent or generally supposed probability, and avoid anything fantastical, it should not be inferred that they expected it to be a photographic reproduction. It was not the poet's task to give an enumeration of particulars; he was rather to select the most salient features, such as constituted the mental aspect of reality rather than reality itself. As Professor Ker says: 'Nature in these discussions generally implied, as it did for Aristotle, the right conception of the true character of the subject by the reason of the poet' [2]. The poet's words were therefore to recall the conceptions that were in everybody's mind. Pope's couplet:

> True Wit is Nature to advantage dress'd
> What oft was thought, but ne'er so well express'd [3];

is the best-known statement of this aesthetic doctrine [4].

The critics of the Johnsonian Age followed their Augustan predecessors in this respect as in so many others, and their conception of the poet's art as well as that of the painter offer a very close resemblance to those of the preceding generations.

Ever since the days of Horace painting and poetry had been considered as sister arts. The Horatian maxim: *ut pictura, poesis* [5]

---

1 *Poetics,* IX.
2 Ker, I, LIX. Cf. R. Wolseley's *Preface to Valentinian* (1685): 'By *Nature* I do not only mean all sorts of material Objects and every species of Substance whatsoever, but also general Notions and abstracted Truths, such as exist only in the Minds of men and in the property and relation of things one to another, ...' (Spingarn, *Crit. Essays,* III, p. 21).
3 *Essay on Crit.,* ll. 297, 298.
4 Cf. Boileau, *préface de l'éd. de* 1701. Cf. Addison's discussion of Pope's *Essay on Criticism,* in which he quotes Boileau and adds: We have little else left us, but to represent the common sense of mankind in more strong, more beautiful, or more uncommon lights (*Spectator,* 253).
5 *A P.* 361.

had been repeatedly quoted and commented on. Sidney had called
poetry 'a speaking picture: with this end, to teach and delight' [1]
and the critics that came after him were equally convinced of the
close relation between the two arts. Arthur Murphy observed
that from the days of Aristotle and Horace down to Dryden and
the Abbé du Bos the two had been 'mutually borrowing side-lights
and reflecting Lustre upon each other' [2]. The only critic who
had a clear notion of the difference between painting and
poetry and their respective means of expression was Edmund
Burke, who must therefore be classed among the forerunners of
Lessing [3].

There was a strong tendency in the eighteenth century to look
for fundamental principles that could be applied to all artistic
productions, and in the numerous essays on aesthetic theory in
general, as well as in treatises concerned with one particular art,
parallels are often drawn. In France the foundation of the *Académie
royale de peinture et de sculpture* (1648) meant the assumption of
authority over art. A system of rules and precepts was invented
which gradually crystallized into a generally accepted doctrine.
The aesthetic ideas of the academic school of painting bear a great
resemblance to those of the neo-classic poets and critics, and many
theorists did for painting what Boileau had done for criticism and
poetry. Their works reveal the same belief in rational truth, and
the same conception of art as imitation of nature. Cartesianism
left on them the same rationalistic impress [4]. Nicolas Poussin, the
chief representative of the French school of painting, accepted
reason as his chief guide and was a great admirer of Greek and
Roman art. His aesthetic theory, based on that of the Italians,
teems with ideas that were the common stock-in-trade of contemporary writers on poetry and literary criticism. The painter's
task was to imitate human actions. Like the poet he was to aim
at general truth, carefully avoiding all that was particular
or individual. This theory of the *beau idéal* repeatedly finds

---

1   Gregory Smith, *Eliz. Crit. Essays,* I, p. 158. Cf. Hobbes (Spingarn, *Crit.
    Essays,* II, p. 71).
2   *Gray's Inn Journal,* March 3, 1753.
3   See PMLA, XXII, p. 608.
4   Cf. L. Hourticq, *De Poussin à Watteau.* Paris, 1921.

expression in the seventeenth and eighteenth centuries, in England as well as in France.

In England a national school of painting was not founded before the second half of the eighteenth century. Apart from Hogarth, who is an isolated figure, there were no painters of outstanding merit before Sir Joshua Reynolds, and there was no definite English theory of the art of painting before he delivered his *Discourses* to the Royal Academy, of which he was the first president. Poetry and architecture could boast of a glorious, time-honoured national tradition, which painting could not, with the result that in the latter half of the seventeenth and the first half of the eighteenth century the treatises on painting show the influence of the continent even more clearly than those on poetic theory. The view that the painter is the idealizer of nature, that he should avoid minuteness and reproduce the universal element in nature, is held by Dryden, Shaftesbury, Roger de Piles, J. Richardson, and others [1].

Dryden's *Parallel of Poetry and Painting* (1695) was prefixed to his version of *De Arte Graphica*, a Latin poem by the French painter Charles Alphonse Dufresnoy. The essay gives utterance to his idealistic conception of both arts, its avowed purpose is to prove that a learned painter should form to himself an idea of perfect nature, 'thereby correcting Nature from what actually she is in individuals, to what she ought to be and what she was created'. From what follows, it appears that Dryden expects the poet to proceed in the same manner. In both arts a close resemblance of nature is recommended. 'But it follows not, that what pleases most in either kind is therefore good, but what ought to please' [2].

Dryden's *Parallel* has been called the prototype of Reynolds's *Discourses*, in which the eighteenth century view of the relation between art and nature finds its best illustration. As Hogarth advocated realism, a literal rendering of nature with all its beauties and imperfections, Reynolds is the typical representative of idealism during the Age of Johnson. In the third discourse, delivered in the year 1770, he expounds his theory of art and discusses the 'great leading principles of the grand style'. The aim of the

---

[1]   See S. H. Monk, *op. cit.*, pp. 168 ff. De Piles's *Principles of Painting*, translated by a Painter, appeared in 1743.

[2]   Ker, II, p. 136.

painter is not to amuse mankind by imitation. A mere copier of
nature could, according to Reynolds, never produce anything really
great [1]. Beauty and grandeur in a work of art, he thought, were
not compatible with a too rigid adherence to reality. The poet as
well as the painter should try to correct nature, which is far from
perfect; ideal beauty should be their leading principle. Like all
other arts, painting receives its perfection from 'an ideal beauty,
superior to what is to be found in individual nature'. This idea
of perfect beauty in the painter's mind, this 'intellectual dignity',
as Reynolds calls it, ennobles his art and distinguishes him from
the mere mechanic. It enables him to discover what is deformed,
'or, in other words, what is particular and uncommon', to 'get above
all singular forms, local custom, particularities, and details of every
kind'. The most dangerous error into which an artist was apt to
fall was, in Reynolds's opinion, minuteness; he should avoid the
exhibition of detailed discriminations of individual nature; what
he had to consider was nature in the abstract [2]. The great Italian
painter in whose works these principles were exemplified was
Raphael, Poussin's master. His simple and unadorned style, his
great charm, his 'grace' and 'greatness' were in strict accordance
with the practice of the ancients, his works represented universal
nature, they were not marred by undue attention to particulars
and by the individuality and eccentricity that characterized those
of the other great Italian painter Michelangelo.

In his three papers contributed to Johnson's *Idler*, Reynolds
had already condemned this love of excessive detail. 'The grand
style of painting requires this minute attention to be carefully
avoided', he says in one of them [3], and the *Discourses* contain
many remarks to the same effect [4].

The general acceptance of this aesthetic theory in the latter
half of the eighteenth century accounts for the inability of the
age to appreciate the paintings of the Dutch and Flemish schools.
They were too much the representation of individual nature, they

---

[1] *Discourses*, p. 23.

[2] *Ibid.*, p. 33.

[3] *Idler*, 79.

[4] Cf. p. 33: The painter of the grand style 'will permit the lower painter, like
    the florist or collector of shells, to exhibit the minute discriminations'.

exhibited, as Reynolds said, 'the minute particularities of a nation differing in several respects from the rest of mankind'[1]. On the other hand it explains why Claude Lorrain, whose pictures represent ideal landscapes and excel principally in their general effects, enjoyed such a high reputation with painters as well as literary critics. Reynolds advised the students of the Academy to adopt the practice of this painter instead of that of the Dutch school. Even portrait-painting was rather to aim at a likeness 'in the general air' than at an exact resemblance of every feature[2].

The same idealistic conception of art was prevalent among literary critics. The author in general, the poet more in particular, was to be no mere copier; what he produced was not to bear a minute resemblance to nature, his task was to rectify its blemishes, to create something that came up to the type of perfection existing in his mind. He was not to depict reality, but the general notion which the mind abstracted from reality. 'Poetry pleases by exhibiting an idea more grateful to the mind than things themselves afford', said Johnson in his *Life of Waller*[3]. He did not think devotional subjects fit for poetic treatment on the ground that religion ought to be shown as it is, whereas poetry idealizes all that it touches on: 'Its effect proceeds from the display of those parts of nature which attract, the concealment of those which repel, the imagination'. It goes without saying that this process of selection which Johnson advocated was mainly determined by ethical considerations. His comment on Aristotle's precepts in the fourth number of the *Rambler* is generally believed to have been prompted by the popularity of Fielding's *Tom Jones* and Smollett's *Roderick Random*. It clearly shows how Johnson's interpretation of Aristotle's maxim that the poet was to imitate nature, was affected by his strong moralistic bent. He thinks it necessary to distinguish those parts of nature which are proper for imitation. If the world were to be described with all its passions and all its wickedness, the account could be of no use to the reader. He might just as well turn his eyes immediately upon mankind[4].

---

1 *Discourses*, p. 49.
2 *Ibid.*, p. 38.
3 *Lives*, I, p. 292.
4 *Rambler*, 4.

Like his friend Reynolds, Johnson insisted that it was the poet's duty to describe the type rather than the individual. Generalized nature was to be his main object of attention. This theory is best of all illustrated by the dissertation upon poetry in *Rasselas*, where Imlac calls it the business of the poet to remark general proportions and large appearances, to exhibit such prominent and striking features as recall the original to every mind. Every reader of the critic remembers the often-quoted dictum about the streaks of the tulips and the different shades of verdure of the forest, which the poet should think it beneath himself to number and describe. Not only does Johnson disapprove of minuteness in descriptions of external nature, but also in pictures of human life. The poet 'must divest himself of the prejudices of the age and country; he must consider right and wrong in their abstracted and invariable state; he must disregard present laws and opinions, and rise to general and transcendental truths, which will always be the same'. Already in the *Rambler* the great critic had explained why minute distinctions were to be avoided: they were not compatible with simplicity and grandeur, and would make poetry lose its power and universal appeal [1]. Johnson was convinced that sublimity was intimately associated with generality and that excessive attention to detail destroyed grandeur and nobility: 'Sublimity is produced by aggregation, and littleness by dispersion' [2]. One of his chief objections to the 'metaphysicals' was, that they forgot that only a strict regard to the common sentiments of humanity could win the approval of a wide circle of readers. Instead of bearing this in mind, they devoted their attention to the unexpected and surprising, which could only appeal to the minds of a few readers: 'Great thoughts are always general, and consist in positions not limited by exceptions, and in descriptions not descending to minuteness' [3]. There is another well-known statement to the same effect in the *Preface to Shakespeare* (1765), where the dramatist is praised for his delineation of character. 'His persons act and speak by the influence of those general passions and principles by which all minds are agitated, and the whole

1   *Rambler,* 36.
2   *Lives,* I, p. 21.
3   *Ibid.*

system of life is continued in motion. In the writings of other poets a character is too often an individual; in those of *Shakespeare* it is commonly a species' [1]. Speaking of Pope's translation of Homer, Johnson characterizes the Greek poet by saying that he has fewer passages of doubtful meaning than any other poet, because 'his positions are general, and his representations natural, with very little dependence on local or temporary customs ....' [2]. Pope's *Temple of Fame*, however, in spite of its many beauties, will never receive much notice, because its sentiments 'have little relation to general manners or common life' [3]. Johnson disliked pastoral poetry because of its narrow range. On the other hand he admired Thomson's broad view of the general aspects of nature in the *Seasons*: 'His descriptions of extended scenes and general effects bring before us the whole magnificence of Nature, whether pleasing or dreadful. The gaiety of *Spring,* the splendour of *Summer,* the tranquillity of *Autumn,* and the horror of *Winter,* take in their turns possession of the mind' [4]. It is remarkable, however, that Johnson not only praises the poet for his 'wide expansion of general views', but also for 'his enumeration of circumstantial varieties', so that even the naturalist is not 'without his part in the entertainment', a remark which would seem at variance with his theory of 'general and large appearances' [5].

As to the use of general terms and conventional generalized descriptions, one of the distinguishing qualities of eighteenth century poetic diction, Johnson's view is that of the ordinary Augustan critic. His own style is marked by a strong predilection for periphrastic phrases, and by a peculiar tendency to use abstract terms for concrete notions. This practice is founded on his belief, expressed in the *Life of Dryden,* that in poetry 'all appropriated terms of art should be sunk in general expressions, because poetry is to speak an universal language' [6].

On the subject of poetic imitation of nature, as on so many others,

---

1   Raleigh, p. 12.
2   *Lives,* III, p. 114.
3   *Ibid.,* p. 226.
4   *Ibid.,* p. 299.
5   See Ch. XXV, infra.
6   *Lives,* I, p. 433.

Goldsmith's opinion agrees almost perfectly with that of his two great contemporaries, Johnson and Reynolds. He, too, thinks that the poet is not to be a copyist: his task is to depict ideal beauty. 'To copy nature is a task the most bungling workman is able to execute; to select such parts as contribute to delight is reserved only for those whom accident has blessed with uncommon talents, or such as have read the ancients with indefatigable industry' [1], he says in his *Life of Parnell*. whom he calls the last representative of that great school of poets who modelled their works on those of the ancients.

In one of the *Essays* (collected for publication in 1765) entitled *Cultivation of Taste*, he draws the Aristotelian distinction between history, which represents what has really happened, and 'the other arts', which exhibit what might have happened; their aim is to surpass nature, to create a perfection that nature would be glad to reach. 'It is the business of art', says Goldsmith, 'to imitate nature, but not with a servile pencil; and to choose those attitudes and dispositions only which are beautiful and engaging' [2]. The poet, like the painter, should therefore abstain from depicting anything disagreeable, anything that might cause abhorrence and disgust. The only restriction that his art is subject to, according to Goldsmith, is that it should never exceed the limits of truth and probability, without which the beauties of imitation cannot exist.

In 1764 the Scottish philosopher Alexander Gerard published his *Essay on Taste*, the fourth section of which deals with imitation. The author deprecates a too high degree of resemblance to the original. A poet has to select judiciously the most striking qualities of a subject, and combine them in such a way that a lively idea of it is impressed on the reader's mind [3]. The philosopher observes and describes minutely all the appearances of his objects which can forward his imagination: the artist catches only such general appearances as are most striking.

The views expressed in the third chapter of James Beattie's *Essay on Poetry and Music* (1776), are almost identical with those of the critics I have just been discussing. The Scottish writer adheres

---

[1] *Works,* ed. J. W. M. Gibbs, IV. 172.
[2] *Ibid.,* I, 338.
[3] P. 48.

to the same idealistic conception of art. 'Poetry exhibits a system of nature somewhat different from the reality of things', he observes. The poet's business is to devise some more pleasing qualities than nature can offer. Nature only supplies 'the ground-work and materials, as well as the standard' of poetical fiction [1]. The true poet must therefore have an intimate knowledge of real life but at the same time he must have sufficient imaginative power to invent additional embellishments. External nature must be more picturesque in poetry than in reality: 'actions more animated; sentiments more expressive of the feelings and characters'. Like Reynolds, Johnson and Goldsmith, Beattie believes that the poet and the painter ought to proceed in much the same manner: they ought to copy after general ideas based on the observation of many individual things, rather than give a faithful reproduction of reality. He compares the Dutch and the Italian artists and shares the opinion of his age as to the superiority of the latter over the former. Teniers and Hogarth are mentioned as representatives of realism, Raphael and Reynolds as painters who took their models from general nature.

Beattie considers pleasure as the only end of poetry and con-sequently approves of any means tending to this end. If poetry were a mere copy of actual life, it would give no greater pleasure than history. If the prototype and transcript were the same, poetry would not be an imitation, but 'a representation, a copy, a draught, or a picture' of reality. 'For that which is properly termed *Imitation,* has always in it something which is not in the original' [2]. The only limits that Beattie sets to the range of poetic fiction are those imposed by the laws of probability, for just as Goldsmith did before him, he thinks that imitation should never be at variance with rational truth. What is unnatural, i.e. not in accordance with the dictates of reason, cannot give pleasure.

In one of the *Dissertations, Moral and Critical* (1783) Beattie condemns too minute descriptions, which in his opinion can only lessen the effect: 'Writers . . . . who describe too nicely the minute

---

[1]   *Op. cit.,* p. 382.
[2]   P. 416. This statement is quoted by Pye in his translation and commentary on Aristotle's *Poetics* (p. 107) as the best expression of his own ideas on the subject.

parts of a grand object, must both have disengaged their own minds and must also withdraw ours, from the admiration of what is sublime in it' [1].

The opinion of one more critic may be added here. In the second of the two essays prefixed to his poems and entitled *On the Arts, commonly called Imitative* [2], Sir William Jones observes that the chief object of a poet, a painter and a musician should be to cause the same effect upon the imagination as the works of nature produce on the senses. Great effects are, however, not brought about by minute details, but by the general spirit of the whole.

It would be wrong to suppose that Johnson's and Reynolds's views were shared by all the critics of the period. We shall see that before the century closed, at least some writers expressed their dissatisfaction with the doctrine of broad effects and general proportions. Their opinions will be discussed when I deal with the reaction against the supremacy of reason.

---

[1]   P. 640.
[2]   Chalmers, *English Poets,* vol. 18.

CHAPTER VII

THE DOCTRINE OF THE LITERARY GENRES

On the whole the veneration for the doctrine of the literary types remained as strong during the Age of Johnson as it had been in the days of Pope and Addison. John Brown, in his *Essay on the Characteristics,* thinks it necessary to ascertain the nature and limits of the different provinces of poetry before he proceeds to determine how far in each of them ridicule can be regarded as a test of truth. Goldsmith is also convinced that the 'kinds' should be carefully distinguished. He praises the ancients for keeping them apart and believes that 'this diversity, which the ancients so religiously observed, is founded in nature itself' [1]. Gerard considers it as an important duty of the critic to make sure if the fable or design of a poem is 'well imagined in congruity to the species of the poem or discourse' [2]. These examples are only some of the many that might be adduced to illustrate the general belief in this neo-classical tenet. The only critic who holds an entirely different opinion and flatly professes disbelief in this arbitrary distinction is Kames, the author of the *Elements of Criticism* [3]. He realizes that there are no insuperable barriers between the various literary types, and that like colours they often run into each other.

On one aspect of the question, however, namely the strict separation of dramatic forms, there is not the same concurrence of opinion. Critics like Kames, Hurd, and Pye reject the mixed drama. Kames thinks that a mingling of the two conflicting elements will produce discordant emotions, which are unpleasant. Pye believes that the intermixture of the comic and the serious 'tends to destroy the efficacy of both', and Hurd is of opinion that the pleasure which it affords will be less in proportion to the mixture. A striking contrast with these purely theoretical objections is formed by Johnson's defence of tragi-comedy in the name of reason and nature [4].

---

[1]   Gibbs, IV, p. 339.
[2]   *An Essay on Taste,* p. 88.
[3]   See Chapter XI, infra, pp. 139, 140.
[4]   See infra, p. 121.

How deeply the system of classification was ingrained in eighteenth century thought is proved by the attitude of the critics towards those forms of literature that had no prototype in the field of classical art. Addison had compared the *Ballad of Chevy Chase* to the *Aeneid,* and had tested its literary merit by the Aristotelian rules of the epic. This method of procedure is ridiculed by Gray in one of his letters to Mason, where he speaks of the old Scottish ballad of *Gil Morrice,* and remarks that 'Aristotle's best rules are observed in it in a manner that shews the author never had heard of Aristotle' [1]. Vicesimus Knox applies the rules of epic unity to Sterne's *Tristram Shandy* and thinks that the necessary requirements, a beginning, a middle and an end, are difficult to find owing to the chaotic confusion of the novel. Characteristic of this period of transition are the remarks of the critics on Macpherson's pretended translations from the Gaelic, and their half-hearted attempts to reconcile them with Aristotelian precepts. Hurd, like Gray and the Wartons, a great admirer of *Fingal,* founds his conviction of its forgery not only on the fact that the poem is 'cloathed in very classical expression', but above all on its construction: it has a *beginning, middle* and *end,* in accordance with its classical prototypes, and is moreover 'enlivened in the classic taste with episodes' [2].

Of Dr. Blair's *Critical Dissertation on Ossian* more will be said later on. Like Addison's essays on the ballads and *Paradise Lost,* it is an example of static criticism. The very instructive remarks of the *Monthly Review* and *Critical Review* will be discussed along with Blair's essay. Both closely follow Aristotle's schedule, even though the critic of the latter periodical is conscious of the absurdity of examining the poems by classical rules. Like Warton's discussion of *The Faerie Queene,* they show that the old leaven had not yet ceased to ferment.

---

1   *Letters of Thomas Gray,* ed. Tovey, I, p. 336.
2   *Letters from a Late Eminent Prelate to one of his Friends,* pp. 244, 245. Warburton's view was at first different. He believed it was an original poem: 'It can be no cheat, for I think the enthusiasm of his specifical sublime could hardly be counterfeit. A modern writer would have been less simple and uniform'. After reading Hurd's letter he changed his mind: 'Your reasons for the forgery are unanswerable'. (*Letters from a Late Eminent Prelate,* p. 246).

PART II

The Believers in the Doctrine of Reason

CHAPTER VIII

A WORD OF INTRODUCTION

After having given a survey of the main tendencies prevailing during the latter half of the century, I now proceed to a discussion of the various critics in particular. My chief purpose is to illustrate the general repugnance for the old critical canons, and at the same time to show in what respect the rules which were the outcome of the renewed analysis differed from them. It will appear that most of the new as well as the old precepts are concerned with the two main departments of poetry, the epic and tragedy. An attempt has been made to classify the critical writers in three different groups. To the first belong those who recognized reason as the highest authority, to the second the champions of taste, whereas the third comprises the leaders of the revolt against the supremacy of reason. It goes without saying that such a division is bound to be more or less arbitrary.

It is undoubtedly true that English criticism of the Age of Johnson appears remarkably shallow, if compared with the work of such a keen observer and shrewd expounder of principles as Lessing. The most prominent minds of the period, like Gibbon, Hume, and Burke, are comparatively unimportant as critics: their main achievements lie in other fields. The majority of the writers with whom we have to deal are men of very modest talents, but for that very reason their essays are perhaps all the more symptomatic of the general course of development. Though no author can wholly emancipate himself from the manners and thoughts of the age and the country in which he lives, the strong individuality of the major figures tends to make them independent of their environment. The minor writers, on the other hand, are to a much higher degree the product of the general intellectual tendencies.

After Pope's death in the year 1744 the position of the highest critical authority was for some time held by the poet's literary executor, Bishop Warburton. In 1747 his edition of Shakespeare saw the light. Some months after its appearance it was attacked by Thomas Edwards. In his pamphlet, *The Canons of Criticism and a Glossary* [1], which went through several editions, the editor's way of handling the text, his 'chimerical conjectures and gross mistakes' and his 'hasty, crude and unedifying notes' were exposed and held up to ridicule. Four years after, Warburton published his edition of Pope, to which he added lengthy and ponderous commentaries full of adulatory remarks on the poet's character and genius. The tedious and verbose notes that accompanied the text teemed with irrelevant matter and far-fetched explanations. Yet Pope had called his burly champion the greatest critic he ever knew [2] and had even suggested in his will that Warburton's interpretations would throw additional lustre on his works. The two abject admirers of the eminent prelate, R. Hurd, and J. Brown, the author of *Essays on the Characteristics* and *An Estimate of the Manners and Principles of the Times,* eulogized him immoderately [3], Johnson repeatedly speaks of him with great respect [4], but the praise that Warburton bestowed upon his *Life of Savage* may have influenced his opinion. It is said that Thomas Warton warmly admired Warburton's learning. In his dissertation *Of the Origin of Romantic Fiction in Europe,* prefixed to his *History of English Poetry,* he followed in the main the fanciful account given by the bishop, which was later on refuted by Thomas Tyrwhitt [5]. Though a critic like J. Warton must have been conscious of the many irrelevancies and misrepresentations in Warburton's edition, there

---

[1] The first edition bore the title: *Supplement to Mr. Warburton's Edition of Shakespeare,* 1747. The later title was suggested by Warburton himself, who in his preface had promised to give the canons of criticism, and to add a glossary.

[2] 'Mr. Warburton is the greatest general critic I ever knew, the most capable of seeing through all the possibilities of things'. (Spence, *Anecdotes,* p. 256).

[3] Dedication to Hurd's ed. of Horace's *Epistola ad Augustum;* J. Brown, *An Estimate of the Manners and Principles of the Times,* 7th ed., 1758, p. 43.

[4] See J. E. Brown, *The Critical Opinions of S. Johnson,* 1926, pp. 536, 537.

[5] *Supplement to the Edition of Shakespeare's Plays, published in 1778 by S. Johnson and G. Steevens.* London 1780, vol. I, p. 373.

is no reference to them in the first volume of the *Essay on Pope*. The second volume did not appear till three years after Warburton's death, and Chalmers suggests that fear of the bishop was probably the reason for this postponement.

When the necessity to apply sound scholarship to poetical texts began to win general recognition, the shortcomings of this editor became more and more evident. In 1782 Hayley says in one of the notes to his *Poetical Epistles on Epic Poetry*: 'What havock has the course of every few years producted in that pile of imperious criticism which he had heaped together! Many of his notes on Shakespeare have already resigned their place to the superior comments of more accomplished Critics; and perhaps the day is not far distant, when the volumes of Pope himself will cease to be a repository for the lumber of his friend'. The reason why J. Warton undertook his edition of the poet in 1797, was, according to the 'Advertisement' prefixed to it, 'the universal complaint that Dr. Warburton had disfigured and disgraced his Edition, with many forced and far-sought interpretations, totally unsupported by the passages which they were brought to elucidate'. In spite of this, however, Warton reproduced much of this worthless matter in his own [1].

Besides this 'Colossus', this 'dreaded Gulliver', as the author of the *Estimate* styled him, there were in the middle of the century a host of minor critics, the members of 'the Lilliputian Tribe', to quote Brown's words once again.

'No Age .... abounded with more Critics, or Pretenders to Criticism, than the Present; yet we have very Few who have Distinguish'd Themselves in any eminent Degree to merit that Title', says N. Weekes in the preface to his Satire *On the Abuse of Poetry*. In *The Universal Visiter and Monthly Memorialist for April 1756*, Johnson speaks of the multifariousness of English writers 'who like wolves in long winters, ... are forced to prey on one another. The *Reviewers* and *Critical Reviewers*, the

---

[1] Cf. Elwin and Courthope, *Pope's Works*, III, p. 14. In Gilbert Wakefield's edition of Pope, of which only one volume appeared in 1794, Warburton's text was adopted, and the preface calls the bishop 'a man .... whose powers of intellect have been surpassed by very few individuals of his species, in any age or nation ....'.

Remarkers and *Examiners* can satisfy their hunger only by devouring their brethren' [1]. And Goldsmith complains that 'attorneys, clerks and raw unexperienced boys are the chief critics we have at present'.

Many of these contributed to one of the literary magazines, in which the age was very prolific, and of which the number increased in the course of the century. The two principal periodicals dealing with criticism were the *Monthly Review* and the *Critical Review*. The former was established in 1749 by Ralph Griffiths and was continued almost uninterruptedly up to the year 1845, the latter was started by Archibald Hamilton in 1756 in opposition to the *Monthly*. They are the first regular literary reviews in England, and may be considered as the forerunners of the *Edinburgh* in the next century.

When Johnson's literary career began, the reputation of the critic in general was lower than it had ever been since the days of Dryden. Dryden himself disliked the critics of his own age. 'Formerly', he says, 'they were quite another species of men. They were defenders of poets, and commentators on their works'. But in his own time 'ill writers are usually the sharpest censors', ... 'the corruption of a poet is the generation of a critic' [2]. And Addison complained that 'a critic is a man who, on all occasions, is more attentive to what is wanting than what is present' [3]. The critical essays of the Popean Age were greatly deformed by the spirit of malignity that pervaded most of them. The literary feuds of the period were characterized by an unlimited use of personal invectives, and the violent denunciations of Warburton and his antagonists tended no less to cast discredit on the critic's office. Arthur Murphy calls them a 'Shoal of Monsters .... prowling about the Main, upon the Look-out, ... for some Object of their Rage'. Criticism is represented by him as the daughter of *Malice* and *Envy*, who is herself the offspring of *Ill Nature* and *Ignorance* [4]. One of the introductory chapters of *Tom Jones* is entitled *A Crust for Critics*, where this kind of writer

---

[1]   *The Universal Visiter And Monthly Memorialist for April* 1756, p. 162.
[2]   Ker, I, pp. 2, 3.
[3]   *Guardian*, 103.
[4]   *The Gray's Inn Journal*, Jan. 13, 1753.

is classed among the most abject slaves of vice and the most odious vermin that society produces [1]. The author of *An Essay on the New Species of Writing founded by Mr. Fielding* (London, 1751) laments that the title of critic, which was once so dignified and venerable, has been reduced to a state of ignominy in his time, and Gibbon speaks of 'the great but prostituted name of critic' [2].

---

[1] Book XI, Ch. I.
[2] *Miscellaneous Works,* IV, p. 113.

CHAPTER IX

SAMUEL JOHNSON [1]

Warburton's reputation was soon superseded by that of Johnson. In March 1750 the first number of the *Rambler* was published and its essays appeared regularly twice a week for the next two years. These papers, but above all his *Dictionary*, which was completed five years later, secured for Johnson the eminent position which he was to hold throughout his life. For a long time his authority as a writer and critic was undisputed. The never failing common sense, the love of truth, the intimate knowledge of human life, and above all the strong didactic tendency that distinguishes nearly every page he wrote, appealed to the wide circle of his readers as well as to his intimate friends. All felt great esteem for his critical powers, and some of his best-known verdicts are quoted by romanticists like the Wartons as well as by staunch believers in the doctrine of reason. The growing discontent with the old rational creed was looked upon by Johnson with disfavour, and there is no doubt that his powerful influence for a time kept the romantic tendencies of some of his contemporaries in check. After his death, however, his reputation rapidly decreased. The pomposity of his style, his awkward inversions, and his antipathy to blank verse, became the objects of abuse [2], and his Lives of Milton, Gray and Prior were considered as unmistakable proofs of his inability to appreciate the higher kinds of poetry [3]. In the third place his

---

[1] It might be objected that the length of this chapter is not in proportion to Johnson's importance as a critic. So much has been written about him, however, that I have thought it superfluous to deal with him at greater length. For more details the reader should refer to Prof. Houston's excellent book: *Doctor Johnson, A Study in Eighteenth Century Humanism*, Cambridge (Mass.), 1923, Dr. Brown's valuable compilation of representative passages from Johnson's works, *The Critical Opinions of Samuel Johnson*, Princeton, 1926, and J. W. Krutch, *Samuel Johnson*. London, 1948 (chiefly biographical).

[2] T. Twining, *Recreations and Studies of a Country Clergyman of the 18th Cent.*, p. 112; J. Warton, *The Works of Pope*, I, XVII note.

[3] Twining, *op. cit.*, p. 120; V. Knox, *Essays, Moral and Literary*, 1824, I, p. 465; II, p. 47; J. Warton, *op. cit.*, I, pp. XVII, 134 (note), 173; Pye,

suggestion to the booksellers to admit writers like Blackmore, Pomfret and Yalden among 'The English Poets' to whose works his *Lives* were to have served as prefaces, caused great discontent among the exponents of incipient romanticism. Though his good sense and originality were still acknowledged, he was pronounced to be deficient in taste, and by soms critics his verdicts were believed to have been instigated by religious and political prejudices [1].

Johnson has been represented as an orthodox believer in neoclassical tenets, and as a thoroughgoing exponent of the narrow doctrine that finds expression in the critical literature from the Restoration till the end of the eighteenth century. It has been said that all his verdicts were passed in strict accordance with certain fixed laws which he considered as final for authors as well as critics [2]. This view of Johnson's critical method has long since been rejected as untenable. His strong individuality, the sanity and independence of his judgment, made it impossible for him to submit to such a narrow code as that of the pseudo-classicists. Johnson's shortcomings as a literary critic are not the result of an implicit faith in pre-conceived standards but rather of a too rigid application of reason to aesthetic problems, of which a rational explanation cannot always be given.

Common sense is in Johnson's opinion the basis of all criticism. The critic is not a specialist endowed with special distinguishing qualities, with great learning, or more than average sensibility. Public opinion is to determine whether an author deserves to be held in esteem, it is the best standard by which literary merit can be evaluated [3].

A Commentary illustrating the Poetic of Aristotle, 1792, p. 473; Cowper, *Works,* (ed. Southey), II, 395, 398; III, 93.

[1] Twining, *op. cit.,* p. 119; Wakefield, *The Poems of Mr. Gray,* Advertisement; *Recollections of Some Particulars in the Life of the Late William Shenstone.* London, 1788, pp. 52, 53.

[2] Cf. E. E. Vaughan, *English Lit. Criticism.* London, 1903, LVI ff.

[3] *Rambler,* 52. Cf. Johnson's opinion of Gray's *Elegy*: 'I rejoice to concur with the common reader; for by the common sense of readers uncorrupted with literary prejudices, after all the refinements of subtlety and the dogmatism of learning, must be finally decided all claim to poetical honours'. *Lives,* III, p. 441.

Personal verdicts, based on emotional appeal, must be rejected.
Reason and life are the two main standards by which all literature
is to be tried. His own writings are the best illustration of this
theory. His poetry was characterized by Thomas Twining as 'good
sense put into good metre', his *Ramblers, Idlers* and *Adventurers*
are a storehouse of thoughts based on good sense and experience
of the world. In none of his works do we find a better reflection of
his never-failing sound judgment and great knowledge of human
life than in his greatest literary achievement, the *Lives of the Poets*.
The task of the critic is, according to Johnson, that of establishing
principles. It is not sufficient to know that a literary work should
please the reader, the critic should try to find out why it pleases,
and 'distinguish those means of pleasing which depend on known
causes and rational deduction, from the nameless and inexplicable
elegancies which appeal wholly to the fancy' [1]. Criticism is therefore entirely an intellectual process, its aim being to lay down
fundamental laws, not imposed by authority but based on rational
grounds. In opposition to Addison, who had advanced the view
that the critic's duty was rather to point out the beauties than the
faults, Johnson asserts that his task is 'to hold out the light of
reason', whatever it may discover [2]. He has a strong word of
warning for the kind of criticism that would permit fancy to dictate
the laws. Instead of following the caprices of this frivolous
mistress, the critic should endeavour to bring the regions of literature
under the dominion of science by a sustained rational process. Like
Kames and other critics of this Age, Johnson thinks that it is
possible to lay down with something like scientific stability, certain
immutable postulates, which have their foundation in human nature.
He is firmly convinced, however, that many of the rules laid down
by earlier generations of critics are mere arbitrary laws, 'not drawn
from any settled principle' or 'adapted to the natural and invariable
constitution of things'. He realizes that rules are based on practice
and not the reverse, and that laws that have thus originated are
always capable of improvement: 'Every genius produces some
innovation, which, when invented and approved subverts the rules

---

[1] *Rambler,* 92.
[2] *Ibid.,* 93.

which the practice of foregoing authors had established' [1]. This recognition of the progressive element in literature, of its capability of development, is widely different from the neo-classic conception of literary art as something static. Johnson blames the critics who follow *a priori* methods. As early as the year 1751, in one of the critical papers in the *Rambler,* we find his first attack on the prevalent critical code of his time. Here he summons the established laws before the tribunal of reason and nature: 'The accidental prescriptions of authority, when time has procured them veneration, are often confounded with the laws of nature, and those rules are supposed coeval with reason, of which the first rise cannot be discovered'. He then distinguishes two kinds of rules, those that are to be considered as fundamental and indispensable, 'dictated by reason and necessity', and others that are merely accidental and the result of custom. Applying this distinction to the rules of the drama, he places in the latter category the precepts that no more than three speaking personages should appear at once upon the stage, that the drama should be divided into five acts, and that the dramatic action should be restricted to a few hours. The passage winds up with the genuinely Johnsonian antithesis: 'It ought to be the first endeavour of a writer to distinguish nature from custom; or that which is established because it is right, from that which is right only because it is established; ....' [2]. He makes fun of the petty modern critics who reiterate the commonplaces of criticism without understanding them. These criticasters are held up to ridicule in the Dick Minim papers of the *Idler.* Dick Minim, after having been an apprentice to a brewer, seeks the company of literary men and picks up a number of cant phrases, the knowledge of which he considers as a sufficient guarantee for his critical abilities.

These passages from Johnson's early work furnish ample evidence of his sturdy independence, and clearly show how absurd it is to call the great critic an unswerving believer in neo-classic dogmas. Of his disbelief in *a priori* methods his later critical writings offer even more numerous illustrations. In the famous

---

[1] *Rambler,* 125.
[2] *Ibid.,* 156. Cf. Dryden's evaluation of French plays by the standard of nature. (*An Essay of Dramatic Poesy,* Ker, I, pp. 67 ff.)

Preface to Shakespeare, that marvellous manifestation of shrewd common sense, he speaks of the danger there is in submitting to the dictates of authority: 'Judgement, like other faculties, is improved by practice, and its advancement is hindered bij submission to dictatorial decisions . . . .' [1]. In his *Life of Milton* he speaks disparagingly of those critics who found their judgments on books instead of on reason, and think it worth while discussing the question whether *Paradise Lost* can be properly termed an heroic poem and who is the hero [2].

Of all the generally accepted postulates, Johnson approves only of those which are consistent with the leading principles of his critical belief: reason and truth. Both are to him absolutely fixed standards. 'Truth indeed is always truth, and reason is always reason; they have an intrinsick and unalterable value, and constitute that intellectual gold which defies destruction', is the dictum with which he opens his discussion of Cowley's style [3]. The critics who followed no other guides than these two were in Johnson's opinion far superior to those who were led by natural taste and feelings, but there was a third group of critics whom he ranked even lower, namely those whose opinions were formed by the rules.

It goes without saying that his denunciation of classical authority for the modern poet does not detract from his great reverence for classical authors and critics. His works leave no doubt about his extensive knowledge of the ancient, especially of the Latin, writers. His *Ramblers* teem with classical allusions. He regretted the neglect into which the great masters of antiquity had fallen at the time when he began his literary career, he proclaimed the superiority of the ancients over the moderns, and was of opinion that the latter often 'shone with reflected light, borrowed from the ancients'. He held that the modern writer was at liberty to borrow from the wealth of thoughts and images contained in their works without running the risk of being condemned as a plagiarist. He distinguished between imitation and servile copying, between 'pursuing the path of the ancients' and

---

1   W. Raleigh, *Johnson on Shakespeare,* p. 54.
2   *Lives,* I, p. 176.
3   *Ibid.,* I, p. 59.

treading in their footsteps [1]. He did not believe, however, that mere imitation could ever make an author great. The study of books, though necessary, was not sufficient, unless it was combined with invention: 'either the effect must itself be new, or the means by which it is produced' [2].

Horace, the idol of the neo-classical writers, was also Johnson's favourite [3]. No classical author is so often alluded to in Boswell's biography. In his *Ramblers* and *Adventurers* he adopted the practice of prefixing mottos to his periodicals, as Addison and Steele had done before him, and many of them are taken from Horace. He often supported his critical dicta by references to the *Ars Poetica* [4]. But even Horace's rules are accepted only if they are reconcilable with the laws of reason. In his review of the *Memoirs of the Court of Augustus* by Thomas Blackwell [5], he speaks of 'the dictates of common sense and common honesty', which he calls 'names of greater authority than that of Horace'. In his *Life of Dryden* he deals with the poet's views on translation. He expresses his agreement with Dryden's method of procedure, which is neither that of 'metaphrase' or translating word for word, nor that of the looser 'imitation', in which both sense and words may be materially different from those of the original, but rather that of 'paraphrase', which follows the sense rather than the words of the author. To justify this practice, the adherents of the new school of translation, inaugurated by Malherbe in France and supported by Balzac, Saint-Évremond and others, often appealed to the Horatian warning against a too close following of the original [6]. Johnson thinks, however, that 'the reasonableness of these rules seems sufficient for their vindication; .... reason wants not Horace to support it' [7].

Johnson's critical works contain very few references to Aristotle, but such as there are, leave no doubt about his high opinion of 'the father of criticism'. There are even some instances where his

---

1   *Rambler,* 143.
2   *Ibid.,* 154.
3   For the influence of Horace on Johnson, see Goad, *Horace in the English Lit. of the 18th Cent.,* 1918, pp. 233 ff.
4   *Ibid.,* p. 254.
5   Lit. Club Ed., New York, 1903, XIII, p. 170.
6   *AP,* ll. 133—134.
7   *Lives,* I, p. 423.

usual independence of judgment forsakes him and he falls back
upon the old method of testing the merit of a work of art by the
laws that the Greek critic had laid down. His analysis of Milton's
Samson Agonistes [1] is based upon 'the indispensable laws of
Aristotelian criticism'. He examines it to see if it has a beginning,
a middle and an end, and overlooking the fact that the speeches
of Samson and the dialogue between him and Dalila manifest the
hero's intention to take revenge, and consequently prepare the
way for the catastrophe, he finds that it has no middle, or as he
puts it later on in his *Life of Milton,* that 'the intermediate parts
have neither cause nor consequence'. In the *Preface to Shakespeare*
he applies the same precept of the Greek philosopher to the works
of the dramatist, and comes to the conclusion that most of his
plays are built upon the plan that Aristotle requires [2]. In his
discussion of Milton's epic Johnson follows Aristotle's method,
which the French commentator, Le Bossu, had made popular,
and Addison had adopted in the Milton papers of the *Spectator.*
After citing Le Bossu's dictum that the first task of the epic poet
is to find a moral, which his fable ought to illustrate, and stating
that in *Paradise Lost* the moral is an essential and intrinsic element,
he closely follows the track of the French critics. He first discusses
the *fable,* then the *characters,* the *probable* and the *marvellous,* the
machinery, episodes and the *integrity* of the design, last of all the
sentiments and *the diction* [3]. Cowley's *Davideis* escapes the same
fate, because only four of the twelve books of which it was to
have consisted, were finished, and so there is 'no opportunity
for such criticisms as Epick poems commonly supply' [4]. The
influence of Le Bossu on English aesthetic theory was still strong
in Johnson's time, so strong that even a critic whose verdicts
generally bear the stamp of an original mind, was not entirely free
from its powerful sway.

Among Johnson's criticisms there are none that illustrate his
independence of established opinions better than his discussion
of tragi-comedy and that of the dramatic unities. His defence of

---

1   *Rambler,* 139.
2   *Op. cit.,* p. 25.
3   *Lives,* I, pp. 171 ff.
4   *Ibid.,* p. 53.

the intermixture of tragic and comic elements in the same play forms a striking contrast with the apologetic attitude which Dryden had adopted in the preface to *Cleomenes,* and Addison's dictum that it is 'one of the most monstrous inventions that ever entered into a poet's thoughts' [1]. The Restoration poet had avoided the introduction of comic scenes because he considered it as contrary to the 'natural and true way' of writing plays. Johnson, on the other hand, thinks that he who is unbiassed by authority, and accepts no other laws than those of nature, can have no objection to the mingled drama. The stage is to Johnson only the mirror of life and the connexion of important and trivial incidents is not only common but perpetual in the world. 'Impartial reason' can therefore find nothing to condemn. Moreover, the great popularity that this kind of drama had always enjoyed in England was for Johnson a sufficient reason for disregarding the established views of criticism. 'Is it not certain', he exclaims, 'that no plays have oftener filled the eye with tears and the breast with palpitation than those which are variegated with interludes of mirth?' [2]. Deference for the popular judgment was a distinguishing trait of his critical creed; the opinion of the multitude, unprejudiced by dictatorial laws, was to him the final test of all literary merit, or, as he expresses it himself, 'the publick, which is never corrupted, nor often deceived, is to pass the last sentence upon literary claims' [3]. At the end of his essay, however, the critic shows that he is not free from the ordinary pseudo-classical prejudices, when he suggests that our interest in the distresses of Shakespeare's heroes might have been much greater, 'had we not been so frequently diverted by the jokes of his buffoons'.

Fourteen years later, in the *Preface* to Shakespeare's plays, we find Johnson's views restated, now much more explicitly. Though the mixing of the comic and the tragic is pronounced to be contrary to the rules of criticism, it 'exhibits the real state of sublunary nature' and nature is a higher authority than the bigoted opinions of the critics.

---

1   *Spectator,* 40.
2   *Rambler,* 156.
3   *Ibid.,* 23. Cf. *Rambler,* 52.

The unities of time and place had never been so popular in England as in France, where, after the *Cid* controversy, they had become a recognized canon of dramatic theory, which found expression in Boileau's well-known dictum [1]. The English critics of the seventeenth century, even those who were on the whole rather dogmatic, treated the unities with considerable latitude. Their views were in the main based on the lenient conception of Corneille, whose critical opinions on the drama were looked upon as an authority up to Johnson's time. Dryden translated the end of Corneille's *Troisième Discours*, and then asserted that the servile observance of the unities of time and place had caused a 'dearth of plot and a narrowness of imagination' in the French drama [2]. In the *Preface to Troilus and Cressida* he called them the mechanic beauties of the plot [3], just as Rymer had done before him [4].

Johnson's first attack is to be found in the *Rambler* [5]. Though he had strictly observed the unities in *Irene,* his own unsuccessful attempt in the field of the drama, in this essay he considers only the unity of action as essential. He grants that probability requires the time of the action not to differ materially from that of the representation, and even thinks it speaks for the dramatic skill of the author, if he crowds the greatest variety into the least space. He adds, however, that minds 'not prepossessed by mechanical criticism', will not object to longer intervals between the acts than the unity of time would allow. This conciliatory attitude, being neither a complete defence nor an open denunciation, had been entirely abandoned by the time he wrote the *Preface to Shakespeare*. Here he waives all belief in authority and founds his discussion of the unities on a purely rational basis. The common sense of the spectators is for Johnson a sufficient guarantee that they will never mistake dramatic representation for reality. They know 'from the first act to the last, that the stage is only a stage, and that the players are only players' [6]. The common objection that it would

---

1 *Art poétique,* III, ll. 45, 46.
2 *An Essay of Dramatic Poesy,* Ker, I, p. 75.
3 Ker, I, p. 212.
4 Spingarn, *Crit. Essays,* II, p. 183.
5 *Rambler,* 156.
6 *Op. cit.,* p. 27.

be impossible for the audience to imagine that they pass the first
hour at Alexandria and the next at Rome, or that the second act
represents an action happening years after the first, is therefore
a mere illusion: 'a lapse of years is as easily conceived as a passage
of hours'. Throughout the performance the spectators are conscious
of fiction; they know that the evils they see before them are not
real, but only such as they *may* be exposed to. If they did think
them real, they would please them no more.

Of *correctness* Johnson was as staunch a defender as the critics
of the reign of Queen Anne. He disapproved of anything that
was not in strict accordance with the laws of reason, nature and
truth. Extravagant diction, far-fetched allusions, and irrelevant
ornaments were an abomination to him. With the Augustans he
shared the view that Waller and Denham had saved poetry from
'forced thoughts and rugged metre' and had been the first writers
to advance it to a state of 'nature and harmony'. He admired the
first for the smoothness of his numbers but considered him deficient
in 'strength'; like Dryden he thought that the latter quality had
been introduced by the author of *Cooper's Hill* [1]. But Johnson
believed that these two had left much to be done by later poets
and that the new versification had not been firmly established
before Dryden, 'from whose time it is apparent that English poetry
has had no tendency to relapse to its former savageness' [2].
According to Johnson, Roscommon was the first example of a really
correct writer who made it his special task to avoid faults, and

---

[1] The notion that Denham was the first poet to give strength to English verse
[cf. Pope's lines in his *Essay on Criticism*:
>   And praise the easy vigour of a line,
>   Where Denham's strength, and Waller's sweetness join.
>   (ll. 360, 361)],
was severely attacked by John Scott of Amwell in his *Critical Essays* (1785).
His criticism is instructive as being indicative of the great change that had
taken place since Pope's juvenile production was written: 'When Denham
wrote, strength was not to be given to verse, it had been already given by
Spenser, Shakespeare, Drayton, Fairfax, Milton, Bishop Hall, Sandys the
translator of Ovid and others. Denham's vigour is not genuine poetical energy,
but harshness and obscurity . . . . Cooper's Hill is an uniform mass of dullness'
(p. 35).

[2] *Lives*, I, p. 421.

Addison, Pope and Prior followed in his track [1]. Johnson admires
the last-named because he 'never sacrifices accuracy to haste, nor
indulges himself in contemptuous negligence or impatient idleness:
he has no careless lines or entangled sentiments; his words are
nicely selected, and his thoughts fully expanded' [2]. Though he
praised *Comus* for being truly poetical, as a drama he thought it
'inelegantly splendid'. A very typical illustration of his views is
a curious passage in his *Life of J. Philips*, where he calls Milton's
verse harmonious, 'in proportion to the general state of our metre
in Milton's Age', and expresses his belief that he would have
attained a much higher degree of perfection, if he had written after
the improvements made by Dryden [3]. He accused Cowley of
negligence and unskilful selection of words [4], and in spite of his
high esteem for Shakespeare he blamed him for corrupting language
'by every mode of depravation' [5]. He held the common view of
the eighteenth century that the beauties of the dramatist were
greatly marred by his serious blemishes. After having compared
a correct writer to a garden 'accurately formed and diligently
planted', he draws the parallel between some poets who 'display
cabinets of precious rarities, minutely finished, wrought into shape
and polished into brightness', and Shakespeare's inexhaustible mine
of gold and diamonds, which are, however, 'clouded by incrusta-
tions, debased by impurities and mingled with a mass of meaner
minerals' [6]. Yet mere correctness does not make a writer a good poet.
Though Addison's poetry is 'polished and pure', it is not 'sufficiently
vigorous to attain excellence' [7]. *Cato*, which was so popular in
the author's own time, finds no favour in Johnson's eyes, because
it is lacking in emotional appeal: 'Nothing here excites or assuages
emotion; here is no magical power of raising phantastick terror
or wild anxiety' [8].

---

1 *Lives,* I, p. 235; II, pp. 145, 208; III, p. 93.
2 *Ibid.,* II, p. 208.
3 *Ibid.,* I, p. 318.
4 *Ibid.,* I, p. 55.
5 *Preface to Shakespeare* (Raleigh), p. 41.
6 *Ibid.,* p. 34.
7 *Lives,* II, p. 145.
8 *Ibid.,* p. 132.

Johnson was conscious of the fluctuating nature of language and literature. He regretted that language was subject to continual change, he was of opinion that no innovation should be made without sufficient reason, and he regarded his dictionary as a means to reduce the English tongue to a greater degree of stability. But at the same time he saw that all attempts to check its growth would prove futile. 'I am not so lost in lexicography, as to forget that *words are the daughters of earth, and that things are the sons of heaven.* Language is only the instrument of science, and words are but the signs of ideas: I wish, however, that the instrument might be less apt to decay, and that signs might be permanent, like the things which they denote', he says in the preface to his *Dictionary* [1].

He rejected the idea of establishing an English Academy for the improvement of the language. He realized that such an institution could never have the desired effect. In his *Life of Swift* he exposes the neo-classical fallacy by the remark that such a certainty and stability of language as Swift had in mind would be contrary to all experience and therefore unattainable [2].

That Johnson recognized the idea of development in literature and saw that it would be irrational to apply a preordained standard to it, is evident from some of his statements. He

---

1   *Preface,* p. 2. We find another interesting passage on page 9: 'Those who have been persuaded to think well of my design, require that it should fix our language, and put a stop to those alterations which time and chance have hitherto been suffered to make in it without opposition. With this consequence I will confess that I flattered myself for a while; but now begin to fear that I have indulged expectation which neither reason nor experience can justify. When we see men grow old and die at a certain time one after another, from century to century, we laugh at the elixer that promises to prolong life to a thousand years; and with equal justice may the lexicographer be derided, who being able to produce no example of a nation that has preserved their words and phrases from mutability, shall imagine that his dictionary can embalm his language and secure it from corruption and decay, that it is in his power to change sublunary nature, or clear the world at once from folly, vanity, and affectation'.

2   Swift's statement that the English language often offends against every part of grammar, a statement illustrative of his complete ignorance of linguistic development and the grammarian's task, is refuted by George Campbell in his very interesting treatise *The Philosophy of Rhetoric.* His remarks sometimes breathe a very modern spirit as will appear from the following passage. Grammar is, according to him, nothing but 'a collection of general observ-

clearly saw that is was impossible to judge of a certain literary product without considering the historical environment, the social conditions of the author's age, and the causal connexion between these and the work of art. 'Every man's performances, to be rightly estimated, must be compared with the state of the age in which he lived, and with his own particular opportunities' [1], is his answer to those critics who blamed Shakespeare for his defective judgment. Nowhere does Johnson stress the necessity of historical approach so much as in his note to the scene of the witches in *Macbeth*: 'In order to make a true estimate of the abilities and merit of a writer, it is always necessary to examine the genius of his age, and the opinions of his contemporaries. A poet who should now make the whole action of his tragedy depend upon enchantment, and produce the chief events by the assistance of supernatural agents, would be censured as transgressing the bounds of probability, be banished from the Theatre to the nursery, and condemned to write fairy tales instead of tragedies; but a survey of the notions that prevailed at the time when this play was written, will prove that *Shakespeare* was in no danger of such censures, since he only turned the system that was then universally admitted to his advantage, and was far from overburthening the credulity of his audience' [2]. In the *Proposals,* which appeared nine years before the *Preface* saw the light, he had dealt with the difficulties that confront the editor of Shakespeare, and had made it clear that only a thorough knowledge of the manners and customs of the author's age, and a careful examination of the books that the dramatist had read, can lead to satisfactory results. He praised Thomas Warton's *Observations on the Faerie Queene,* because it drew the attention of the reader to the sources from which Spenser took his material, and compared this method to that followed by previous critics like Hughes and others. 'The reason why the authours, which

---

ations, methodically digested and comprising all the modes previously and independently established .... (the modes or fashions) no sooner obtain and become general, than they are laws of the language and the grammarian's only business is to note, collect and methodise them'.

(*The Philosophy of Rhetoric,* 1816, II, Ch. I).

Kames falls into the same error as Swift when he thinks that language can be fixed by authoritative rules.   (*Elements of Criticism,* II, p. 13).

[1] Raleigh, p. 30.
[2] *Ibid.,* p. 167.

are yet read, of the sixteenth century, are so little understood, is, that they are read alone; and no help is borrowed from those who lived with them, or before them' [1]. These dicta show at least that Johnson knew how well a critic should be equipped before embarking upon an edition of Elizabethan poetry. It follows naturally from his words, however, that his own imperfect knowledge of the dramatists before Shakespeare, and of the great poet's contemporaries was a serious shortcoming in himself, when he undertook his task as an editor.

Johnson's insistence on reason as the sole criterion by which literary art should be tested made him an incompetent judge of aesthetic qualities for which it is impossible to find a strictly rational foundation. The work of the poet was in his eyes an intellectual process, a certain skill in arranging words. It has repeatedly been said that the lives of Dryden and Pope were the only two that he wrote with great sympathy. The works of the latter poet offered the best exemplification of his aesthetic conceptions. Johnson enumerates all the great qualities that Pope possessed. Among these the first is 'good sense', which he calls 'the constituent and fundamental principle of his intellectual character'. The idea of *inspiration* is rejected by him with disdain. The days of his own hard struggle with poverty had taught him that literary production was possible whenever circumstances made it necessary. 'A man may write at any time, if he will set himself *doggedly* to it', he is reported to have observed on the occasion of his visit to Parliament-House at Edinburgh, when one of the other visitors spoke about happy moments for composition [2]. He thought it easier for himself to write poetry than to compose his dictionary [3]. He makes fun of Milton's statement in the *Latin Elegies* that with the advance of spring he felt the increase of poetical force: 'This dependance of the soul upon the seasons, those temporary and periodical ebbs and flows of intellect, may, I suppose, justly be derided as the fumes of vain imagination' [4]. Gray's notion that

---

1   Boswell, I, p. 270.
2   *Ibid.*, V, p. 40.
3   *Ibid.*, p. 47.
4   *Lives,* I, p. 137.

he could only write at certain times when he felt inspired, is called a 'fantastic foppery' [1].

As has been observed before, Johnson by no means ignored the fact that the poet's first duty was to move, and it is beside the point to assume that he was not capable of any poetic feeling, as the nineteenth century critics would have us believe. His great love of Shakespeare and his genuine, though not unqualified, admiration of *Paradise Lost* are perhaps the best arguments to refute this erroneous view. But he hated affectation, he strongly disliked any form of emotionalism that he suspected to be mere false parade. He was out of sympathy with the incipient romanticism of the grave-yard school of poetry. To Joseph Warton he referred as 'an enthusiast by rule', he ridiculed his brother Thomas's fondness for obsolete words and his turgid diction. 'He puts a very common thing in a strange dress till he does not know it himself, and thinks other people do not know it', he said to Boswell. His distaste for Gray's mannerisms prevented him from recognizing this poet's great qualities. His *Odes* were to him 'forced plants raised in hot-beds'. He failed to see the merit of Collins's poetry, though in this respect he was no better and no worse than his contemporaries. He could not appreciate his love of fairies, genii, giants and monsters, which lay so far outside the bounds of nature that one could only be reconciled to them by 'a passive acquiescence in popular tradition' [2]. Johnson's love of truth drove him into opposition to the sentimental revolt that rose as a reaction against the long-lived sway of reason. The strong tidal wave of individualism, the personal way of looking at life which characterized the resurrection of romanticism, found no favour with the critic who had laid so much stress on the necessity for the poet to depict the general aspects of human nature. He denied any merit to *Ossian* which, from the very beginning, he suspected to be a forgery. He despised the conventional sentimentalism, affectation and hollow, declamatory style, which he thought too facile substitutes for genuine emotion [3]. Pastoral poetry was Johnson's pet aversion. In his opinion the writers of pastorals forgot that the

---

[1] *Lives,* III, p. 433.
[2] *Ibid.,* III, p. 337.
[3] Boswell, IV, p. 183; V, p. 388.

two most important subjects of all literary art were life and nature. They filled their poems with incredible fictions and with sentiments, 'which neither passion nor reason could have dictated' [1]. The best-known and most often quoted illustration of Johnson's low opinion of this sort of poetry is his severe criticism of Milton's *Lycidas*. It has been attributed to prejudice, and to the critic's toryism and High-Churchmanship, which are said to have prevented him from acknowledging the poetic genius of a man whose political and religious views were so different from his own. But if we bear in mind what are the fundamental principles of Johnson's critical creed, we see that there is nothing to justify these assumptions. His sweeping condemnation is only a vigorous repetition of similar statements in a milder form in the *Rambler*. His chief objection to *Lycidas* is that it is not the effusion of real passion and is full of far-fetched allusions: 'In this poem there is no nature, for there is no truth; there is no art, for there is nothing new'. Moreover Johnson objected to the pastoral form. He thought that, owing to its artificiality, it could never satisfy the mind of the reader.

It was only natural that a critic whose interest in poetry was almost exclusively restricted to those kinds which deal with the realities of life, could find little to admire in *Paradise Lost*. Though he praised Milton's masterly skill in expanding the small amount of material that the Scriptures afforded him, the poem had one serious defect for which all its beauties could not make up, namely its want of universal human interest.

Poetry dealing with subjects outside the bounds of empirical fact, sentiments and images not consistent with the experiences of common humanity, did not lie within Johnson's sphere of interest. He condemned Milton's invocation of Arethuse and Mincius in *Lycidas*, because it was at variance with genuine passion. He blamed Waller and Granville for borrowing sentiments and illustrations from classical mythology. He believed that it was illogical to plead the example of the ancient poets because to them the pagan deities had been realities, at least had been accepted as such, 'whatever sober reason might even then determine'. But in modern poetry such allusions were out of place. Tested by truth and nature, they were no more than absurdities.

---

[1] *Rambler*, 37.

CHAPTER X

HENRY FIELDING. LAURENCE STERNE

Henry Fielding, the great novelist, did not write any work dealing exclusively or even chiefly with literary criticism. His critical observations have to be culled from various prose-writings, from dedications, prefaces, certain articles in his *Covent Garden Journal,* and principally from those delightful introductory chapters to the different books of his masterpiece *Tom Jones.* Here, as Austin Dobson has observed, 'he takes us, as it were, into his confidence and discourses frankly of his aims and his way of work' [1]. All these scattered passages taken together constitute a critical output that gives Fielding a right to a prominent place among the rationalistic critics of the time.

In his article on *Fielding's Library,* the author of the interesting *Eighteenth Century Vignettes* defends the novelist against Thackeray's unfounded charge of bragging of his 'two-penny learning'. 'For if Fielding was anything at all, he was a genuine scholar', the critic observes, and supports his statement by references to Murphy's *Life,* all pointing to great versatility in and genuine admiration for the classical writers. Allusions to them are very numerous in his work and there is no doubt that his first-hand knowledge of them was considerable [2]. Like some of his contemporaries [3] he regretted the decline of classical scholarship which characterized his age, and repeatedly attacked the ignorance of the numberless petty writers, whom he ridiculed in the first number of his *Covent Garden Journal.* In one of his articles in *The Champion* [4] there is the ironical suggestion 'to banish from among us those dead tongues, which are not only useless, but as I am informed, have much contributed to introduce the religion of the ancients as well as their language' [5].

---

[1] Austin Dobson, *Fielding,* (*Eng. Men of L.*), p. 122.
[2] Cf. *Quarterly Review,* vol. XCVIII, 1856.
[3] Cf. V. Knox's vindication of classical learning in his *Essays, Moral and Literary,* (number III).
[4] Tuesday, Dec. 25, 1739.
[5] For other references see Jensen, *Covent Garden Journal,* II, p. 149.

An extensive knowledge of classical literature is in Fielding's opinion one of the necessary qualifications for a critic. Aristotle, Horace, and Longinus, are held up as examples of what a good judge of poetry should be, and are called writers to whom the learned world is greatly indebted [1]. In his third paper of the *Covent Garden Journal* he proposes to exclude anyone from the office of criticism that has not read over and understood the works of these three masters of antiquity in their original languages [2]. Besides these authorities he mentions two others, the French critics Dacier and Le Bossu. *Amelia* is defended against the charges of the 'Court of Censorial Enquiry' on the ground that the author has followed the rules 'of all those who are acknowledged to have writ best on the subject', which neither Homer nor Virgil could have pursued with greater care than he [3]. He even tells us that Virgil was the model on which his favourite *Amelia* was written.

In spite of all these reverential allusions to the great Latin and Greek authors, Fielding does not unreservedly accept their dicta as a standard for modern authors. Truth and nature in the strictly pseudo-classical sense are his supreme tests as well as Johnson's, reason and common sense the never-failing guides. All laws of writing are first summoned before these tribunals before they are pronounced to be of any practical merit. In the opening chapter of the fifth book of *Tom Jones* (1749) he denounces the authority of such rules as have no adequate foundation, and blames the critics whose laws are not based on *essential* qualities in great writers. 'They acted as a judge would who should adhere to the lifeless letter of law, and reject the spirit. Little circumstances, which were perhaps accidental in a great author, were by these critics considered to constitute his chief merit, and transmitted as essentials to be observed by all his successors; . . . .' and this is in Fielding's opinion the reason why so many rules have been established that are not founded on truth and nature and merely tend to restrain the genius of the author [4]. Dogmatic methods of

---

[1] *TJ*, Book XI, Ch. I.
[2] *CGJ*, 3. (Jensen, I, p. 150).
[3] *Ibid.*, 8.
[4] *TJ*, Book V, Ch. I.

criticism do not find favour in Fielding's eyes. The world has had far too high an opinion of critics and this has emboldened them to assume a dictatorial power. Precepts which originated from the practice of previous generations of writers can never have binding force for the modern author. They can only be a means to an end, but their guidance, however safe it may be, is not the only way to excellence. Fielding's remarks in this chapter illustrate his consciousness of the relationship that exists between criticism and creation: 'The critic, rightly considered, is no more than the clerk, whose office it is to transcribe the rules and laws laid down by those great judges, whose vast strength of genius has placed them in the light of legislators in the several sciences over which they presided'.

In number sixty-two of the *Covent Garden Journal* we find a letter, sent by a fictitious contributor and addressed to Sir Alexander Drawcansir, Knt., the Censor of Great Britain. It is supposed to have been written by a madman, who calls himself Tragicomicus, and contains a criticism of a drama thrown into his cell at Bedlam. As appears from the further particulars (the five letters prefixed — the fact that the author lives at Pembroke Hall in Cambridge) it is a skit on Mason's *Elfrida*. Fielding makes fun of Mason's design to follow ancient models and of his assertion that good sense prescribes an adherence to the three unities [1]. He speaks of 'the abominable Rules of Aristotle', and censures their curbing effect on the genius of the modern playwright. 'If Shakespeare had observed them', he says, 'he wou'd have flown like a *Paper-Kite, not soar'd like an Eagle*'. He next holds up to ridicule Scroddles's attempt to restore the ancient chorus. The passage, full of excellent banter, is as follows: '. . . . methinks this *Mr. Chorus* would be a very impertinent Fellow if he was to put in his Observations on any of Shakespeare's interesting Scenes; as for Example, what do you think of this same *Chorus*, if he was to be upon the Stage when, in the Play of Othello, Iago is imprinting those exquisite Tints of Jealousy upon Othello's Mind in the third Act; or suppose when Desdemona drops the fatal Handkerchief, the *Chorus* was to call after her to bid her take it up again, or tell the Audience what

---

[1] First letter, prefixed to *Elfrida*. See infra, pp. 159, 160.

was to happen in Case she did not. — Or suppose, Sir, this same *Chorus* was to stand by, and tell us Brutus and Cassius were going to differ, but that they would make it up again — would not this prevent the noble Anxiety this famous scene in Julius Caesar raises in the minds of a sensible Audience?' Mason had asserted that the chorus tended to explain the characters to the audience; Fielding recommends a still better practice, namely that of the Chinese, 'who always make the Characters of the Drama come upon the Stage before the Play begins' [1].

In the chapter of *Tom Jones* where Fielding rejects the judicial procedure of some critics, he also expresses his disbelief in the unities of time and place, which he ranks among the dogmatic rules that have been accepted without any rational inquiry: 'What critic hath been ever asked, why a play may not contain two days as well as one? Or why the audience (provided they travel, like electors, without expense) may not be wafted fifty miles as well as five?' In a similar manner he suggests the absurdity of the division of a drama into five acts: 'Hath any commentator well accounted for the limitation which an ancient critic hath set to the drama, which he will have contain neither more nor less than five acts?'

One of the few serious critical papers of the *Covent Garden Journal* deals with the complicated question of *taste* on which, as he says, 'scarce two authors have agreed in their notions of it'. He himself calls it a 'nice Harmony between the Imagination and the Judgment', which, he thinks, sufficiently accounts for its rare occurrence: 'Neither of these will alone bestow it; nothing is indeed more common than to see Men of very bright Imaginations, and of very accurate Learning (which can hardly be acquired without Judgment) who are entirely void of Taste' [2]. Though he grants that the highest consummation of taste can only be attained if there is a natural disposition, his opinion is that art can greatly improve it, and that a proper education is therefore an indispensable means to this end. As naturally follows from his insistence on learning as a necessary qualification for the critic, he does not

---

[1]   *CGJ*, 62, Jensen, II, pp. 93, 94.
[2]   *Ibid.*, 10.

accept popular applause as a sufficient guarantee of literary merit:
'as for the Bulk of Mankind, they are clearly void of any Degree
of Taste'.

Fielding's rational conception of literary art plainly appears in
his 'Wonderful long Chapter concerning the Marvellous' [1], which
the novelist considered as an adequate introduction to the strange
and surprising matters related in the following chapters. His views
are midway between those of Dacier, who in accordance with
Aristotle's doctrine had admitted even the impossible if it was
only probable [2], and others who were unwilling to believe anything
that had not actually been the object of their observation.
Fielding's final criterion is *possibility*, not *probability:* 'what it is
not possible for man to perform, it is scarce possible for man to
believe he did perform'. But he grants that the doctrine of popular
belief, which had been advanced by the pseudo-classical critics
to defend Homer's use of the supernatural, is perhaps an excuse for
his extravagancies: 'the poet himself wrote to heathens to whom
poetical fables were articles of faith'. Yet he wishes that the great
Greek poet had known Horace's precept to introduce supernatural
agents as seldom as possible: he would not have indulged his love
of the marvellous to such a degree. 'We should not then have seen
his gods coming on trivial errands, and often behaving themselves
so as not only to forfeit all title to respect, but to become the
objects of scorn and derision; a conduct which must have shocked
the credulity of a pious and sagacious heathen; and which could
never have been defended, unless by agreeing with a supposition
to which I have been sometimes almost inclined, that this most
glorious poet, as he certainly was, had an intent to burlesque the
superstitious faith of his own age and country'. To Christian poets
he denies the right to make use of pagan machinery; the only
supernatural agents that he would allow them are ghosts, but even
these should be seldom resorted to. He compares them to arsenic

---

[1]   *TJ,* Book VIII, Ch. I.
[2]   Dacier's explanatory note to the passage in his translation of Aristotle's *Poetics*
is as follows: 'Le poète doit plutôt choisir les choses impossibles pourvu qu'elles
sont vray-semblables, que les possibles qui sont incroyables avec toute leur
possibilité'. Of course the *vraisemblance* of Dacier and other French critics
simply means accordance with the laws of experience.

and other dangerous drugs, which ought to be used with the utmost caution. It is curious to notice his conciliatory attitude towards elves, fairies and 'other such mummery', which in spite of their unreality, he does not openly reject. He insists, however, that the historian as well as the poet should take care not to transgress the bounds of human reason when relating human actions, for like a true child of the age of Enlightenment, Fielding looks upon man as the highest subject of their works. The historian is obliged to record matters as he finds them, even if they are not consistent with probability. As Boileau had done before him [1], Fielding denies the poet the right to excuse his departure from the credible by asserting that what he relates is matter of fact. For the poet it is not sufficient that the events he tells have really happened, they must be such that the reader can believe them. Rational belief is a higher authority than empiric fact.

The attitude which another great novelist of the eighteenth century, Laurence Sterne, maintained towards classical canons, was no less sceptical than that of Fielding. The few references that we find in his works show clearly enough that he doubted the validity of all external rules; he generally speaks of them in a tone of good-humoured raillery. The ancient writers are often mentioned with respect, but of the critics there is only one that has won his esteem: Longinus. In his forty-second sermon he calls him 'the best critic the eastern world ever produced'.

In one of the first chapters of *Tristram Shandy* (1759—61), he makes fun of Horace's famous precept, when he remarks that he has traced the story of himself *ab ovo*, even though he knows that the author of the *Ars Poetica* has not recommended this procedure. At the same time he expresses his intention not to confine himself to his directions, 'nor to any man's rules that ever lived' [2].

Sterne's banter is unsurpassed in a well-known chapter of the third book [3]. It is directed against the 'connoisseurs', who are 'so

---

[1]   Jamais au spectateur n'offrez rien d'incroyable;
      Le vrai peut quelquefois n'être pas vraisemblable.
                              (*Art Poétique*, III, ll. 47, 48).

[2]   Book I, Ch. IV.

[3]   Ch. XII.

hung round and *befetish'd* with the bobs and trinkets of criticism',
whose heads 'are stuck so full of rules and compasses, and have
that eternal propensity to apply them upon all occasions, that a
work of genius had better go to the devil at once, than stand to
be prick'd and tortured to death by 'em'. The author has a fling at
the critic, who, unable to appreciate the great talents of the actor
David Garrick, measures the pauses he makes in speaking a soli-
loquy by a stop-watch, and then examines if they are in accordance
with the rules of grammar. — 'But in suspending his voice — was
the sense suspended likewise? Did no expression of attitude or
countenance fill up the chasm? — Was the eye silent? Did you
narrowly look? — I look'd only at the stop-watch, my lord. —
Excellent observer!'

In a similar way the novelist ridicules the narrow-minded judges
that test a new book by mechanical rules or weigh the merit of an
epic poem 'upon an exact scale af *Bossu's*', and then gives his final
verdict: 'Of all the cants which are canted in this canting world —
though the cant of hypocrites may be the worst — the cant of
criticism is the most tormenting!'

One more illustrative passage may be adduced: the fourth
book of *Tristram Shandy* opens with the grotesque tale of Hafen
Slawkenbergius de Nasis, where Sterne once again rallies the
rules of Aristotle. The story, he says, has all the essential parts that
the Greek critic thought necessary for the drama: 'it has its *Protasis*,
Epitasis, *Catastasis*, its *Catastrophe* or *Peripetia*', and he follows
it up with the satirical remark that without these a tale had better
not be told, 'but be kept to a man's self'.

Both Sterne and Fielding were thoroughgoing rationalists. They
were among the earliest critics who had completely freed themselves
of the old shackles of the rules. Neither of the two thought the belief
in authoritative precepts worth any serious discussion; ridicule was
in their eyes the proper means to expose it.

CHAPTER XI

HENRY HOME, LORD KAMES

One of the large number of eminent writers that the Scotch centre of culture, Edinburgh, could boast of in the eighteenth century, was Henry Home, Lord Kames. Like Lord Monboddo and Lord Hailes he belonged to the legal profession [1]. His *Elements of Criticism* appeared in 1762, and was several times reprinted.

As the author states in the 'Dedication to the King', his work endeavours to unfold the principles of art by which the taste of every individual ought to be governed. His design is twofold: in the first place he wants to ascertain, as Burke had done before him, what objects are naturally agreeable or naturally disagreeable; in the second place his intention is to examine 'the sensitive branch of human nature' and to give a psychological analysis of all the aesthetic emotions that these objects cause in the human mind.

The common sense of mankind is, in Kames's opinion, the only standard in the fine arts, as well as in morals. Aesthetic principles must therefore be founded on the mental experience of the people in general, not on that of a selected few [2]. Like Johnson, the author believes that 'the general taste is seldom wrong' and he himself is prepared 'to submit to it with entire resignation'.

It is not my intention to follow Kames in his abstract inquiry. Some of its results have already been touched on in the preceding pages. The greater part of the elaborate treatise, however, falls outside my scope. Moreover, the importance of the book in the history of the development of aesthetic theory has already been discussed in Dr. W. Neuman's dissertation: *Die Bedeutung Home's für die Ästhetik und sein Einfluss auf die deutschen Ästhetiker.*

---

[1] For biographical details see A. F. Tytler, *Memoirs of the Life and Writings of the Honourable Henry Home of Kames.* Edinburgh, 1807, 2 vols.; H. G. Graham, *Scottish Men of Letters in the Eighteenth Century.* London, 1901.

[2] At the end of the second volume, Kames makes the following curious restriction: 'Those who depend for food on bodily labour, are totally void of taste; of such a taste at least as can be of use in the fine arts. This consideration bars the greater part of mankind; and of the remaining part, many by a corrupted taste are unqualified for voting.' (Vol. II, p. 499).

(Halle, 1894). What concerns us mainly here are the practical rules which Kames derives from the principles he has established, and more in particular their application to the two main departments of poetic art, the epic and the drama.

Johnson's opinion of the essay appears to have been far from unfavourable. We have Boswell's account of a dinner-party at his own house, where, in the presence of Reynolds, Garrick, Goldsmith, Murphy and others, the Doctor expressed his approval of the method that Kames had followed and said: 'I do not mean that he has taught us anything; but he has told us old things in a new way' [1]. Those who are acquainted with Kames's *Elements* will hardly wonder at this, for, if we except what Johnson called 'chimerical matter', it cannot be denied that there is more similarity between the views of the great English critic and those of his Scottish contemporary than the superficial reader would believe.

There is in Kames the same disinclination to accept anything on mere authority; all the aesthetic problems discussed in the *Elements* are subjected to a new analysis. Like Johnson he believes in independent rational deduction and despises slavish submission to the dictates of classical and French critics. 'Rude ages exhibit the triumph of authority over reason .... In later times, happily, reason hath obtained the ascendant: men now assert their native privilege of thinking for themselves' [2], he observes in the introductory chapter. Kames regrets that in spite of the general spirit of scientific investigation in his time, criticism still obeys arbitrary rules based merely on custom. He attacks Le Bossu, who could find no better foundation for the rules than 'the practice of Homer and Virgil, supported by the authority of Aristotle', and never tried to find out how far they agree with human nature. 'It could not surely be his opinion', queries Kames, 'that these poets, however eminent for genius, were intitled to give law to mankind: and that nothing now remains but blind obedience to their arbitrary will;

---

[1] Boswell, II, pp. 89, 90. There is another remark in the first volume of the biography, where Johnson is reported to have called the *Elements* 'a pretty essay', deserving 'to be held in some estimation, though much of it is chimerical'. (Boswell, I, pp. 393, 394). The statement of the *D. of N. B.* that 'Dr. Johnson formed a poor opinion of him' is founded on a passage in Boswell, II, p. 53.

[2] Sixth ed., Edinburgh, 1785, I, p. 12.

if in writing they followed no rule, why should they be imitated? if they studied nature and were obsequious to rational principles, why should these be concealed from us?' [1] Human nature is to Kames the only true source of criticism, and from human nature all the principles of art must therefore be drawn. If this method is followed, he expects that criticism will become a regular science which will improve the heart as well as the understanding, and will even prove to be 'a great support to morality'. By working the underlying principles into a system, Kames hopes to find an immutable standard of taste by which all works of art may be tried. In one of the later chapters he speaks about the influence of custom on taste, and attacks the unscientific methods that both the ancients and the moderns followed in the well-known controversy. The ancients thought it sufficient that ancient manners were supported by custom, their antagonists refused to submit to custom as a standard of taste and 'condemned ancient manners as in several instances irrational'. Aş the critics in the two hostile camps based their verdicts on entirely different principles without trying to fix a common standard, the dispute could not lead to any definite conclusion [2].

Let us now consider the practical results in the field of poetics to which Kames's investigations lead him. Chapter XXI, dealing with Narration and Description, has already been referred to. The next chapter contains the author's remarks on the epic and the drama.

On the doctrine of the 'kinds' Kames holds views which are diametrically opposite to those of his contemporaries. He accepts the distinction between tragedy and the epic. They do not differ 'in substance', both have the same ends: instruction and amusement. But they are unlike in the manner of imitating; epic poetry employs narration, tragedy represents its facts as passing in our sight. 'In the former, the poet introduces himself as an historian; in the latter, he presents his actors, and never himself' [3]. The distinction between the epic and other literary types is, however,

---

1   I, pp. 12, 13.
2   I, p. 422.
3   II, p. 370.

rejected by Kames on the ground that it is impossible to mark off the different compartments of literature by definite bounds. The critics that have tried to do so, such as Le Bossu and Voltaire, have arrived at widely different conclusions, he thinks. The passage is so remarkable for the eighteenth century and so flagrantly opposed to the orthodox views that it is worth quoting in full: 'It is not a little diverting to see so many profound critics hunting for what is not: they take for granted, without the least foundation, that there must be some precise criterion to distinguish epic poetry from every other species of writing. Literary compositions run into each other, precisely like colours: in their strong tints they are easily distinguished; but are susceptible of so much variety, and of so many different forms, that we never can say where one species ends and another begins' [1].

The discussion of the three unities breathes a spirit of independence, of disbelief in the dogmatic precepts advocated by the French critics and some of their English followers. Kames exposes the misconception under which they have been labouring by taking the practice of Greek and Roman authors as the determinant for modern writers. The argument that the time of the dramatic fable should not exceed that of the performance would at least have had the appearance of plausibility, but no critic, not even the most rigid adherent to classical canons, has ever insisted that the dramatic fable ought to be confined within such a narrow compass. The only way to account for the observance of the unities by the Greek dramatic writers is therefore to consider the question historically. In Greece the unities of place and time 'were a matter of necessity, not of choice', Kames observes. 'The Greek drama is a continued representation without interruption . . . . (it) affords not opportunity to vary the place of action, nor to prolong the time of the action beyond that of the representation'. It is therefore 'an egregious blunder' to establish rules, merely based on a practice imposed by the conditions of the Greek stage. If the modern dramatist submits to such fetters, he must do it from choice, not from necessity. The modern drama is no longer trammelled by the chorus, and consequently it is possible to divide the representation

---

[1]   II, p. 370, note.

by intervals of time. During these intervals the spectator can easily imagine any length of time to elapse, and any change of place to happen [1].

Kames then attacks the neo-classic fallacy that the dramatic performance should be a kind of deception, as the audience mistake it for reality. 'It is abundantly ridiculous', he says, 'that a critic, who is willing to hold a candle-light for sunshine and some painted canvasses for a palace or a prison, should be so scrupulous about admitting any latitude of place or of time in the fable....' [2]. But though Kames's purpose is to rescue modern poets from the despotism of modern critics, he does not approve of an unbounded license, as far as place and time are concerned, on the ground that it would endanger the unity of action. The unities of time and place should therefore be strictly observed during each separate act. Kames considers the unity of action as the only one of the three that is essential, and time and place have to adapt themselves to its requirements. The French neo-classical critics had followed a different method, and had subordinated the unity of action to the observance of the other rules [3]. Kames thinks it absurd to consider the three as equally important, which he calls contrary to the nature of the modern drama. By insisting on a strict adherence to Greek and Roman models, many interesting subjects, fit for dramatic performance, would be excluded from the modern stage. If the critics really want to bring about a reformation, there is only one means to do so, namely by restoring the Greek chorus, which would prevent discontinuity of action. It would at least have one advantage, the author believes: 'it not only preserves alive the impressions made upon the audience, but also prepares their hearts finely for new impressions'. One of the drawbacks of a modern theatrical representation is, according to him, that the break at the end of each act prevents a sustained emotion on the part of the audience. As the chorus would, however, revive the 'slavery of place and time', Kames suggests another means to

---

[1] II, p. 415.
[2] II, p. 416.
[3] It is evident that Kames's views on this important problem of poetics closely resemble those laid down by Lessing in his *Hamburgische Dramaturgie,* Sechsundvierzigstes Stück.

attain the same result: the introduction of music between the acts, adapted to the subject [1].

Though Kames calls a plurality of unconnected fables a great deformity, not only in the drama but also in the epic, he does not want the dramatist to stick rigidly to one single plot. A too narrow interpretation of the Aristotelian precept had already been condemned in England by Ben Jonson and Dryden. The latter had been of opinion that the 'Unity of Action is sufficiently preserved, if all the imperfect actions of the play are conducing to the main design' [2]. For the sake of variety Kames would allow an underplot, provided that it is closely connected with the main action. A double plot one part of which would resemble an episode in an epic, is looked upon by him as an inexcusable blemish, as it distracts the attention of the spectator instead of entertaining him. He thinks that it might be tolerated in a comedy, as the end of comedy is exclusively to please, but even here it should be used with moderation. On no account should the tone of the secondary plot vary greatly from that of the main plot, 'for discordant emotions are unpleasant, when jumbled together'. Unlike Johnson he considers this as an insuperable objection to comedy [3]. To preserve the unity of action, Kames thinks it requisite that the stage should be always occupied. Each personage introduced during an act should 'be linked to those in possession of the stage, so as to join in one action'. This is evidently what Corneille called *la liaison des scènes* [4] or 'the continuity or joining of the scenes', as Crites translates in Dryden's *Essay of Dramatic Poesy*, and which he calls 'a good mark of a well-contrived play' [5]. In his discussion of 'the marvellous' in an epic poem, Kames again manifests his rational outlook on literature. It follows naturally from his theory of *ideal presence* that anything transgressing the laws of probability ought to be excluded from an epic poem. Human reason revolts against improbable incidents. As soon as the reader begins to doubt

---

1   II, p. 421.
2   Ker, I, p. 71. Cf. Corneille, *Troisième Discours.*
3   II, pp. 397 ff.
4   *Discours des trois Unités, Oeuvres,* 1862, I, 101 ff.
     Examen de La Suivante, ibid., II, 123 ff.
5   Ker, I, p. 40.

of their reality, the *waking dream* will be dispelled, and it is
not likely to be restored. In an epic, which pretends to give a
copy of human actions and manners, such blemishes should therefore be carefully avoided. The objection against the introduction
of imaginary beings is still much more serious than that against
improbable facts. *'But waiving authority, which is apt to impose
upon the judgment,* let us draw what light we can from reason' [1],
the critic observes, before he proceeds to account for his rejection of
this absurd neo-classic conventionality. He denounces 'machinery'
for two reasons: in the first place, it gives an air of fiction to the
whole work and prevents an impression of reality, in the second
place, because virtuous emotions can only be roused by the actions
of persons who are endowed with the same passions and affections
as the reader, so by those of human beings only. In Homer the
use of poetic machinery is not so unnatural, since the Greeks
believed that the gods 'often interpose visibly and bodily in human
affairs'. But Kames thinks that even Homer's fictions seldom do
the poet credit: 'they may inflame the imagination for a moment,
but will not be relished by any person of correct taste' [2].

The passage leaves no doubt that Kames is unable to appreciate
anything that reason does not approve of. In the third chapter
of his essay, where he attempts to establish practical rules for the
fine arts, he lays great stress on regularity, uniformity, order and
simplicity and mentions them among the chief qualities that
constitute beauty: 'Profuse ornament in painting, gardening or
architecture, as well as in dress or in language, shows a mean
or corrupted taste'. He quotes Pope's lines from the *Essay on
Criticism,* directed against an excessive use of 'glittering thoughts' [3].
In the section dealing with versification he advocates a rigid correspondence between sound and sense in the heroic couplet and insists
that the break in the sense ought to coincide with the end of the
distich: 'Licenses must be used with discretion'. In a footnote he
attacks French versification. Boileau, the great champion of correctness, is taken to task for his neglect of this important rule;
he often closes one subject with the first line of a couplet, and

---

[1]   II, p. 386. Italics are mine.
[2]   *Ibid.,* p. 388.
[3]   ll. 289 ff.

begins a new subject with the second. 'Such license', Kames continues, 'however sanctified by practice, is unpleasant by the discordance between the pauses of the sense and of the melody' [1].

On the other hand Kames grants that genuine poetry must possess other qualities than these formal excellencies. Shakespeare's plays are indeed defective in the mechanical part, but this is 'less the work of genius than of experience'. The critic also realizes, just as J. Warton did, that in the higher sense of the word Shakepeare is just as 'correct' as any other writer: 'wherever passion is to be display'd, Nature shows itself mightily in him, and is conspicuous by the most delicate propriety of sentiment and expression' [2]. He is therefore far superior to Racine, who, though generally correct and seldom 'falling low', is a stranger to the genuine language of fervid passion.

Kames thus manifests great independence of judgment. He discards all *a priori* rules and accepts nothing on mere authority. Like Johnson he is an unalloyed supporter of the cause of reason. He measures literary merit exclusively by logical tests, he accepts emotion and even thinks it indispensable, so long as it is conformable to the laws of common sense.

---

1 II, p. 160, note.
2 I, pp. 502, 503.

CHAPTER XII

SOME MINOR CRITICS

William Cooke was a poet, dramatist and critic. His *Elements of Dramatic Criticism,* which saw the light in 1775, purports to be a renewed inquiry into the nature and principles of dramatic art. Cooke's purpose is to rescue the drama from the arbitrary and flimsy restrictions imposed upon it by the petty critics. His essay is an attempt to find more permanent foundations, to rescue the theatre from such 'usurpers' and 'restore it to that respectable character it originally possessed — *a Public School of Virtue, and of Manners'*. Cooke was evidently a careful reader and a great admirer of the *Elements of Criticism* by Lord Kames, to whom he expresses himself obliged for several statements, but whose influence is also evident in passages where there is no acknowledgement.

The author considers classical rules binding for the modern dramatist only if they are consistent with reason and modern dramatic manners. He calls it absurd to insist on a rigid adherence to precepts which had their origin in the peculiar character of the Greek stage. After having given a sketch of the origin and nature of the ancient drama [1], he begins his discussion of tragedy, in which he strictly follows the Aristotelian method: first the *Fable,* then the *Manners,* the *Sentiments* and last of all the *Diction* [2]. The fable may be *simple* or *compound,* as the Greek critic has stipulated. In the compound fable, care should be taken that 'everything proceeds from the very constitution of the subject'. An underplot is permissible, it even has the advantage of contributing to variety [3]. It should, however, be closely connected with the main plot. 'All the incidents in a dramatic fable ought to have a mutual connection by their common relation to the grand event; and in this relation consists the *Unity of Action'* [4]. Two unconnected

---

[1] Chapters I, II, III.
[2] He leaves out *decoration* and *music,* which he calls 'little more than ornamental appendages to the modern tragedy' (p. 33).
[3] Cf. Kames, supra, p. 142.
[4] P. 87.

10

plots are a serious blemish; the audience are compelled to divide their attention between two equally interesting events [1].

Cooke does not agree with the critics who would exclude the love-element from modern tragedies. The objection of the extreme devotees of classical propriety that the passion of love is a human infirmity incompatible with the character of a great man, must in his opinion be disclaimed as invalid.

As to the unities of time and place, Cooke stands up for greater latitude than the French and some English critics would allow. He exposes their narrow views in the same way as Kames had done; the uninterrupted performance of Greek drama afforded no opportunity to prolong the time of the action beyond that of the representation, and a deviation from the established practice would therefore have been preposterous. Not only the substance of these and the following observations was probably suggested by Kames's treatise, even the very words bear a close resemblance to those of the *Elements,* as for instance in the following statement: 'the unities of time and place, so much vaunted of, were in Greece a matter of necessity, not choice, and if *we* submit to such rules, it must be from choice, not necessity' [2]. Like Kames, Cooke disapproves of a too liberal use of freedom: 'an unbounded licence with relation to *place* and *time,* is faulty for a reason that seems to be overlooked; that it seldom fails to break in upon the *unity of action*' [3]. In themselves Cooke thinks the limitations of time and place an advantage, as they contribute to the unity of the drama; he condemns them, however, for their restraining influence on the poet's imagination. He follows Kames again when he suggests the restoring of the Greek chorus or the introduction of music between the acts.

Of the minor rules Cooke defends the Horatian precept of five acts and that of restricting the dialogue to two or three persons [4]. He blames modern dramatists for their neglect of the laws of decorum in exhibiting to the audience that which should take place behind the scenes. His denunciation of tragi-comedy is also founded

---

1   P. 35.
2   Pp. 98, 99.
3   Cf. Kames: 'An unbounded licence with relation to place and time . . . . seldom fails to break the unity of action.' (Vol. II, p. 417).
4   *AP,* l. 192.

on the essential requisite of the unity of action [1]. The basis of this type of drama is moreover 'egregiously unnatural': 'as Aristotle has justly laid down *compassion* to be one of the great springs of tragedy, how incompatible is *mirth,* or, more commonly *low humour,* with so refined and exalted a sensation? and, is it not evident, that the poet must destroy the former, by mixing it with the latter?' [2]. The author then expresses his satisfaction that tragi-comedy left the country about half a century ago and he hopes 'for the credit of posterity, no succeeding age will relapse into a species of the drama, at once so repugnant to all the laws of art as well as nature'.

In the fifteenth chapter of his essay Cooke advises any writer who intends to devote himself to dramatic art to make himself acquainted with the rules before entering upon his task. Though he admits that they are not sufficient without the help of genius, he is firmly convinced that all attempts to dispense with their guidance are bound to fail.

Percival Stockdale's *An Inquiry into the Nature, and Genuine Laws of Poetry* (1778) is one of the critical treatises elicited by Joseph Warton's *Essay on Pope,* and contains a defence of this poet's writings and genius. Although, as he himself avows, this is the principal object of his essay, it aims at being something else at the same time, namely a strong plea for *nature* and *reason* against authority. Its critical value is indeed very small; Stockdale is not a critic with the same keenness of insight and the same strongly individual judgment as either Johnson or Kames. The *Inquiry* is instructive, however, in that it once again shows the great confusion and lack of any definite critical creed that caracter-ize this transitional period. It illustrates how wrong it would be to suppose that only the so-called romantic critics insisted on freedom from dictatorial restraint. In many respects the rationalists are even more averse to dogmatic methods than the so-called precursors of romantic theory. Joseph Warton, whose *Essay on Pope* may be called the first open attack on the neo-classical citadel,

---

[1] Cf. Kames, supra, p. 142.
[2] P. 119.

is classed by Stockdale among 'the mechanical critics', whereas Johnson is held up as the exponent of independence and disbelief in authority. Warton is called an author whose taste is vitiated, 'a man of mere erudition', who 'was intended by nature for a diligent and reputable schoolmaster .... not for a poet'; he is blamed for his inordinate desire to show off his book-learning.

Stockdale is obviously out of sympathy with the prevailing trend of romantic literature. *Fingal* is dubbed 'the very froth of puerile declamation', Gray is declared to show 'a depravity of judgment' in preferring it to Rousseau's *Nouvelle Héloïse,* and he is censured for choosing as subjects and ornaments of his poetry 'the dreary heaths, the howling caves; the warp and woof, and vile webs of the North'; Akenside on the other hand is designated a great poet.

Stockdale is a genuine admirer of the classical poets; he has a special reverence for Horace, for hardly any author has afforded him so much 'moral and poetical' pleasure. But there are principles that weigh even heavier with him than the authority of the Roman poet, and he hopes he can distinguish between him and truth, 'when he deserts the bright and infallible Goddess'. He strongly condemns imitation and severely inveighs against his compatriots, 'the degenerate English coxcombs', for following too closely in the track of the French and adopting their contemptible manners and fopperies. The truly poetical genius takes nothing on trust and thinks for himself. He may now and then borrow from other writers but he will always impart a new spirit and new vigour to what he borrows. This was, according to Stockdale, Pope's way of working, and it would therefore be absurd to accuse him of plagiarism [1].

Stockdale's reverence for Johnson is apparently unreserved. To support one of his statements, Warton had quoted the opinion of the author of the *Rambler,* whom he had commended as 'a rational and free Being' whose 'masterly learning is chastified and brightened by genuine taste'. Stockdale advises him, however, not to call in the assistance of the great critic, who might prove a dangerous ally. He then refers to the well-known dictum from the

---

[1]　Pp. 82, 83.

156th number of the *Rambler* [1] and the other, equally sweeping, contained in number 158, both directed against 'the arbitrary edicts of legislators'. Numerous are the passages which illustrate Stockdale's rejection of the rules as a touchstone for literary excellence. 'The ample and inexhaustible page of nature' is to him, as to many other rationalists of the period, the highest tribunal of art. 'So little is effected by scholastick education and so much by nature, and our own generous cultivation of noble talents, that I think a poet may be illustrious in his divine art; — .... without ever having read Aristotle, or Quintilian, or Warton', he says. He condemns Warton's conciliatory attitude towards classical precepts [2]. The latter's statement that the rules of the *Poetics* are as indispensable for the critic as Euclid to the geometrician is called absurd: the nature of geometry and that of poetry are so heterogeneous that a comparison between the two only shows Warton's defective judgment [3].

The last few pages contain a brief summary. Stockdale once more advocates a complete emancipation from authoritative prescriptions. His intention has been 'to vindicate the laws of nature from the laws of Aristotle'. He regrets that in his enlightened age taste and reason are not yet allowed to choose their own way and decide for themselves: 'The fascination of Greek and Latin is yet unbroken; and every impartial scholar deserves encouragement from the Republick of Letters who endeavours to dissolve the spell'. The critics are still too much shackled by prejudices, they condemn an epic if it is not modelled on Homer or Virgil and has not the generally accepted epic requirements, such as episodes like the descent into hell. Instead of attaching so much importance to such trivial matters, they ought to pay regard to human life and take nature as their only guide. Stockdale does not agree with the common objection of contemporary critics to the love-plot in Addison's *Cato*; it is this very love-plot that saves the play from flatness [4]. He opposes the attempts of other writers to revive the 'old impertinent Chorus',

---

[1] 'It ought to be the first endeavour of a writer to distinguish nature from custom; or that which is established because it is right, from that which is right only because it is established; ....'

[2] 'A petulant rejection and an implicit veneration of the rules of the ancient critics, are equally destructive of true taste'. (*Essay on Pope*, p. 120).

[3] See Warton, infra, pp. 214, 215.

[4] Cf. Blair, infra, pp. 184, 185.

and blames Hurd, 'that modern Aristarchus, without *his* fire', for his defence of the unities in a dramatic composition [1].

The treatise winds up with an invocation to the shade of Pope and a eulogy on the great merits of this poet.

In 1795 Stockdale began his *Lectures on the Truly Eminent English Poets;* thirteen years passed before they were brought to a conclusion. We learn from the preface that the word 'truly' in the title has been put in by way of protest against Johnson's *Lives of the Poets,* where many names occur of poets that have not the least pretension to fame. For Stockdale's feelings towards the Doctor have undergone a remarkable change since the date of his earlier essay. The critic himself attributes it to the prejudices and lack of critical justice that some of the *Lives* manifest. He thinks it surprising that Johnson has been so long considered as an absolute poetical lawgiver in a free and enlightened country. 'His name shall never circumscribe *my* range in the persuit, and publication of truth', Stockdale exclaims in his lecture on Dryden, '. . . . I will not be so profane to the genius of my great master whom I am now contemplating; . . . . as to rank the feeble *Pomfret; Yalden;* good *Isaac Watts;* and *Sir Richard; . . . .* with *our most eminent English Poets*' [2]. The reader is inclined to believe that this revolution in Stockdale's attitude is chiefly due to the fact that his own poetical genius and critical talents, of which he never seems to have entertained the least doubt himself, were not sufficiently appreciated by the literary dictator. He tells us that Johnson had read his *Inquiry* with great pleasure and had promised him to make mention of it in his *Life of Pope,* but that he had not kept his word, owing to his prejudices in favour of Dr. Warton [3].

The lectures are twenty in number: one on Spenser, one on Shakespeare, two on Milton, three on Dryden, one on Pope, two on Young, one on Thomson, six on Chatterton and two on Gray.

In the first, that on Spenser, we clearly trace the influence of Thomas Warton's *Observations on the Faerie Queene,* to which the author acknowledges his indebtedness. Stockdale, like Warton,

---

[1]   Cf. Hurd, infra, pp. 259, 260.
[2]   *Lectures on the Truly Eminent English Poets.* London, 1807, pp. 232, 233.
[3]   *Lecture on Pope.*

admires Spenser in spite of his serious shortcomings: his defective judgment, his inability to make proper selection, and his mixing of pagan mythology with the images of Christian revelation. These faults are attributed to the depraved taste of the Elizabethan Age, which the critic considers in many respects as a barbarous time. As Warton had done before him, Stockdale states the necessity of following the historical method in criticism. 'A poem must as certainly take its complexion from the religion, policy, customs and manners of the time at which it is written, as from the genius of the authour, and from the external objects of nature that surround him', he observes, and in his opinion the reader can only arrive at a just estimate of its merits if he takes all these external circumstances into consideration.

There is one statement in Warton's treatise with which Stockdale does not agree. The author of the *Observations* had strongly disapproved of a method followed by such critics as 'criticize from the imagination rather than from the judgment', and 'exert their admiration instead of their reason'[1]. This passage is called by Stockdale the most exceptional and erroneous of the whole book. Poetry is pre-eminently addressed to the sentiments, he thinks, and all good criticism must therefore appeal '*from* the imagination to the imagination'. 'In the province of which we are treating', he goes on to say, 'the imagination and taste of the critick must mingle their rays with the glory that beams from the page of the poet. Else, why did our great forefather Dryden say (I tremble while I quote my oracle!) that "no man is fit to comment upon a poet *but* a poet?" ' The critic must feel the same enthusiasm that the poet has felt before him; with the workings of the intellect neither of the two has anything to do. This effusion might almost incline us to believe that Stockdale has given up his rationalism and now poses as the herald of a new critical outlook. His allegiance to truth and nature (in the neo-classic sense) are, however, hardly less strong than in the *Inquiry*. He has no sympathy with Ariosto, because his adventures are not within the compass of possibility, and he thinks that fiction can be tolerated only if it does not exceed the limits of truth. For the critic as well

---

[1] Vol. II, p. 263.

as the poet reason is represented as a safeguard against a too exuberant imagination. Reason must play a part in all that relates to fine art, 'for fancy, without the direction of reason is not better than insanity'. Enthusiasm is necessary; it must be, however, a kind of enthusiasm which is not hostile to argument and truth but is their best friend.

Henry James Pye was a poet, playwright, and critic whose name is now deservedly forgotten. His appointment as Poet Laureate after the death of Thomas Warton as a reward for his support of Pitt in the House of Commons, of which he was a member for many years, caused great indignation in the literary circles of the time. His verses bear evidence of a total lack of poetic feeling and power of expression, and were treated with contempt by the great exponents of the Romantic movement.

His only contribution to criticism worthy of a short discussion is his translation of Aristotle's *Poetics,* to which he added a commentary. It is remarkable for the traces it shows of Lessing's influence on English critical thought. The first reference to the *Hamburgische Dramaturgie* that I have been able to find, occurs in an edition of the *Poetics* by T. Winstanley (1780) [1]. Lessing's essay also excited the interest of Thomas Twining but, as he could not read German, he had to resort to a French translation of the work: *Observations critiques sur plusieurs pièces de théâtre, tant anciennes que modernes* (Paris, 1785). He praised Lessing for his 'strength of feeling and strength of thought', the two qualities upon which, in Twining's opinion, good and original criticism depended, and regretted that the book had not fallen into his hands before he embarked upon his own translation, so that he might have paid more attention to it.

Pye inserts large sections from the *Dramaturgie* into his Commentary. He probably read it in the original version, for Pye was one of the very few people in England at that time who had some knowledge of German, and he actually wrote a translation

---

[1] *Aristotelis de Poetica liber ex versione Theodori Goulstoni,* Oxford, 1780. Winstanley is described in *The Gentleman's Magazine* (1823, II, p. 643) as a most distinguished scholar, well versed in many of the modern languages.

of Bürger's *Lenore* in the same year as Scott published his [1].

The first edition of Pye's commentary on and translation of Aristotle's *Poetics* [2] was published in the year 1788; the book was reissued in 1792. The author wrote it because a good English version of the Greek treatise did not exist. An edition belonging to the year 1705 was a translation from the French by Dacier and in addition there was another, published anonymously in the year 1775, which Pye thinks 'as much beneath criticism as it is above comprehension'. A year after he had brought his own before the public, Twining's book saw the light. In the preface to the second edition of 1792 Pye calls it 'a work of distinguished excellence' which would have kept him from writing his own, if it had appeared earlier.

Pye's purpose is to make Aristotle's precepts accessible to the general reader, that he may judge for himself how far these rules, which have so often been quoted and misinterpreted, are 'consonant with truth and nature'. As far as they are founded on these two principles, they are applicable to the modern as well as to the classic drama, but if they are exclusively based on the practice of the Greek dramatic writers, on Greek customs, laws and superstitions, they have authoritative force only in so far as the modern drama resembles the Greek. The lack of a good English translation had made it necessary for those who could not read Aristotle's treatise in the original to resort to Dacier's commentary, which was the reason why the critic's precepts were always read through French spectacles. This had led to the general belief that the rules laid down by the French interpreter were part and parcel of the Aristotelian doctrine. Among the arbitrary precepts of the French critics which are not supported by the authority of the Greek, Pye mentions the dramatic unities and the 'bloodless action'.

The author quotes the remarkable passage from Morgann's *Essay*

---

1   These references to Lessing's *H. D.* are ignored by E. Margraf, *Einfluss der deutschen Litteratur auf die englische am Ende des achtzehnten und im ersten Drittel des neunzehnten Jahrhunderts.* Diss. Leipzig, 1901; and more recently by T. W. Stokoe, *German Influence in the English Romantic Period.* Cambridge, 1926.

2   *A Commentary illustrating the Poetic of Aristotle, by Examples taken chiefly from the Modern Poets, to which is prefixed a new and corrected Edition of the Translation of the Poetic, by H. J. Pye, Esq.* London 1792.

on the Dramatic Character of Sir John Falstaff [1] directed against
the dictatorial ways of critics like Rymer and adds: 'The age of
blind veneration is now over, and Aristotle, like other writers, can
only be estimated by his merit'. Then he states emphatically that
the rules have only relative force for modern compositions. Aristotle
could never have foreseen the changes that were to take place
in succeeding centuries, the difference in manners, customs and
opinions, and the growth of science. The modern critic should
therefore not expect a work of art to conform to canons based
on altogether different dramatic conditions. Only a new analysis
on rational grounds, taking truth and nature as guiding principles,
will lead to satisfactory results. This method is applied by Pye
to the unities. He follows Johnson and others in rejecting the
notion of the French critics that dramatic imitation can ever be
mistaken for reality. Their interpretation of the unity of time,
their dictum that the time of the action should not exceed that of
representation, is neither warranted by Aristotle's authority nor
by the practice of the Greek tragedians. This strikes Pye as 'a
strange perversion of common sense'. He agrees with Johnson and
Blair that it is easy for the audience to imagine that a much longer
time passes during the intervals between the acts, but thinks it
inconsistent with probability, if 'without an interruption during a
dialogue of six minutes, six hours are supposed to have elapsed'.
After quoting this statement from Lessing, he adduces the opinion
of Brumoy, who, though 'a staunch advocate for the doctrine of the
French school', shows more leniency here. The difference between
the time of the action and that of the performance must not be
too great, because a too great divergence would be against truth
and nature. Pye thinks that Shakespeare's genius makes us forget
his glaring irregularities but that it is dangerous for a modern
poet to follow his example.

In Chapter XII Pye traces the fluctuations of Shakespeare's
reputation from the dramatist's own time to the end of the
eighteenth century. He once more stigmatizes the slavish acceptance of French critical opinions, which had led to a complete
misapprehension of his art and to animadversions like those of

---

[1] See Morgann, *infra*, pp. 287, 288.

Rymer and the 'superficial and pedantic *Shaftesbury*'. Pye calls it a happy symptom that at last English criticism had outgrown French influence and ventured to walk alone.

The rule that a tragedy should consist of five acts is looked upon by Pye, as by so many other critics of the latter half of the eighteenth century, as an absurd requirement founded on obedience to the *ex post facto* law of Horace. He would consider a division into three acts, in accordance with the division of the epic fable (a beginning, a middle and the end), as a much more reasonable arrangement. As an example of a defective middle he mentions the 'premature catastrophe' in *The Merchant of Venice*; the punishment of Shylock in the fourth act takes away the interest of the reader in the rest of the play.

Pye shares the opinion of Brumoy that the modern dramatic writer must introduce a chorus wherever it can be admitted with propriety, as for instance between the acts [1]. Mason's *Elfrida* and *Caractacus* are regarded as being above all criticism and commendation.

Tragi-comedy finds no favour in Pye's eyes. The mixing of serious and comic elements in one play must be considered as a heinous offence against the laws of decorum. Shakepeare's transgression of these laws is extenuated in the usual neo-classic manner: it was imposed upon him by the taste of the public [2].

A staunch upholder of the neo-classic creed is James Harris. He is now best known as the author of *Hermes*, of which the subject is almost exclusively grammatical. The short but interesting *Dialogue concerning Art* is a philosophical disquisition on art in general, dedicated to the Earl of Shaftesbury, and showing the influence of that writer's aesthetic theories. Of the other essays the *Philological Inquiries* (1781), written when the author was already advanced in years, is the only one that deals with the subject of literary criticism.

---

[1] Brumoy in *Le Théâtre des Grecs*. Paris, 1730 speaks of the great advantage the Greek drama had over the modern drama by the use of the chorus. He calls its loss 'une perte considérable' and does not think it right, as some critics do, to condemn the chorus 'uniquement par la raison que nous ne sommes pas avisés de nous en servir . . . .' (pp. LXXVIII ff.).

[2] Cf. Rowe's opinion. See Nichol Smith, *Eighteenth Century Essays on Shakespeare*, 1903, p. XIII.

In the first part of this work, Harris discusses the rise of criticism and gives an account of its different species. These are three in number. The first is the *philosophical* kind, dealing with the causes and principles of good writing in general. In its original form it was 'a deep and philosophical Search into the primary Laws and Elements of good Writing, as far as they could be collected from the most approved Performances'[1]. The other two are *historical* criticism, by which Harris means the commentaries on and explanations of particular authors, and *corrective* criticism, concerned with *collation* and its dangerous ally *conjecture*. Harris is convinced that nothing in literary art depends on chance and that for all the effects it produces there is some rational cause. As all writers draw from two immutable sources, namely nature and truth, their works must be governed by identical basic principles: 'If Truth *be always the same,* no wonder *Geniuses should co-incide*'[2].

The catchwords 'nature' and 'truth' are of course used in the strictly neo-classical sense. Harris speaks contemptuously of those writers who manifest a too great fondness for the marvellous and the incredible, and forget that common life is the proper subject of literary art. The first poets of England were, according to him, 'prone to a turgid Bombast'. Gradually the style improved, but 'a classical purity' was not reached before Tillotson, Dryden, Addison, Shaftesbury, Prior, Pope and Atterbury[3]. Perspicuity, simplicity and correctness are Harris's idols. The French critics Rapin, Bouhours, Boileau and Le Bossu, 'the most methodic and accurate of them all', are the great exponents of philosophical criticism; in England they are Roscommon, Buckingham and Pope[4].

After having touched on the essential requisite that a work of art should be *a whole,* having a beginning, middle and end, Harris proceeds to give a lengthy discussion of 'the constitutive Parts of every Drama'. They are the Aristotelian elements: the fable, the manners, the sentiments, the diction, the scenery and the music. In accordance with the neo-classic conceptions 'the fable' is allotted the most important place.

---

[1] *The Works of James Harris,* ed. by his son. London, 1803, IV, p. 9.
[2] *Ibid.,* p. 234.
[3] *Ibid.,* p. 51.
[4] *Ibid.,* p. 20.

The second part of the *Philological Inquiries* winds up with a defence of the rules [1]. Harris does not agree with those who think that they cramp genius. If they are good, they never take away privileges but can only prevent writers from falling into errors. Even on those who possess genius, rules will have a beneficial influence, for neglect of them means want of accuracy. That Harris is not averse to dogmatic methods is clear from his statement that the study of rules, if it cannot make good authors, will at least make tolerable critics. For rules are to Harris 'a Part of that Immutable Truth, the natural object of every penetrating Genius'. For the rest we find the ordinary neo-classic platitudes. The Greek authors are pronounced to have been rules unto themselves, for they excelled not by art, but *nature*. We are once again reminded of the old beauty-blemish cant when reading Harris's assertion that Shakespeare's innumerable beauties are all conformable to the rules of sound and ancient criticism.

The third and fourth parts trace the development of literary art during the Middle Ages. They may be safely passed over as they betray absolute ignorance of the facts and a total lack of historical perspective.

It has repeatedly been observed by critics of eighteenth century poetry that the reputation which William Mason, a very multifarious writer, enjoyed during his lifetime, was far higher than his moderate talents justified. Among his admirers were Gray, Hurd and his friends Balguy and Warburton, Walpole, Hayley and others. All of them were equally liberal in their praise. Hurd, who was one of his earliest friends and thought him the best poet of his time [2], acted as a kind of literary adviser. In Mason's sonnet to the Bishop of Worcester, Hurd is called 'the critic of my youthful lay', and in one of his elegies the poet says that this critic saw 'the fresh seeds their vital powers diffuse' and fed them 'with the fost'ring dew of praise' [3]. Hayley addressed his *Essay upon Epic Poetry* to him, Reynolds annotated his *Art of Painting;* his *English*

---

1   *The Works of James Harris,* IV, pp. 220 ff.
2   Kilvert, *Memoirs of the Life and Writings of the Right Rev. Richard Hurd.* London, 1860, p. 247.
3   Mason, *Works.* London, 1811, vol. I, p. 104.

Garden was considered by Warton as the highest perfection of didactic poetry.

In the first chapter of his study on William Mason [1], Professor Draper speaks of the gradual decline of his fame during the nineteenth century, and observes that after Macaulay's complimentary notice in his review of Moore's Byron, all the opinions of the critics are unfavourable. His name is now almost exclusively mentioned in connection with the poet Gray. The *Memoirs of the Life and Writings*, which he prefixed to an edition of Gray's poetry, was the prototype of several other works of the same kind [2].

Both his poetry and his criticism mark him as a neo-classicist. Only here and there, but very rarely, do we find symptoms of a wider outlook.

In *Musaeus*, a pastoral monody on the death of Pope, Mason gives utterance to his great reverence for the English Augustan. Excessive praise having been bestowed on him by Tityrus (Chaucer), Colin Clout (Spenser), and Thyrsis (Milton), Musaeus (Pope) himself speaks. Disclaiming the merit of his juvenile verse, he sums up the main qualities which constitute poetic genius:

> To sway the judgment, while he soothes the ear;
> To curb mad passion in its wild career;
> To wake by sober touch the useful lyre,
> And rule, with reason's rigour, fancy's fire:
> Be this the poet's praise. And this possest,
> Take, Dulness and thy dunces! take the rest.

The reader cannot help feeling that in this short characterization of Pope's poetry Mason gives expression to his own conception of the poet's task.

Mason's only critical work consists in the letters to an anonymous correspondent, prefixed to his *Elfrida* in the year 1752 [3]. They contain a justification of the method he adopted in this dramatic poem, a method which he was to follow again in *Caractacus*,

---

[1]   J. W. Draper, *William Mason, A Study in Eighteenth Century Culture*. New York, 1924.

[2]   *The Poems of Mr. Gray. To which are prefixed Memoirs of the Life and Writings by W. Mason*. York, 1775.

[3]   According to Nicholls, Gray disliked these letters. He thought *Elfrida* far inferior to *Caractacus*. (Tovey, *Letters*, II, p. 282).

published six years later. Both tragedies are attempts to reproduce
the form and spirit of the Greek drama as far as this was possible
for the modern dramatist. In spite of their lack of dramatic interest
they seem to have found a favourable reception among the critics.
Elfrida was put upon the stage by Colman in 1772, though according
to the author himself, it was not meant for performance.

In the first letter Mason expresses his intention of following the
ancient method in so far as it can be adapted to modern conceptions. Everything that nature and Aristotle — which he evidently
uses as equivalent terms — could dispense with, has been left out
as a concession to the taste of the time. No modern refinement
has been introduced, however, which is inconsistent with 'antient
judgment'. The unities are strictly observed because they are prescribed by 'good sense as well as antiquity' [1]. On the other hand
he has followed the moderns in making love the predominant
passion, which it may claim to be, owing to the universality of
its influence.

The next letter contains a refutation of the main objections that,
according to Mason, are generally raised against the Greek drama:
that the adherence to the unities restrains the genius of the poet,
that the simplicity of the fable diminishes the pathos, and the chorus
prevents a proper interest in the passions. He believes that the
example of Shakespeare is the chief cause of this false criticism,
because his irregularity was looked upon as the distinguishing mark
of his genius. Mason endorses Voltaire's opinion that Shakespeare
is the main cause of the corruption of the English drama. He fears
that the erroneous notions which the popularity of the great
Elizabethan has engendered, will never be relinquished until a
poet arises 'with a genius as elevated and daring as Shakespeare's
and a judgment as sober and chastis'd as Racine's'.

He thinks that his own way of proceeding is intermediate between
the unlicensed deference which the Elizabethans manifested for the

---

[1]   In the third letter Mason observes that the use of the Chorus requires a strict
adherence to the unities of place and time, which ought to be restored to
the rights 'which they anciently enjoyed and yet claim, by the *Magna Charta*
of Aristotle'. From this one would be inclined to infer that Mason had not
read the *Poetics* itself, but like so many critics of the eighteenth century,
derived his knowledge of Aristotle's aesthetic creed from some commentator.

corrupted taste of their age, and the method adopted by Milton, whose contempt for public opinion made him choose a model still more severe and simple than even an Athenian audience would have required. Mason's attitude towards the great period of dramatic activity in England is still that of the extreme neo-classicist. He blames the dramatists for the servility with which they have humoured 'that illiterate, whimsical, or corrupted age, in which it was misfortune to be born'. Regularity in the construction of the fable is in Mason's opinion the only means to reconcile tragedy with 'the approbation of judgment', which is an indispensable requisite for success.

Lastly Mason states his reasons for introducing the chorus. The rejection of this classical element, and the consequent neglect of the unities of time and place, have caused the loss of simplicity and nature. Moreover the chorus gave the author the opportunity to introduce what Mason calls 'pure poetry' into the drama. Though Shakespeare had the natural gift of combining it with 'pure passion', his tragedies would have excelled even much more if they had been built on classical models. Mason then gives an enumeration of all the advantages that the introduction of the chorus brings with it. As a true child of a strongly moralistic age he attaches by far the greatest importance to its ethical function. The chief actors of a tragedy are too much agitated by passion to pay any attention to moral reflection, for which the chorus is therefore the proper vehicle. It heightens the pathos, inspires awe for the deity, and in general advances the cause of honesty and truth.

The majority of the critics that have hitherto been discussed had so much in common that they felt how absurd it was to accept a fixed code of rules. They realized that any tendency to stereotype the principles of art was inconsistent with the laws of reason. Common sense was the quality they valued above all others. They failed to understand, however, that the true merit of art cannot be determined by a judgment too rigidly intellectual.

PART III

The Champions of Taste

CHAPTER XIII

INTRODUCTION

From the very beginning of the Age of Johnson there were traces of a reaction against the absolute power of common sense. The leaders of the revolt, the two Wartons, Bishop Hurd, and a few minor figures, whose works contain open attacks on the Augustan ideals of reason and correctness, will be discussed in the next part of this treatise. Besides these, however, there were some others, who did not deny that reason was the supreme guide of poet and critic, but who recognized that works of art do not exclusively and not even primarily address themselves to the intellect. Instead of founding their decisions on purely logical considerations they cast about for a new and juster standard, and vaguely labelled it *taste*. I had occasion to refer to *the school of taste* when discussing the critical currents of the latter part of the seventeenth and the beginning of the eighteenth century. Originally meant to denote something falling outside the scope of reason, something individual which could not be reduced to any special laws, the word 'taste' changed its meaning when the rationalistic movement grew in strength. The critics of the latter half of the eighteenth century who accepted this principle all agreed that like genius it was a natural quality which might be developed by art. In investigating the nature of beauty and the various ways in which man's feelings respond to impressions received through the senses, they followed the methods of empiric philosophy. They tried to find a rationalistic basis, founded on a new psychological analysis, to disprove the popular notion that taste was something essentially individual, based on personal sensibility, which could not be defined, analysed and subjected to rules. The title of Hogarth's *Analysis of Beauty, written with a view of fixing the Fluctuating Ideas of Taste* (1753)

11

clearly indicates what purpose the author had in view [1]. These investigators did not deny that there was something indefinable, something capricious and irregularly varying about taste, but this did not prevent them from looking for principles in art that might be accepted as fundamental, and it was on these that a universal standard of taste was to be founded. According to Hume the general principles of taste are uniform in human nature, they are 'nearly, if not entirely the same in all men'. The general opinion of such people as have 'strong sense, united to delicate sentiment, improved by practice, perfected by comparison, and cleared of all prejudice, is the true standard of taste and beauty' [2] and the rules of art are based on experience and the observation of the common sentiments of human nature. By thus accepting the joint verdict of all just critics as the principal criterion Hume tried to reconcile his views with the neo-classic conception of a universal standard and universal appeal and the same was done by other rationalistic writers on the subject [3].

In France the sole authority of reason had been attacked by the Abbé du Bos. He did not consider 'la raison' as the final test of art, but 'le sentiment'. What the earlier French critics had called the *je ne sais quoi*, was looked upon by him as an altogether independent faculty, a definite physical sense, 'un sixième sens'.

---

[1] See E. N. Hooker, *The Discussion of Taste, from 1750 to 1770, and the New Trends in Literary Criticism* (PMLA, XLIX, 1934).

[2] *Op. cit.*, I, p. 278.

[3] Cf. Hogarth, *op. cit.*, Introduction: 'I now offer to the Publick a short Essay, accompanied with two explanatory Prints, in which I shall endeavour to shew what the principles are in Nature, by which we are directed to call the forms of some bodies beautiful, others ugly;....'
Burke, *op. cit.*, Introduction: 'On a superficial view, we may seem to differ very widely from each other in our reasonings, and no less in our pleasures; but notwithstanding this difference, which I think to be rather apparent than real, it is probable that the standard both of reason and taste is the same in all human creatures.'
Kames, *op. cit.*, Dedication: '.... the following work, which treats of the Fine Arts, and attempts to form a standard of taste, by unfolding those principles that ought to govern the taste of every individual.'
Blair, *op. cit.*, p. 22: 'I by no means pretend that there is any standard of taste, to which, in every particular instance, we can resort for clear and immediate determination'. At the same time Blair is convinced that taste is far from being an arbitrary principle.

Rational analysis could, in his opinion, do nothing but confirm the verdicts of this higher authority. Any conclusion, not in accordance with what the critic feels, must therefore be renounced.

Whether Du Bos is responsible for the views expressed by English critics like Goldsmith and Reynolds, is difficult to say, though one feels inclined to believe that there are traces of his influence. Goldsmith attaches great value to the operations of reason, and thinks it necessary that it should restrain emotion and the imagination within their proper bounds. But mere reason according to him is not sufficient for the critic: it should be guided by 'taste', which Goldsmith considers as a separate quality. The principal ingredient of it is a natural sensibility which enables one to feel the impressions of beauty [1]. This is of course a significant change in attitude: by making 'taste' the final criterion, Goldsmith reserves a much more important function for emotion than the rationalistic critics allowed it.

Reynolds inveighs against the popular opinion that taste is independent of reason, precept, and experience. 'One can scarce state these opinions', he says, 'without exposing their absurdity; yet they are constantly in the mouths of men, and particularly of artists'. Like Hume, Reynolds is of opinion that the artist's taste can be regulated and formed 'by those works which have approved themselves to all times, and all persons'. Reason and philosophy must help the man of taste 'to weigh and estimate the value of every pretension that intrudes itself on his notice'. All that falls outside the pale of reason must be considered rather as 'the dreams of a distempered brain, than the exalted enthusiasm of a sound and true genius'. A man of taste is therefore always a man of judgment [2]. But on the other hand reason and taste are not identical. In the thirteenth of the *Discourses* we find the important statement that all arts address themselves only to two faculties of the mind: the imagination and sensibility. Reynolds grants that ultimately reason decides everything, but the first appeal of art is to 'a sagacity which is far from being contradictory to right reason' [3].

---

[1] Gibbs, I, p. 327. See infra, chapter XIV, pp. 174, 175.

[2] *Op. cit.,* pp. 117, 118.

[3] *Ibid.,* p. 195. See infra, chapter XV, pp. 182, 183.

The views of some literary critics can be traced back to the philosophy of Shaftesbury. The author of the *Characteristics* draws a close analogy between morality and art. What *Taste, Good Taste* or *Relish* is for the connoisseur, the *moral sense* or *conscience* is in the domain of ethics. Both are natural principles, which can be cultivated by experience. In their natural conditions they are emotional, but their improvement is chiefly due to reason and reflection [1]. Shaftesbury's influence on ethical and aesthetic theory in the eighteenth century was considerable, especially after 1730. His principle of 'benevolence', directed against Hobbes's egoistic doctrine, affected poets like Thomson and Akenside and theorists like Francis Hutcheson and John Gilbert Cooper [2]. As has been mentioned above, Hutcheson distinguishes internal or reflex senses besides the five external senses. One of the first group is *the sense of beauty* or *taste*, another is the *moral sense of beauty in actions and affections.* The former, with which we are concerned here, is defined as 'a passive power of receiving ideas of beauty from all objects in which there is Uniformity amidst Variety'.

The term 'internal sense' is accepted by John Gilbert Cooper in his *Letters concerning Taste* (1757), addressed to three fictitious correspondents. Cooper keeps taste distinctly apart from reason: a man of strong understanding may be devoid of a delicate sense of beauty. As he expresses it, '*Taste* does not *wholly* depend upon the natural Strength and acquired Improvement of the *Intellectual* Powers; nor *wholly* upon a fine Construction of the *Organs* of the Body; nor *wholly* upon the intermediate Powers of the *Imagination*; but upon a Union of them all happily blended, without too great a Prevalency in either' [3]. It is a kind of intuitive power, which fills the heart with rapture before reason can give its approbation and prove the beauty of a work of art by comparing the imitation with the original. It is therefore 'the herald of the whole human system'. Beauty and truth are in Cooper's opinion coincident, they are celestial twins. *Truth* and *nature* are the criteria of perfection. This

---

1   See Fowler, *Shaftesbury and Hutcheson*. London, 1882.
2   Cf. C. A. Moore, *Shaftesbury and the Ethical Poets in England 1700—1760.*
    (PMLA, XXXI, 1936). Shaftesbury's school was ridiculed by Armstrong in
    his poem *Taste*.
3   P. 27.

explains why the critic is so very severe in his condemnation of
Italian poetry; he thinks that the frequent reading of Tasso's epic
will vitiate a person's taste. Akenside's poem on the *Pleasures of
Imagination,* however, manifests the 'glorious enthusiasm', the
'fine frenzy' that characterize poetical genius.

Hutcheson's influence was greatest in Scotland. In 1759
Alexander Gerard gained a prize offered by the Philosophical
Society of Edinburgh for his *Essay on Taste* (1759) [1]. A fine taste
is in his opinion 'neither wholly the gift of *nature,* nor wholly the
effect of *art.* It derives its origin from certain powers natural to
the mind; but these powers cannot attain their full perfection unless
they are assisted by proper culture'. The author reduces it to
various principles: the sense of novelty, of sublimity, of beauty,
of imitation, of harmony, of ridicule and of virtue, and then gives
a lengthy explanation of each in particular. A detailed discussion
of this part falls outside the scope of this thesis [2]. The second part
of his essay is devoted to the formation of taste by the union and
improvement of its simple principles. Here the critic discusses the
functions that the different elements have in artistic creation. He
does not deny that the first duty of the poet as well as the painter
is to affect us, but he does not agree with the 'very ingenious'

---

[1]   The edition which I consulted is the second (Edinburgh, 1764), to which
      were annexed three dissertations on the same subject by Voltaire, d'Alembert
      and Montesqieu.
[2]   PART I comprises the following *sections:*
      I. Of the Sense or Taste of Novelty.
      II. Of the Sense or Taste of Grandeur and Sublimity.
      III. Of the Sense or Taste of Beauty.
      IV. Of the Sense or Taste of Imitation.
      V. Of the Sense or Taste of Harmony.
      VI. Of the Sense or Taste of Ridicule.
      VII. Of the Sense or Taste of Virtue.
      PART II consists of five *sections:*
      I. Of the Union of the Internal Senses and the Assistance they receive from
      Delicacy of Passion.
      II. Of the Influence of Judgment upon Taste.
      III. Taste improveable; by what Means; and in what Respects.
      IV. Of Sensibility of Taste.
      V. Of Refinement of Taste.
      PART III. The Province and Importance of Taste.
      I. How far Taste depends on the Imagination.
      II. Of the Connexion of Taste with Genius.

Abbé du Bos, who had called it the *only* business of these arts. He allows the imagination a large share in descriptive poetry, but even here subjects of an emotional nature should be introduced. In the dramatic kind, however, the pathetic element is by far the most important and determines the merit of the work of art. In general he considers the capacity to move so essential that a man destitute of sensibility can hardly be called a competent judge.

In the next section: *Of the Influence of Judgment on Taste* [1], Gerard's veneration of reason becomes manifest. He thinks even the most complete union of the internal senses insufficient. They are of no use to the critic if not supported and governed by judgment, which ought to accompany them in all their operations. He therefore calls good sense 'an indispensable ingredient in true taste', though the relation between the powers of the imagination and the rational faculty need not be the same in all critics: 'one *feels* what pleases or displeases; the other *knows* what ought to gratify or disgust'. This diversity of taste is illustrated by two examples from antiquity: Longinus, in whom the acuteness of the senses was the predominant quality, and Aristotle, who was known for the accuracy of his judgment. The former excelled in *sensibility*, the latter in *refinement*. The same difference existed, according to Gerard, between Bouhours and Le Bossu [2].

Both Blair and Beattie avow their indebtedness to Gerard's treatise. Their views will receive treatment under the respective headings.

The opinions of one more critical writer may follow here. Edmund Burke discusses 'taste' in the introduction to his *Enquiry into the Origin of our Ideas on the Sublime and Beautiful*. He opposes the view that 'taste' is a separate faculty of the mind, distinct from judgment and imagination, a species of instinct, by which a person is struck at the first glance, without any previous reasoning [3]. He does not consider it as a simple idea: the two main constituent elements are sensibility and judgment. From a defect in the first elements arises 'a *want of taste*', an imperfection in the

---

1   P. 84.
2   P. 91.
3   *Op. cit.*, p. 19.

latter faculty causes 'a *wrong* or *bad* taste'. A certain degree of sensibility is therefore necessary to form a good judgment, but a good judgment does not always co-exist with great sensibility.

It was to be expected that in their definitions of taste, their descriptions of its operations and the practical rules deduced from its general principles the aestheticians of the Age of Johnson would show some diversity. As they all considered the senses as the ultimate source of knowledge, their conclusions could only be founded on their own experiences and reflections, and in their attempts to arrive at a standard of taste, they could only start from their own individual response. The attention was shifted from the qualities residing in the object to the effects the object had on the mind of the subject. Though the investigations were made under the guardianship of 'reason and philosophy', there was something irrational in founding conclusions on what were ultimately no more than personal reactions. Thus the way was gradually prepared for the subjective conception of art in the nineteenth century. Hume, for example, observes that 'Beauty is no quality in things themselves: It exists merely in the mind which contemplates them; and each mind perceives a different beauty' [1]. Burke, too, rigidly restricts his enquiry to sensation [2] and examines his own physical and mental responses stimulated by the contemplation of the outer world. By thus stressing individual sensibility he turned his back upon the neo-classic standard of objective beauty.

In the course of the eighteenth century the two most important aesthetic concepts — beauty and sublimity — began to be differentiated [3]. The first critic to distinguish the two was Addison, though he uses the term 'great' instead of sublime [4]. Akenside's

---

1 *Op. cit.*, I, p. 268.
2 *Op. cit.*, Part IV, Sect. I: 'When we go beyond the immediate qualities of things, we go out of our depth.'
3 See the elaborate discussion of this question in Professor S. H. Monk's *The Sublime, A Study of Critical Theories in XVIII-Century England*. New York, 1935, to which this survey is indebted.
4 *Spectator*, 412. 'I shall consider those pleasures of the imagination which arise from the actual view and survey of outward objects; and these, I think, all proceed from the sight of what is great, uncommon, *or* beautiful' (my italics).

poem *The Pleasures of Imagination* made this distinction popular [1]. Both writers considered the wild and the vast as the two most important constituent elements of the sublime [2]. Burke looks upon 'terror' as its principal source, 'as it is productive of the strongest emotion which the mind is capable of feeling' [3] 'Whatever therefore is terrible, with regard to sight, is sublime, too . . . .' [4]. Burke follows his predecessors in keeping sublimity apart from the other category — beauty — and sees a remarkable contrast between the two: 'sublime objects are vast in their dimensions, beautiful ones comparatively small'. Speaking of the nature of each of these categories, he observes that 'the great ought to be dark and gloomy; beauty should be light and delicate; . . . . .' [5]. These views are obviously the reflection of a changing taste, as it is exemplified in the work of the early romanticists. They are a justification of the prevailing tendencies in the literature of the period, of the spirit of melancholy, gloom and despair that pervades the poetry of the graveyard and the charnel-house, of ruins and haunted castles, of the conventional machinery of the Gothic novels and all the other crude expedients that the writers of the second half of the century employed to create terror. Burke's ideas of sublimity fell in with the growing love of sensation, the strong predilection for the wilder aspects of nature, which found their best illustration in the enthusiastic welcome given to the Ossianic poems.

The glamour of Ossian strongly attracted and influenced the Edinburgh professor of rhetoric and belles lettres, Hugh Blair, for a time the Scottish 'arbiter of taste' [6]. He was of opinion that the works of Ossian 'abound with examples of the sublime', and that 'the subjects of which that author treats, and the manner in which he writes, are particularly favourable to it', for 'amidst the rude scenes of nature and of society, such as Ossian describes; amidst

---

[1] Book I, ll. 139 ff.
[2] *Spectator*, 412. Examples of greatness are: 'the prospects of an open champaign country, a vast uncultivated desert, of huge heaps of mountains, high rocks and precipices, or a wide expanse of waters'.
[3] *Op. cit.*, Part I, Section 7.
[4] *Ibid.*, Part II, Section 2.
[5] *Ibid.*, Part III, Section 27.
[6] H. G. Graham, *Scottish Men of Letters in the Eighteenth Century*. London, 1901, p. 126.

rocks, and torrents, and whirlwinds, and battles, dwells the sublime, and naturally associates itself with that grave and solemn spirit which distinguishes the author of Fingal' [1]. The emotional effects of the wild scenery and the supernatural elements in Ossian left a strong impress on eighteenth century aesthetic theory and helped to free it from the neo-classic conceptions of art.

The association of terror with sublimity was supported by the landscapes of the seventeenth century Neapolitan painter Salvator Rosa, who had found little appreciation among the Augustans, but who strongly appealed to the early romanticists. His pictures showed the wilder aspects of nature, similar to those that were familiar to the readers of Ossian [2]. Reynolds thought them lacking in 'that elevation and dignity which belongs to the grand style', though he admitted that the savage and uncultivated scenery they represented had a certain dignity of its own. When the distinction between beauty and sublimity became generally recognized, Claude Lorrain's name came to be associated with the first quality, Salvator Rosa's with the second.

The believers in 'taste' occupy an intermediate position between the extreme devotees of reason and the precursors of a new critical outlook. Their essays show certain tentative efforts to free themselves from the pseudo-classical conventionalities, but it will appear from the following chapters that the rationalistic spirit of the age looms behind most of their critical verdicts.

---

[1] *Lectures on Rhetoric and Belles Lettres,* p. 42.
[2] J. Warton sees a similarity between the scenes of Thomson's *Seasons* and those of Salvator Rosa. (*Essay on Pope,* p. 43).

CHAPTER XIV

OLIVER GOLDSMITH

Goldsmith's poetry as well as his criticism marks him in the main as a staunch supporter of the Augustan tradition. His strong didactic tendency, his rigid adherence to the regularity of the heroic couplet in his longer poems, his fondness for abstractions and the artificial diction of the Popean style connect the bulk of his poetical works with those of the preceding age. As his critics have pointed out, however, there is in Goldsmith a warmth of temperament, a marked individuality which often makes him transgress the narrow confines of neo-classicism.

The same may be said of his critical essays. His sympathies, like those of Johnson, are clearly with the writers of the Age of Pope, but at the same time many of his statements bear evidence of a delicacy of taste which is entirely Goldsmith's own. Hazlitt refers to his 'fine tact, the airy, intuitive faculty with which he skimmed the surfaces of things, and unconsciously formed his opinions' [1]. It was this quality that prevented him from basing his verdicts exclusively on rational grounds.

In one of the papers contributed to the short-lived *Bee*, there is the following passage, which leaves no doubt about Goldsmith's general critical outlook: 'Some have looked upon the writers in the times of Queen Elizabeth as the true standard for future imitation; others have descended to the reign of James I; and others still lower, to that of Charles II. Were I to be permitted to offer an opinion upon this subject, I should readily give my vote for the reign of Queen Anne, or some years before that period. It was then that taste was united to genius . . . . they (viz. the writers of that time) have cast such a lustre upon the age in which they lived that their minutest transactions will be attended to by posterity with a greater eagerness than the most important occurrences of even empires, which have been transacted in greater obscurity [2]. In

---

[1] *Essay on Genius and Common Sense. (Table Talk,* ed. World's Classics, 1925, p. 39).

[2] *An Account of the Augustan Age of England.* (Gibbs, II, p. 444.)

the *Poetical Scale,* attributed by Gibbs to Goldsmith, and drawn up
for the *Literary Magazine* (January, 1758), the merits of the
various English poets from Chaucer onward are compared with
those of the author's own time as to genius, judgment, learning and
versification. Pope and Dryden occupy prominent positions. Both
have attained eighteen degrees of genius (the scale consists of
twenty for each column), the former exceeds the latter in judgment
and versification. Dryden ranks just as high as Milton, Shakespeare
occupies the highest place in the Temple of Fame for genius, his
judgment, however, is below Ben Jonson's and that of the Augustans.
Only Spenser, Chaucer and some minor poets are inferior to him
in this respect. This will hardly astonish us, when we learn what
the critic means by judgment. It is 'that probability in conducting
or disposing a composition that reconciles it to credibility and the
appearance of truth' [1]. Waller on the other hand, the favourite
of Pope and his contemporaries, has, in Goldsmith's opinion, been
too much praised.

In the *Life of Parnell* (published 1770), used by Johnson in an
abridged form as one of his *Lives* with a very complimentary notice
of its author, he lauds the correctness of this poet's language and
the high degree of refinement that the English tongue had attained
in the works of Dryden, Addison and Pope. There is a strong
Johnsonian note in Goldsmith's complaint of the decay that it has
suffered since the death of the greatest of Augustans. Like the
Doctor he speaks of 'the misguided innovators' who have done
their best to 'involve it in pristine barbarity'. 'They have not
been content with restoring antiquated words and phrases, but have
indulged themselves in the most licentious transpositions and the
harshest constructions, vainly imagining, that the more their writings
are unlike prose, the more they resemble poetry: they have adopted
a language of their own and call upon mankind for admiration' [2].
It is obvious that this is a hit at the strained diction of some of
the author's contemporaries, at the Wartons and especially at Gray,
whose poetry Goldsmith could no more appreciate than his learned
friend. In his review of the two Odes, *The Progress of Poesy* and

---

[1] Gibbs, IV, pp. 417 ff.; Appendix, pp. 513 ff.
[2] *Ibid.,* IV, p. 173.

The Bard for the *Monthly,* he censures their irregularity and
unnatural flights [1]. The *Elegy* is called 'a fine poem but overloaded
with epithet', and pronounced to be inferior to Parnell's *Night
Piece on Death* [2]. One of the *Chinese Letters,* later on collected
and published under the title of *Citizen of the World,* contains
an adverse criticism on contemporary poetry: 'A parcel of gaudy
images pass on before his (i.e. the reader's) imagination like the
figures in a dream; but curiosity, induction, reason and the whole
train of affections are fast asleep' [3]. All these utterances offer
a sufficient proof that as far as their attitude towards the coming
romantic vogue in poetry was concerned, Goldsmith and Johnson
were remarkably at one. Both measured the new movement by
the standard of reason and correctness and found it wanting. In
his criticism of the *Faerie Queene,* written for the *Critical Review* [4],
Goldsmith ventured to predict that the highest degree of perfection
in English poetry was past in his time, and that it would gradually
decline. He expected that there would be a close resemblance
between the poetry of the latter half of the century and that of
the Elizabethan period.

Particularly characteristic is his confession that he likes Spenser's
poem in spite of its many improbabilities, which he apparently
considers as serious blemishes. 'We have always two passions
opposing each other', he says, 'a love of reality which represses the
flights of fancy, and a passion for the marvellous, which would
leave reflection behind' [5]. As I observed already, the only restriction Goldsmith makes, when he speaks of the freedom of the poet
to surpass nature, is that he should keep within the pale of probability and truth. His definition of judgment excludes anything
not conformable to these two. But he, like some of his contemporaries, considers popular belief as the ultimate criterion. From
his review of Wilkie's *Epigoniad* we learn that he agrees with this
author's dictum in the preface that 'tradition is the best ground
on which a fable can be built'. This explains why he is willing to

---

[1]   Gibbs, IV, p. 297.
[2]   *Ibid.,* p. 176. Cf., however, infra, p. 173.
[3]   *Ibid.,* III, p. 358.
[4]   *Ibid.,* IV, p. 335.
[5]   *Ibid.,* p. 335.

accept Homer's deviations from rational truth; on the same ground
he defends Tasso's witches and enchanters.

Goldsmith's conception of the relation between reason and
emotion or imagination is that of the neo-classical critics. He looks
upon great indulgence of the two latter faculties with suspicion.
Reason ought to keep them in check. For the cultivation of taste he
thinks it necessary that reason should be developed and the judgment refined in order to restrain 'the luxuriancy of the young
imagination, which is apt to run riot' [1]. Of more than ordinary
interest is one of the critic's contributions to the *British Magazine*
(May, 1760), entitled *A Dream*, wherein he gives a description of
many writers ascending a steep mountain with two fountains, one
half-way up, and the other at the summit, which can be reached
only with considerable difficulty. The water of the first fountain
intoxicates those that drink of it; they are 'the enthusiasts', aiming
at being sayers of good things, who often speak without understanding what they say. Those that reach the top and drink there,
are the authors of real genius, among whom Goldsmith mentions
especially Metastasio, Maffei and the English poets Johnson, Gray
and Mason, who all 'convey strong sense in the wildest sallies of
poetical enthusiasm'. The benefit that is to be derived from this
imaginary journey is to Goldsmith the conviction that reason ought
to preside over the other faculties and should constantly exercise
its restraining power: 'A shallow understanding generally aspires
at the reputation of wit; but true genius ever chooses to wear the
appearance of good sense' [2].

Though Goldsmith warns his readers against excessive indulgence
of the emotional element in literary art, he by no means seeks to
exclude sentiment and passion. 'Invention and enthusiasm constitute
genius, in whatever manner it may be displayed', we read in one of
his *Essays*. Lien Chi Altangi, the Chinese correspondent in the
Citizen of the World, complains of the insipidity of modern poetry.
He thinks it sadly deficient in reason and emotion: 'The *jucunda
et idonea vitae* — those sallies which move the heart, while they
amuse the fancy — are quite forgotten; ....' [3]. The same letter

---

[1]   Gibbs, I, p. 336.
[2]   *Ibid.*, IV, p. 479.
[3]   *Ibid.*, III, p. 358.

contains a mock eulogy on the lifeless tragedies of his day in which the genuine effusions of the human heart are replaced by languor, affectation and false sublimity [1]. Poetic fire and real pathos would reconcile him to a tragedy which is far from faultless in other respects.

Johnson and Goldsmith are equally emphatic in their insistence on 'correctness'. Like the great dictator, Goldsmith thought that English diction reached its highest pitch of refinement in the days of Parnell, whom he praised for keeping up the standard of perfection which it had attained through the improvements of Dryden, Addison and Pope. We trace Johnson's influence in Goldsmith's violent attack on the romantic poets of his own day, who were trying to undo what the preceding generations of writers had achieved. 'It is indeed amazing, after what has been done by Dryden, Addison, and Pope, to improve and harmonize our native tongue, that their successors should have taken so much pains to involve it in pristine barbarity', he observes. Measuring their verses by the even flow of Augustan precision, Goldsmith, just like his friend, finds fault with their 'licentious transpositions', their 'harsh constructions', their use of antiquated words, their borrowings from Spenser and Milton, and other absurd mannerisms.

When Goldsmith comes to speak about the qualities that a good critic should possess, we see that there is an important difference between his views and Johnson's. Reason alone is in his opinion an incompetent judge; it must be guided by 'taste', which in all critical verdicts should have the final decision. He does not consider it as a natural talent, wholly independent of art. Like Reynolds he believes that it cannot be brought to perfection without proper cultivation. What Horace says of genius is just as applicable to taste [2]. It may be developed by culture, experience and instruction, on the other hand it may be corrupted by bad precepts or bad examples [3]. It is, as the author expresses it, 'composed of Nature improved by Art; of Feeling tutored by Instruction'. Feeling

---

[1] Gibbs, IV, p. 251.
[2] *AP*, ll. 408 ff.
[3] Gibbs, I, p. 324 ff. According to Miss Caroline E. Tupper (PMLA, XXXIX, p. 325) the seven essays republished by Gibbs from the *British Magazine* (July 1761—January 1763) have been erroneously attributed to Goldsmith.

and sagacity are the two powers that constitute the faculty of taste. Its most important ingredient is a natural sensibility; it will teach the critic what to accept and what to reject in literary art. A capacity to acquire learning and philosophy is not sufficient for him, 'he must have also sensibility before he feels those emotions with which taste receives the impressions of beauty' [1]. For the cultivation of taste the formation of the heart is of primary importance, it should precede that of the understanding. In this way, by making the emotional appeal the ultimate test of art, Goldsmith limits the sphere of reason. The man of taste stands, according to him, half-way between 'the world and the cell, between learning and common sense'. In the controversy between the scholar who never has leisure to think for himself but merely investigates the thoughts of authors minutely, and the man of the world who looks down on such laboured nonsense with great contempt, the man of taste stands neutral [2].

It follows naturally from what has been said about his conception of the critic's task, that Goldsmith does not believe in neo-classic criticism by rule. In the ninth chapter of *An Inquiry into the Present State of Polite Learning* (1759), there is an attack on those who judge by *rules* and not by *feeling*. He calls the dogmatic belief in pre-conceived standards 'the most severe misfortune in the commonwealth of letters'. 'At such a tribunal no work of original merit can please. Sublimity, if carried to an exalted height, approaches burlesque, and humour sinks into vulgarity. The person who cannot feel may ridicule both as such, and bring rules to corroborate his assertion . . . . Rules render the reader more difficult to be pleased, and abridge the author's power of pleasing' [3]. Criticism by rule is the destroyer of all polite learning. Like Joseph Warton and other contemporaries, Goldsmith looks upon criticism of this kind and creative literature as hostile forces; an increase of the first has always portended a decay of the latter. If rules have been properly deduced from the practice of good writers, an author will always endeavour to observe them, but it should be borne in mind that 'a failure in this respect should

---

[1]   Gibbs, I, p. 327.
[2]   *Ibid.*, III, p. 499.
[3]   *Ibid.*, p. 510.

never induce us to reject the performance.... If sublimity, sentiment, and passion give warmth and life and expression to the
whole, we can the more easily dispense with the rules of the
Stagyrite; but if languor, affectation, and the false sublime are
substituted for these, an observance of all the precepts of the
ancients will prove but a poor compensation' [1].

Several statements from Goldsmith's critical works might be
quoted to illustrate the author's conviction that the standard of
literary excellence is relative, and that it is therefore irrational to
assign to classical canons an absolute value. One of the passages
from the first edition of the *Inquiry* (it is excluded from the second),
contains some noteworthy remarks on the controversy between
the Ancients and Moderns. The absurdity of this quarrel, which
from its very nature could never lead to any definite conclusion,
is sufficiently exposed in the following observation: 'The reflecting
reader need scarcely be informed, that this contested excellence
can be decided in favour of neither. They have both copied from
different originals, described the manners of different ages; have
exhibited nature as they found her, and both are excellent and
separate imitations. Homer describes his gods as his countrymen
believed them. Virgil, in a more enlightened age, describes his
with a greater degree of respect; .... Had Homer wrote like Milton,
his countrymen would have despised him; had Milton adopted
the theology of the ancient bard, he had been truly ridiculous'.
Goldsmith thinks that the only sensible way of drawing a parallel
between ancient and modern learning is not to treat them
as two entirely independent things but to compare the rise
and progress of ancient and modern learning together. The causes
of the corruption of taste in a certain period would induce us to
be on our guard against decay in our own time. Here we find
the idea of progress in art clearly enunciated. It is not that of the
moderns, who founded their superiority merely on the ground that
they had been born in a later age and could thus profit by the
experience of preceding generations of writers. Goldsmith recognizes
that art does not progress along a straight line but that periods
of rise and fall follow each other. 'Learning and language are ever

---

[1] *Review of Home's Tragedy of Douglas* (1757), Gibbs, IV, p. 251.

fluctuating, either rising to perfection or retiring into primeval barbarity', he says in his discussion of Spenser's great epic [1]. In his view of relativity in aesthetics he even goes so far as to think that there is a particular standard of taste in every country, and that therefore the critics of one country can never be proper guides for the writers of another. The laws that are laid down by them to improve the taste of readers should be adapted to the genius of the nation. This especially holds good for English taste, which by the insular position of the country is materially different from that on the continent. 'English taste, like English liberty, should be restrained only by laws of its own promoting' [2].

---

[1] Gibbs, IV, p. 533.
[2] *Ibid.*, III, p. 533.

CHAPTER XV

SIR JOSHUA REYNOLDS

In the account of Reynolds's life and writings, prefixed to his edition of the painter's works [1], Edmund Malone prints a sketch of a discourse which Reynolds had contemplated but had left unfinished. In this document, found by the editor among some loose papers, the painter acknowledges how much he has profited by his friendship with Johnson. Though he denies that the Doctor has had a hand in the composition of any of his *Discourses*, he openly avows that their merit is chiefly due to 'the education' he has received from his friend. 'The observations which he made on poetry, on life, and on everything about us, I applied to our art', are the words in which he acknowledges his great indebtedness [2]. Though this statement must of course not be taken too literally, it cannot be denied that the views of the two men manifest a marked similarity. Even the form in which some of the painter's dicta are couched, bears a distinctly Johnsonian impress. One of the questions on which they were in perfect agreement has already been mentioned, namely the Aristotelian maxim that the artist is to imitate nature. A short discussion of a few other aspects of aesthetic theory will not be out of place.

The *Discourses*, a series of lectures delivered to the Royal Academy during the years 1769—1790, were not meant to be a historical and critical survey of the art of painting. Nor do they treat of technical matters, but they deal with general principles founded on the painter's own experience, and exemplified in the works of the great artists. In spite of the circumstances under which they were composed they constitute a unified doctrine, which is the embodiment of the traditional views that prevailed in the latter part of the eighteenth century and the first part of the nineteenth. They derive their interest to the student of literary criticism

---

[1] *The Works of Sir Joshua Reynolds, Knt., in two Volumes, to which is prefixed 'An Account of the Life and Writings of the Author'*, by Edmund Malone. London 1797.

[2] *Ibid.*, I, p. XX.

from the fact that the author often draws analogies between painting and the sister arts, especially poetry, and he lays great stress on 'the common congeniality' which they all bear to human nature. As Reynolds says: 'Each art will corroborate and mutually reflect the truth on the other', so that the artist may 'habitually transfer the principles of those arts to that which he professes: which ought to be always present to his mind, and to which everything is to be referred' [1]. Poetry and painting address themselves to the same faculties, they both try to accommodate themselves to 'the natural propensies and inclinations of the mind'. They only differ in the means they employ to attain the same result. Reynolds rejects the view that rules are the fetters of genius and his intention is 'not so much to place the artist above rules, as to teach them their reason'. It appears that, like Johnson, he accepts only those that are based on the passions and affections of the human mind. Reynolds advises the student never to lose sight of them, for they are collected from the full body of the best general practice. In the last discourse he expresses the conviction that he has succeeded in establishing the rules and principles of his own art on a more firm and lasting foundation than that on which they had formerly been placed [2].

Some of Reynolds's conceptions had already found expression in the three letters that the painter contributed to the *Idler* in the year 1759. They were elicited by the satirical *Dick Minim* papers, in which Johnson made fun of the petty critics who are unable to form an opinion themselves but merely repeat the cant phrases of others. In this first letter Reynolds closely follows his friend and ridicules 'the connoisseurs' who have no knowledge of art beyond the few platitudes they have picked up among the painters. The second and third letters contain his first exposition of the grand style, of which the *Discourses* were to give a more elaborate discussion. In the author's eyes, imitating nature does not mean mere copying; if it did, painting would not be a sister to poetry. Both arts are concerned only with universal nature, and minute attention to reality should be carefully avoided, for both require

---

[1]   *Discourses,* ed. Dobson (World's Classics), p. 199.
[2]   *Ibid.,* p. 232.

ideal and not literal truth. Painting like poetry addresses itself to
the imagination, which would have no scope if a strict adherence
to fact were required. Reynolds adds, however, that imagination
and enthusiasm should only be indulged to a certain extent,
though he grants that the exact degree of enthusiasm that the arts
of poetry and painting admit is difficult to determine. 'There may
perhaps be too great an indulgence, as well as too great a restraint
of imagination; and if the one produces incoherent monsters, the
other produces what is full as bad, lifeless insipidity' [1]. The limits
must be determined 'by an intimate knowledge of the passions and
good sense, but not *common sense*' [2]. To the painter's or poet's
individual reason is therefore assigned the task of keeping the
imagination in check. This dread of excessive indulgence of the
imaginative faculty repeatedly finds expression in the *Discourses.*
Reynolds warns the student of art not to try the power of his
imagination until his judgment has been duly trained and his
memory been properly stored with knowledge. 'The mind that has
been thus disciplined may be indulged in the warmest enthusiasm,
and venture to play on the borders of the wildest extravagance' [3].
But without the restraint of reason the imagination is a dangerous
guide for the artist: 'Mere enthusiasm will carry him but a little
way' [4].

Like Johnson, Reynolds has no patience with 'the enthusiasts'
who assert that taste and genius are in no way connected with
reason and common sense. There is little doubt that the passage
in the seventh Discourse, where Reynolds speaks of inspiration, was
influenced by Johnson's vigorous maxims on the same subject.
'The temporary and periodical ebbs and flows', which were in
Johnson's opinion merely 'the fumes of vain imagination' [5], are
treated with no less contempt by the painter. 'When, in plain
prose, we gravely talk of courting the Muse in shady bowers;
waiting the call and inspiration of Genius, finding out where he
inhabits, and where he is to be invoked with the greatest success;

---

[1] *Discourses,* p. 254.
[2] My italics.
[3] *Discourses,* p. 12.
[4] *Ibid.,* p. 16.
[5] *Lives,* I, p. 137.

of attending to times and seasons when the imagination shoots with
the greatest vigour, whether at the summer solstice or the vernal
equinox; . . . . how this same imagination begins to grow dim in
advanced age, smothered and deadened by too much judgement;
when we talk such language, or entertain such sentiments as these,
we generally rest contented with mere words, or at best entertain
notions not only groundless but pernicious' [1]. Reynolds disdainfully
rejects the belief in such vanities; the poet's physical conditions
may make him less fit for his task at one time than at another,
his imagination may decline in later life if it has not constantly
been cultivated, but generations of writers from Homer to Dryden
have proved that it may be as strong in the last works as in those
produced in the poet's youth.

Nor does Reynolds agree with the romanticist's conception of
genius. He denies that it has nothing to do with reason, that it is
an intuitive power which allows of no restraint and is therefore
exempt from rules. If art were an inspiration, a gift divinely
bestowed upon the artist at birth, a long and severe course of
study would be unnecessary for him. Against this mistaken opinion
Reynolds raises his voice: 'Excellence is never granted to man but
as the reward of labour' [2]. Whatever natural talents the poet or
painter may possess, only a constant application to his art can
ensure lasting success. In painting, more than in any other art,
the imitation of great masters should be carefully practised by
the student: 'The greatest natural genius cannot subsist on its own
stock' [3]. Reynolds does not agree with Bacon that the painter
must attain excellence by 'a kind of felicity . . . . and not by rule'.
The notion that all rules are worthless is false. Nothing is attained
by mere chance. The pleasure that we derive from a work of art
is founded on certain principles, and the artist, who by constant
practice strives to develop his talents, should keep these principles
in view so that they may direct him. Like Johnson, Reynolds
carefully distinguishes between rules merely founded on authority
and 'the precepts of the mind'. The student who in the beginning
of his career has to follow the examples of great masters, because

---

[1] *Discourses,* pp. 93, 94.
[2] *Ibid.,* p. 19.
[3] *Ibid.,* p. 75.

his judgment is not yet sufficiently mature, must gradually emancipate himself from them, and trust to his own reason.

Taste, which is according to Reynolds the same as genius but without the power of execution, can only be cultivated by a strict adherence to the dictates of reason and philosophy. The painter admits that it is impossible to trace it back to its first principles; yet he thinks that much of what is called taste, can be brought under the dominion of reason, and as reason is something immutable, some invariable laws may be laid down to which most of the beauties of art can be reduced. What is not reducible to rational principles is treated with suspicion by Reynolds as well as by Johnson. 'Those inventions which either disdain or shrink from reason, are generally, I fear, more like the dreams of a distempered brain, than the exalted enthusiasm of a sound and true genius. In the midst of the highest flights of fancy or imagination, reason ought to preside from first to last, though *I admit her more powerful operation is upon reflection*' [1], he says in the seventh discourse. The last restriction connects the passage with the thirteenth discourse, delivered ten years later (1786). In spite of the fact that Reynolds attaches so much importance to the function of reason, he warns his hearers against a purely rational conception of art. He distinguishes truth in art from mathematical truth [2]. Minds which admit only the latter are unfit to judge, for ultimately 'common sense must give way to a higher sense'. What all arts have in common, 'the fundamental ground' of them all in the painter's opinion, is that they address themselves to two faculties of the mind, its imagination and its sensibility. He grants that in the last resort everything in art ought to be weighed in the balance of reason, but before it is ready with its deductions, the intuitive faculty of the imagination has already formed its conclusion. 'A man endowed with this faculty, feels and acknowledges the truth, though it is not always in his power, perhaps, to give a reason for it' [3]. Reynolds looks upon this impression, this 'first effect', as the result of collective observation and of accumulated experience. It is a kind of 'habitual reason', which ought to be the

---

[1] *Discourses,* p. 118. My italics.
[2] *Ibid.,* p. 102.
[3] *Ibid.,* p. 196.

guiding principle in life as well as in art. 'If we were obliged to enter into a theoretical deliberation on every occasion, before we act, life would be at a stand, and art would be impracticable'. Theories of art, built exclusively on a rational basis and ignoring the important factor of the first impression on the mind are therefore worthless. Not reason, but imagination, is the residence of truth.

The conflict between reason on the one hand and emotion and imagination on the other hand explains Reynolds's hesitation when evaluating the respective merits of the two great Italian painters Raphael and Michelangelo, and accounts for a few inconsistencies between his various dicta. Reason would make him yield the palm to Raphael in accordance with the traditional conception of the French Academy, because he is the only painter who is able 'to get above all singular forms, local customs, particularities, and details of every kind' [1]. He is the painter of universal nature, his pictures are the best exponents of the *beau idéal*. Yet the reader feels all the time that Reynolds's sympathies are on the side of the Florentine in spite of the latter's strong individuality and his capricious inventions. Though his judgment must therefore decide in favour of Raphael, who possesses more excellent qualities than any other painter, 'yet he never takes such a firm hold and entire possession of the mind as to make us desire nothing else, and to feel nothing wanting', as the works of Michelangelo do [2]. In the last Discourse Reynolds openly expresses his predilection: 'were I now to begin the world again, I would tread in the steps of that great master: to kiss the hem of his garment, to catch the slightest of his perfections, would be glory and distinction enough for an ambitious man' [2]. For more than a century sublimity had been associated with large proportions and generalized nature, but Reynolds, quoting Longinus' opinion that true sublimity can compensate for the absence of all other beauties, feels inclined to call the works of Michelangelo with their strongly individualistic character the best examples of the true sublime.

In making the appeal to the imagination and sensibility the test

---

[1] *Discourses*, p. 61.
[2] *Ibid.*, p. 245.

of art and the arbiter of truth, Reynolds differs widely from the orthodox believers in reason. The painter's aesthetic creed shows in this respect an important divergence from that of his friend and avowed master Dr. Johnson, and approaches that of Goldsmith [1].

---

[1] In his *Essay on Genius and Common Sense* (*Table Talk*, World's Classics, pp. 38 ff.) Hazlitt deals with the same question and follows Reynolds very closely. He says: 'In art, in taste, in life, in speech, you decide from feeling, and not from reason; that is, from the impression of a number of things on the mind, which impression is true and well founded, though you may not be able to analyse or account for it in the several particulars'; and somewhat later on: 'He must be a poor creature indeed whose practical convictions do not in almost all cases outrun his deliberate understanding, or who does not feel and know much more than he can give a reason for'. What Reynolds calls 'habitual reason' — the result of various impressions collected in the memory, — is called by Hazlitt 'common sense', which he considers as *tacit* reason, just as conscience is a tacit sense of right and wrong.

CHAPTER XVI

WILLIAM SHENSTONE

Shenstone's critical opinions must be sifted from his *Essays on Men and Manners* (1764), his letters to particular friends, published in the third volume of *The Works in Verse and Prose* (1769), those beween the Duchess of Somerset and other members of the Warwickshire circle, collected by Thomas Hull, the actor, in 1778[1], and the *Recollection of Some Particulars in the Life of the late William Shenstone, Esq., in a Series of Letters from an intimate Friend of his to . . . ., Esq. T. R. S.* (London, 1788).

So far as the scattered, aphoristic remarks contained in these volumes enable us to judge, Shenstone shows much of the influence of the old and very little of that of the new school of criticism. Apart from their strong ethical bent, which is a widespread characteristic of this moralizing age, they betray the influence of the pseudo-classical creed in some other respects as well. Simplicity and correctness are the critic's two objects of devotion. They are the chief traits that he admires in the Greek and Roman poets. 'Every noble truth and sentiment was expressed by the former (the ancients) in the natural manner; a word and phrase, simple, perspicuous and incapable of improvement. What then remained for later writers but affectation, witticism and conceit?' [2]

His attitude towards Pope shows, however, that Shenstone does not consider these two qualities as the sole essence of the poet's art. He admires him for his ease and perspicuity, his 'consolidating or condensing sentences', the smoothness of his verse; but he feels at the same time that he is wanting in invention. He calls Pope 'the most correct writer since Virgil' and knows no English poet who could condense so much sense in such small compass. On the other hand he thinks that Pope had not enough genius to justify

---

[1] *Select Letters between the Late Duchess of Somerset, Lady Luxborough, Miss Dolman, Mr. Whistler, Mr. R. Dodsley, William Shenstone, Esq. and others, by Mr. Hull.* London, 1778. The letters from Lady Luxborough to Shenstone were published by Dodsley three years earlier.

[2] *Essays on Men and Manners: On Writing and Books.*

the high esteem in which he was held by his contemporaries. Though he is the most correct writer since Virgil, he is 'the greatest genius only since Dryden'.

His critical remarks on Spenser illustrate the usual pseudo-classical prejudices: the plan of the *Faerie Queene* is imperfect, 'much art and judgment are discovered in parts, and but little in the whole', his descriptions show a lack of true taste, his imagination is immoderately indulged, 'he expands it beyond its due limits'. Shenstone sums up his views in the following thoroughly Augustan dictum: 'there are many favourite passages in the *Faerie Queene* which will be instances of a great and cultivated genius misapplied'. We know from a letter to his friend R. Graves [1] that the reading of Spenser's epic prompted him to write *The Schoolmistress* and that he originally meant this 'trifling imitation' only as a burlesque, but was converted while he was writing it. What attracted him particularly in the Elizabethan poet was the obsolete language, his simplicity, and 'a peculiar tenderness of sentiment', as he states in the short advertisement prefixed to the poem. Simplicity was the main feature that Shenstone admired in the ballad. In his *Essay on Writing and Books* he speaks of a certain 'flimsiness' which this kind of literature requires and which a poet like Pope would not have been able to produce. He himself wrote some imitations and encouraged Percy to publish his *Reliques*. It was owing to bad health that he had to give up his plan of assisting him [2]. It was at his advice, too, that Percy complied with the taste of his time, and Shenstone seems to have been in perfect agreement with his friend as to the way in which the latter treated his material.

As is apparent from a letter to Mac Gowan, dated 24 Sept. 1761, Shenstone was greatly interested in *Ossian:* he considered it as a welcome antidote to the laboured productions of his age. 'The taste of the age, so far as it regards plan and style, seems to have been carried to its utmost height, as may appear in the works of Akenside, Gray's *Odes and Churchyard Verses*, and Mason's *Monody* and *Elfrida*. The public has seen all that art can do and

---

[1] Dated Jan. 19, 1741.
[2] *The Works in Verse and Prose*, III, p. 321.

they want the more striking efforts of wild, original, enthusiastic genius.... Here is indeed, pure original genius! the very quintessence of poetry; a few drops of which, properly managed, are enough to give a flavour to quart bottles. And yet one or two of these pieces.... are undoubtedly as well planned as any ode we find in Horace' [1].

Shenstone had read Goldsmith's *Inquiry into the Present State of Polite Learning*, and agreed with the author's censure of the inflated language used by contemporary poets to make up for their lack of sentiment [2]. A year later he writes to Percy in a similar strain. He trusts that the *Reliques* will meet with general approval, because the poems contain 'ye true C h e m i c a l Spirit or Essence of P o e t r y', and then adds: 'Tis ye voice of Sentiment rather y^n the L a n g u a g e of R e f l e x i o n, adapted peculiarly to s t r i k e ye P a s'si o n s, which is the only Merit of Poetry that has obtained my regard of late' [3]. It is evident from this passage that Shenstone looks upon emotion as an indispensable element of poetry. There is a remark to the same effect in one of his *Essays* [4]: 'I think nothing truly poetic, at least no poetry worth composing, that does not strongly affect one's passions'. The importance of this statement is lessened, however, by what immediately follows: 'and this is but slenderly affected by fables, allegories and lies. Incredulus odi.... Hor'. If the critic means — and it is apparently the only plausible interpretation — that no poetry other than that dealing with the actual or the probable can rouse genuine emotion, it is a dictum that connects him with the Augustans rather than with the early romanticists [5].

---

[1] Quoted by Hecht: *Thomas Percy und William Shenstone, Ein Briefwechsel aus der Entstehungszeit der Reliques of Ancient English Poetry.* Strassburg, 1909, p. 124. Percy had a high opinion of Shenstone's writings and his taste. He regrets that Macpherson had not shown his *Fingal* to Shenstone before sending it to the press. He would have disapproved of the turgid diction, the affectation and stiffness of the images (p. 77).

[2] *Ibid.,* p. 18.

[3] *Ibid.,* p. 46.

[4] *On Writing and Books.*

[5] The passage has been quoted without the additional remark, and this may give rise to wrong conclusions. See Miss Hazeltine, *A Study of William Shenstone and his Critics.* Menasha, Wisconsin, 1918, p. 54. Cf. also O. Doughty, *English Lyric in the Age of Reason,* London, 1922, p. 106, where it is adduced as a proof that 'Shenstone's poetic theory was indeed far better than his practice'.

There was one thing in Goldsmith's *Inquiry* that Shenstone read with great interest, as appears from one of his letters to Percy [1]: it was his discourse on 'taste', by which Shenstone sets great store, and which he carefully distinguishes from judgment and wit. He, too, was of opinion that this should be the leading principle of the critic, its function being 'to reconcile Literature and the Sciences to Common Sense'. Percy refers to a history of *false taste* that Shenstone intended to write [2]. The plan was never carried out, but in the essay *On Taste* there is an allusion to the 'counter-taste', which again illustrates Shenstone's fear of the unduly fantastic and marks him as a champion of correctness. 'It is founded on surprise and curiosity, which maintains a sort of rivalship with the true: and may be expressed by the name Concetto'.

To summarize, Shenstone's critical work shows all the wavering and the half-heartedness which characterizes that of several other writers in this transitional period.

---

[1]   Hecht, p. 31.
[2]   *Ibid.,* p. 38.

CHAPTER XVII

HUGH BLAIR

Gerard's *Essay on Taste* did not fall on barren ground. His ideas were taken up and developed by a number of followers. The chief of them was Hugh Blair. In literary history his name is best known in connection with the *Ossian* controversy. He encouraged Macpherson to publish his *Fragments of Ancient Poetry* and praised them excessively in his *Dissertation concerning the Poems of Ossian* (1762). His other important contribution to the field of literary criticism is his *Lectures on Rhetoric and Belles Lettres,* delivered in the University of Edinburgh, where he was made a professor of rhetoric in 1760. It was not published till the year 1783. Its object is to arrive at a just estimate of a literary work by distinguishing what is beautiful from what is faulty. The critic's duty is, according to Blair, to admire as well as to blame. If reason might prompt him to be on the look-out for deviations from established principles, 'taste' will prevent him from paying a too rigorous attention to them. This 'beauty-blemish' theory, as it has been called by Professor Saintsbury, was often resorted to by the critics of Dryden's time and especially by the Augustans. Instead of judging exclusively by faults, they had insisted on a more appreciative sort of criticism which attempted to find out the merits rather than the defects [1]. Blair's definition of taste as 'the power of receiving pleasure from the beauties of nature and of art' proves that he shares this view.

In the second of his *Lectures,* entitled *Taste,* Blair sets out to explain what this quality is like and answers the question 'whether it is to be considered as an internal sense or as an exaction of reason'. It appears that he, too, looks upon reason and taste as two separate criteria. The pleasure the mind receives from the contemplation of beauty is, in his opinion, not the result of a purely intellectual process: a beautiful object or a fine poem strikes us intuitively, and it is often impossible to state the reasons why we

---

[1] Cf. supra, p. 22.

are pleased. Taste is therefore ultimately founded on 'a natural and instinctive sensibility', though Blair grants that it usually acts in conjunction with the rational faculty: 'reason assists taste in many of its operations and serves to enlarge its power'. He calls good taste a compound power, of which natural sensibility and improved understanding are the two main constituent qualities [1]. As a further requisite he mentions a good heart, without which the critic will be unable duly to appreciate the human actions and affections depicted in a literary work. Like Reynolds and Gerard, Blair thinks that taste is primarily a natural gift, which can be greatly improved by frequent attention to beautiful objects and generally approved models. When it is brought to its highest degree of perfection, it is reducible to two characteristics: *delicacy*, which enables the critic to discover beauties hidden from vulgar eyes, and *correctness*, whose chief function is to trace the principles from which beauties derive their power of pleasing. Of the critics distinguished by delicacy, Longinus and Addison are mentioned, of those possessing a high degree of correctness, Aristotle and Swift [2].

The great value attached by Blair to the function of taste explains why he cannot agree with Kames's conception that criticism is a rational science. He grants that there are some principles of reason and sound judgment which can be applied to matters of taste as well as the subjects of science and philosophy [3]. But reason can help the critic only up to a certain limit, and can never lead to final conclusions.

That the importance of the reactionary tendencies of the School of Taste against the supremacy of reason can easily be exaggerated, is made obvious by Blair himself. He rejects the notion that taste is an arbitrary principle, dependent on individual whim, and insists that it should be tested by some immutable criteria. They are *nature*, if it concerns descriptions of human characters or human actions, and 'the common opinion of men placed in such situations as are favourable to the proper exertions of taste'. For just as Johnson and Kames do, the author of the 'Lectures' considers the public, 'unprejudiced and dispassionate',

---

[1] *Lectures on Rhetoric and Belles Lettres.* London, 1833, p. 14.
[2] Cf. Gerard, supra, p. 166.
[3] *Op. cit.*, p. 20.

as the supreme judge to whom the final appeal must be made.

A significant note to the second lecture clearly illustrates that the advocates of 'taste' did not see a great diversity between their own guiding principles and those of the thoroughgoing rationalists. I subjoin the passage *in extenso*: 'The difference between the authors who found the standard of taste upon *the common feelings of human nature* ascertained by general approbation, and those who found it upon established principles which can be ascertained by reason, is more an apparent than a real difference. *Like many other literary controversies, it turns chiefly on modes of expression* [1]. For they who lay the greatest stress on sentiment and feeling, make no scruple of applying argument and reason to matters of taste. They appeal, like other writers, to established principles, in judging of the excellencies of eloquence or poetry; and plainly show, that the general approbation to which they ultimately recur, is an approbation resulting from discussion as well as from sentiment. They, on the other hand, who, in order to vindicate taste from any suspicion of being arbitrary, maintain that it is ascertainable by the standard of reason, admit nevertheless, that what pleases universally, must on that account be held to be truly beautiful; and that no rules or conclusions concerning objects of taste, can have any just authority, if they be found to contradict the general sentiments of men' [2].

This observation throws some light on the uncertainty and confusion that characterize eighteenth century criticism and proves how intimately the schools of Reason and Taste are related.

Like the majority of his contemporaries Blair is a disbeliever in external laws and *a priori* rules are rejected. The critic should follow experimental methods and should come to no decisions merely by a train of abstract reasoning. He illustrates this statement by a reference to the critics of antiquity who proceeded in the same way: Aristotle's rules about unity in the drama and the epic were founded on the practice of Homer and the Greek dramatists, and were therefore the result of experience. They appeared to be consonant with the principles of reason and human nature, and have therefore passed into established rules [3]. Such rules may

---

[1] Italics are mine.
[2] P. 21.
[3] P. 24.

be of great help to the poet and teach him to avoid faults, but
'beauties' can only be attained by a close attention to nature.

It is by following the method discussed in the first few lectures
that Blair wants to examine the comparative merits of the Ancients
and the Moderns, disregarding authority except when it is founded
on 'good sense and reason'. The chief qualities in which the moderns
excel the classics are in their regularity and accuracy, and (in the
drama) an improvement in the conduct of the plot and a greater
attention to probability and decorum. On the other hand the Greek
and Roman writers were superior in fire, enthusiasm and genius;
Milton and Shakespeare alone are exceptions to the rule. Blair's
neo-classic leanings are evident from his enumeration of the
most distinguished men of genius that the world has known. As
has already been observed, he recognizes four periods of history
which have been curiously productive. They are the time from
the Peloponnesian war to the reign of Alexander the Great, the
Roman Age of Caesar and Augustus, the period of the Revival
of Learning and, last of all, the reigns of Lewis XIV in France
and of Queen Anne in England. The Age of Elizabeth apparently
ranks below that of Pope and the list of the great men includes
such names as Parnell, Atterbury, Young and Rowe, but neither
Shakespeare nor Spenser, nor Milton finds mention.

In the succeeding lectures Blair applies the principles laid down
in the first to the various departments of poetical composition. His
analysis is less purely rational than that of Johnson and Kames
and is therefore bound to lead to somewhat different results. An
instance in point is his attitude towards the use of the marvellous
or 'the machinery' in an epic poem. He does not agree with the
French critics of the preceding century who had considered it as
an essential element, an opinion which could, according to Blair,
only be founded on 'a superstitious reverence for the practice of
Homer and Virgil'. Though he denies that 'machinery' cannot be
dispensed with in an epic, he by no means shares the view of 'some
late critics of considerable name' who reject it on the ground that it
is not consistent with reality and probability. The author probably
alludes to Kames, who disapproved of its use in an heroic poem
and would admit it only in a burlesque. 'Mankind do not consider
poetical writings with so philosophical an eye', Blair says. The

reader wants to be pleased and 'the marvellous' is one of the greatest charms of poetry and particularly of epic poetry. Blair makes the restriction, however, that the machinery should be used with moderation and should have its foundation in popular belief. The chief task of the poet is to depict human actions and human nature. In his discussion of Tasso's *Jerusalem Delivered* [1] the Italian poet is taken to task for his excessive fondness of the supernatural. In his epic the use of the marvellous is carried to a degree of extravagance: 'The objects which he presents to us, are always great; but, sometimes, too remote from probability' [2]. But, as Thomas Warton does in his *History of English Poetry,* he acknowledges that in this respect Tasso is not more to be blamed than Homer and Virgil, the only difference being that in the classical epics we find the romance of paganism, in the *Jerusalem Delivered* that of chivalry.

Though machinery may therefore be tolerated in epic poetry, Blair objects to its use in tragedy, where it would be contrary to the laws of reason. Tragedy has an altogether different aim; its end is not to elevate the imagination but to affect the heart, and passion can only be raised 'by making the impressions of nature and of truth upon the mind'. Ghosts are an exception to the rule; not only are they founded on popular belief, but also they conduce to heighten the terror of the tragic scenes. The *deus ex machina,* the unravelling of the plot by the interposition of deities, an expedient to which Euripides resorted in his tragedies, is looked upon by Blair as a serious blemish.

In the same lecture the critic delivers his opinion on the absence of the chorus in the modern drama. One of the questions in controversy between the 'Ancients' and the 'Moderns' had been whether this absence was to be considered as a loss or a gain. Blair grants that the chorus rendered the tragedy more instructive by contributing to its moral teaching, and he thinks it therefore far preferable to the unmeaning and irrelevant music which is introduced into the modern play to entertain the audience during the intervals [3]. But at the same time he realizes that serious drawbacks would attend

---

[1]   Lecture XLIV.
[2]   P. 605.
[3]   Cf. Kames, supra, p. 141.

the reintroduction of the chorus; it would be an unnatural con-
finement of the poet, the scope of the action would be too narrow,
and this would require too great a sacrifice of probability.

Blair's views of the unities resemble those of Kames. He thinks
that the unity of action is even more necessary for dramatic art
than for the epic. Two independent actions in the same tragedy
cannot be tolerated. There may be underplots, but by the poet's
art they must be rendered completely subservient to the main plot
and lead up to the catastrophe. He distinguishes between 'the
simplicity of the plot' and 'the unity of action' in a dramatic composition. A plot is simple when it contains a small number of
incidents. But a tragedy may be *implex*; it may have a considerable
number of persons and incidents and yet preserve its unity, if
only the incidents 'tend towards the principal object of the play
and be properly connected with it' [1]. Addison is censured for
introducing irrelevant scenes in his *Cato* for no other reason than
that of contributing variety to a barren subject. Congreve is blamed
for falling into the other extreme, namely that of overcrowding
the fable with incidents.

The Horatian precept [2] that each play is to consist of five acts,
is called by Blair a purely arbitrary division, not even supported
by the Greek dramatists and Aristotle's *Poetics*, but founded only
on common practice. It would have been much better, if such a
number had never been fixed, and every play was divided into as
many acts as the subject requires. Now that the division has become
a recognized rule, the dramatist should take care that the pause
is in the right place, so that the thickening and unravelling of the
plot is properly managed [3]. The action of the play should continually
advance. Shakespeare is praised for his great dramatic skill; his
scenes are full of sentiment, 'never of mere discourse', whereas
the French tragedians 'allow the action to languish for the sake
of a long and artful dialogue'. From the discussion of the division
of a tragedy into acts, the critic passes on to that of acts into scenes.
Here his remarks bear a close resemblance to those of Kames. The

---

[1] P. 623.
[2] *AP*, l. 189.
[3] P. 625.

scenes should be closely connected, the persons appearing in one
scene should never go off together, lest the next scene should be
quite independent of the preceding one. If this rule is not kept up,
the union of the scenes will be broken and there will be an interruption in the representation in the middle of an act. Blair thinks
that the French writers have in this respect far excelled the English
dramatists.

The unities of time and place are considered by Blair in their
relation to the most important of the three: the unity of action.
A strict observance of them is difficult and unnecessary. Like
other critics of his age he considers the question historically. With
the Greeks the representation of a tragedy was uninterrupted and
the stage was continually occupied, so that there was little room
for the imagination of the audience to go beyond the time and
place of the representation. The intervals between the acts in a
modern play make it much easier for the spectators to imagine that
a few hours elapse, and that they pass from one apartment of a
palace, or one part of a city, to another. It is clear that Blair will
allow only a comparatively slight deviation from the classical
practice. He does not insist on a close adherence, especially if this
would have to be at the cost of the higher beauties of the drama.
But the concession is by no means unlimited; indeed, as appears
from what follows, it is considerably restricted: 'hurrying the
spectator from one distant city, or country, to another; or making
several days or weeks to pass during the course of the
representation, are looked upon as unpardonable violations of
dramatic correctness [1]. During each act the unities should be strictly
kept up, the scene must be the same throughout, the time that
is supposed to pass must not be greater than that actually taken
up by the representation. Addison's *Cato* is held up as a favourable
exception to the deplorable irregularity of the English drama.
Blair believes no more than Kames and Johnson that even the most
rigorous adherence to the classical unities will make the spectators
believe that the actions seen on the stage are real. They are
conscious that it is only an imitation, but this imitation should at
least have the air of probability and verisimilitude. Improbable

---

[1] Pp. 630, 631.

circumstances would shock their imagination and deprive them of
their pleasure.

It goes without saying that, judged by this severe standard,
Shakespeare is found to be sadly lacking in dramatic decorum.
Blair grants he had genius, but it was 'genius shooting wild;
deficient in just taste, and altogether unassisted by knowledge or
art'. The whole passage is thoroughly pseudo-classic. 'Long has
he been idolized by the British nation', the critic exclaims, 'much
has been said, and much has been written concerning him; criticism
has been drawn to the very dregs, in commentaries upon his words
and witticisms; and yet it remains, to this day, in doubt, whether
his beauties or his faults be greatest' [1]. Among the latter Blair lays
particular stress on his mixing of serious and comic scenes, his
harsh diction, his bombast and his plays upon words.

In another lecture there is a discussion of comedy, which, being
an imitation of familiar life, is pronounced to require an even
stricter attention to dramatic rules. There is a vehement attack
on the Spanish drama and more in particular on the irregular plays
of Lope de Vega, which transgress all the laws of propriety. They
are compared with the products of the French comic theatre, the
exemplifications of correctness, taste and decency.

Blair's *Dissertation concerning the Poems of Ossian,* in which
Macpherson's *Fragments of Ancient Poetry* are immoderately
eulogized, is one of the attempts, common among neo-classic
critics, at testing 'romantic' poetry by Aristotelian canons. Instead
of adapting their standard of judgment to the new literary form
which Aristotle did not know and to which consequently his
rules did not apply, these writers adopted the opposite method,
namely that of explaining the popularity of the new species of
composition by its accordance with generally accepted laws. The
Elizabethan critic Sir John Harington had defended Ariosto's
Orlando Furioso on similar grounds in his *Briefe Apologie,* prefixed
to his translation of the poem (1591) [2], where he had taken Virgil
as a pattern and Aristotle's rules as his standard. Addison had

---

[1] P. 645.
[2] *A Preface, or rather a Briefe Apologie of Poetrie, and of the Author and
Translator,* 1591. (Greg. Smith, *Eliz. Crit. Essays,* II, pp. 194 ff.).

proceeded along analogous lines when trying the merit of *Chevy Chase* by the precepts of the Greek critic and by the models of Homer and Virgil; he had compared the *Children in the Wood* to a passage in Horace and last of all had judged Milton's great poem by the rules of the epic.

Blair draws a parallel between Ossian and Homer's *Iliad;* the manners which the Greek poet describes, resemble those of Ossian's time, for both represent an early stage of social development. Both writers were ignorant of the laws of criticism, both were only guided by nature. It is therefore no wonder that there should be great conformity between the two. Then follows an examination of *Fingal* on Aristotelian principles to prove that 'it has all the essential requisites of a true and regular epic'. It possesses the unity that the Greek critic prescribed; it has a beginning, a middle and an end; it observes the unity of place, the scene being the heath of Lena throughout the poem; it is characterized by the grandeur of sentiment, style and imagery required in an epic [1]; the poet has followed Horace's advice of 'hastening to the main action' [2]; the episodes are introduced with great propriety, the human characters are naturally represented, and in both poems the machinery is founded on popular belief.

It is interesting to compare the comments of the two leading literary periodicals on Blair's dissertation. The *Critical Review* for 1762 condemns his practice of testing a work of extraordinary merit like *Fingal* by the rules of the Greek critic. This method of procedure is designated as absurd as 'to judge a Lapland jacket by the fashion of an Armenian gaberdine'. The writer of a poem 'has a natural right to choose the manner in which it shall be presented'. Ossian was therefore perfectly free to disregard the rules of a critic whose works he could not possibly know. This is certainly one of the most unreserved statements of the historic point of view that we find in the critical literature of the eighteenth century. Still, even this reviewer is not altogether exempt from the influence of the dominant creed, as appears from what follows: 'Nevertheless, this admirable piece will, even according to Aristotle's

---

[1] *The Poems of Ossian,* ed. Leipzig, 1847, p. 64.
[2] *AP*, ll. 148, 149 (in medias res .... auditorem rapit, ...).

definition, be found a truly epic poem and (under correction be it spoken) in many places superior even to Homer and Virgil'.

The *Monthly Review* [1] for the same year, though acknowledging the extraordinary merit of the poem, cannot join in the excessive praise that is being bestowed on it. The attitude of the *Monthly* is diametrically opposed to that of the *Critical*. After admitting that established laws should be applied with a certain latitude, as 'the noble flights and native excursions of true genius are indeed frequently too eccentric to be exactly measured by critical rules', the reviewer states his reason for disagreeing with the general opinion: 'It is expedient, that the mechanism and execution of every considerable performance should be compared with that standard, and examined by those laws, which have for many ages been allowed to constitute the perfection of that species of writing, under the denomination of which such performance is presented to the world. Criticism degenerates, otherwise, into a servile echo of the leading voices of the times, and gives encouragement for every rising genius to indulge the luxuriance of his imagination, at the hazard of being hurried, by the impetuosity of unbridled fancy, into bombast, extravagance, and absurdity'. The critic then observes that Aristotle's rules are not the result of abstract reasonings, but were rationally deduced from the practice of the Greek poet. They are therefore not 'arbitrary assumptions *a priori*' but deductions *a posteriori*. Genius need not conform to them in all respects, but experience has taught that those who deviate from models of the ancients will never attain to their perfection. The reviewer is a firm believer in the doctrine of the literary *genres*. He does not dispute the right of a poet to indulge his genius and invent a new species of writing, but he is not allowed 'to corrupt and destroy the old'. A poem cannot claim the merit of the epopee, if it is not distinguished by what for ages have been considered its essential characteristics. The critic then follows Blair's example and tests *Fingal* by the rules of the epic; he is compelled to do so, he says, because many admirers have allowed it great merit as such. The result is not very satisfactory.

---

[1] Vol. 26.

CHAPTER XVIII

JAMES BEATTIE

Another critic who was influenced by Gerard's *Essay on Taste* is James Beattie, the author of *The Minstrel*. This long, though unfinished poem in the Spenserian stanza shows many traces of incipient romanticism, and stamps its author as a pioneer of the reaction against the school of Pope. Gray, whose favour he was very anxious to procure and whose poetry he greatly admired, praised it and wrote a criticism on the first book [1].

His *Essay on the Nature and Immutability of Truth* (1770), containing a vigorous attack on Hume's philosophy, gained him much fame among his contemporaries and won the approbation of Johnson, who seems to have had a high opinion of its critical value [2].

Beattie's reputation as a critic is founded on one of the essays that accompanied the new edition of his *Essay on Truth* in 1776, entitled: *On Poetry and Music as they affect the Mind*, and on the *Dissertations Moral and Critical*, published in the year 1783. Of these latter essays it is especially the second, *On Memory and Imagination* that belongs to literary criticism. It was warmly commended by Cowper, who in a letter to his friend and biographer Hayley, spoke of Beattie as the only author 'whose critical and philosophical researches are diversified and embellished by a poetical imagination, that makes even the driest subject, and the leanest, a feast for epicures' [3].

On the whole the author does not give evidence of great originality. His remarks are the usual stock-in-trade of the lenient neo-classical critic. The rules are interpreted with a certain latitude, but an open rejection of them, such as we meet with in other rationalistic writers, is nowhere to be found. In discussing the influence of science on aesthetic theory it has already been observed that Beattie divides these rules into two groups, those which are *essential,* because they are necessary to the accomplishment of the

---

[1] Tovey, *The Letters of Thomas Gray,* III, pp. 305 ff.
[2] Boswell, V, p. 274.
[3] April 5, 1784. (*Works,* ed. Southey. London 1854, III, p. 98).

end the artist has in view, and those that are *ornamental* or
mechanical, as being merely based on the practice of one or more
great artists whose works have become established models for
imitators. Only the former category can be investigated on the
principles of 'Reason and Philosophy'. As the critic tells us, some
of his friends had pleaded against him that Aristotle's *Poetics*, being
founded on the practice of Sophocles and Homer, for that reason
could not be applied to poetry of other nations and other ages.
This point of view is accepted by Beattie only to a degree, namely
in so far as the rules are local and temporary. The *essential* rules,
however, having their foundation in nature, which he considers as
an immutable criterion, ought not to be violated. It is therefore
absurd to excuse the transgression of such indispensable laws by
a disbelief in Aristotle. The influence of the scientific cast of
thought becomes evident when Beattie compares this method to that
of a mechanic who wants to construct an engine on principles
inconsistent with the laws of motion and who excuses himself by
rejecting the authority of Sir Isaac Newton [1]. In his *Dissertations
Moral and Critical* he grants that even the greatest genius is
to a certain extent influenced by the manners of his age and
is consequently determined by outward circumstances. For this
statement of the historical conception Beattie avows his indebtedness
to Thomas Blackwell, under whom he had studied Greek in Aber-
deen. Blackwell is one of the critics who had, long before the
Wartons and Hurd, embraced the historical method of criticism,
and applied it consistently to the works of Homer.

Beattie's conception of the poet's art is scarcely less intellectual
than that of Johnson or Kames. In spite of 'its apparent
licentiousness', he holds that poetry is 'a thing perfectly rational and
regular' [2]. Fiction is only permissible in poetry if it accords with
received opinions. Probability, not possibility, is the standard of all
poetical invention. He warns his readers against the notion that
reason should be a quality of minor importance for the poet and that
genius should be nothing but 'a certain warmth of fancy or

---

[1] J. Beattie, *Essays*, 1776, I, p. 350.
[2] *Ibid.*, p. 350.

enthusiasm of mind', which has no need of judgment to direct its course. The truth of the Horatian maxim that good sense is the source of all good writing, has in the critic's opinion been sufficiently proved by many illustrious examples from literary history: '*Arts and sciences* [1] owe their improvement, and genius its most illustrious displays, not to monks, and hermits, and half-witted enthusiasts, but to such men as Homer, Socrates, Xenophon, Sophocles, Demosthenes, Cicero, Caesar, Bacon, Shakespeare, Milton, Clarendon, Addison, Lyttelton, men who .... gave proof of the soundest judgment, as well as of a most comprehensive mind' [2].

In the fourth chapter of the same essay Beattie considers the question of *Taste and its Improvement*, and here the influence of Gerard is distinctly traceable. He enumerates the different elements that constitute that complex critical quality. The first requisite for a person of taste is 'a lively and correct imagination', the others are 'the power of distinct apprehension', 'the capacity of being easily and agreeably affected', 'sympathy or sensibility of heart', and last of all 'judgment or good sense'. Beattie looks on the last as by far the most important ingredient and thinks that it 'may not improperly be said to comprehend all the rest'. A few pages further on he gives a definition of what he understands by judgment and what he considers as its main functions. It strongly smacks of Johnson's conceptions. He calls it 'such a constitution of mind as disposes a man to attend to the reality of things, and qualifies him for knowing and discovering the truth'. It enables the critic to compare the imitation with the natural object and to trace the points of resemblance and difference [3]. Now the violation of an essential rule discovers want of sense in an author and consequently want of taste, '*for where sense is not, taste cannot be*' [4]. On the other hand a departure from an ornamental rule is consistent with sound judgment [5].

---

[1] My italics.
[2] J. Beattie, *Dissertations Moral and Critical*, 1783, p. 148.
[3] *Ibid.,* p. 182.
[4] My italics.
[5] Beattie supports this statement by quoting Pope's lines:
    Great wits sometimes may gloriously offend,
    And rise to faults true Critics dare not mend.
                    (*Essay on Crit.* ll. 159, 160).

Among the essential rules he classes the probability of fictitious events, decorum in the characterization, a faithful description of natural objects, a perspicuous style, the unity of design, and a moral tendency. The second group comprises among others the Horatian precept on the division of a tragedy into five acts and the unities of time and place.

PART IV

The Revolt against the Supremacy of Reason

CHAPTER XIX

INTRODUCTION. JOSEPH WARTON

Hitherto I have almost exclusively dealt with one of the two antagonistic forces that were fighting for supremacy in the latter half of the eighteenth century. The critics that have been discussed, fully acknowledged the superiority of reason, and I have tried to show that this rationalistic outlook on literary art survived up to the last decades of the period. There was, however, an undertone of dissent, which was gradually increasing in force. Emotion, which had long been repressed, and had grown strong behind the bars of reason, at last broke through the restraints, and reasserted its powerful sway.

From the beginning of the Georgian Era there had been symptoms that the rational system of theology, which accepted no guide but common sense in the solution of religious problems, had begun to lose its hold. It could no longer satisfy the emotional craving, the vague religious instincts that were felt by the great mass of the English people. For a time the 'enthusiast' William Law was the only divine to raise his voice against the cold intellectualism of his day; his *Serious Call* forms an important landmark in the history of religious thought. Among its admirers was John Wesley. Though he was repelled by Law's mysticism, he was no less firmly convinced of the impotence of the rational faculty; his stern teaching appealed to the believer's heart rather than to his intellect. Wesleyanism and Evangelicalism were the two chief movements in which the resurgence of religious emotion found its outlet.

A strong wave of emotionalism began to sweep through imaginative literature. Dissatisfaction with the conventionalities of the Augustan school gave rise to the renascence of sentiment which affected both prose and poetry. Sentiment, often degenerating into morbidity, is the characteristic feature of Richardson's novels, sentiment of a subtler and strongly individual kind is exemplified in Sterne's *Tristram Shandy* and *A Sentimental Journey*. The reaction was strengthened from abroad by the influence of Rousseau, the greatest of all sentimentalists, whose philosophy profoundly affected English thought in the latter half of the century. He subordinated judgment to sensibility and thus stimulated the revolt of passion against reason. The poets, too, began to free themselves from rationalistic trammels. Blair's *Grave*, Young's *Night Thoughts* and Gray's *Elegy* exemplify the resurrection of the spirit of melancholy, of gloomy meditation and despair which had been characteristic of Puritan England and had never completely died out, not even immediately after the Restoration. The Ossianic poems took England — and not only England — by storm. They were widely read and enthralled their readers by their atmosphere of gloom, their mysterious beauty and their wild, 'sublime' scenery. The Age of Johnson is characterized by a growing interest in a sort of poetry that was unclassical in form and subject matter, in 'poetry of nature' like the ballad, Hebrew poetry, and the poems of old Norse and Welsh bards, all of which formed a striking contrast with the 'artificial' poetry of more civilized ages. The old national vigour returned, the renewed study of the Elizabethans tended to restore to poetry the lyric impulse and the old unchecked spontaneity.

It is only natural that this stream of emotional fervour should have influenced criticism and should have led to the development of a new critical outlook.

The leaders of the attack on the stronghold of reason were the two brothers Joseph and Thomas Warton. Their father, Thomas Warton senior, Professor of Poetry at Oxford, was a fervent admirer of Milton, when the great merits of the Puritan poet were far from being generally recognized, and, if we may believe his son, drew Pope's attention to the beauties of the minor poems. His experiments in poetry showed traces of the romantic revival at a time when the Augustan ideals were still paramount. The enthusiasm for the older poets, for Chaucer and Spenser as well as for Milton, passed from the father to the sons.

The elder of the two, Joseph, published a volume of verse including *The Enthusiast, or the Lover of Nature,* in the year 1744; according to his biographer, the Rev. J. Wooll, it had been written four years earlier. It is an immature attempt to give expression to that love of nature and solitude to which both the Wartons remained true throughout their lives. It is full of conventional images and turgid diction, and destitute of genuine poetic feeling. From an historical point of view, however, it has much interest. Its very title is indicative of a new poetic ideal, of a reaction against the depreciation of enthusiasm. The theme of the poem is the conventional antithesis between nature and art. Pope's friend, William Kent, is praised for his bold attempts to imitate nature in landscape-gardening and for scorning formality and method. Warton's 'Enthusiast' prefers wild scenery ('some pine-topped precipice', 'a foamy stream', 'some black heath') to the formal style and cultivated beauty of Versailles. The same fondness for romantic effects in landscape-gardening had been expressed by earlier writers like Temple and Pope. What was new, however, was that Warton made a similar distinction in poetry:

> What are the lays of artful Addison
> Coldly correct, to Shakespeare's warblings wild?

These lines contain the first intimation of Warton's unorthodox views, of his disapproval of neo-classic elegance and polish and so foreshadow his attack on correctness in the *Essay on Pope.*

It was followed by the *Odes on various Subjects* (1746). The original intention had been to publish them together with those of William Collins, his schoolfellow at Winchester, but when the plan failed, they appeared separately. The 'Advertisement' which was prefixed to it contains an open avowal of Warton's dissatisfaction with the Augustan conception of poetry. He fears that some critics may think the odes 'too fanciful and descriptive', if measured by the prevailing standard. He is convinced, however, that the didactic tendency has been too obtrusive in the preceding age, and the *Odes* must therefore be considered as 'an attempt to bring back Poetry into its right channel'. There is moreover the important statement that he considers invention and imagination as the chief factors in artistic creation. The poems that were meant to bear out this theory have no great merit. They are devoid of the

genuine emotionial ring that characterized those of his friend
Collins, whose genius was so little appreciated by his contemporaries, even by the Wartons and Gray.

When he came back to England after his travels abroad with his
patron, the Duke of Bolton, he worked for a time on a new edition
of Virgil in Latin and English, which was published in four volumes
in the year 1753 and, according to Chalmers, 'raised him to a very
high reputation among scholars and critics' [1]. The translation of
the *Aeneid* was by Pitt, that of the *Eclogues* and *Georgics* by
Warton. To this edition he added a life of Virgil, and essays on
pastoral, didactic and epic poetry. The first was Johnson's
discussion of the subject in the *Rambler* [2], the two others were by
himself. The *Dissertation on the Nature and Conduct of the Aeneid*
avowedly follows Le Bossu's schedule and successively deals with
the fable, the characters, the sentiments, and the language. In the
Reflections on Didactic Poetry Warton stands up for emotion even
in this department of poetic art; he advises the poet to introduce
digressions of a pathetic nature. 'A stroke of passion is worth a
hundred of the most lively and glowing descriptions. Men love
to be moved much better than to be instructed' [3], he says, and
quotes a long passage from Du Bos's *Réflexions critiques sur la
poésie et sur la peinture,* where the French critic expresses a similar
opinion.

It is rather disappointing, however, after this plea for the
pathetic element in poetry, to find that Mark Akenside's *Pleasures
of the Imagination* is held up as one of the best examples of
didactic poetry and is lauded for 'its glowing and animated style',
'its noble spirit of poetical enthusiasm, which breathes thro' the
whole work' [4]. But Warton is not the only critic of that time who
bestows abundant praise on this long, very unimaginative poem
with its conventional display of emotion and inflated diction [5].

---

[1] Chalmers, *English Poets,* vol. 18.
[2] Warton says that of all the treatises, both of French and Italian critics, on
the pastoral kind of poetry he has never found any 'so rational, so judicious
and yet so new'.
[3] Vol. I, p. 400.
[4] P. 436.
[5] Cf. Cooper's *Letters concerning Taste,* 3rd ed. London 1757, p. 95; T. Twining,
Recreations and Studies of a Country Clergyman, p. 120.

Johnson asked Warton to contribute to the *Adventurer*, and in
the years 1753 and 1754 he wrote several essays, of which the
greater number deal with literary subjects. The forty-ninth [1]
contains the well-known attack on the French moralists and critics.
Warton censures the common practice among the critics of his day
of founding their opinion of Greek and Roman writers exclusively
on the dissertations of Rapin, Bouhours and others, without having
recourse to the classical writers themselves. Rapin is accused of
ignorance of the Greek language, and blamed for his vague critical
verdicts, Saint-Évremond for his florid and verbose style. Le Bossu
on the other hand is praised for the regularity of his plan and 'the
exactness of his method', and Brumoy for his judicious remarks on
Greek Tragedy. But however excellent these two commentators
may be, Warton thinks that they cannot give the student an
adequate knowledge of Aristotle and Sophocles: 'To contemplate
these exalted geniuses through such mediums, is like beholding the
orb of the sun, during an eclipse, in a vessel of water' [2].

In the sixty-third number Warton complains of the paucity of
original writers. His conception of originality is practically the
same as that of Boileau and Pope. The essence of art is imitation
of nature. All writers draw from a common source which
can only be diversified by differences in climate and custom.
Resemblances are therefore bound to occur. Passages are quoted
from Pope to show that a poet may improve what he borrows from
others [3].

The first volume of the *Essay on the Genius and Writings of
Pope* was published in the year 1756, five years after the poet's
fame had received additional support by the publication of
Warburton's bulky edition of his works. Though many of its most
important statements may be mere truisms in the eyes of the
modern reader, at the time when the *Essay* saw the light they must

---

[1]   April 24, 1753.
[2]   Ferguson, *The British Essayists*. London 1819, XXIV, p. 41.
[3]   *Ibid.*, p. 132.
    Joseph Warton contributed five other papers to the *Adventurer*, viz. two on
    The Tempest and three on *King Lear*, which call for no comment in this
    connection.

have had a startling novelty. In spite of its faults, which have been pointed out by many critics — its ponderousness, its unscholarly method, its many irrelevancies, its pedantic display of book-learning — it is undoubtedly one of the most remarkable critical documents of the Johnsonian Age. It is the first open declaration of war against the rational creed of the Augustan Age. The 'Advertisement' to the *Odes* had been an earlier indication that the tide was on the turn, but it was still characterized by an apologetic tone which is completely absent from the *Essay*. On the one hand it is a conscious effort to detract from Pope's fame, on the other an elaboration of the principles laid down in the 'Advertisement', a renewed statement that poetry is something other than moralizing and reasoned expression. The two are of course intimately connected: the exaltation of imagination and invention over reason and morality would necessarily lead to a lower estimate of Pope's poetical talents. The following is the gist of his dedication to the author of the *Night Thoughts:* 'I revere the memory of POPE, I respect and honour his abilities; but I do not think him at the head of his profession. In other words, in that species of poetry wherein Pope excelled, he is superior to all mankind: and I only say, that this species of poetry is not the most excellent one of the art' [1]. Warton then distinguishes between a 'MAN OF WIT, a MAN OF SENSE and a TRUE POET', and follows it up with the rather infelicitous remark that Donne and Swift 'were undoubtedly men of wit and men of sense' but that they have left no traces of pure poetry. He insists that the province of these two and that of the poet of true lineage should be carefully kept apart, and emphatically postulates 'that a clear head, and acute understanding are not sufficient, alone, to make a POET; that the most solid observations on human life, expressed with the utmost elegance and brevity, are MORALITY, and not POETRY; that the EPISTLES of Boileau in RHYME, are no more poetical, than the CHARACTERS of Bruyère in PROSE; and that it is a creative and glowing IMAGINATION, "acer spiritus ac vis" and that alone, that can stamp a writer with this exalted and very uncommon character, which so few possess, and of which

---

[1] P. IV. The references are to the fifth ed. in 2 vols., 1806.

so few can properly judge' [1]. The ascendancy of reason over imagination and emotion had so repeatedly been advocated that this sudden reversal of the relation between them must have struck the orthodox rationalistic critics of the day as an important deviation from the traditional creed. For the first time after a long and undisturbed reign of common sense the appeal to the emotions is pronounced to be the one supreme test of poetry, 'the sublime and the pathetic' its two chief nerves. Judged by this new standard of imagination and pathos, the kind of poetry in which Pope excelled cannot be called the highest manifestation of art. What Voltaire said of Boileau, is applied by Warton to the English Augustan: he is 'le poète de la raison'.

Of course the question recurs: What did Warton mean by the term 'imagination'? There is no reason to assume that his interpretation of the term would have been materially different from that of the contemporary philosophers, especially as his own poetry is characterized by conventional imagery and generalized diction. Yet his repeated insistence that Spenser, Shakespeare and especially Milton surpass all the later English poets by their bold flights of imagination, would make us believe that he was not merely thinking of the assembling and adorning of sense-impressions, to which the Augustan critics had restricted the operations of this faculty.

Warton falls into the same error as the neo-classic critics had done, when he ranks the different poets in four classes. The neo-classicists had judged every production of literary art by the uniform test of reason. Warton's test is as uniform, only his criteria are not reason and common sense, but emotion and imagination. A rigid application of these would of course lead to the same absurdities. The only three sublime and pathetic poets

---

[1] P. V. Chalmers in the *Life of Dr. Joseph Warton,* prefixed to his poetry, suggests that this passage was probably taken from Edward Philips's *Preface to Theatrum Poetarum.* Chalmers refers here to the following distinction which shows indeed a striking similarity to that in Warton's *Essay:* 'Wit, Ingenuity, and Learning in Verse, even Elegancy it self, though that comes neerest, are one thing, true Native *Poetry* is another; in which there is a certain Air and Spirit which perhaps the most Learned and judicious in other Arts do not perfectly apprehend, much less is it attainable by any Study or Industry;...' (Spingarn, *Crit. Essays,* II, p. 271).

that deserve to be put in the first class are in his opinion Spenser, Shakespeare and Milton. To the second belong those that excelled in the didactic kind and possessed true poetic genius, only in a lower degree, such as Dryden, Prior, Addison, Cowley, Waller, Garth, Fenton, Gay, Denham, Parnell, whereas he places in the third class 'the men of wit, of elegant taste and lively fancy in describing familiar life', like Butler, Swift, Rochester, Donne, Dorset, Oldham. The fourth class comprises the mere versifiers: Pitt, Sandys, Fairfax and others.

The idea of classifying authors into different groups according to their merits was not new, and had been rather common ever since French influence made itself felt in England. Several controversies among the French critics had turned upon the relative merits of different classical writers; Dryden in his *Discourse concerning the Original and Progress of Satire* followed their example in trying to determine the respective claims of Horace, Juvenal and Persius in the field of literary fame [1]. Goldsmith composed a very interesting *Poetical Scale* for the *Literary Magazine,* where the English poets from Chaucer onward are arranged according to their genius, judgment, learning and technical skill [2]. Warton himself speaks of a *Temple of Modern Fame* in the 'Musaeum' — by which he means *Dodsley's Museum* — where to his great dissatisfaction Milton was mentioned in the eighteenth place among the twenty great men of modern times [3]. In Volume II, no. 19 of the same periodical we find a *Balance of Poets,* where the ancient and modern writers are grouped alphabetically and are compared according to the various qualities that constitute poetic genius: Shakespeare and Ariosto are sadly lacking in 'critical ordinance', by which is probably meant methodical arrangement of poetic material. In 'taste' Shakespeare, unlike Milton, ranks far below the Augustans. But in 'pathetic ordinance' and 'dramatic expression' he and Homer are superior and according to the 'final estimate' excel all the other poets of ancient and modern times. Shakespeare,

---

[1] Ker, II, p. 69.
[2] Gibbs, IV, p. 418. (See supra, p. 171). Cf. also the *Considerations on the Similitude of Genius between Horace, Boileau and Pope* in the *British Magazine,* August, 1760, reprinted in Clark, *op. cit.,* pp. 462 ff.
[3] *Dodsley's Museum,* no. 13. The first number appeared 29 March, 1746.

Milton and Spenser are held in higher estimation than Boileau and Pope.

That Warton ranked Pope beneath the great Elizabethan is not surprising: he simply followed the neo-classic convention of considering the epic and the tragedy as the higher forms of poetic art. What was new, however, was that he measured them by a different standard. The doctrine of the *genres* was used for a new purpose: to emphasize the superiority of imagination and sentiment over reason and correctness.

Throughout the *Essay* Warton remains true to the principles stated in the *Dedication*. In one of the digressions from the main theme he deals with Milton's minor poems — references to the great Puritan poet are very numerous — and discusses at some length the *Ode on the Morning of Christ's Nativity,* which he praises as an early manifestation of that boundless imagination which was later to produce *Paradise Lost.* 'Shall I offend any rational admirer of *Pope*', the critic exclaims, 'by remarking that these juvenile descriptive poems of Milton, as well as his latin elegies, are of a strain far more exalted than any the former author can boast?' [1] Commenting on Pope's couplet:

> In Poets as true genius is but rare,
> True Taste as seldom is the Critic's share;

he distinguishes between the poetaster, the 'man of rhymes' and the genuine poet, 'the true MAKER or CREATOR' [2], who must be a man of 'a lively plastic imagination'.

In another passage Warton touches on Pope's early ambition to write an epic poem and expresses the opinion that he would never have succeeded. His didactic genius would have been unable to rise to the high level of the epopee, of which 'the sublime and the pathetic' are the distinguishing qualities. There would have been 'elegant' descriptions and well-drawn characters, but he would have failed to set before our eyes the reality of these objects and the actions of these characters: his 'close and constant reasoning

---

[1] *Op. cit.,* I, p. 38.
[2] *Ibid.,* p. 108.

had impaired and crushed the faculty of imagination' [1]. Instead of sharing the neo-classic conception that it was necessary for judgment to keep a restraining influence on the 'wild, vast and unbridled' quality of fancy, reason is here represented as the mortal enemy and suppressor of genuine poetic genius. Warton expects that the projected epic would rather have resembled Voltaire's *Henriade* than Homer's *Iliad* or even Tasso's *Gierusalemme Liberata*. 'The man', he proceeds, 'that is skilful in painting modern life, and the most secret foibles and follies of his contemporaries, is, THEREFORE disqualified for representing the ages of heroism, and that simple life, which alone epic poetry can gracefully describe'; Pope's composition 'would have shown more of the PHILOSOPHER than the POET' [2]. The latter part of this verdict is a restatement of a remark in his early satire *Ranelagh House,* where he had assigned Pope a place in the Elysian Fields among the philosophers, not among the poets.

Of all the compositions of the Augustan poet there are, according to Warton, only two that must be excepted from this general condemnatory judgment. They are of course those which have found most favour with the romantic critics in general: the *Epistle of Eloisa to Abelard* and the *Elegy to the Memory of an Unfortunate Lady.* They are called the only instances of Pope's mastery over the pathetic. At the end of the first volume of the *Essay* the critic expresses his belief that the poet's reputation with posterity will principally rest on these two poems and on *Windsor Forest* and the *Rape of the Lock,* though the two latter do not belong to the most poetic kinds. His other writings will soon be forgotten, for 'WIT and SATIRE are transitory and perishable, but NATURE and PASSION are eternal' [3].

The commentary on lines 536—537 of the *Essay on Criticism* contains an attack on the prevailing taste among the critics of the Restoration. Warton disagrees with the common opinion that this was the Augustan Age in England. 'What was called SHEER WIT, was alone studied and applauded. Rochester, it is said, had no idea that there could be a better poet than Cowley' [4]. The neglect

---

[1]   *Op. cit.,* pp. 275, 276.
[2]   P. 276.
[3]   P. 330.
[4]   P. 153.

of *Paradise Lost* is mentioned as a manifestation of the bad taste
of the period. The critic then inveighs against the scientific spirit
of the time and the institution of the Royal Society, which
turned the thoughts of men of genius to physical enquiries and
'obstructed . . . . the progress of philological learning, and of what
is called the belles lettres'. The attack on science is renewed at the
end of Section III, where Warton tries to account for the disparity
between the lofty flight which criticism had taken, and the
uninteresting, though faultless tragedies. He mentions as the two
probable causes the strict adherence to dictatorial laws and the
rationalistic bent of contemporary thought. The rigid regard paid to
the dictates of art tended to confine and weaken the natural powers,
whereas 'that philosophical, that geometrical and systematical spirit,
so much in vogue, which has spread itself from the sciences even
into polite literature, by consulting only REASON' has in Warton's
opinion 'diminished and destroyed SENTIMENT and made our poets
write from and to the HEAD, rather than the HEART'. Last of all,
the imitation and emulation of classic models led to affectation
and stiffness [1].

Pope's praise of his friend Walsh in the *Essay on Criticism*
prompted Warton's severe denunciation of correctness. He quotes
Walsh's advice to the Augustan poet to try and become a correct
writer and then adds the following remark: 'Correctness is a vague
term, frequently used without meaning and precision. It is perpe-
tually the nauseous cant of the French critics, and of their advocates
and pupils, that the English writers are generally *incorrect*. If
correctness implies an absence of petty faults, this perhaps may
be granted. If it means, that, because their tragedians have avoided
the irregularities of Shakespeare, and have observed a juster
oeconomy in their fables, therefore the Athalia, for instance, is
preferable to Lear, the notion is groundless and absurd'. Warton
then asserts the superior merit of *Paradise Lost* over Voltaire's
Henriade, however faultless the French poem may be. He thinks
moreover that some absurdities in the French tragedies are as inconsistent with this kind of writing as the fools or grave-diggers
of Shakespeare's plays [2]. Thus the reaction against the Augustan

---

[1]   P. 199.
[2]   Pp. 196, 197.

ideal takes the form of a direct attack on French critics and French literature.

The fifth Section contains a eulogy on Dante's *Inferno*, which Warton thinks the next composition to the *Iliad* as far as originality and sublimity are concerned, while the pathetic has never been carried to a greater length. On the other hand he severely censures Addison's *Cato*, which Voltaire had considered as a perfect model of dramatic art and had contrasted with the coarse productions of the barbarian Shakespeare. He blames it for the pompous declamation, which takes the place of genuine passion and pronounces it to be destitute of action and pathos, 'the two hinges .... on which a just tragedy ought necessarily to turn and without which it cannot subsist' [1].

This strong and repeated insistence on sentiment and enthusiasm in all departments of literary art, together with the severe strictures on the sacred idols of the common-sense poets and critics, stamp the appearance of Warton's essay as a remarkable landmark in the history of critical literature.

On the other hand, it would be wrong to represent its author as a thoroughgoing romanticist. There are several passages in his treatise which clearly show that he by no means rejects all belief in external rules; there is sufficient evidence to assume that at this early period of his career Warton is in many respects even more conservative than some of his rationalistic contemporaries, than Johnson and Kames for instance. His laudatory observations on Le Bossu have already been quoted. In the *Essay* there is moreover a staunch defence of Aristotle's precepts 'against the fashionable and nauseous petulance of several impertinent moderns' who had called their authority in question. After bestowing abundant praise on the Greek philosopher's other works, on his *Physics*, his *Morals*, his *Politics*, and his *Rhetoric*, and impugning the 'redundant and verbose systems' founded on Locke's *Essay concerning Human Understanding*, he expresses his high veneration for the *Poetics* as follows: 'To attempt to understand poetry without having diligently digested this treatise, would be as absurd and

---

[1]   P. 257.

impossible, as to pretend to a skill in geometry, without having studied Euclid' [1].

Warton's observations on Pope's couplet:

> Those RULES of old discovered, not devis'd,
> Are Nature still, but Nature methodiz'd; [2]

bear the mark of the same half-heartedness that we have met with in some of the devotees of reason. He neither absolutely denies their value for the modern poet, nor recommends a strict obedience to them: 'A petulant rejection, and an implicit veneration, of the rules of the ancient critics, are equally destructive of true taste'. He quotes Johnson's famous dictum on rules from the *Rambler* [3], 'this liberal and manly censure of critical bigotry', as Warton calls it, but adds that this rejection of external laws does not refer to those 'which nature and necessity dictate and demand to be observed'. Among this category he classes the Aristotelian injunctions that the action of the epic should be one, great and entire, that the hero should 'be eminently distinguished', that the episodes should rise naturally out of the main fable, and that the action should begin as near the catastrophe as possible. It is surprising, however, to read what Warton considers as essential requisites of the drama. They are 'that no more events be crowded together then can be justly supposed to happen during the time of representation, or to be transacted on one individual spot'. Here we have the unities of time and place in their narrowest sense! He moreover suggests that Johnson had included these among the group of 'fundamental and indispensable rules' which he had put over against those that were merely 'useful and convenient'. Surely Warton must have been a careless reader of the 156th number of the *Rambler* to have arrived at this conclusion. In a later passage he calls it one of the blemishes of Addison's *Cato* that the unity of time is not strictly maintained. The time of the action should not have exceeded that of the representation.

---

[1] P. 162.
[2] *Essay on Crit.,* ll. 88, 89.
[3] 'It ought to be the first endeavour of a writer to distinguish nature from custom; or that which is established because it is right, from that which is right only, because it is established'; etc. (*Rambler,* 156).

The group of 'frivolous and unimportant laws' that the critic deprecates, comprises the precept that an epic poem should consist of no fewer than twelve books, that in a tragedy only three personages should appear at the same time, and that it ought to consist of five acts [1].

It is only natural that the *Essay* caused great dissatisfaction among the admirers of Pope, and elicited some answers which were meant to defend the poet against his detractor [2]. Among these we may reckon the new edition of his works by Owen Ruffhead, a London lawyer (1769). It was accompanied by a *Life of the Author* and a *Critical Essay on his Writings and Genius*. Warburton, Pope's executor and staunch upholder of his fame, seems to have furnished the editor with the necessary material. Johnson passed the annihilating verdict that 'Ruffhead knows nothing of Pope or of poetry' [3], and Webb, the author of *Remarks on the Beauties of Poetry, Painting and Music* (1762), called it 'a very feeble attack'. The essay is not worthy of a detailed discussion. There are no new views; Ruffhead is a neo-classicist to the backbone and shows very little critical insight. Many of his commonplaces do not concern us here; there are some, however, that bear more specially on the subject in hand. On Warton's statement that some kinds of verse are morality, but not poetry, Ruffhead passes the trite remark that if they are 'embellished with beautiful figures, illustrating images, and the whole expressed in harmonious numbers; they cannot be denied a place, and perhaps a first place, among poetical compositions' [4]. To try if a composition is essentially poetic, Warton had applied the Horatian test of dropping the metre and transposing and inverting the order of the words to the opening

---

[1] Pp. 121, 122.
[2] Cf. supra, pp. 147 ff.
[3] J. Wooll, *Biographical Memoirs of the late Rev^d. Joseph Warton*. London, 1806, p. 35. The review in the *Gentleman's Magazine* originally ran as follows: 'Mr. Ruffhead says of fine passages that they are fine and of feeble passages that they are feeble; but recommending poetical beauty is like remarking the splendour of sunshine — to those who can see it is unnecessary; to those who are blind, absurd'. It was later on changed by Johnson into the passage quoted. Cf. *Gentleman's Magazine*, 1799, II, pp. 283, 388.
[4] Vol. V, p. 331.

lines of Pope's *Epistle of the Knowledge and Characters of Men*, and had compared the result with that of any ten lines from the *Iliad, Paradise Lost* or the *Aeneid*, if subjected to the same treatment. Ruffhead objects to this experiment, — and not without reason — because of the great difference in nature between a familiar epistle like Pope's and any of the great epics. 'Our poet had transgressed common sense and decorum, had he displayed all that *acer spiritus ac vis* of which our critic is so fond, on an epistle intended to represent the stile of familiar conversation.' The editor thinks, however, that the *Essay on Man* and the *Moral Essays* contain plenty of passages that 'breathe nothing but fire and sublimity' [1].

Ruffhead consciously misinterprets the words of his adversary, when he insinuates that, according to Warton, the true poet should write nothing but what bears the stamp of poetic fire and inspiration, and that he has inherited the sublime taste of Martinus Scriblerus, 'who required everything to be in the buskin or florid style'. How greatly the editor is influenced by the strong moralistic and rationalistic bent of his age, becomes apparent when he refuses to rank among the most excellent of its species such poetry as appeals exclusively to the imagination. For true poetry ought to have some moral or intellectual purpose, 'the pleasures of the imagination are more obvious, but they are not so refined as those of the understanding', they hold a middle space between 'the gross enjoyments of sense' and the more refined delights of the understanding [2]. This passage was probably inspired by Addison's papers on the *Pleasures of the Imagination* (*Spectator*, 411).

Warton had called 'the sublime and the pathetic' the two chief nerves of genuine poetry. Ruffhead's stricture that in these two kinds 'nature is generally represented in the *outré*' throws a curious light upon his conception of the word *nature*.

Sixteen years elapsed before Warton embarked on his second volume. Johnson attributed this delay to his not having been able to persuade the world to be of his opinion [3], and Chalmers suggests

---

[1]   Pp. 334, 335.
[2]   Pp. 340, 341.
[3]   Cf. J. Allison, Joseph Warton's Reply to Dr. Johnson's *Lives* (JEGP, XL, 1952).

that fear of or respect for Warburton was the cause of it. Three
years after the latter's death it was published. The 'Advertisement'
prefixed to the second volume contains an allusion to some of the
author's critics, who had misinterpreted his words and insinuated
that he had denied to Pope the name of a great poet, whereas his
intention had only been to show he was not the greatest, and to
oppose the view held by many contemporary critics that he was
superior to Milton.

In this second volume Warton stands up for the same ideals
as in the first, for enthusiasm and imagination. Instead of insisting
on 'the sublime and the pathetic', he now considers it the highest
duty of the poet 'to strike the imagination with what is Great,
Beautiful and New' [1]. Many of his earlier dicta are repeated here,
some of them in a milder form, which might be looked upon as a
partial revocation of his statements in the first volume. Spenser
and Milton are again highly commended for their transcendent
qualities. The former is admired for his rich imagery and boundless
fancy. 'Here all is in life and motion; here we behold the true
Poet or *Maker*, this is creation' [2], Warton exclaims, and proceeds
to distinguish two kinds of imitators of the great Elizabethan, those
who succeed in catching some of his ancient expressions without
possessing his spirit, and the genuine Spenserians. In the latter
category he ranks Thomson and Shenstone [3].

For a moment he seems to waver in his once accepted opinion
of Pope, when he quotes the well-known lines from the *Essay
on Man*: 'All are but parts of one stupendous whole', etc. 'Whilst
I am transcribing this exalted description of the omnipresence of
the Deity, I feel myself almost tempted to retract an assertion in
the beginning of this work, that there is nothing transcendently
sublime in Pope', he observes, but in the short summary with
which the second part of the essay winds up, he repeats his
objections. He recapitulates that 'the largest part of Pope's works

---

[1] Cf. Addison's papers on the *Pleasures of the Imagination*.
[2] P. 34.
[3] Cf. Johnson's criticism of Prior's *Ode to the Queen*: 'His imitation of Spenser,
which consists principally in *I ween,* and *I weet,* without exclusion of later
modes of speech, makes his poem neither ancient nor modern'. (*Lives*, II,
p. 204).

is of the *didactic, moral* and *satyric* kind; and consequently not of the most *poetic* species of poetry, and 'that good sense and judgment were his characteristic excellencies rather than *fancy* and *invention*'. The only difference is that he does not deny that Pope possessed the necessary constituents of a genuinely poetic nature; he only maintains that imagination was not his predominant talent and that he 'withheld and stifled whatever poetic enthusiasm he felt'. He cannot therefore be placed in the same rank with Spenser, Shakespeare and Milton, the three truly sublime and pathetic poets, but to him must be assigned the prominent position in the second rank, 'next to *Milton* and just above *Dryden*' [1].

In 1797 Warton's edition of Pope's works in nine volumes appeared. As has been repeatedly stated, the preface and notes contain very few new observations: the large majority of them are simply restatements of those in the *Essay* [2]. We find a repetition of the distinction between didactic, moral, and satiric poetry on the one hand, and the higher departments on the other. There is further the old tendency to dethrone reason and replace it by 'feeling', 'passion', 'temper', or similar ideas. Warton takes exception to Pope's line: 'Fools admire, but men of sense approve' and quotes from Dr. Aikin's *Letters from a Father to his Son*. Both critics reject the contrast expressed in this Popean maxim [3]. The opinion of Longinus, Pope's favourite critic, is cited to disqualify cool approbation [4]. In Vol. IV he endorses that of Hurd in his commentary on verse 214 of the *Epistle to Augustus*, where feeling

---

1   There are no instances pointing to a change in Warton's attitude towards neo-classic formalism; indeed, the subject is hardly touched on. The Italian critic Gravina is praised for founding his critical opinions on the principles of Aristotle or in other words 'on nature and good sense', the French critics are taunted with their inability to appreciate the 'bold and severe strokes of our irregular Shakespeare', and are termed 'effeminate judges'.

2   Cf. Miss E. J. Morley, *Joseph Warton: A Comparison of his Essay on the Genius and Writings of Pope, with his edition of Pope's Works*. [*Essays and Studies by Members of The English Association*, vol. IX].

3   Vol. I, p. 226. Cf. infra, p. 293.

4   When still a student at Oxford, Warton had already expressed his admiration of Longinus as follows: 'I shall read Longinus as long as I live; it is impossible not to catch fire and rapture from his glowing style . . . .' (Wooll, p. 9). In the *Essay* he praises his taste and sensibility but thinks his observations too general and his method too loose. (Vol. I, p. 177).

or sentiment is called not only the surest but the sole ultimate arbiter of works of genius [1].

Warton is never tired of blaming the Age of Pope for its shameful neglect of Milton's poetry, and his remarks in the first volume of Pope's works are even more explicit than those in the *Essay*. Again he attributes this undervaluation to an excessive respect for French critics. If the Augustans had only tried to understand Milton's genius instead of looking to France, 'they might have acquired a manner more correct and perfect than French authors could or can teach them. In short, unless correctness signify a freedom from little faults, without enquiring after the most essential beauties, it scarce appears on what foundation the French claim to that character is established'. This distinction between mere technical precision and correctness of artistic conception marks an important change in the use of this pseudo-classic term and foreshadows Macaulay's and De Quincey's observations in the following century [2].

The few references to 'the rules' that the nine volumes contain are all illustrative of a remarkable change in Warton's opinions, in particular in that on the unities. The conciliatory attitude of which the Essay bore evidence has been replaced by one of unconditional rejection. The critic is now completely in agreement with Johnson, and considers his refutation of the unities in the *Preface* as final. He praises Metastasio for proving that those of time and place were not always observed even by the Greek writers of tragedies.

His condemnation of French criticism, too, is much more thoroughgoing than in his earlier work. Excessive attention to it

---

1 See the article on Hurd, infra, p. 254.
2 Macaulay, Review of Moore's *Life of Byron;* De Quincey, *Alexander Pope,* (*De Quincey's Literary Criticism*. Oxford, 1909, p. 103). In a letter written by the great scholar T. Tyrwhitt to J. Warton (dated 22 Jan. 1782) to thank him for sending the second vol. of his *Essay,* there is another attack on the rage for correctness. I quote the following passage: '. . . . I am in hopes that your book may form a timely antidote to that poison, (sweet, sweet poison, and suited, I fear too well, to the age's tooth), with which we have been lately overflowed; under the shelter of your authority, one may perhaps venture to avow an opinion, that Poetry is not confined to riming couplets, and that its greatest powers are not displayed in prologues and epilogues.'

is looked upon by Warton as the main cause of the depraved taste among the Restoration poets and the neglect that Milton suffered at their hands. And in the note to Pope's *A Receipt to make an Epic Poem,* which was intended as a severe animadversion on Le Bossu, he at last openly renounces the latter critic's claim to the high authority he had so long enjoyed on epic poetry. 'After he has been so many years quoted, commended, and followed, by a long train of respectable disciples', Warton observes, 'he must at last be deserted and given up as a visionary and fantastical critic; especially for imagining among other vain and groundless conceits and refinements that Homer and Virgil first fixed on some one moral truth or axiom, and then added a fable or story, with suitable names and characters, proper to illustrate the truth so fixed upon' [1]. The passage forms a striking contrast to the appreciative comment on the French critic in one of the contributions to the *Adventurer* in 1753. More than forty years lie between the two judgments and these four decades had been detrimental to the reputation of the once so famous Le Bossu. His authority had already been rejected by Kames, and his precept that the writer of an epic poem has to choose his moral first, had been ridiculed by Blair, Hayley and Twining. Warton's words are like the deathbell rung by the departing century over the grave of the writer whose schedule had been the basis of criticism on the epic in England for more than a hundred years.

---

[1]   Vol. V, p. 267.

CHAPTER XX

THOMAS WARTON

Like his brother Joseph, Thomas Warton began his literary career as a poet. His early verses are for the greater part imitations of his two great Elizabethan idols, Spenser and Milton. Though devoid of true poetical feeling, they are interesting as historical documents, as they bear all the traces of incipient romanticism: love of nature, interest in 'the Gothic', and the devotion to solitude and gloom, which was the characteristic trait of 'the grave-yard school of poetry'. His long poem *The Pleasures of Melancholy* (1745) is full of Miltonic phrases and diction, *The Triumph of Isis* (1749), a reply to William Mason's *Isis: An Elegy*, which had appeared a year earlier, marks a relapse into the conventional measure and imagery of the neo-classicists. But most of his other contributions exemplify Warton's intention to strike out a new path, though at the same time they clearly illustrate his lack of creative genius.

The Observations on the Faerie Queene of Spenser (1754) primarily derives its importance from the strong impetus it gave to the revival of interest in mediaeval art. Warton tries to rescue chivalry from the censure of barbarism and extravagance to which it had so long been subjected, recommends the study of the romances, and points out their great importance for the student of ancient customs and manners. Last of all he draws attention to the wealth of material which the Age of Chivalry offers to the poet.

One of the merits of the book is that it marks a change in attitude towards Spenser's poetry. Warton's appreciation, unlike that of Augustan England, is not principally based on the poet's moral teaching. What attracts him in the *Faerie Queene* are the 'careless exuberance of a warm imagination and a strong sensibility' [1]; he does not lay stress on its ethical, but upon its emotional side. The essay is memorable as a strong plea for

---

[1] Second ed., 1762, vol. I, p. 15.

enthusiasm and imagination at a time when the main body of literature was still under the sway of reason. As his brother Joseph did two years later in the *Essay,* Thomas Warton elevated the emotional appeal over the old ideals of common sense and correctness. He, too, realized that mechanical finish was not the beginning and the end of art and defended Spenser against the common charge of irregularity. The poet did not live in 'an age of planning'; his exuberant fancy and his unbridled emotion were averse from restraint and could not subject themselves to the severe laws of epic arrangement. 'Exactness in his poem would have been like the cornice which a painter introduced in the grotto of Calypso. Spenser's beauties are like the flowers in Paradise' [1].

When Warton discusses the decay of allegorical poetry after Spenser, he sums up his main objections to Augustanism, expressing his regret that 'a poetry succeeded, in which imagination gave way to correctness, sublimity of description to delicacy of sentiment, and majestic imagery to conceit and epigram'. Then he continues: 'Poets began now to be more attentive to words, than to things and objects. The nicer beauties of happy expression were preferred to the daring strokes of great conception. Satire, that bane of the sublime, was imported from France. The muses were debauched at court, and polite life and familiar manners became their only themes' [2].

On the other hand, it is absurd to represent Warton's essay as an entirely new departure in English literary criticism, or as a document in which the critical outlook of the preceding generations was for the first time exposed [3]. Such a contention is untenable, for throughout the book there is evidence that the critic is hampered by pseudo-classic prejudices which are constantly at war with his romantic leanings. If we compare his criticism with that of his brother in the *Essay on Pope* we cannot but be struck by a remarkable difference in spirit, which is only partly explained by the nature of the subject. The deliberate aim of Joseph Warton was to detract from the reputation of a poet who had for many years been considered as an absolute law-giver in

---

[1] Vol. I, p. 16.

[2] Vol. II, p. 111.

[3] Cf. Miss Rinaker, *Thomas Warton* (University of Illinois Studies in Lang. and Lit., II), 1916, p. 58.

literary taste, whereas the *Observations* was a vindication of
an author whose essential characteristics had not been duly
appreciated. There is in the latter treatise much more compromising,
much less of the spirit of open revolt than in the former. There is
a strong remnant of Augustanism in Thomas Warton's attempt to
do justice to Spenser's epic in spite of the poet's transgression of
classical propriety. He thinks that the want of epic unity is amply
compensated by something that attracts the reader more powerfully,
'something, which engages the affections, the feelings of the heart,
rather than the cold approbation of the head'. As has been observed
before, this contrast between head and heart (*esprit et coeur*) was
a favourite antithesis with the more lenient neo-classic critics,
especially the members of the School of Taste, and was often
resorted to to soften down purely rationalistic dicta. Warton continues: 'If there be any poem whose graces please, because they
are situated beyond the reach of art and where the force and
faculties of creative imagination delight, because they are unassisted
and unrestrained by those of deliberate judgment, it is this' [1].
Here again he falls back on the thoroughly Augustan tenet of
'graces beyond the reach of art', so well-known from Pope's *Essay
on Criticism*.

The discussion of Spenser's plan in Section I is another proof
that Warton had not yet freed himself from the old shackles. In
spite of his assertion that Ariosto and Spenser should be tested
by another standard than that of the classics, he examines the
Faerie Queene according to the classical principle of unity, and
finds it wanting. All he can do is to account for this imperfection
by a reference to the predominant taste of Spenser's time, and
to draw the attention of the reader to the many beauties of the
poem that make up for this defect. It is the same kind of conciliatory criticism that the Augustans had so often applied to
Shakespeare. 'In regarding Spenser, if the critic is not satisfied,
yet the reader is transported', is the final verdict with which this
section closes.

In the brief summary at the end of the essay Warton again
admits that the imperfect construction is a serious drawback, and

---

[1]   I, p. 16.

that the nature of the poet's material did not justify such a glaring divergence from epic rules. 'It is true', he says, 'that his romantic materials claim great liberties; but no materials exclude order and perspicuity' [1]. In the critic's opinion Spenser's excellencies as well as Ariosto's would have appeared to much greater advantage, if the poets had taken care to observe classical propriety.

H. E. Cory has already pointed out that Warton follows Dryden [2] and Hughes [3] in his discussion of the unity of the *Faerie Queene*. He recognizes the unity of design in Spenser's choice of the hero, who is perfect in the virtues attributed to the knights of the several books, but regrets that Spenser neglected the unity of action, which was necessary to carry out his design. 'The poet ought to have made this "brave knight" the leading adventurer, (instead of merely lending his respective assistance to each of the twelve knights) .... At present he is only a subordinate character.... On the whole, the twelve knights do too much for ARTHUR to do anything' [4]. Warton does not agree with Dryden that 'magnanimity, which is the character of Prince Arthur, shines throughout the whole poem; and succours the rest, when they are in distress' [5], nor with Hughes that 'if we consider the First book as an Entire work of itself, we shall find it to be no irregular Contrivance' [6]. He thinks that the poet should have made each book an independent poem without any connection with the rest: 'The Poet might either have established TWELVE KNIGHTS without an ARTHUR, or an ARTHUR without TWELVE KNIGHTS.' Spenser's plan, as it is now, is called by Warton 'highly exceptionable': its faults can only be extenuated by comparing it with that of the much more irregular Ariosto, his master [7].

---

[1]   II, p. 268.
[2]   *Essay on Satire* (1693).
[3]   *The Works of Mr. Edmund Spenser in six Volumes with a Glossary* (1715), I, p. LVIII.
[4]   I, pp. 6, 7.
[5]   *Essay on Satire*, Ker, II, p. 28.
[6]   *Op. cit.*, I, p. LXVII.
[7]   Another eighteenth century editor of Spenser's poem defends the poet against the strictures made by Dryden and Hughes. He thinks that Spenser has carefully observed the unity of action. The fable has a *beginning*: the British Prince sees the F. Q. in a vision, *a middle*: he goes in search of her and has

The main reason why the *Observations* has been so highly praised
is that it contributed largely to the progress of the historical method
in criticism. 'It is absurd', Warton says, 'to think of judging
either Ariosto or Spenser by precepts which they did not attend
to. We who live in the days of writing by rule, are apt to try every
composition by those laws which we have been taught to think
the sole criterion of excellence. Critical taste is universally diffused,
and we require the same order and design which every modern
performance is expected to have, in poems where they never were
regarded or intended'. This passage has been termed the first clear
enunciation of the new way of approach, and the *Observations*
has for that reason been said to mark the beginning of a new
era in criticism [1]. This is of course not quite true. The historical
point of view had been repeatedly stated before the appearance of
this essay, and H. E. Cory has even drawn attention to Warton's
indebtedness for this dictum to Hughes [2]. What was new, however,
was not the statement itself, but the consistent application of it to
the subject in hand. Warton realized that the only method of
explaining Spenser's extravagant incidents and fantastic descriptions, which he had invented 'to engage the fancy', was to consider
the customs and manners of the age about which he wrote, of
which Spenser's poetry was the reflection. The Augustans had
weighed the manners of chivalry in the balance of reason and
had condemned them for their extravagance. It is against this un-
historical conception, this viewing with modern eyes, that Warton's
warning is mainly directed. 'We should endeavour to place ourselves in the writer's situation and circumstances. Hence we shall
become better enabled to discover, how his turn of thinking, and
manner of composing, were influenced by familiar appearances
and established objects, which are utterly different from those
with which we are at present surrounded' [3]. Warton censures the
previous critics of the poet for forgetting that the manners and

---

all sorts of adventures, *an end*: he finds her whom he sought. (John Upton:
Spenser's Faerie Queene, A new Ed. with a Glossary. London, 1758, vol. I,
p. XXI).
[1]   See Miss Rinaker, *Thomas Warton*, p. 58.
[2]   *The Critics of Edmund Spenser*, p. 147.
[3]   II, pp. 87, 88.

customs he depicted really existed in his time, and that the great interest taken in the achievements of chivalry induced him to choose this subject for his epic. Spenser is therefore represented as a realist as well as Homer; the disparity between Spenserian and Homeric manners is ascribed to the difference in historical background [1].

In the same way Warton explains the allegorical character of Spenser's poetry. Allegory was an important element of public shows in Spenser's time, and the poet merely painted what he saw around him. To elucidate many other features of the *Faerie Queene* the critic has traced the influence of Spenser's reading; he has searched contemporary writers and examined the books 'on which the peculiarities of his style, taste and composition are confessedly founded' [2], while several passages are adduced to illustrate his borrowings from old romances, from Ariosto and Chaucer.

The *Observations* was very favourably received by the rationalistic critics. Johnson's letter to Warton, quoted by Boswell, lays great stress on the new method and contrasts it with that which the critics of Spenser before him had followed [3]. 'Of this method', he says, 'Hughes and men much greater than Hughes, seem never to have thought'. There is no reason to assume that this new way of illustrating older writers was not appreciated by the Doctor. He had defended Shakespeare's use of the witches in Macbeth on the ground that it is impossible for a critic to form a true estimate of a writer without considering 'the genius of his age and the opinions of his contemporaries' [4], a statement which he was to repeat in the *Proposals* (1756) [5] and the *Preface* (1765) [6]. Warton's method of procedure must therefore have fallen in with

---

[1] Warton confirms Gray's criticism of Spenser's poetry: 'Truth severe, by fairy fiction drest' (Cf. Rymer's view). In the second edition (1762) Warton opposes Hume, who had praised the Greek poet for his picture of natural manners and had blamed the author of the *Faerie Queene* for drawing 'the affectations and conceits and fopperies of chivalry'. The passage referred to is to be found in Hume's *History of England under the House of Tudor,* 1759, vol. II, p. 739.

[2] II, p. 264.

[3] Boswell, I, p. 270.

[4] *Observations on Macbeth* (1745). See p. 126, supra.

[5] Raleigh, *Johnson on Shakespeare,* p. 4.

[6] *Ibid.,* pp. 30, 31.

his views and there is no doubt that his commendatory notice was given ungrudgingly [1].

None of the other contemporary critics [2] discovered anything strikingly new in the essay, which perhaps more than anything else speaks for the strong admixture of the old leaven. Its spirit was by no means so revolutionary as has often been imagined.

Something has already been said about the important service Warton's *History of English Poetry* did to the cause of English literature. It professed to be an investigation of the progress of art 'from a rude origin and obscure beginnings, to its perfection in a polished age'. As such it showed the indebtedness of modern literature to its earlier stages of development and helped to remove the neo-classic notion that poetry before Waller deserved no serious attention.

The purpose of the book is therefore mainly historical and not critical, but nevertheless it abounds in passages illustrating the author's critical opinions. Emotion and imagination are repeatedly represented as the indispensable requisites of poetry, and reason and correctness as the suppressors of genuinely poetic feeling. The first volume (1774) furnishes ample evidence of Warton's admiration for Chaucer. He discusses this poet's period at great length, and it is with reluctance that he leaves it behind and passes on to the literature of the barren age [3]. The *Knight's Tale* is praised for striking the fancy of the reader and interesting the heart by pathetic situations. Pope's 'correct' imitation of Chaucer's *House of Fame* finds no mercy in the critic's eyes. He thinks that the

---

[1] The references to Johnson are all equally reverential. One of Warton's dicta was probably inspired by a passage in the *Rambler*. On one of the last pages of the *Observations* the author expresses his conviction 'that nothing is more absurd or useless than the panegyrical comments of those who criticise from the imagination rather than from the judgment, who exert their admiration instead of their reason, and discover more of enthusiasm than discernment'. (II, p. 263). Cf. Johnson's statement: 'criticism has sometimes permitted fancy to dictate the laws by which fancy ought to be restrained and fallacy to perplex the principles by which fallacy is to be detected' (*Rambler*, 156).

[2] Cf. Warburton's opinion, *Letters from a Late Eminent Prelate*, CLVII; Walpole's *Letters*, VII, p. 144; *Monthly Review*, vol. XI, pp. 112 ff.

[3] 'I consider Chaucer as a genial day in an English spring.... But winter returns with redoubled horrors' (Vol. II, p. 51).

extravagances of the original are essentials in such a poem and
that Pope, by leaving them out and replacing them by beauties
of another kind, spoilt its character: 'An attempt to unite order
and exactness of imagery with a subject formed on principles so
professedly romantic and anomalous, is like giving Corinthian
pillars to a Gothic palace' [1].

His observations on the *Not-browne Mayde* in Vol. III (1781)
afford a striking contrast to Johnson's depreciatory verdict
in his *Life of Prior*. Warton realizes the difference between
the truly pathetic simplicity of the old ballad and the modern
adaptation, which had long been looked upon as an improvement.
He felt that Prior had 'misconceived and essentially marred the
poet's design', by making Henry talk in a manner inconsistent
with the rigour and reserve of the old ballad.

Warton shows a marked predilection for the Age of Gothic
romance. He thinks that the customs, institutions, traditions and
religious ceremonies of the Middle Ages were the true sources of
imaginative poetry and regrets that these essentially poetic elements
decayed at the Revival of Learning. 'Romantic poetry gave way
to the force of reason and inquiry; as its own inchanted palaces
and gardens instantaneously vanished, when the Christian champion
displayed the shield of truth and baffled the charm of the necro-
mancer'. In the following passage the critic deals with the detrimental influence which the study of the classics and the consequent
desire to emulate the ancient writers by imitating them, had on
poetic art: 'The study of the classics, together with a colder magic
and a tamer mythology, introduced method into composition: and
the universal ambition of rivalling those new patterns of excellence,
the faultless models of Greece and Rome, produced that bane of
invention, IMITATION' [2]. Like his brother, Thomas Warton sees
in the scientific spirit of the latter part of the seventeenth and
first half of the eighteenth century the mortal enemy of the higher
qualities of poetry. It advanced reason above imagination, perfection of form and refinement were ranked higher than original
genius. Warton grants that on the one hand this revolution brought

---

[1]   I, p. 396.
[2]   II, p. 463.

great gain: good sense, good taste, and good criticism. On the other hand, however, 'a set of manners' was lost, which were pre-eminently fit for poetic treatment. 'We have parted with extravagancies that are above propriety, with incredibilities that are more acceptable than truth, and with fictions that are more valuable than reality'.

The Elizabethan Age was, according to Warton, the golden age of English poetry. Reason had not yet entirely suppressed the extravagances of mediaeval art. 'It had suffered a few demons still to linger, which she chose to retain in her service under the guidance of poetry.' This 'civilized superstition', neither too much chastened by reason nor degenerating into absolutely fanciful chimeras, was the best generator of truly poetic imagery.

The third volume contains a defence of Tasso and Ariosto. During the reign of neo-classicism in England, the two great Italian poets had gradually lost the high reputation which they had enjoyed in the days of Spenser. Tasso's withstood the turning of the tide much longer than that of his more irregular compatriot. Davenant still considered the author of the *Gierusalemme Liberata* as 'the first of the Moderns', but would not give Ariosto a prominent place among them. Even Tasso was censured for his use of Christian machinery [1]. As has been said before, Rymer blamed Spenser for allowing himself to be misled by Ariosto 'with whom blindly rambling on *marvellous* Adventures, he makes no Conscience of *Probability*' [2], though the critic showed considerable appreciation of Tasso. The loss of the latter's fame was much furthered by Boileau's notorious judgment in the ninth satire, where he contrasted Virgil's gold and Tasso's tinsel [3]. This verdict was repeatedly echoed by English critics. The best-known attack on the two Italian writers is that by Addison in the fifth number of the *Spectator*, where Boileau's statement is quoted and commented upon. Addison's strictures are mainly directed against

---

[1]   Spingarn, *Crit. Essays,* II, pp. 4, 5.
[2]   *Ibid.,* p. 168.
[3]   Tous les jours, à la cour, un sot de qualité
      Peut juger de travers avec impunité,
      A Malherbe, à Racan préférer Théophile,
      Et le clinquant du Tasse à tout l'or de Virgile.
                                    Satire IX, 173—6.

'the florid form of words and such tedious circumlocutions as are
used by none but pedants in our own country'. Another champion
of correctness, the Earl of Shaftesbury, called them 'the Corrupters
of true Learning and Erudition' [1]. Mr. Clark in his *Boileau and
the French Classical Critics in England* (1925) has traced the revival
of interest in Italian poetry about the middle of the eighteenth
century, but, curiously enough, he does not say anything of the
attitude of Thomas Warton. In his *Observations* this critic had
compared Spenser's manner with that of Ariosto and denounced
the latter's irregularities. 'Spenser, amidst all his absurdities,
abounds with beautiful and sublime representations; while Ariosto's
strokes of true poetry bear no proportion to the sallies of merely
romantic imagination' [2]. Moreover, as has already been said,
Warton voices the truly neo-classic fear of a too great licence in
the use of fiction by making the Abbé du Bos's opinion on the
subject his own. There is evidence that Warton's views had
changed by the time the third volume of his *History* saw the
light. It contains an unreserved defence of the practice of the
Italians and a direct attack on the 'precise and servile critics' who
had condemned their poetry for its whimsical absurdities and
manifold deviations from the practice of Homer and Virgil. Blackwell, after eulogizing Homer's faithful pictures of nature, had
contrasted them with the excessive use of fiction in which Tasso
and Ariosto had indulged. 'Quitting life, they betook themselves
to aerial beings and Utopian characters and filled their works with
Charms and Visions, the modern Supplements of the Marvellous
and Sublime.' It is against this thoroughly rationalistic conception
of poetry that Warton's attack is mainly directed. He compares
the fanciful conceits of the Italians with those of Homer and Virgil
and finds them equally extravagant. 'The hippogrif of Ariosto may
be opposed to the harpies of Virgil. If leaves are turned into
ships in the Orlando, nymphs are transformed into ships in the
Eneid .... Nor am I convinced, that the imagery of Ismeno's
necromantic forest in the Gierusalemme Liberata .... is less
marvellous and sublime than the leap of Juno's horses in the
Iliad, celebrated by Longinus for its singular magnificence and

---

[1] *Op. cit.*, I, p. 335.
[2] *Ibid.*, p. 225.

dignity' [1]. The ancients are therefore pronounced by Warton to be no more 'correct' in the Augustan sense of the word than the great epic writers of the Renaissance; their works offer plenty of instances where the bounds of nature are transgressed.

Thomas Warton agrees with his brother Joseph in considering criticism and creative literature as two hostile forces [2]. He understands that an orthodox belief in pre-ordained canons will suppress individuality and exercise a restraining influence on poetic composition, and believes that the absence of critical treatises during the Elizabethan Age, as supposed by him, was one of the reasons for its unimpeded growth. 'Sentiments and images were not absolutely determined by the canons of composition: nor was genius awed by the consciousness of a future and final arraignment at the tribunal of taste .... The poet's appeal was chiefly to his own voluntary feelings, his own immediate and peculiar mode of conception' [3].

In his edition of Milton's minor poems (1785), praised by Masson as 'one of the best books of comment in the English language' [4], Warton follows the same method as he had adopted in his *Observations*. He adds copious notes to explain the poet's allusions, to illustrate his beauties and point out his imitations [5].

In the days of the Augustans the appreciation of these earlier works of the Puritan poet had sunk to a much lower ebb than that of *Paradise Lost,* and their popularity was still small, when the vogue of the epic was already at its height [6]. The reason is obvious;

---

[1]   III, p. 498.

[2]   Reynolds opposes this view at the end of Discourse VII: 'some of the greatest names of antiquity, and those who have most distinguished themselves in works of genius and imagination, were equally eminent for their critical skill — Plato, Aristotle, Cicero, and Horace; and among the moderns, Boileau, Corneille, Pope, and Dryden, are at least instances of genius not being destroyed by attention or subjection to rules and science'.

[3]   III, p. 499. That Warton in spite of this denunciation of authoritative laws, could not always free himself from them, is apparent from his comment on *Gorboduc,* where he observes that 'in the dramatic conduct of this tale, the unities of time and place are eminently and visibly violated: a defect which Shakespeare so frequently commits, but which he covers by the magic of his poetry'.

[4]   D. Masson, *Life and Times of John Milton,* III, p. 341.

[5]   P. XIX.

[6]   The subject is discussed in R. Havens: *The Influence of Milton on English Poetry.* Cambridge (Mass.), 1922, pp. 9 ff.

the Age of Reason was insensible to spontaneous flow of feeling
and *L'Allegro, Il Penseroso, Lydicas* and *Comus* naturally shared
the fate of all lyric poetry. Joseph Warton referred to the attitude
towards the minor poets in his *Essay on Pope*. The fact that the
Nativity Ode was very little known prompted the critic to give a
detailed description of it, which he did not think necessary for
L'Allegro and *Il Penseroso*. They were, according to him,
universally known, but 'by a strange fatality lay in a sort of
obscurity, the private enjoyment of a few curious readers, till they
were set to admirable music by Mr. Handel'[1].

Both Joseph and Thomas Warton were as fervent admirers of
Milton as their father had been before them, and several passages
in their works give utterance to their devotion. Both thought the
shameful neglect he had suffered at the hands of the preceding
generations an irrefutable proof of the bad taste that was then
prevalent. J. Warton's opinion of the Duke of Buckingham is an
instance in point; the coldness with which he speaks of Milton is
mentioned to illustrate his lack of critical discernment[2]. In Thomas
Warton's *Observations* there is the following remark on the taste
of the Restoration poets: 'The simple dignity of Milton was either
entirely neglected or mistaken for bombast and insipidity, by the
refined readers of a dissolute age, whose taste and morals were
equally vitiated'[3]. In the edition of Milton's earlier poems the
accusation is repeated. Only one critical document is excepted,
namely Edward Phillips's *Preface to Theatrum Poetarum*, which, in
Warton's opinion, contains criticism far above the taste of the period[4].

The shortcomings of the pseudo-classic writers are summed up
as follows: their fondness of wit and rhyme, their exclusive attention
to polish, to 'sparkling couplets and pointed periods', and their
undervaluation of fancy, picturesque descriptions and romantic
imagery. The renewed interest in Milton's poetry is considered
by Warton as the chief motive power in the revolt against reason
and the resurrection of imagination and sentiment. 'A visible
revolution succeeded in the general cast and character of the

---

[1] *Essay on Pope,* I, p. 38.
[2] *Ibid.,* p. 198.
[3] II, pp. 111, 112.
[4] P. 60.

national composition. Our versification contracted a new colouring, a new structure and phraseology, and the school of Milton rose in emulation of the school of Pope' [1].

Warton's estimate of *Lycidas* is symptomatic of the great change in critical outlook that had taken place since the publication of Johnson's *Lives,* and forms a striking contrast with Johnson's notorious strictures. This poem, in which, as Mark Pattison has put it, 'we have reached the high-water mark of English Poesy', had had to wait a long time before it was given the praise to which its merit entitled it [2]. As long as purely rational standards were applied, it was only natural that a poem like *Lycidas* should not be duly appreciated. Johnson had examined it by his standard of strong common sense, and had found it lacking in truth and nature.

In 1785, the year in which Warton's edition saw the light, a collection of *Critical Essays on some of the Poems of several English Poets* by John Scott of Amwell was published. Among these there is a rather long critical discussion of Milton's *Lycidas,* in the course of which Scott defends the poem against Johnson's disparaging judgment. He denies the justice of the statement that it is not an effusion of real grief; Milton did not want to express the sorrow immediately following the great loss, but rather 'a grief softened by time' [3]. Warton admits that the poem is deficient in genuine pathos and is full of conventionalities, he agrees with Johnson that 'passion plucks no berries from the myrtle and ivy, nor calls upon Arethuse and Mincius, nor tells of rough Satyrs with cloven heel' [4]. But at the same time he realizes that it should be judged by other criteria, that its merit should be determined by another test: 'In this piece there is perhaps more poetry than sorrow. But let us read it for its poetry'.

In a note, contributed by Joseph Warton [5], we find *Lycidas*

---

[1] P. X.

[2] R. Havens, *op. cit.,* p. 427.

[3] *Critical Essays on some of the Poems of several English Poets* by John Scott, Esq. *With an account of the Life and Writings of the Author,* by Mr. Hoole. London 1785.

[4] *Lives,* I, p. 163.

[5] The second edition also contains some observations of Bishop Warburton and Bishop Hurd which were sent to Warton by the latter of the two critics. They are distinguished by the initials W. and H.

represented as a touchstone of poetic taste: '.... perhaps it may be said, that He, who wishes to know whether he has a true taste for Poetry, or not, should consider whether he is highly delighted or not with the perusal of Milton's *Lycidas*' [1].

In his eulogy on *Comus* Warton once again denounces the bad taste of his time and its excessive dread of anything not reconcilable with the laws of reason. If Milton had lived in the critic's own age he would have avoided 'palpable absurdities' and 'monstrous conceits', but he would not have left us such delightful specimens of true poetry as this fantastic masque contains: 'In the present Age, correct and rational as it is, had *Comus* been written, we should not perhaps have had some of the greatest beauties of its wild and romantic imagery.'

Warton's firm conviction that common sense is an altogether incompetent judge of artistic merit, his repeated insistence that emotion and imagination are the primary factors in poetic creation, give him a right to an important place among the advocates of a new critical outlook. He has a special claim to our attention, because he did more than any of his contemporaries to further the literary interest in the past and to lead the eighteenth century reader back to the two great poets whose influence played an important part in the English Romantic Revival, Spenser and Milton.

---

[1]   Cf. R. D. Havens, *op. cit.*, p. 419.

CHAPTER XXI

IMITATION AND ORIGINALITY. GENIUS AND LEARNING.
EDWARD YOUNG

One of the symptoms of the wider outlook was a change in the attitude of the critics towards the doctrine of imitation. The humanists had made it their chief dogma; for two centuries it had dominated aesthetic theory and prevented a free development of poetic art. Professor Spingarn has given us a clear exposition of the way in which it affected the classical canon that art is imitation of nature, and of the different interpretations the Aristotelian maxim received in the successive stages through which classicism progressed from Vida to Boileau [1]. By the latter critic and his English disciple Pope, nature and the classics were considered as identical.

The Augustan critics misinterpreted Aristotle in two respects: they expected the poet to restrict his operations to the limited sphere of town life, and they advised him to copy the accepted masterpieces of antiquity. Their implicit belief in universal nature, in uniformity and immutability made them suspicious of anything that was not common property, so that any form of 'originality' consisting in personal thoughts and sentiments, was under suspicion. The classics formed a vast storehouse of universally human ideas and permanent truths from which any writer was allowed and was even advised to borrow. New thoughts and experiences were out of the question, the only thing the modern writer could do was to 'convert the substance or Riches of another Poet to his owne use' [2] and to represent 'the common sense of mankind in more strong, more beautiful, or more uncommon lights' [3]. No originality could therefore be expected in the choice of subject-matter, it was to be restricted to the treatment of old material, to the expression [4].

---

[1] *A Hist. of the Lit. Crit. of the Ren.*, pp. 132 ff.
[2] Ben Jonson, *op. cit.*, p. 25.
[3] Addison, *Spectator*, 253.
[4] Cf. Pope's letter to Walsh, July 2, 1706; 'I would beg your opinion, too, as to another point: it is how far the liberty of borrowing may extend? I

This is the view that continued to prevail in the first half of the century and even later. Gray, for example, was no less an imitator than Pope and was equally ready to acknowledge his indebtedness to his predecessors [1], and the critics of his time persisted in defending this practice [2]. The question of borrowing from older writers and the extent to which it was permissible is a problem that looms large in eighteenth century criticism. Mere plagiarism was strongly disapproved of, no imitation could be accepted if the writer did not succeed in adding something personal by showing old thoughts in a new light. 'Poets, like merchants, should repay with something of their own what they take from others; not like pirates, make prize of all they meet', Pope wrote to Walsh [3]. And much earlier Dryden had said: 'Without invention a painter is but a copier, and a poet but a plagiary of others. Both are allowed sometimes to copy, and translate; but, as our author (Walter Moyle) tells you, that is not the best part of their reputation. *Imitators are but a servile kind of cattle,* says the poet; or at best, the keepers of cattle for other men: they have nothing which is properly their own: that is a sufficient mortification for me, while I am translating Virgil' [4]. Virgil was generally considered to have been an imitator himself, a borrower from Homer, but, as Dryden puts it,

---

have defended it sometimes by saying that it seems not so much the perfection of sense to say things that had never been said before, as to express those best that have been said oftenest; ....'.

And Walsh's answer, July 20, 1706: 'The best of the modern poets in all languages are those that have the nearest copied the ancients. Indeed, in all the common subjects of poetry, the thoughts are so obvious, at least if they are natural, that whoever writes last must write things like what have been said before, but they may as well applaud the ancients for the arts of eating and drinking, and accuse the moderns of having stolen those inventions from them.' (*Works,* ed. Elwin and Courthope, VI, pp. 52, 53.)

[1] Cf. John Butt, *The Augustan Age.* London, 1950, p. 106.

[2] Cf. Warburton's comment on Young's *Conjectures*: '.... had he known that *original composition* consisted in the manner and not in the matter, he had wrote with common sense, and perhaps very dully under so unsufferable a burthen'. (*Letters from a Late Eminent Prelate to one of his Friends.* London, May 17th, 1759).

V. Knox expresses the traditional view: 'if novelty is necessary, it may be exhibited in the style, though not in the matter' (*op. cit.,* p. 241).

So does J. Warton in the *Adventurer* (89).

[3] *Works,* ed. Elwin and Courthope, VI, p. 52.

[4] Ker, II, pp. 138, 139.

'descriptions, figures, fables, and the rest, must be in all heroic poems; they are the common materials of poetry, furnished from the magazine of nature; every poet hath as much right to them, as every man hath to air or water' [1]. Dryden's opinion is re-echoed by later critics. 'Though Virgil copied Homer perhaps more than is generally imagined .... yet he copied him no farther than he found Homer and Nature to agree', says Robert Wood in *An Essay on the Original Genius and Writings of Homer* (1775) [2]. In the eyes of the neo-classicists the Roman poets, who borrowed from their Greek predecessors, had often excelled their models. Henry Felton, the author of *A Dissertation on Reading the Classics and Forming a Just Style* (1713), of which Professor R. S. Crane has given an analysis, even thinks that the Romans 'have been such happy Imitators that the Copies have proved more exact than the Originals' [3]. And John Douglas, who defended Milton against Lauder's charge of plagiarism, observes: 'There may be such a thing as an *original* Work without Invention, and a writer may be an Imitator of authors without *Plagiarism*' [4]. The idea that a great genius who occasionally borrows from older writers is much to be preferred to an inferior writer who does not, is attributable to Longinus, whose opinion is quoted by Douglas. Though Longinus was regarded as the champion of originality by critics like Young, Duff and others, he did not disapprove of every form of imitation. He advised the poet to try and recapture the spirit of the older writers and rejected imitation only if it degenerated into slavish copying [5]. This view was widely accepted by the neo-classicists who distinguished between the plagiarist and the imitator and

---

[1]   Ker, II, p. 198.
[2]   P. 28. Cf. J. Beattie, who does not deny that Virgil is an imitator, but thinks that 'his style and manners and the numbers of his verse are altogether his own'. (*Dissertations Moral and Critical*, p. 159.)
[3]   R. S. Crane, *Imitation of Spenser and Milton in the Early Eighteenth Century: A New Document* (SP, XV, 1918).
[4]   John Douglas, *Milton vindicated from the Charge of Plagiarism, brought against him by Mr. Lauder*, etc. London, 1751, p. 7.
[5]   Longinus, XIII. The passage from Longinus is quoted bij Dryden in the *Preface to Troilus and Cressida* (Ker. I, p. 206). Dryden adds: 'Those great men, whom we propose to ourselves as patterns of our imitation, serve us as a torch, which is lifted up before us, to enlighten our passage, and often elevate our thoughts as high as the conception we have of our author's genius.'

insisted that an imitation should be an improvement on the original. Even J. Warton, who accused Pope of being deficient in 'invention', admitted that he was 'a most excellent *improver*, if no great original *inventor*' [1]. And orthodox critics like Ruffhead and Stockdale defended their idol against his detractors on the same grounds. 'There are few passages in Pope which our poet borrowed without improving them', Ruffhead says [2], and Stockdale compares him with Midas, who converted everything he touched into gold. Stockdale, too, draws a parallel between the plagiarist, 'a creature of a sordid spirit' and the imitator who mixes borrowed ideas 'with the effusions of his own imagination' [3]. Beattie contrasts Dryden, whose writings 'are stamped with originality, but are not always the better for that circumstance', with Pope, 'who is an imitator professedly and of choice; but to most of those whom he copied he is at least equal and to many of them superior' [4].

The practice of imitating older writers received a fresh impetus from the works of Spenser and Milton. The high reputation they enjoyed among the neo-classicists led to the conviction that these two English poets were equally proper models for imitation as the great masters of antiquity, as is evident from Felton's *Dissertation*. Thus the field of operation for imitators was considerably enlarged [5].

From the beginning of the humanistic movement, however, and throughout the period of pseudo-classicism, there were critics who did not put implicit faith in the imitation of the Greek and Roman writers and exalted the freedom of genius. Sidney allowed the poet, at least the non-dramatic poet, unlimited freedom of

---

[1] *Essay on Pope*, p. 298.

[2] *The Works of Alexander Pope,* vol. V, p. 31. Cf. p. 95: 'He invades authors like a Monarch; and what would be Theft in other Poets is only Victory in himself'.

[3] *Op. cit.,* p. 74.

[4] *Essays,* note to p. 358.

[5] Felton is a thoroughly conservative critic who believes in imitation, though he objects to servile copying. He reminds us of Longinus, when he observes: '*To imitate Horace* then, is to write as himself would have done upon the same Occasions, on which we propose him to Imitation. We must have the same Turn of Thought, the same Faculty of Expression, and in a word, the same Genius with himself' (SP, XV, p. 199). Cf. Longinus, XIV.

imagination. In his opinion he differed from all other men who made the works of nature the principal object of their study in 'freely ranging onely within the Zodiack of his owne wit'. Bacon, to whom the author of the *Conjectures* often refers and under the shadow of whose name he takes shelter, called poetry a part of learning 'extreamely licensed', except in its expression. In the middle of the century, Davenant in his *Preface to Gondibert* advocated originality and compared an imitator to him 'that sailes by others Mapps' and can never make a new discovery [1]. Saint-Évremond deprecated the practice of the modern poets who follow too closely in the track of the ancients [2]. The essay of his friend Sir William Temple *On Ancient and Modern Learning*, may be considered as the immediate forerunner of Young's *Conjectures*. One of Young's chief statements, namely that a too great awe for the classics may exercise a restraining influence on a writer's genius, finds a much earlier expression in Temple. 'Nay, 't is possible, men may lose rather than gain by them (viz. the Ancients)', he says, and then expresses his fear that 'learning' may weaken the poet's invention. He suggests that 'the weight and number of so many other mens thoughts and notions may suppress his own, or hinder the motion and agitation of them from which all Invention arises' [3].

Most of the seventeenth and eighteenth century critics accepted Horace's statement that genius is indispensable to the poet, but that it cannot do anything without the aid of art and learning [4]. '.... They each require | The aid of each and must as friends conspire', as Howes translates. Dryden contrasts natural endowments

---

[1] Spingarn, *Crit. Essays*, II, p. 7.
[2] 'C'est à une imitation servile et trop affectée qu'est due la disgrâce de tous nos poèmes', (*Oeuvres mêlées*, ed. cit., vol. II, p. 502).
[3] *Op. cit.*, p. 18.
[4] *AP*, 408 ff. Cf. Milton, who thought that 'a strong propensity of nature' was not sufficient to produce a great poem, it must be accompanied by 'labor and intent study' (*The Reason of Church Government*, Book II).
Cf. Bouhours: 'la nature ne fait pas toute seule un bel esprit. La plus heureuse naissance a besoin d'une bonne éducation' (*Le Bel Esprit*).
Cf. Shaftesbury: '.... No more can a Genius alone make *a Poet*; or good Parts *a Writer*, in any considerable kind. The Skill and Grace of Writing is founded, as our wise Poet tells us, in *Knowledg* and *good Sense*'. (*op. cit.* I, p. 193).

with 'acquired parts' and considers their importance for dramatic and epic art [1]. Johnson, Reynolds and others all endorse Horace's dictum. 'Genius is nothing more than knowing the use of tools; but there must be tools for it to use', Johnson is reported to have said [2]. He rejects the idea of 'unassisted genius' and 'natural sagacity' and believes that such gifts of providence may be more properly urged as sentiments to labour, than encouragement to negligence [3]. Reynolds even denies that the art of painting is accessible only to those that have a natural gift. He is probably thinking of Temple's *Essay* when he says that 'the mind, or genius, has been compared to a spark of fire, which is smothered by a heap of fuel, and prevented from blazing into a flame' [4]. He does not believe that there is any danger 'of the mind's being overburthened with knowledge', and compares 'these acquisitions' to 'a supply of living embers, which will contribute to strengthen the spark'.

In Temple's *Essay* we find the first intimation of the danger that excessive attention to learning may involve. The warning is repeated in Leonard Welsted's *Dissertation concerning the Perfection of the English Language, the State of Poetry*, etc. (1724). Welsted avows his indebtedness to Temple for his statement that *'the least Grain of Wit one is born with, is worth all the Improvements one can make afterwards by Study'*, to which he adds that a great part of what is called learning 'consists in such Things, as a Wise Man, to use Seneca's words, if he knew 'em, would labour to forget' [5]. But most critics consider genius as a divine gift or at least an inborn aptitude which should be carefully nourished and cultivated.

Like Dryden and Temple the critics of the Age of Johnson are of opinion that genius manifests itself chiefly in 'invention'. 'The highest praise of genius is original invention', says Johnson himself

---

[1] Ker, II, p. 43.
[2] D'Arblay, *Diary and Letters*. See Brown, *op. cit.*, p. 123.
[3] *Rambler*, 154.
[4] *Op. cit.*, pp. 76, 77. Cf. Temple's *Essay*, p. 18. Cf. *The Memoirs of The Life of Edward Gibbon*, p. 143: 'After his oracle Dr. Johnson, my friend Sir Joshua Reynolds denies all original genius, any natural propensity of the mind to one art or science rather than another'. Blake's marginal note runs: 'The man who says that Genius is not Born but Taught, is a Knave'.
[5] Durham, *Essays*, p. 391.

in his *Life of Milton* [1] and Goldsmith calls invention and enthusiasm its constituent elements [2]. Gerard, the author of *An Essay on Genius* (1774) thinks that 'genius is properly the faculty of invention: the degree of this faculty is always judged to be proportioned to the novelty, difficulty or dignity of the invention', and Gerard's opinion is considered as authoritative by the other members of the 'Common Sense School'. The question for the inquirers was: what mental powers qualify a man for invention, but, as V. Knox tells us: 'the noble distinction denominated genius has been the subject of much inquiry, though the results are very unsatisfactory'. Duff thinks invention chiefly depends on imagination and grandeur of sentiment. True genius is, according to him, characterized by 'Irregular Greatness, Wildness, and Enthusiasm of Imagination' [3]. Gerard, too, looks upon imagination as the chief source, 'for only imagination invents', but it cannot attain perfection unless it is combined with a 'sound and piercing judgment' [4]. It goes without saying that both critics take for granted that the imaginative faculty operates in accordance with the laws of association.

Professor Brandl has pointed out that the veneration for Shakespeare tended to lessen the belief in imitation [5]. However firmly the pseudo-classic critics were convinced that the Elizabethan dramatist was sadly deficient in dramatic propriety, none of them denied that his genius was superior to that of all other English writers. Ben Jonson, referring to his flagrant neglect of classical rules, pronounced him to be wanting in 'art' and this statement was echoed over and over again by the pseudo-classicists after him. It became a commonplace among them to call Shakespeare the representative of 'nature' [6], the learned Ben that of 'art'. Rowe

---

[1] *Lives*, III, p. 247.
[2] Gibbs, I, p. 352.
[3] *An Essay on Original Genius*, p. 152.
[4] *An Essay on Genius*, Part. I.
[5] *Jahrbuch der Deutschen Shakespeare-Gesellschaft*, vol. XXXIX, pp. 1 ff.
[6] Cf. Dryden: 'he was naturally learn'd; he needed not the spectacles of books to read Nature; he looked inwards, and found her there'. *(An Essay of Dramatic Poesy*, Ker, I, p. 78). Cf. Hooker, *Dennis*, II, pp. 428 ff.
  Cf. Pope: 'The poetry of Shakespeare was inspiration indeed; he is not so

expressed the general belief that strict attention to classical models would have been injurious to his genius. There were others, however, who were of opinion that a closer acquaintance with the ancients would have made him still greater than he was [1]. His originality was taken for granted by both groups of critics and so the increase of his fame naturally tended to lessen the belief in imitation.

In one of the *Spectators* Addison distinguishes between two kinds of geniuses, those who 'have excelled by the mere strength of natural parts, and without any assistance of art or learning' and 'those that have formed themselves by rules, and submitted the greatness of their natural talents to the corrections and restraints of art'. The critic believes that the latter kind are apt to 'cramp their own abilities too much by imitation', and adds that 'an imitation of the best authors is not to compare with a good original' [2].

L. Welsted regrets that so many English writers in the past and in his own time have been servile copiers. He calls imitation 'the Bane of Writing' and thinks that imitations differ from originals 'as Fruits brought to Maturity by artificial Fires, differ from those that are ripen'd by the natural Heat of the Sun, and the Indulgence of a Kindly Climate' [3].

Before Young wrote his essay, Johnson had championed the cause of originality in the *Rambler*: 'No man ever yet became great by imitation', he says in number 154. The author who hopes to win the veneration of mankind, must have invention. Borrowed sentiments can never secure him any lasting esteem. 'There are qualities in the products of nature yet undiscovered and combinations in the powers of art yet untried', he observes in a later

---

much an imitator as an instrument of Nature'; etc. (*Preface to the Works of Shakespeare,* ed. Elwin and Courthope, X, p. 534).

[1] Dennis. See D. N. Smith, *Eighteenth Century Essays on Shak.,* p. 26.

[2] *Spectator,* 160. The passage has already been quoted by Professor Brandl, who also refers to a similar one in Shaftesbury's *Characteristics,* where a distinction is made between 'the natural and simple genius of antiquity' and 'another . . . . which has its rise chiefly from the critical art itself, and from the more accurate inspection into the works of preceding masters'. (*op. cit.,* p. 4).

[3] Durham, *Essays,* pp. 377, 378. Cf. T. Warton's *History of English Poetry,* vol. III, where Warton says that the ambition of rivalling the models of Greece and Rome produced 'that bane of invention, *Imitation*'.

number, and calls it the duty of every writer to add something to the general stock of knowledge.

More than thirty years before the appearance of the *Conjectures on Original Composition*, Young had touched on the question of imitation in the *Preface to the Satires* (1728), where he owns his indebtedness to Juvenal, though he adds that he has tried to emulate rather than to imitate him. At the same time he blames Boileau for following Juvenal too closely. In his discourse *On Lyric Poetry* (1728) he again speaks about imitation. In the eyes of the neo-classicists the ode occupied a special place among the various poetic *genres*. It was considered to be the most emotional kind of poetry, characterized by sublimity of thought, elevated and fiery in spirit, abrupt and irregular in construction. It required a greater indulgence of emotion and imagination than the other *genres*. Young takes the traditional view, he thinks that the nature of the subject is incompatible with scrupulous exactness or, as he expresses it: 'That apparent order and connexion which gives form and life to some *compositions*, takes away the very soul of *this*. Fire, elevation, and select thought are indispensable' [1]. But, though the imagination should have a freer course, Young warns the writer of odes against excessive indulgence: 'Judgment, indeed, that masculine power of the mind, in ode, as in all compositions, should bear the principal sway'. Above all, like every work of genius, the ode should be characterized by originality, for 'originals only have true life, and differ as much from the best imitations, as men from the most animated pictures of them' [2]. Young therefore advises the poet to imitate the example of the ancient writers 'in the general *motives*, and fundamental *methods* of their working' rather than 'in the *works* themselves'. This advice is repeated in the preface to *Imperium Pelagi: A Naval Lyric* (1730). Young says that he has written the poem 'in Imitation of Pindar's Spirit', not by following one of Pindar's works closely, for the genius and spirit of great men like Pindar and Raphael 'must be collected from the *whole*' [3].

---

[1] *Conjectures*, ed. Miss E. Morley, p. 58.
[2] *Ibid.*, pp. 60, 61.
[3] *Ibid.*, p. 63.

These Longinian views of imitation and originality are elaborated in the *Conjectures on Original Composition,* written in the form of a letter, addressed to the Author of *Sir Charles Grandison* and composed, as the author says himself, for amusement and as a consolation in his old age. As I have pointed out, the subject was not so new as Young thought it to be, though it had never been discussed at such length and with so much enthusiasm. Young distinguishes two kinds of imitations, 'one of nature and one of authors'. He calls the first kind 'originals' and restricts the term 'imitation' to the latter. An original composition is the spontaneous production of genius, 'it grows, it is not made', whereas an imitation is the fruit of art and labour and is composed of material which is not the author's own. The number of originals is small, not because there are no new subjects to write upon, or because modern writers are lacking in productive power, but because classical models engross their attention so much that they are not conscious of their own capacities. Young is a great admirer of the classical poets, 'they afford the best nourishment for the understanding', but, as he says, 'let them nourish, not annihilate our own. When we read, let our imagination kindle at their charms; when we write, let our judgment shut them out of our thoughts'. Young's conception of imitation is that of Longinus: 'Imitate; but imitate not the *Composition,* but the *Man* .... The less we copy the renowned antients, we shall resemble them the more .... Let us build our Compositions with the spirit, and in the taste, of the antients; but not with their materials'. The modern poet should therefore not follow the beaten track but deviate as much as possible, for 'the more remote your path from the highway, the more reputable'. A too great respect for the ancients would prevent genius from having free scope [1].

Young compares learning, which is only an instrument and is 'a great lover of rules', with genius, 'the master workman', who has the power of achieving great things without the means that are generally considered indispensable. Like Temple and Welsted, he thinks learning is not essential and is most required where there is least genius. It is 'borrowed knowledge', whereas genius

---

[1] *Op. cit.,* pp. 10 ff.

is 'knowledge innate, and quite our own'. As examples of poets who had genius but lacked learning, Young mentions Shakespeare and Pindar, two stars of the first magnitude. He contrasts 'the well-accomplished scholar, and the divinely-inspired enthusiast; the *first* is, as the bright morning star; the *second*, as the rising sun'. A distinction is made between two species of genius: *adult* and *infantine*. The first, of which Shakespeare's is a good example, is wholly a gift of nature, the second, exemplified in Swift, must be educated and nursed by learning [1].

Young then deals with the effects of 'that meddling ape *Imitation*': it deprives the artist of the opportunity to surpass his predecessors, it destroys all mental individuality and thus interferes with nature's design to make us all originals, and, last of all, it 'makes us think little, and write much' [2]. Young does not believe that genius is rare; like Gray he is convinced that it is often not discovered. Many men are unaware of their own abilities and this is mainly due to the neglect of two golden rules: '1. *Know thyself*; 2ndly *Reverence thyself*' [3]. If these are carefully observed, the modern poet will no longer be inferior to the ancients. As the various departments of science are constantly progressing, so arts will also gradually advance to perfection.

Too great an admiration for older writers may prostrate the modern poet's creative powers. To illustrate this statement, Young compares Pope's translation of Homer with the original. 'What a fall is it from *Homer's* numbers, free as air, lofty and harmonious as the spheres, into childish shackles, and tinkling sounds!' Milton's genius should have warned Pope and dissuaded him from using rhyme, 'that *Gothic* dæmon, which modern poesy tasting, became mortal' [4]. By using the heroic couplet Pope murdered Homer's music. Pope was not only 'an avowed professor of imitation', but at the same time 'a zealous recommender of it'. Young is convinced that he would have succeeded better in an original work, for 'Imitation is inferiority confessed; emulation is superiority contested, or denied; imitation is servile, emulation generous; that

---

[1] *Op. cit.*, pp. 13 ff.
[2] *Ibid.*, p. 20.
[3] *Ibid.*, p. 24.
[4] *Ibid.*, pp. 26, 27.

fetters, this fires'. Pope would have obliged us much more than he did, if instead of giving us Homer he had followed his boyish ambition of writing an original epic [1].

Young thinks that England has excelled other countries in 'polite composition' as well as in science, and that it has had great originals like Bacon, Boyle, Newton, Shakespeare and Milton. He compares Shakespeare, the original writer, with Jonson, the imitator, and follows Temple when he says that the latter's learning diminished rather than increased his invention; 'he pulled down all antiquity on his head and buried himself under it' [2]. Shakespeare, however, was without learning: he drew only from two important sources: the book of nature and that of man. Dryden was without Shakespeare's genius, he was destitute of genuine feeling and showed lack of taste in writing tragedies in rhyme. On the other hand his *Ode* is an inimitable original. Young's *Conjectures* winds up with a eulogy on Addison, who had a warm, feeling heart, but unfortunately kept it too much under restraint when writing *Cato*. In spite of its many beauties, this tragedy is without any real pathos and shows much more of art than of nature. But Addison's 'sweet, elegant, Virgilian prose' will continue to be greatly appreciated. Yet Addison's name deserves immortality for another reason: 'His compositions are but a noble preface; the grand work is his death'. Of Addison's last hours and the heroic words spoken to 'a youth nearly related', Young gives a circumstantial account.

From this summary it will be clear that Young's views did not deviate materially from those of his contemporaries, so that Johnson's remark, quoted by Boswell, that 'he was surprized to find Young receive as novelties what he thought very common maxims' [3], was quite justified.

In the tenth chapter of *Rasselas*, which appeared in the same year as Young's *Conjectures*, Johnson repeated what he had said in the *Rambler*, and made Imlac, the poet, say that he soon learned to turn his attention to nature and life instead of following the poets of Persia and Arabia.

---

[1] *Op. cit.*, p. 30.
[2] *Ibid.*, p. 36.
[3] *Journal of a Tour to the Hebrides,* 1785. Thursday, 30th Sept.

Goldsmith, too, repeatedly expressed his dissatisfaction with the neo-classic doctrine of imitation. In the second chapter of *An Enquiry into the Present State of Polite Learning* he speaks about those writers who 'instead of aiming at being originals themselves, became imitators of that merit alone which was constantly proposed for their admiration. In exercises of this kind, the most stupid are generally most successful; for there is not in nature a more imitative animal than a dunce' [1]. In one of his contributions to *The Bee*, entitled *The Characteristics of Greatness*, Goldsmith complains of the common tendency among the writers of his time to follow the beaten track instead of striking out new paths [2]. True greatness, he thinks, can only be attained by originality. The reputation of a work of art is not determined by the number of its faults, but by the greatness of its beauties [3].

Neither Young, nor any of the other champions of originality threw any new light on the problem they discussed. They left it as far from solution as it had been before them. There is hardly any attempt to refute the argument of the neo-classicists that nature has always been and will always be the same, that 'whatever is very good sense, must have been common sense in all times'. Young vaguely suggests that originality can easily be attained by the bold excursions of the human mind 'in the vast void beyond real existence', where 'it can call forth shadowy beings, and unknown worlds, as numerous, as bright, and, perhaps, as lasting, as the stars'. That the imaginative faculty enables the poet to place the most common things in a new light, and that therefore the number of poetic subjects is unlimited, of this the critics hitherto discussed

---

[1] Gibbs, III, p. 475.

[2] *Ibid.*, II, pp. 374, 375.

[3] Cf. *The Vicar of Wakefield*, Chapter XV. Another plea for originality, an anonymous review in the *Critical Review* for Jan. 1760, is attributed to Goldsmith by Professor Crane (PQ, XIII, 1934). Cf. also the anonymous *An Essay on the New Species of Writing founded by Mr. Fielding with a word or two upon the Modern State of Criticism*. London, 1751, p. 33.
Some critics who advocated originality in the second half of the century were W. Duff, whose *An Essay on Original Genius* appeared in 1767, R. Lloyd in his poem *Shakespeare*, Launcelot Temple (J. Armstrong) in *Sketches or Essays on various Subjects*, London, 1758 and H. J. Pye in *A Commentary illustrating the Poetic of Aristotle*, London, 1792.

had no idea. A more truthful conception of originality was fostered when the doctrine of generalized nature began to lose its firm hold on the critics and a renewed interest began to be taken in individual thoughts and feelings and in minute discriminations. The Wartons, Hurd, and other critics expressed their dissatisfaction with general ideas and stereotyped diction and praised the use of particular images and detailed descriptions. The problem that confronted them was in how far the subject-matter of a poem could be transmuted in the poet's mind, and in their mania for collecting parallel passages they tried to ascertain in what cases coincidences in subject matter in different writers could be considered as proofs of plagiarism, and under what circumstances the critic was justified in taking resemblances and possible borrowings for thefts. More will be said of this, when I discuss Hurd's *A Discourse on Poetical Imitation* [1].

Young's total neglect of this side of the question, his ignorance of the fact that the poet does not represent objects as they are but, to use Hazlitt's words, 'as they are moulded by other thoughts and feelings', explains why so little attention was paid to his essay, at least in England.

---

[1] See also the concluding chapter of this study.

CHAPTER XXII

RICHARD HURD

Among the critics that showed a marked dissatisfaction with neo-classic principles, and may be considered as the heralds of a new critical theory, Bishop Hurd occupies a prominent position. The importance of his work has been greatly undervalued by the critics of the nineteenth century, and for this his priggishness and his abject servility towards his friend and benefactor Warburton will at least partly account. In his own age, however, Hurd's reputation as a critic was considerable. Gray, with whom he occasionally corresponded, and both the Warton brothers mentioned his name with great respect; so did Twining in his translation of Aristotle's *Treatise on Poetry,* and Vicesimus Knox called the bishop 'a critic whose genius and judgment keep pace with each other and illustrate every subject on which he treats' [1].

This fame among his contemporaries was chiefly due to the *Letters on Chivalry and Romance* (1762), but his earlier essays and his Commentary and Notes on Horace's *Epistolae ad Pisones et Augustum* are also mentioned with respect. A commendatory notice of Hurd's edition of the *Ars Poetica* is to be found in Gibbon's *Miscellaneous Works,* where the great historian praises the editor's learning and critical discernment, and expresses the opinion that he knows 'few writers more deserving of the great but prostituted name of critic' [2]. Hurd's main point at issue is that Horace's *Epistola ad Pisones* is not an unmethodical collection of criticisms on poetry in general, based on the doctrines of Aristotle, but that its subject is exclusively the state of the Roman drama [3].

The whole of the commentary and most of the notes fall outside the scope of this essay, as they merely contain explanations and illustrations of various Horatian dicta. In some of them, however, Hurd goes beyond the narrow bounds of his task and touches on more general questions of literary criticism. On the whole they

---

[1] *Essays, Moral and Literary,* II, p. 242.
[2] *Miscellaneous Works,* III.
[3] This view was disputed by G. Colman in the preface to his translation (1783).

bear evidence of that mild form of neo-classicism, which is so characteristic of this transitional period. As some scattered allusions to the works of the French critics show, Hurd does not believe in their narrow interpretations of classical canons [1]. Brumoy, the author of the *Théâtre des Grecs*, is called the only one of the French nation who saw through 'the foppery, or, as some affect to esteem it, the refinement of French manners' and his view of the Greek drama is pronounced to be based on the solid principles of 'nature and common sense' [2]. Hurd agrees with this 'sensible' French critic that Racine diminished the merits of his play *Iphigénie* by modelling it, not on the practice of Euripides, as he ought to have done, but on Aristotle's comment.

Like Brumoy, Hurd is a great admirer of the chorus in a classic drama and regrets that Racine's revival of it in *Athalie* and *Esther* and Milton's in *Samson Agonistes* have not found more imitators. He thinks it an indispensable element, as it tends to correct the judgment of those among the audience who are liable to mis-interpret the poet's intentions. The modern stage, by not possessing this element is, according to Hurd, 'but a very faint shadow of the old'. He praises his friend Mason for introducing the chorus in his two tragedies *Elfrida* and *Caractacus* [3].

Nature and common sense are Hurd's final criteria; they are higher authorities than classical canons. In a note to line 286, in which Horace recommends the use of domestic subjects for the drama, he observes that this precept was not followed by later dramatists, who generally reverted to the Greek practice. He calls Shakespeare the first great dramatist 'that broke through this bondage of classical superstition', and thinks that his want of

---

[1]   *Q. Horatii Flacci Epistolae ad Pisones et Augustum: with an English Commentary and Notes: to which are added Critical Dissertations by the Reverend Mr. Hurd*, 3 vols. London, 1776, I, pp. III, IV: '.... the world hath been nauseated with insipid lectures on *Aristotle* and *Phalereus;* whose solid sense hath been so attenuated and subtilized by the delicate operation of French criticism, as hath even gone some way towards bringing the *art* itself into disrepute'.

[2]   Note to *AP*, 127, *op. cit.*, I, p. 116. Cf. J. Warton's equally complimentary reference to Brumoy (*Essay on Pope*, p. 74). Brumoy's defence of the chorus for the modern drama occurs in the twenty-ninth chapter of his *Théâtre des Grecs*. Paris, 1730, I, pp. LXXVI ff.

[3]   See Mason, supra, pp. 158, 159.

learning and consequent freedom from prejudices had a beneficial
influence on his dramatic power. 'Thus uninfluenced by the weight
of early prepossession, he struck at once into the road of nature
and common sense' [1].

Acting up to his rationalistic principles, Hurd denounces anything
savouring of affectation and bombast, the tendency of some
dramatists to fill their plots with unnatural incidents, and the
introduction of violent scenes, which he calls a violation of 'the
laws of decency and common sense' [2].

The highly complimentary reference to Warburton in the
introduction to Hurd's edition of the *Ars Poetica* was returned
by the editor of Pope in a no less laudatory form in a note to the
Essay on Criticism (line 632) [3], and in the very first of the *Letters
from a Late Eminent Prelate,* addressed to Hurd, the notes are
called one of the most masterly pieces of criticism ever written.
Warburton suggested to his friend that he should write a comment
on the *Epistola ad Augustum* and sent him the manuscript notes
on Pope's imitation of the epistle 'to convince him how much a
comment on that piece of Horace is wanting'. It appeared in 1751.
The dedication contains an interesting sketch of the history of
criticism, marred by the adulatory encomium on the bishop of
Gloucester at the end. According to Hurd, two qualities are
necessary for the critic: a *philosophic spirit* which helps him to
trace the reasons of excellence in the various forms of literary
composition and *a strong imagination.* The latter is called 'the
parent of true taste', as it enables the critic to feel the full force
of his author's excellence and to impress a lively sense of it upon
others. Like Johnson and Kames he holds that the critic's statements
should be primarily founded on reason, and agrees with them that
by the unwearied application of the philosophic spirit, criticism
will acquire 'the soundness and solidity of science'.

The first stage of development through which criticism passed
was naturally characterized by a preponderance of the power of
fancy: criticism among the Greek Rhapsodists became identical
with admiration, in which true judgment had no share. The later

---

[1]   Note to l. 286, I, p. 245.
[2]   Note to l. 185, I, p. 127.
[3]   *The Works of Alexander Pope.* London 1751, I, p. 202.

Greek critics, who began to comment upon and praise the great
writers of their own nation, proceeded on different lines: 'The
researches grew severe, inquisitive and rational'. 'Scientific or
speculative criticism', as Hurd calls it, attained its utmost degree
of perfection in the writings of the great philosopher of antiquity,
Aristotle. But he thinks that this critic was merely going to the
other extreme; reason had to concede part of its power to fancy,
criticism 'wanted to be *relieved* and set off to the common eye by
the heightenings of eloquence', for the readers would not allow
themselves to be convinced if there was nothing to admire in the
works of the critical writers.

Longinus was the critic in whom the two necessary qualities
were happily combined. Unfortunately, however, he relapsed too
often into the manner of the Rhapsodists, and the many imitators
who sprang up everywhere at the revival of learning, were much
worse than their master; criticism degenerated into the 'most
unmeaning, frivolous, and disgustful jargon, that ever discredited
polite letters' [1]. From this state of decay it was at length saved
by Warburton; his editions of Pope and Shakepeare marked,
according to Hurd, an entirely new phase of criticism, in which
strictest rationality was illuminated by imagination. The happy
union of the two requisites, together with a perfect insight into
human nature, enabled the learned editor to add new lustre to the
art and advance it to its full glory.

Among the notes there are some that still betray the old neo-
classic prejudices; only here and there do we find traces of a new
critical trend. To the first group may be reckoned to belong the
disquisition on tragedy and comedy in his comment on line 169.
Hurd does not find fault with the mixing of tragic and comic
scenes in comedy, but thinks it a serious blemish in tragedy,
where 'the serious and solemn air must prevail throughout'. The
end of tragedy is to excite the stronger passions, and a mingling
of the two elements will break their even flow and consequently
lessen the effect. There is evidently an allusion to Johnson's defence
of tragi-comedy in the *Rambler* [2], when Hurd says: 'We are told

---

[1] *Op. cit.*, II, p. XIII.
[2] *Rambler*, 156.

that this is nature, which generally blends together the *ludicrous* and the *sublime*' [1]. He waives this objection, however, by observing that 'art is nature to advantage dress'd' and that the end of tragedy requires that comic scenes should not be introduced.

Of much more importance is the note on lines 210 ff., which reveals the influence of contemporary philosophy. Hurd agrees with Horace that feeling should be the test of poetic merit [2], and in the succeeding passage he openly rejects the pseudo-classic belief in reason and the rules: 'For the *pathos* in tragic, *humour* in comic, and the same holds of the *sublime* in the narrative, and of every other *species* of excellence in universal poetry, is the object not of *reason*, but *sentiment*; and can be estimated only from its *impression* on the mind, not by any speculative or general *rules*. Rules themselves are indeed nothing else but an appeal to *experience*; conclusions drawn from wide and general observation of the aptness and efficacy of certain *means* to produce those *impressions*. So that feeling or sentiment itself is not only the surest but the sole *ultimate* arbiter of works of genius' [3].

The appeal to the emotions is therefore considered by Hurd to be the one thing necessary, its effect is irresistible and instantaneous. '*Rules, art, decorum,* all fall before it. It goes directly to the *heart,* and gains all purposes at once' [4]. As an instance of a dramatic composition of great merit in spite of its transgression of essential rules, he adduces Corneille's *Cid.* It continued to enjoy great popularity even after Chapelain's severe strictures in the *Sentiments de l'Académie sur le Cid,* which Hurd calls 'one of the justest pieces of criticism in the French language'.

But, though Hurd grants that there are higher qualities than a faithful adherence to classical precepts, it does not follow that he thinks all rules worthless. He only holds that those which have hitherto been established are inadequate. He, too, like Johnson, Kames, and other contemporaries, insists on a new analysis to arrive at the establishment of some general principles to which the merits and demerits of literary works may be referred. Hurd would

---

[1] *Op. cit.,* II, p. 105.
[2] *Epistola ad Augustum,* ll. 210 ff.
[3] *Op. cit.,* II, p. 108.
[4] *Ibid.,* p. 116.

consider it the highest perfection of the art of criticism if all these rules were ultimately reducible to one common principle, but he fears that such a scientific perfection is difficult to attain. He has no doubt, however, that by the laborious attention of the critics to the invention of general rules it may at last be possible 'to direct the caprices of *taste* by the authority of rule, which we call *reason*' [1]. He examines the methods adopted by three of the most popular critics, Longinus, Bouhours and Addison, and comes to the conclusion that none of these could lead to satisfactory results. They all indulged too much in generalities. Instead of pointing to general beauties as they did, they ought to have found out the peculiar qualities and sentiments that occasioned them. Their manner of criticizing was, according to Hurd, unscientific. Scientific criticism would have attempted 'to lay open the more secret and hidden springs of that pleasure, which results from poetical composition' [2].

Hurd's opinion of Addison's critical talents is very much the same as Johnson's. He grants that his taste was 'elegant', but thinks that he wanted the 'vigour of understanding' and the philosophical spirit which Hurd considers as the first requisites of a critical writer.

He allows Addison's Milton papers the merit of having made an excellent poet popular, but for the rest he does not believe that they deserved the praise that was generally bestowed upon them. His plan lacked originality, as it was based on Aristotle and Le Bossu, and his own observations were too general to be of any value.

To the *Epistola ad Augustum* was appended a critical essay entitled *A Discourse on Poetical Imitation*. The two epistles were reprinted with additional critical appendices in 1753, 1766 and 1776. In 1753 Hurd added a second essay: *Dissertation on the Provinces of the Drama*. Another, *On the Marks of Imitation*, written in the form of a letter to Hurd's friend, William Mason, appeared in 1757, and a fourth, *A Dissertation on the Idea of Universal Poetry* followed in 1766, four years after the appearance of the *Letters on Chivalry and Romance*. In the 1776 edition of

---

[1]   II, p. 110.
[2]   II, p. 113.

Horace's two epistles in three volumes it precedes the other three essays, and that on the drama opens with the following remark: 'In the former Essay I gave an idea, or slight sketch, of *Universal Poetry*. In this, I attempt to deduce the laws of one of its kind, the Dramatic, under all its forms.' So *A Dissertation on the Idea of Universal Poetry* was apparently meant as an introduction to the other three essays. It contains some general conclusions on the art of poetry, which were meant to serve as preliminary remarks to more special disquisitions upon its various species. Hurd thinks that of these the dramatic kind has received an adequate treatment in Aristotle's *Poetics*, but not until all the others have been dealt with in a similar way, can it be said that a complete Art of Poetry has been written.

It is therefore advisable to deviate from the chronological order and examine first what Hurd has to say about poetry in general. As some of his remarks in his edition of Horace had already made clear, Hurd was a firm believer in the doctrine of the literary *genres* and in his dissertation on *Universal Poetry* he stands up for a rigid adherence to the laws of each particular kind. Far from considering them as arbitrary things, he believes that they have their foundation in *nature* and *reason* and that they cannot be multiplied or varied at pleasure. He strongly censures the practice of mixing elements fundamentally opposed to each other: 'true taste requires chaste, severe and simple pleasures; and true genius will only be concerned in administering such'. As he had said in the 'Notes on the Epistle to Augustus' criticism was to him 'a species of didactic writing, which *refers to general rules the virtues and faults of composition*'. In its most perfect form criticism should be capable of reducing any beauty and blemish to a certain class, and any class to one single principle. Hurd is convinced, however, that this degree of perfection has not yet been reached and that only the most general rules hitherto discovered will apply to any sort of poem. Like his contemporaries, Johnson, Reynolds, Hume and Burke, he recommends the empiric methods of scientific criticism; which will 'contribute to the *confirmation* of rules already established, or the *invention* of new ones' [1].

---

[1]   *Op. cit.,* p. 109.

The one universal principle that underlies poetry is that it is meant to afford pleasure, and in this respect it differs from all other kinds of literary composition, where pleasure is subordinate to use [1]. To explain the nature of poetic art and to distinguish it from other kinds of writing the critic cites the passage from Bacon's *Advancement of Learning* in which the Elizabethan philosopher dwells upon the perfect freedom that the poet enjoys. All other kinds of writing are under the control of *reason,* poetry only 'accommodates itself *to the desires of the mind* and doth not . . . . *buckle and bow the mind to the nature of things'* [2]. Hurd allows poetry an almost unlimited range and rejects all the limitations that had been imposed on it by the rigid pseudo-classicists. Its task is not to deal with the actual, with what is credibly true, its essential element is fiction [3]. Its purpose is not 'to reflect the real face of things, but to illustrate and adorn it; not to represent the fairest objects only, but to represent them in the fairest lights . . . . to *outstrip* nature, and to address itself to our wildest fancy, rather than to our judgement and cooler sense' [4]. The first part of this quotation might be interpreted as being a restatement of the Augustan conception of idealized nature, but it is apparent from what follows that Hurd's poetic world extends far beyond the narrow confines of actuality and verisimilitude. Hurd allots to the imagination the most important share in poetic creation and considers judgment as something secondary. He goes even much further than either of the Warton brothers, who were both convinced that poetic license should be used with moderation, and that ultimately fiction had to submit to rational truth. Hurd does not draw a line of demarcation between the credible and the incredible. 'Poetry' he says, 'peoples all creation with new and living forms; calls up infernal spectres to terrify, or brings down celestial natures to astonish, the imagination'. He then quotes the well-known passage from Shakespeare's *Midsummer Night's Dream* to support his statement that, poetry 'prefers not only the agreeable

---

[1] A similar opinion had already been expressed in the essay on the drama. (*Op. cit.,* II, p. 238).
[2] II, p. 136. For Bacon's words see supra, p. 43.
[3] The *style* is, as it were, the body of poetry; *fiction* is its soul. (II, p. 143).
[4] II, p. 141.

17

and the graceful, but, as occasion calls upon her, the vast, the incredible, I had almost said, the impossible, to the obvious truth and nature of things' [1].

There is the same longing for the world of romance that we have met with in the critical writings of the Wartons, the same conviction that mediaeval manners and religion acted as a strong stimulant on the poet's imagination and suited the extravagant turn of the human mind. Of all poetic forms he considers the pagan fable and Gothic romance as the most interesting.

The *Dissertation on the Provinces of the Drama* likewise owed its origin to the belief that is was necessary to distinguish the several species of dramatic art more rigorously than had been done by previous writers on the subject. Though he is aware that such essays will offer little assistance to the author, he thinks that they are not altogether useless; he believes with Fontenelle that they 'lead up *to the first principles of beauty* such persons as love reasoning, and are fond of reducing, under the controul of philosophy, subjects that appear the most independent of it, and which are generally thought abandoned to the caprice of taste' [2]. Most of Hurd's dicta are restatements of Aristotelian canons. His definition of tragedy as a dramatic representation whose end is to evoke the passions of pity and terror; the great stress he lays on the fable as its principal element, as opposed to that of comedy, which is character and not action; his assertion that the persons of a tragedy ought to be '*of principal rank and dignity*', whereas the characters of comedy should be taken from private life, are all based on the *Poetics*. So is Hurd's statement that the manners of the persons in a tragedy ought to be imperfect, since absolutely *good* as well as absolutely *bad* characters are out of place in this department of the drama [3].

In accordance with the practice of the Greek dramatists for which Hurd repeatedly expresses great deference, he insists that the action of a tragedy should be of sufficient importance to rouse the interest of the audience, and deprecates the common

---

[1] II, p. 142.
[2] *Op. cit.*, II, 247.
[3] Cf. Lessing's discussion of the dissertation in his *Hamburgische Dramaturgie*, zweiundneunzigstes Stück, etc.

practice of introducing the passion of love into modern tragedy. Shakespeare made it the subject of *Romeo and Juliet,* and it invaded nearly all the great tragedies of the French dramatists in the seventeenth century. The immense popularity it enjoyed across the Channel influenced the English drama after the Restoration, even to such a degree that one of the means to adapt Shakespeare's tragedies to the popular taste was the introduction of amorous scenes [1]. The staunch upholders of the classical doctrine had looked upon this preponderance of the love-element with great disfavour. Rapin had called it a sign of degeneracy in the modern drama and his translator and disciple Rymer had protested against it. Dennis had expressed his disagreement with these two critics in his *Remarks on Prince Arthur* [2]. Joseph Warton compared the Greek and the French drama; 'the greater passions' were the subject of the former, 'the tenderer passions' of the latter. He praised Racine's *Athalie* and Voltaire's plays because they were free from love-scenes, and quoted Shakespeare's *Macbeth* and *Lear* as examples of genuinely great tragedies [3]. Hurd's denunciation of love-subjects is based on similar grounds to Rapin's. They lack the dignity with which the tragic action should be invested. Only the rank of the characters is in keeping with its heroic nature. But the action, 'when stripped of its accidental ornaments and reduced to the essential fact', is nothing more than what might as well have passed in a cottage as in a king's palace. He recommends the method of the Greek poets, who always took as subjects events of the grandest kind.

Of the three unities, those of time and place are not discussed, from which we may infer that the unity of action is the only one that Hurd considers essential. On this his views are very strict. Not only does he reject a double plot, because it would divert and weaken 'the course of the *affections*' [4], but even 'a multiplicity

---

[1] See Lounsbury, *Shakespeare as a Dramatic Artist,* pp. 309 ff.

[2] Hooker, *op cit.,* I, pp. 129, 438. Cf. Corneille, *Premier Discours;* Boileau, *Art poétique,* III, ll. 93 ff.

[3] Voltaire did not condemn the love-element in tragedy. Cf. his *Discours sur la tragédie* (Vial et Denise, *Idées et doctrines littéraires du XVIIIe siècle,* p. 186): 'Vouloir de l'amour dans toutes les tragédies me paraît un gout efféminé; l'en proscrire toujours est une mauvaise humeur bien déraisonnable'.

[4] *Op. cit.,* II, p. 178. Cf. Kames, supra, p. 142.

of *subordinate events*, though tending to a common *end*; and of *persons*, though all of them, some way, concerned in promoting it'. His views are therefore even less latitudinarian than those of Dryden, which have already been quoted. Hurd calls the neglect of simplicity in the conduct of the fable one of the serious defects of the modern drama and agrees with Riccoboni, who in his *Histoire du théâtre italien* had contrasted the simple structure of the Greek drama with the intricate plots of the French dramatists. He admits that a good plot is not so essential to comedy as to tragedy [1]. Pathos in the latter kind of dramatic art can only be effected by the entire action and will be disturbed by a defective arrangement. Humour on the other hand is not 'the effect of the *whole*', it may be restricted to a few scenes of a comedy, so that this department of the drama does not require the same rigid exclusion of accessory events. But even the writer of comedy should be careful not to divert attention from the main theme by an immoderate use of underplots. The intricate plots of the Spanish romantic models and their French and English imitations [2] do not find favour in Hurd's eyes.

In spite of Hurd's great deference to Greek drama and the Aristotelian maxims he understands that it would be absurd to insist on a rigid conformity to classical models and precepts in modern plays. Since the nature of the Greek drama was determined by its origin, it follows that 'the practice of the ancient stage is then of no further authority than as it accords to just criticism' [3]. For the French weeping comedy, '*la comédie larmoyante*', Hurd considers the laws of the classical drama as invalid, because the classical poets have left no examples of this species of writing. Their merit should therefore be tried by other tests, namely 'the success of this new practice, compared with the general dictates of common sense'. In the passage that follows he even waives all authoritative claims of established canons, and agrees with Fontenelle that these precepts are often merely the result of established customs, 'for *rules* they will not deserve to be esteemed,

---

[1] Cf. again Kames, supra, p. 142.
[2] Cf. *Cambr. Hist. of E. L.*, VIII, 124 ff.
[3] *Op. cit.*, II, p. 208.

till they have undergone the rigid scrutiny of reason' [1]. One of these rational deductions is that no comic scenes should ever be introduced into tragedy, with which the ridiculous cannot be associated. Correct writers have therefore always abstained from mixing grave and pleasant scenes in this department of the drama, though in comedy it has often been done.

To sum up, Hurd's *Dissertation on the Provinces of the Drama* evinces hardly any traces of dissatisfaction with the neo-classic doctrine. Some of its canons are even accepted in their severest form. The author's absolute rejection of subordinate plots in a tragedy and his denunciation of tragi-comedy characterize him as a staunch opholder of the old creed. It is true that Hurd admits the necessity of reconsidering all accepted postulates, but with him this renewed analysis on rational lines does not lead, as it did with Johnson, to any conclusions that differ materially from the rules of the preceding generation of critics.

The last two essays deal with poetical imitation. They were probably prompted by the *Essay on Milton's Use and Imitation of the Moderns in his Paradise Lost* by W. Lauder (1750), in which the Puritan poet was accused of having borrowed his material from several modern writers, of whom Jacobus Masenius, professor of rhetoric and poetry at Cologne, was the most important. Milton was charged with having wilfully concealed his obligations 'notwithstanding his high pretensions to truth and integrity', so that the reading public had been deluded into the false opinion that he was an original writer. Warburton observed in a letter to Hurd, dated December 1749, that Lauder's book had again proved clearly how little the term 'imitation' was understood by contemporary critics and he heartily welcomed his friend's plan to discuss the subject in a note to his *Epistle to Augustus* [2]. Instead of a note Hurd

---

[1] *Ibid.*, p. 220. Fontenelle's words are: 'Toujours il me paraît certain que nous sommes en droit d'examiner si, en fait de théâtre, nous n'aurions pas quelquefois des *habitudes* au lieu de *règles;* car les règles ne peuvent l'être, qu'après avoir subi les rigueurs du tribunal de la raison'; ... (Vial et Denise, *Idées et doctrines littéraires du XVIIIe siècle*, p. 232).

[2] *Letters from a Late Eminent Prelate*, p. 24. Lauder's *Essay* is an expanded version of his articles in the *Gentleman's Magazine* for 1747. It appeared at the close of the year 1749, but is dated 1750.

composed a lengthy discourse, to which he added a dissertation, entitled *On the Marks of Imitation,* at the request of his friend William Mason [1].

The two essays voice the general opinion of the eighteenth century about this much discussed problem of poetics, a fact which explains why they found much more appreciation than Young's ardent plea for originality in his *Conjectures on Original Composition.* Hurd defends imitation, though at the same time he praises invention, 'which unquestionably holds the first place in the virtues of a poet'.His main purpose is to show how unreasonable it is to charge an author with plagiarism, if close parallels of certain images or sentiments in his works can be found in earlier writers. It is against the 'parallelists' — the word is Hurd's own — against their inveterate prejudice of taking all *resemblances* for *thefts* that his dissertation is directed. Originality in the sense they attach to it is hardly to be expected, as the objects of imitation and the materials of human knowledge have for the greater part been the same in all ages. It is therefore only in the *manner* of imitating, in the operation of the human mind on this material, that the invention of the poet can have full play. Hurd thinks, however, that conformity cannot always be considered as a sure proof that the writer has borrowed from others. Identity of phrase and diction can least of all be defended, though even here Hurd makes some restrictions. On the other hand he believes that imitations by a genuine poet need not be without merit; it may even be greater than that of the originals. Imitation does not exclude invention; the poet should always try to 'improve the *expression,* where it is defective, or barely passable: he must throw fresh light of fancy on a common *image*: he must strike out new

---

[1] This dissertation elicited an answer by E. Capell, the Shakespearean scholar. It is entitled *Reflections on Originality in Authors: being Remarks on a Letter to Mr. Mason on the Marks of Imitation* (London, 1766). Hurd had attempted to point out that coincidences of a certain kind prove that an author is an imitator. Capell believes that he went too far in his tracing of resemblances, and quotes two lines from Milton, which Newton had supposed to have been borrowed from Shakespeare, Warton from the *Cuckow* by Nichols, whereas he himself adduces a similar passage from Spenser. To make sure that a writer has borrowed from others, Capell thinks that historical evidence is necessary, and that mere coincidence of sentiment is an insufficient criterion.

hints from a vulgar *sentiment*' [1]. Hurd then proceeds to show that a strong desire to be original may often induce the poet to have recourse to forced conceits and affected expressions and points out that Davenant, an early champion of originality [2], has fallen into this error. He goes even much further and asserts that the chief cause of the degeneracy of taste in any country has always been and will always be 'this anxious dread of imitation in polite and cultivated writers'.

The *Discourse on Poetical Imitation* betrays the influence of empiric philosophy; to arrive at his conclusions Hurd follows the methods of Hume and Burke. When summarizing at the beginning of the second section, he says: 'The *objects* of imitation, like the *materials* of human knowledge, are a common stock, which experience furnishes to all men. And it is in the *operations* of the mind upon them, that the glory of *poetry*, as of *science*, consists. Here the genius of the *poet* hath room to shew itself; and from hence alone is the praise of *originality* to be ascertained' [3]. Originality is therefore never impossible, some grace of novelty can always be added, because 'the *properties* of things are numerous, and the *lights* in which they shew themselves to a mind uninfluenced by former prejudices' are always different [4]. This statement, strongly reminiscent of Addison's in the *Spectator* [5], gives the clue to the solution of the problem of imitation and to the distinction between plagiarism and imitation. Poetry does not reproduce what is really seen or experienced, it does not represent reality but the mental response to reality, which is always influenced by personal sensibility and coloured by the poet's own imagination.

Hurd's treatise was not without influence on his contemporaries. Warburton and V. Knox echo his statement that originality in composition consists in the manner and not in the matter. Both the Warton brothers disapprove of the too common tendency to take resemblance for theft. The author of the *Essay on Pope* believes that uniformity in description or sentiments is frequently

---

[1] *Op. cit.*, III, pp. 135, 136.
[2] *Preface to Gondibert* (Spingarn, *Crit. Essays*, II, pp. 1, 2).
[3] *Op. cit.*, III, pp. 73, 74.
[4] *Ibid.*, p. 118.
[5] See supra, p. 236.

due to 'invincible necessity and the nature of things'. He points
out that several passages in Pope's works are apparent borrowings,
but that in many cases the Augustan poet has greatly improved upon
his original. Thomas Warton did the same for Spenser. According
to this critic the 'malicious triumph' in detecting a source from
which the author drew his material, soon gives way to rapture
when contemplating 'the chymical energy of true genius, which
can produce so noble a transmutation' [1].

Both Hurd and Thomas Warton were therefore conscious of the
fact that, however limited the number of subjects may be for the
poets to choose from, the forms which the poetic material can
assume in their minds are numberless, even though coincidences
may occur. The same idea is expressed much more explicitly in
Daniel Webb's *Remarks on the Beauties of Poetry* (1762). At
the end of the dialogue between Aspasia, Hortensius and Eugenio,
the last, who evidently voices the opinions of the critic himself,
speaks of 'the power of giving an advantage to the most familiar
objects, by some unexpected happiness in their use and application'.
He then observes that a rich imagination can give 'a second vegeta-
tion' to the beauties of nature and calls this the reason why every
enlightened age has had and must continue to have its original
writers. In the following passage the pseudo-classical theory of
imitation receives its death-blow: 'We have no right, therefore,
to complain, that Nature is always the same; or that the sources
of Novelty have been exhausted. It is in Poetry, as in Philosophy,
new relations are struck out, new influences discovered, and every
superior genius moves in a world of his own' [2].

Of the *Moral and Political Dialogues*, published in the year
1759, only one belongs to the field of literary criticism. It is the
third, a dialogue between Mr. Digby, Dr. Arbuthnot and Mr.
Addison on the *Golden Age of Queen Elizabeth*. In the summer
of 1716 they take a journey into Warwickshire, where they visit
the ruins of Kenilworth. The contemplation of what remained
of this once famous castle leads to a discussion of the political and

---

[1] *Observations*, I, p. 54.
[2] Daniel Webb, *Ein Beitrag zur englischen Ästhetik des achtzehnten Jahrhunderts,* ed. by H. Hecht. Hamburg, 1920, p. 112.

social conditions of the Elizabethan Age. There is a wide divergence
of opinion between the two principal interlocutors, Mr. Addison
and Dr. Arbuthnot. The former, who expresses himself 'with a
vehemence, so uncommon, and not suited to his natural temper',
thinks there are no sufficient grounds to justify the excessive praise
that is generally bestowed on what is called the 'golden reign' of
the Virgin Queen. Arbuthnot, however, who apparently expresses
the views of Hurd himself, admires it on account of its many
distinguished qualities. The dialogue anticipates the *Letters on
Chivalry and Romance* in its encomium of the deeds of chivalry.
Arbuthnot defends them against Addison's charge of fierceness and
barbarism and even thinks the 'Gothic Tilts and Tournaments'
superior to the Grecian gymnastics. As Thomas Warton had done
before him, Hurd refutes the common censure of his day that the
poets and romance-writers who had immortalized these heroic feats,
had exceeded the limits of credibility. What was called false and
unduly fantastic, was merely a copy of life, of truth and reality [1].
Like the author of the *History of English Poetry,* he considers the
Elizabethan Age as the period of the highest manifestation of poetic
art, and thinks that the main reason for the superiority of the
writers in the reigns of Elizabeth and James I over all their
successors is to be found in the prevalent mode of thinking. Though
Arbuthnot cannot deny that Shakespeare and Spenser would have
been great poets at any time, yet he is of opinion that what
particularly attracts the reader in these writers is due to the spirit
of the age. Imagination was on the wing, art and genius were close
friends, 'the high figurative manner, which fits a language so
peculiarly for the uses of the poet, had not yet been controlled by
the prosaic genius of philosophy and logic' [2]. The acme of poetic
achievement lies for Hurd, as it does for Thomas Warton, 'between
the rude essays of uncorrected fancy, on the one hand, and
the refinements of reason and science, on the other' [3]. The early

---

[1] Hurd here acknowledges his indebtedness to the *Mémoires de littérature,
tirés des registres de l'académie royale des inscriptions et belles lettres,* tome
vingtième. Paris, 1753.

[2] *Hurd's Letters on Chivalry and Romance with the Third Elizabethan Dialogue,*
ed. Miss E. J. Morley. Oxford, 1911, p. 72.

[3] *Ibid.,* p. 71.

attachment of the English to the old mysteries and moralities of which the spirit was kept awake in the Elizabethan masques and pageants, prevented poetry from submitting entirely to the supremacy of reason at the dawn of rationalism.

The *Letters on Chivalry and Romance,* which saw the light in 1762, were meant to serve as an illustration of some passages in the *Third Dialogue,* as is evident from the title-page of the edition of 1788. The critic begins by stating his plan. It is to give an explanation of the rise, progress and genius of Gothic chivalry, to point out the elements in Gothic fictions and manners that are peculiarly fit for poetic treatment, and last of all to trace the reasons for the decline of the 'Gothic taste'. Hurd acknowledges that he himself has not been able to consult the only proper authority on the subject: the 'barbarous volumes of the old romances'. To anyone who wants to know what chivalry really was, he once again recommends the reading of the French memoir which had already been referred to in the Dialogue [1]. After having traced the origin of chivalry to the feudal system and having accounted for its main distinguishing qualities, he tries to prove that there is a close similarity between the Greek manners of Homer's time and those reflected by the mediaeval romances, between heroic and Gothic manners, and he thinks it expedient to draw a close parallel between the two. He looks upon this resemblance as a sufficient explanation for the constant blending of paganism and the Gothic machinery in the *Faerie Queene* and in Tasso's great epic; the great love of classical learning which characterized both these poets was apt to lead them into a practice which the 'correct' critics had so often treated with contempt.

Hurd goes even further, and maintains that the circumstances under which 'the Gothic designers' wrote their poetry were more felicitous than those of Homer's Age. Much stress had been laid on the happy conditions of the Homeric Age by Blackwell and Wood [2] and others. Hurd ventures to say that if the Greek poet

---

[1] Hurd's *Letters,* at least the first few, seem to have been inspired by the *Mémoires sur l'ancienne Chevalerie* par La Curne de Sainte-Palaye. Paris, 1759. The two books have too little in common, however, to speak of a direct influence.

[2] *An Essay on the Original Genius and Writings of Homer.* London 1775.

could have known the manners of the feudal ages, he would undoubtedly have preferred them for their dignity, magnificence, and variety. The religious machinery of the days of chivalry gave more scope to the imagination, the tales of elves and fairies exercised a greater charm than those of classical mythology.

In Letter VII Hurd discusses the effect that feudal manners had on the two greatest English poets, Spenser and Milton: the first preferred the Gothic plan to the classical, Milton only relinquished his favourite subject of Arthur after long hesitation, and his poetry bears ample evidence of his predilection for the legends of chivalry. Shakespeare, too, is greatest when dealing with Gothic manners and machinery, which, in Hurd's opinion, is one more proof that they have the advantage over classical manners in producing *the sublime*.

In accordance with the views laid down in his dissertation on *Universal Poetry* Hurd looks upon the *Faerie Queene* as a special 'kind' of poetry [1]. The rules to which it is subject are therefore different from those of the classical epic and its nature must be explained in connection with its origin. Spenser might have built his epic on the classical model or he 'might have trimmed between the Gothic and Classic', as Tasso did, but the charms of fairyland prevailed. The *Faerie Queene* should therefore be read, not as a classical, but as a Gothic poem. The critics of Spenser before Hurd — Thomas Warton among the rest — had fallen into the error of applying classical canons to a poem essentially romantic. Hurd censures these 'austerer and more mechanical critics'. He is aware that a just appreciation can only be arrived at if the critic accepts the principles that guided the author in writing, and he regrets that such a method has never yet been followed. 'On these principles, it would not be difficult to unfold its merit in another way than has been hitherto attempted' [2]. Though the general plan of the *Faerie Queene* may be faulty in the eyes of readers who judge by a classical standard, it will prove to be quite regular when tested by the laws according to which it was constructed. In the next letter the critic compares the method of procedure of the 'classical

---

[1]   Cf. H. Trowbridge, *Bishop Hurd; A Reinterpretation* (PMLA, LVIII, pp. 450 ff.).

[2]   P. 115.

reader' to that of an architect who 'examines a Gothic structure
by Grecian rules and finds nothing but deformity. But the
Gothic architecture has it's own rules, by which when it comes
to be examined, it is seen to have it's merit, as well as the
Grecian' [1].

Hurd then explains that Spenser's design, stated by the poet
in his letter to Sir Walter Raleigh, is founded on the common
practice in the days of chivalry of holding a feast for twelve
successive days, each day being marked by one separate adventure.
The subject therefore made it necessary to adopt the plan that the
author chose: 'It was as requisite for the Faery Queen to consist
of the adventures of twelve knights, as for the Odyssey to be
confined to the adventures of one Hero: Justice had otherwise not
been done to his subject' [2]. That is why it is wrong to judge the
Faerie Queene by the classical idea of unity, which consists in the
representation of one entire action. The unity of Spenser's epic is
one of *design,* not of action. Hurd disagrees with Upton [3], who
had defended the unity of Spenser's poem on the ground that the
hero Prince Arthur has a share in each of the adventures, and that
his going in quest of Gloriana is, as the poet himself suggested,
the proper theme of the epic. He thinks that this attempt to reconcile
its structure with classical canons is a blemish rather than a merit,
as it is inconsistent with the Gothic design. The critic therefore
looks upon it as an afterthought, prompted by Spenser's extreme
reverence for the classics; the poet ought to have considered that
it is impossible to reconcile two things so diametrically opposite
as classic and Gothic unity.

If we compare Hurd's attitude towards this problem with that
of Thomas Warton, we notice that the first critic is much more
consistent than the last. Warton, though he acknowledges the
necessity of judging Spenser by another standard than Homer or

---

[1] P. 118. Hurd's comparing the romantic epic to a Gothic building was probably
suggested by Hughes's *Remarks on the Faerie Queene,* where we find this
passage: '.... to compare it (i.e. the F. Q.) therefore with the models of
antiquity would be like drawing a Parallel between the Roman and the
Gothick Architecture' (p. LX).

[2] P. 121.

[3] *Spenser's Faerie Queene, A new Edition with a Glossary and Notes Explanatory
and Critical* by John Upton, two vols. London 1758, vol. I, pp. XX, XXI.

Virgil, thinks the plan of the epic 'highly exceptionable', because
it does not accord with these classical models and with classical
precepts. The *Faerie Queene* is to him 'the careless exuberance of
a warm imagination' and the poem deserves admiration in spite
of its serious shortcomings. Hurd states the historical point of view
just as his fellow-critic had done before him, but he does not
show the constant wavering which is so characteristic of Thomas
Warton. Having once accepted the Gothic unity of design, he
abides by it. There is no attempt to compromise; on the contrary,
the only thing Hurd disapproves of is Spenser's own conciliatory
attitude in consequence of his deference for the great masters of
antiquity.

So far Hurd has approached the *Faerie Queene* merely as a
narrative poem. When he considers its allegorical character, he
is perfectly at one with Thomas Warton, whom he calls 'Spenser's
best critic', that there is a serious imperfection in the management
of the story. He quotes his predecessor's words that 'the part of
Arthur in each book is *essential* and yet not *principal*', and agrees
with him that this blemish breaks the unity of the poem and that
'the hero must either have had no part at all in the other adventures
or the main part' [1]. He does not object to the management of the
allegory itself. It is in keeping with Spenser's plan of attributing
all the virtues of the twelve knights to the chief hero. The defect
is simply the result of the union of the two designs, each of which
is perfect in itself: that of a *narrative* poem and that of an
allegorical poem [2].

In the ninth letter Hurd compares Spenser's method with that
of Tasso, which is intermediate between the purely classic and
the Gothic manner. The Italian poet's strict regard to the Homeric
and Virgilian unity of action secured him from the severe censure
that his countryman Ariosto had to undergo at the hands of the
French critics. But the strong admixture of Gothic elements in
the *Gierusalemme Liberata* lowered their estimation of this poem
also. This leads Hurd to the bitter indictment of the narrow
principles of the French school of critics and their obsequious

---

[1]   Thomas Warton, *Observations,* I, p. 7.
[2]   Pp. 126, 127.

English followers. He thinks that the substance of their views is
to be found in Davenant's *Preface to Gondibert* and Hobbes's
answer to it: 'Succeeding wits and critics did no more than echo
their language. It grew into a sort of cant, with which Rymer, and
the rest of that School filled their flimsy essays and rambling
prefaces' [1]. Hurd next denounces the narrow views of the Earl
of Shaftesbury, who in his *Advice to an Author* had spoken with
contempt of the Gothic manner; he censures the one-sidedness of
this writer, who tests any kind of literary excellence by classical
standards and 'will fight with any man who contends, not that his
Lordship's mistress is not fair, but that his own is fair also'. Critics
like Shaftesbury willingly adopt 'the authorized *lyes* of Greece'
but find fault with any departure from truth in the Italian poets,
who choose to lie in their own way.

Hurd regrets that the words of 'the exact, but cold Boileau',
who had contemptuously spoken of 'le clinquant du Tasse', were
taken up by Addison in England, and became the common cant
of those who looked upon this critic as the law-giver in matters
of taste. Then he examines the charge so often brought against the
Italian poets, namely, that their fictions are beyond the bounds
of credibility, and this gives Hurd the opportunity to expose the
false belief in the rational criteria of truth and probability. The
poets do not expect their fictions to be believed: 'They think
it enough, if they can but bring you to *imagine* the possibility of
them.' For the doctrine of *rational* truth Hurd substitutes that
of *poetical* truth, which cannot be tried by common sense but only
by the imagination of the reader.

Having thus attacked one of the main tenets of Augustanism,
Hurd turns to another pseudo-classical commonplace, namely the
maxim that the poet is to follow nature. In his later dissertation,
On the Idea of Universal Poetry he rejects the recognized
Augustan conception that the poet should be careful not to depart
from 'obvious truth', and observes that it is his right, even
his duty, 'to *outstrip* nature'. In the *Letters on Chivalry and
Romance* he attacks the cramped sphere to which the writers of
the preceding age had restricted the term *nature*, and he emphatic-

---

[1] P. 131.

ally states that the poet's world has a much wider area, far
removed from 'the real face of things', a world, as he expresses
it, 'where experience has less to do, than consistent imagination' [1].
This deviation from actuality is the privilege of 'the more sublime
and creative poetry'. In those kinds of poetry which have men and
manners for their theme, that is the dramatic kinds, Hurd, too,
expects a close resemblance to human nature [2]. He considers the
extension of dramatic precepts to poetry in general to be one of
the main causes of the narrow interpretations of the Aristotelian
doctrine. He thinks that the Horation canon: 'Quodcumque ostendis
mihi sic, incredulus odi' [3] was erroresously applied to all the kinds
of poetry, and Hurd, in accordance with the views stated in his
'Commentary', only allows its force for the drama.

Hurd refutes the charge brought against the Italian poets that
magic and enchantments, which they use so freely, are 'senseless
things'. Like Thomas Warton he holds that the same extravagant
use of the supernatural is to be found in Homer and Virgil and
that therefore their poems must be pronounced to be 'good for
nothing' on the same grounds. Rationalists like Hobbes had
asserted that the invention of things lying 'beyond the conceived
possibility of nature', was a perfectly easy expedient [4]. Hurd
rightly objects that, though the invention of such supernatural
elements may be easy, the superior management of them, which
the Italians manifest in their poetry, requires something more than
mere courage.

Hurd, however, makes one restriction with respect to the 'fairy

---

[1] P. 138.
[2] 'That, which passes in *representation* and challenges as it were, the scrutiny
of the eye, must be truth itself, or something very nearly approaching to it'.
The epic 'appeals neither to the *eye* nor to the *ear*, but simply to the
imagination, and so allows the poet a liberty of multiplying and enlarging his
impostures at pleasure, in proportion to the easiness and comprehension of
that faculty'.
[3] *AP,* 188.
[4] *Answer to Davenant,* Sping. *Crit. Essays,* II, pp. 61, 62: 'There are some that
are not pleased with fiction, unless it be bold, not onely to exceed the *work,*
but also the *possibility* of nature: they would have impenetrable Armors,
Inchanted Castles, invulnerable bodies, Iron Men, flying Horses, and a
thousand other such things, *which are easily feigned by them that dare'*
(my italics).

way of writing'. He distinguishes between 'the *popular belief*, and *that of the Reader*', and is of opinion that 'The fictions of poetry do, in some degree at least, require the *first*; (They would otherwise, deservedly pass for *dreams* indeed): But when the poet has this advantage on his side, and his fancies have, or may be supposed to have, a countenance from the current superstitions of the age, in which he writes, he dispenses with the *last*, and gives his Reader leave to be as sceptical and as incredulous, as he pleases' [1]. From another passage it appears, however, that he insists on this deference to popular opinion mainly for practical reasons, namely, because 'readers do not usually do, as they ought, put themselves in the circumstances of the poet, or rather of those, of whom the poet writes' [2]. On this ground he praises Milton for using angels and devils instead of Gothic fairies, as the latter were no longer founded on popular belief. He also advises modern poets not to revive these fictions in the epic.

Hurd then accounts for the fact that classical manners are still the object of general admiration among poets, whereas Gothic manners have almost completely gone out of vogue. As the reason he mentions that the latter had been disgraced by bad writers before justice was done to them by later writers of genius: 'Real genius was even very early employed against it.' Here Hurd alludes of course to Chaucer's *Rhyme of Sir Topas*. The neglect into which they fell, is attributed by him to their exceptional character, which made them liable to be misunderstood and misinterpreted, whereas the manners of the Homeric age are those peculiar to any rude stage of civilization, and are therefore more generally appreciated.

The last letter deals with the decay of chivalry and romance. Spenser's popularity was favoured by the romantic tendencies of the Elizabethan Age, which kept the spirit of chivalry alive for

---

[1] P. 136.

[2] P. 143. Miss E. J. Morley in the introduction to her edition of Hurd's *Letters* (Oxford, 1911) regrets that there is 'no record to tell us how he (H.) greeted *The Ancient Mariner* and *Christabel*', and thinks that '*The Letters on Chivalry and Romance* incline one to believe his criticism would have been more just than that of *Quarterly* and *Edinburgh* reviewers'. I am not so sure about that. The words quoted above give us reason to suppose that his opinion of Coleridge's poetry would have been anything but favourable.

a time. When the power of reason increased, the Gothic fictions lost their magic charm: 'It's growing splendour, in the end, put them all to flight and allowed them no quarter even amongst the poets' [1]. Hurd thinks that even Milton was so much influenced by the rising rationalism that he had to relinquish his favourite plan and restrict his use of romance to similes and illustrations. For a time the fictions of chivalry survived in an allegorical form and then reason 'drove them off the scene, and would endure these lying *wonders*, neither in their own proper shape, nor as masked in figures'. There is a close resemblance between Hurd's pathetic lament at the end of the twelfth letter and that of Thomas Warton in the third volume of his history. Both critics bewail the loss of the unrestrained freedom of fancy, both regret that imagination was forced to be the handmaid of reason, or, as Hurd says 'constrained against her will, to ally herself with strict truth, if she would gain admittance into reasonable company'. Both critics acknowledge that there was a gain of good sense but they are conscious that it was dearly bought by the loss of something that ranks far higher than this. For Warton it consists in 'the extravagancies that are above propriety', 'the incredibilities that are more acceptable than truth' .... 'fictions that are more valuable than reality'; to Hurd it is 'a world of fine fabling', which will always be attractive to anyone except to 'earth-born critics'.

If after discussing Hurd's greatest achievement in the field of literary criticism, we try to give a short estimate of his importance in the development of aesthetic theory in the Johnsonian Age, two salient, but contrasting features strike us. On the one hand his earlier essays clearly bring out his reverence for classical precepts and his acceptance of some of them as authoritative laws, at least for one of the literary genres, the drama. His observations on tragi-comedy, the unity of action, and the chorus, leave no doubt about this. We must not forget, however, that his interpretation of one of the most important classical documents, the *Ars Poetica*, differs from that of his contemporaries in that Hurd considers it only as a criticism of the Roman drama but denies its authority for any other literary *genre*. For he insists on judging every kind

---

[1] P. 153.

of literary composition by the laws of its own being. In the *Letters on Chivalry and Romance* he applies the neo-classic tenet of the 'kinds' to new material, cast in a new poetic form. Like most of his contemporaries he adopts the historical way of approach and examines Spenser's epic by its own underlying principles. Even in his early work he takes his stand against the ruthless denunciations by the French critics and their English followers of anything not compatible with reason's laws. From the very beginning of his literary career, he expresses his dissatisfaction with their narrow interpretations of the terms *truth, nature* and *verisimilitude.* He speaks contemptuously of the neo-classic precept that the poet is to imitate nature, which he calls 'a trite maxim', and after stating that 'the source of bad criticism, as universally of bad philosophy, is the abuse of terms', he blames the preceding generations of critics for restricting the poet's world to a narrow range. With the Wartons, Gray, and many minor critics, he champions the cause of imagination and emotion. In his plea for these two essential elements of poetry he shows a thoroughness, an absence of compromise that is unparalleled in the critical literature of the eighteenth century. I cannot therefore accept the view, held by some recent writers on the subject, that he is merely an 'enlightened' neo-classicist like Hume, Kames, Reynolds and Burke. No doubt Hurd was influenced by the empirical methods of his contemporaries, as I have had occasion to point out, but on the other hand his criticism is openly directed against reason, correctness and rational truth, the main pillars of Augustanism. Therefore the importance of the *Letters on Chivalry and Romance* in the history of the emancipation of critical thought from the bondage of rationalism cannot easily be over-estimated. As I hope to have made clear, his attitude was not due to a sudden 'volte-face': even as early as in his commentary on Horace's *Epistola ad Augustum* we find traces of this same incipient romanticism [1].

---

[1]   His devotion to Spenser and Milton, the two chief writers of what Hurd called *pure poetry,* did not lead with him to an under-estimation of the great English Augustan poet, as it did with Joseph Warton. In his edition of Horace he repeatedly expresses his high opinion of Pope's poetical merits, and we can hardly expect a different attitude from the slavish devotee of the poet's editor. In his later treatises there is no evidence to show that he altered his views, though I am inclined to think that he ranked the writers of 'sublime poetry'

In the last few decades of the eighteenth century Hurd's influence on his contemporaries is unmistakable. The two critics discussed in the next chapter avow their indebtedness to him [1].

---

higher than Pope. In Hurd's *Commonplace Book,* in which the critic was accustomed to register his thoughts on different subjects and from which extracts have been added by Kilvert to his biography, we find an entry from which I quote the following passage: 'The greater, and what may be called pure poetry came to perfection in the hands of Spenser and Milton.
.... The humbler sorts of poetry, under whatever name, but chiefly satire and ethic, have been carried to all the excellence their nature admits, and adorned with the utmost grace and harmony of versification and expression, by Dryden and Pope'.

[1] Cf. Audley L. Smith, *Richard Hurd's Letters on Chivalry and Romance* (ELH, VI, 1939).

CHAPTER XXIII

THOMAS TWINING. JOHN HOOLE

Thomas Twining's reputation as a critic is chiefly founded on his translation of Aristotle's *Poetics,* which appeared in the year 1789, one year after Pye had published his. Like the Poet Laureate he was convinced that such a translation would supply a want, as only two imperfect renderings of the treatise were extant when he embarked on his task, one a mere retranslation from that of Dacier, though professing to be from the original Greek (1705), and an anonymous one published in the year 1775.

Twining is obviously a critic with romantic leanings and his book is an important contribution to the new critical movement. His dissent from the pseudo-classic doctrine is clearly brought out in the notes, and by the two accompanying dissertations, entitled *On Poetry considered as an Imitative Art* and *On the Word Imitative, as applied to Music* [1]. It is moreover apparent from his interesting correspondence, of which selections were published by his grand-nephew Richard Twining under the title of *Recreations and Studies of a Country Clergyman of the 18th Century* (1882), to be followed in 1887 by the *Selections from the Papers of the Twining Family.* The letters contain very few observations belonging to literary criticism, but such as there are leave no doubt about Twining's sympathies. He was passionately fond of *Percy's Reliques,* and was a great admirer of the *Rowley Poems,* even though he believed they were, at least partly, a forgery. What makes the correspondence especially worthy of attention are the enthusiastic descriptions of mountain-scenery, expressing the same admiration of external nature as we meet with in Gray's letters.

I have already had occasion to speak of his attitude towards Johnson, whose poetry he qualified as 'only good sense put into good metre' and whose estimate of Gray's *Odes* he called 'a mere school-boyish criticism'. His dissatisfaction with the heroic couplet is sufficiently illustrated by the following passage: 'To me, a work of length in the rhymed heroic of Pope....

---

[1] See J. W. Draper, Aristotelian 'Mimesis' in Eighteenth Century England (PMLA, XXXVI).

is insufferably monotonous, and cloying to the ear. It should be appropriated, I think, to short poems and gay subjects' [1].

His edition of the *Treatise on Poetry* is based on a reconsideration of Aristotle's principles, independent of the interpretations of the French critics which had so long been considered as final. His attack is principally directed against their narrow views, and against those of Dacier in particular. Twining is of opinion that great injustice has been done to the Italian commentators of the Renaissance, of whom he mentions Castelvetro and Beni, who had been treated with disdain by the French arbiters of taste in the 17th century. He blames Harris because in his *Philological Inquiries* he had deserted Aristotle for Le Bossu, 'who with little reason, in my opinion, passed with him, as well as with Lord Shaftesbury, for Aristotle's best interpreter'.

Before proceeding to his task, Twining waives all belief in authority, that of the ancient critics as well as that of their French interpreters. 'The time is come', he observes, 'when we no longer read the antients with our judgments shackled .by determined admiration; when even from the editor and the commentator, it is no longer required as an indispensable duty, that he should see nothing in his author but perfection' [2]. The conclusions to which the new analysis had led him are widely different from the conceptions of the Augustan critics and their masters on the other side of the Channel. They had considered the Aristotelian precepts as thoroughly rational and therefore as the summary expression of their own narrow views. Against this opinion Twining protests; he characterizes the principles of the Stagyrite as truly *poetical*, 'and such as afford no countenance to that sort of criticism which requires the Poet to be "of *reason* all compact" ' [3]. As a natural consequence his conceptions of 'nature' and 'truth' show an equally wide divergence from the pseudo-classic interpretations of these terms. In the discussion of the word 'nature' the influence of Hurd's *Letters on Chivalry and Romance* is distinctly to be traced. Twining realizes that the Augustans, by limiting the sphere of nature to the manners of everyday life, and qualifying anything

---

[1] P. 120.
[2] P. XXII.
[3] P. XXVII.

that lay beyond the bounds of reality as absurd and extravagant, misinterpreted Aristotle's intention. He believes that the Greek critic would have approved of any means that conduces to the only end the poet ought to have in view, namely that of giving pleasure. 'He sees fully, what the *rationalists* among modern critics have not always seen, the power of popular *opinion* and *belief* upon poetical credibility' [1], he remarks, and agrees with Hurd that a legend, tradition or superstition may be the sole basis of a poet's visions. He has a right 'to impose upon the imagination, as far as imagination, for the sake of its own pleasure, will consent to be imposed on', and if only the one supreme end of poetic art is attained, he is free to introduce impossibilities, even absurdities. 'Poetry can do no more than this, and, from its very nature and end, ought not to be required to do less. If it is our interest to be cheated, it is her duty to cheat us' [2].

Hurd's influence is again to be discerned, when he comes to speak about poetic truth. Passages from the *Letters* are adduced as being the best comment on Aristotle's discussion of the improbable and the incredible. Far from restricting the range of poetry to that of immediate reality or 'the vraisemblable' of the French critics, he wants to extend it far beyond the narrow limits of actual experience. Aristotle's 'probable impossibilities' include in Twining's opinion 'all that is called *faery, machinery,* ghosts, witches, enchantments, etc.' — things, as Hobbes had said, lying 'beyond the actual bounds of nature, and only within the conceived possibilities of nature'. As an example of an impossible character, made probable by the poet's artistic skill, he mentions Caliban; he contrasts it with Richardson's Lovelace and comes to the conclusion that the latter is much more improbable than the former, which is at least consistent. 'I can *imagine* such a monster as Caliban: I never could imagine such a man as Lovelace'. Shakespeare has made his character appear probable, not to *reason* but to *imagination*, and it is by imagination that poetic truth should be tried.

In the second volume Twining discusses Aristotle's use of the word 'fiction'. The poet's art of feigning consists according to the

---

[1]　P. XXVII.
[2]　P. XXVIII.

Greek critic in a kind of fallacy: 'For, assuming that if one thing is or becomes, a second is or becomes, men imagine that, if the second is, the first likewise is or becomes' [1]. Dacier and the other pseudo-classic interpreters had thought that Aristotle was merely thinking of the narration of real events, in which fiction should be blended with historical or acknowledged truth, so that the latter element would impart an air of truth to the former and as Twining puts it, 'make the false pass glibly with the true' [2]. In his commentary on this passage in the *Poetics* Twining denounces this narrow interpretation; he is one of the first to see that the critic was rather thinking of certain extraordinary characters, incidents and situations which are made acceptable by the genius of the poet: 'When the actions, and the language, of those characters and in general, the *consequences* of those events or situations, as drawn out into detail by the Poet, are such as we know, to be *true* — that is to say, poetically true, or *natural*; such, as we are satisfied must necessarily, or would probably follow, if such characters and situations actually existed; this probability, nature, or *truth*, of representation, imposes on us, sufficiently for the purposes of Poetry' [3]. Instead of insisting on rational tests as the Augustan critics had done, he advances the view that the reader ought *to feel* the truth of fiction. The following passage is important enough to quote in full because it clearly points to a new manner of approach: 'The reader of a play, or a novel, does not, indeed syllogize, and *say* to himself — "Such beings as are here supposed, had they existed, *must* have acted and spoken exactly in this manner; therefore, I believe they *have* existed" — but he *feels* the truth of the premises and he *consents* to feel the truth of the conclusion.... the probability and truth of nature, in the *consequences*, steals, in a manner, from our view, even the *impossibility* of the cause and flings an air of truth over the whole' [4]. In this sense of the word not only Homer's fiction, which Aristotle had in mind, but even the extravagancies of Ariosto are true,

---

[1] *Poetics*, XXIV, 9. (Butcher, *op. cit.*, p. 95).
[2] Vol. II, pp. 346 ff.
[3] II, p. 349.
[4] II, p. 350.

though they are nothing but revolting lies, if examined by purely rational standards. The readiness with which the reader yields himself up to these absurd fictions is in Twining's opinion partly due to the 'truth and nature which he has contrived to fling into the *detail* of his description', a statement illustrating an important dissent from the pseudo-classic doctrine of general nature.

There is another point on which Twining disagrees with the French critics. In their eyes, he reminds us, scenes of violence, murders and bloodshed were inconsistent with the laws of decorum and were therefore looked upon as unpardonable defects in a tragedy. Saint-Évremond, during his long stay in England had been particularly struck by the relish of English people for cruel acts and bloody scenes, which he considered as a sign of their bad taste. His severe censure affected the opinions of the English critics. Though Addison did not approve of the French practice of banishing all deeds of violence from the stage, he condemned the monstrous atrocities that disfigured some of the English trage-dies. His own contribution to dramatic art, *Cato*, was held up by Voltaire as a model worthy of imitation, as a favourable contrast with the works of the barbarian Shakespeare. Twining opposes these views and asserts that the great delicacy of the French theatre is by no means in keeping with the character of the Greek drama. The rule of the French critics that the dramatist should take care 'de ne pas ensanglanter le théâtre' was not always observed by the ancients, and Sophocles' *Oedipus* is no more perfect in this respect than Shakespeare's *King Lear* [1].

In another passage Twining attacks the pseudo-classic delusion that the Greek tragedies were models of correctness. Critics who think so, merely echo what others have said before them without examining if their opinions are consistent with fact. Against this 'conventional and *hearsay* kind of praise' Twining raises his voice, and makes the important statement that in the Popean sense of the word, the Greek writers are no less correct than the English dramatists of the Elizabethan Age. 'The true praise of Aeschylus, Sophocles, and Euripides is, (in *kind* at least, though not in *degree*,)

---

[1] J. Warton had made a remark to the same effect (*Essay on Pope*, vol. I, p. 73, note).

the praise of Shakespeare; that of strong, but irregular, unequal and hasty genius. Everything, which this genius and the feeling of the moment could produce, in an early period of the art, ... these writers possess in great abundance: what meditation, and *"the labour and delay of the file"* only can effect, they too often want [1]. Of Shakespeare, however, compared with the Greek poets, it may justly, I think, be pronounced, that he has *much* more, both of this *want,* and of that *abundance'* [2].

It is a great merit of Twining's edition of the *Poetics* that for the first time in England it drew the attention to the mistaken notion of the pseudo-classicists that the rule for the unity of time by which they set such great store, was supported by Aristotle's authority. He shows conclusively that this view is not in any way founded on the *Poetics,* that the rule about this unity had never been explicitly laid down by *Aristotle,* and that the only one of the three which he had considered as indispensable was that of action: 'In his view it was no duty incumbent on the dramatic Poet even to *aim* at the observance of such a rule' (the unity of time) . . . . 'His rule is, as *generally* understood, "confine your action, as nearly as you can, to a single day" or as . . . . it *should* be understood, to a single revolution of the sun or twenty-four hours' [3]. Dacier, whose conception had for such a long time been paramount, had postulated that the dramatic action was never to exceed the limit of twelve hours, and that for the sake of verisimilitude the time of the action and that of the representation were to be about the same. Twining made it clear that this interpretation of Aristotle's words could not be right. He respectfully mentions Johnson, who had long before denounced the minor unities of time and place, and recommends the reading of Metastasio's *Estratto dell' Arte poetica d'Aristotele,* which had not come into his hands until his notes had already been written.

---

[1] Twining's expression: 'the labour and delay of the file' was probably suggested by Horace's *Ars Poetica,* ll. 289 ff. Howes translated:

> Nor would the name of Latium stand renowned
> On martial more than on Parnassian ground,
> Were not our every bard so loth the while
> To brook *the pause and labor of the file.*

[2] I, p. 311.

[3] I, p. 341.

Another writer who underwent the influence of the *Letters on Chivalry and Romance* is John Hoole, the translator of Tasso's *Gerusalemme Liberata* (1763) and Ariosto's *Orlando Furioso* (1783) [1]. Johnson encouraged the translation of the first work and wrote the dedication to the Queen, which we find prefixed to it in Chalmers's edition. It received moreover a complimentary notice in the critic's *Life of Waller* [2].

The only things that concern us here are the prefaces. That preceding Tasso's epic contains a defence of the poem against Boileau's animadversion in his ninth satire. Hoole does not contradict the view that Tasso has 'tinsel', by which, as he says, the French poet meant false thought or incredible fiction. He is convinced, however, not only that the gold preponderates, but also that proportionally the tinsel is not more prevalent than in some works that have received the approbation of generations of critics. The same extravagancies and improbabilities are to be met with in Ovid, yet his *Metamorphoses* have always found admirers. Then Hoole clearly follows in the track of Hurd, when he accounts for these incredible elements historically. 'It is very likely that magic and enchantment were as generally and firmly believed, when Tasso wrote his *Jerusalem*, as the visible agency of the Pagan deities at the writing of the *Iliad*, the *Odyssey* and *Aeneid*.' If therefore the *Jerusalem Delivered* is to be condemned on these grounds, the high merit of Virgil and Homer can no longer be maintained. Hoole agrees with Hurd, from whose *Letters* he quotes, that the Gothic machinery is more adapted to the great ends of epic poetry than the tales of antiquity. It is therefore clear 'that a reader may be pleased with Tasso and not disgrace his judgment'.

The Preface to the translation of *Orlando Furioso* is a strong plea for the other Italian poet, whose work had met with still more disapproval at the hands of the neo-classical critics. Hoole thinks that they were too rash in their contempt for the tales of chivalry, which had so long been the delight of their ancestors. Besides the

---

[1] The only complete translation of Tasso's epic that existed before Hoole embarked on his, was that by Fairfax (1600). Hoole translated the first ten books of the *O.F.* According to the D.N.B. the first vol. was published in 1773; in 1783 five vols. appeared.

[2] *Lives*, I, p. 296.

charge of its many absurdities, another grave objection had been raised against Ariosto's epic, namely that there was an indecorous intermixture of comic and serious elements in the poem. Hoole is of opinion, however, that it would be unjust to condemn it for this reason. On similar grounds praise would have to be withheld from Shakespeare, for he has not written pure tragedies. We discern the influence of Johnson's defence of tragi-comedy in Hoole's remark that the poet drew his picture of life from nature, where the comic and the serious are often blended, and where the same characters are seen in different lights at different times. He is indebted to Hurd again for his statement that most of the censures on Ariosto 'are founded on the mistaken opinion that the *Orlando* is to be tried by the rules of Aristotle and the examples of Homer and Virgil'. As a counterpart to these criticisms he adduces passages from Gravina's appreciative discussion of the epic in his *Ragion Poetica.*

Though the marvellous is carried to an extreme in Ariosto's poem, Hoole considers that most of his fictions are not more incredible than those of Greek and Latin poets. He allows that the *Orlando* contains passages that have justly been reprehended, but still maintains that far too much importance has been attached to the strictures of the French critics, who have little taste for the works of imagination of other nations, having no good examples themselves. 'Yet while the enthusiastic spirit, that hurries away the reader, continues to be regarded as the glorious criterion of true poetry, every follower of the Muses will find ample subject for admiration in the perusal of the *Orlando Furioso* of Ariosto.' This unreserved admission that the emotional appeal is the only determining factor in testing the merit of literary work stamps Hoole as an antagonist of rationalism and gives him a place among the romantic critics.

CHAPTER XXIV

OTHER VOICES OF DISSENT

The conflicting tendencies of this transitional period cannot be illustrated better than by Thomas Percy's dedication and preface to one of the most remarkable books the eighteenth century produced, the *Reliques of Ancient English Poetry* (1765). The editor's wavering attitude and his apologetic tone have not escaped the notice of any of his critics. They were the outcome of his fear that 'the barbarous productions of unpolished ages', as he called his *Reliques*, might not be deemed worthy of the aesthetic standard of his time. Percy had the same unalloyed reverence for the literature and the highly cultivated taste of his own era as the Wartons and other contemporary critics. Convinced as he was that the ballads lacked the higher beauties of art which the 'present state of improved literature' required, he hesitated long before he gave them to the public. At last he did so only in the hope that the names of the 'many men of learning and character' who had encouraged his publication, might 'serve as an amulet to guard him from every unfavourable censure'. He did not recommend the ballads as 'labours of art' but merely as 'effusions of nature', showing the first efforts of ancient genius. He ranked Prior's *Henry and Emma* far higher than the old pathetic song of the *Not-browne Mayde* and considered the beauty of the modern imitation as the principal reason why the original should be rescued from oblivion. The insertion of the modern pieces to make up for the rudeness of the 'reliques' of antiquity is another proof of Percy's inability to appreciate their literary merit. Equally instructive is his way of dealing with the text. The critic of the *London Magazine* for 1767 observed that 'he looked on it as a young woman from the country with unkempt locks, whom he had to fit for fashionable society' [1]. Alterations were made wherever the 'polite' taste of the time made it necessary to improve upon the text. This manner

---

[1] Quoted by Furnivall, *Bishop Percy's Folio Manuscript,* ed. by W. Hales and F. J. Furnivall, vol. I, p. XVI.

of proceeding excited the displeasure of Ritson, the antiquarian, but the majority of contemporary critics had no fault to find with Percy's adaptations. In an age of forgeries his method could hardly be expected to meet with any serious objection.

Percy's letters clearly show that in his later life the bishop regretted having bestowed so much attention on 'a parcel of old ballads'. He had come to consider these frivolous occupations merely as follies of his youth, and could not be induced by his friends to publish some more volumes, even though they assured him that the 'inditing of dulcet ditties was in nought misbeseeming to a mitred clerk' [1].

The third volume of the *Reliques* opened with an essay on *The Ancient Metrical Romances*. Some of Percy's remarks in this essay were obviously prompted by Thomas Warton's *Observations on the Faerie Queene*. The author praised the songs of the ancient minstrels for their poetic merit, and recommended the study of them for another reason, namely their value as historical documents. As Warton had done before him, he pointed out how much light they throw on the manners and opinions of former times, and that they illustrate many passages in the older poets, in Chaucer, Spenser and Shakespeare. The second essay of the first volume is entitled: *Observations on the Origin of the English Stage* and on *The Conduct of our first Dramatic Poets*. Like the first, that on the minstrels, it naturally contains statements that later investigations have proved to be unfounded, and it is not free from fanciful theorizing.

Percy's comment on *Everyman* betrays the influence of the neo-classic doctrine. He observes that it is strictly built on the model of the Greek tragedy and thinks the plan even severer than that of Milton's *Samson Agonistes*: the action is simple, the time of the action is that of the performance, the scene is not changed, and the stage is never empty. Everyman leaves the stage only once to receive the sacraments and during this time 'KNOWLEDGE discants on the excellence and power of the priesthood, somewhat after the manner of the Greek Chorus'. Percy even detects in the

---

[1] A. C. C. Gaussen, *Percy: Prelate and Poet,* p. 54.

morality something of the Aristotelian katharsis: 'It is not without some rude attempts to excite terror and pity', he says, 'and therefore may not improperly be referred to the class of tragedy'.

When discussing the Elizabethan drama, he alludes to Polonius' enumeration of the various subdivisions [1], and then denounces the practice of applying the rules of one kind of dramatic composition to that of another. He thinks it absurd to try Shakespeare's histories by the laws of tragedy. The passage winds up with an important statement, in which he rejects all attempts at judging a work of art by pre-ordained standards: 'Certainly we ought to examine a work only by those principles according to which it was composed. This would save a deal of impertinent criticism' [2].

The Essay on the Dramatic Character of Sir John Falstaff by Maurice Morgann was written in 1774, and not published till the year 1777. As the author states in the preface, he maintains, contrary to the general opinion [3], that the humorous knight was not regarded by Shakespeare as a coward. It is therefore primarily an early instance of the kind of Shakespearean criticism which was to become so very common in the nineteenth century, namely the study of single characters [4]. But it is more than that. There are some digressions from the main theme — consistent arrangement is not Morgann's strong point — which mark the essay as an important contribution to the advance of Romantic aesthetic theory. The author does not enumerate the demerits of Shakespeare's works and put them over against their many beauties, as had so often been done before him. He does not test them by a rigid schedule of *a priori* rules, nor does he apply the rational criteria 'nature' and 'truth'. Earlier critics who had followed this method, had all

---

[1] *Hamlet,* Act II, Sc. II.

[2] Cf. Hurd, supra, p. 267.

[3] Cf. Johnson's: 'Falstaff is a character loaded with faults, and with those faults which naturally produce contempt. He is a thief, and a glutton, a coward, and a boaster, always ready to cheat the weak, and prey upon the poor; to terrify the timorous and insult the defenceless' (Raleigh, *Johnson on Shakespeare*, 1925, p. 125).

[4] Johnson had discussed some of Shakespeare's characters in his notes, J. Warton in his contributions to the *Adventurer*. For other instances see D. Nichol Smith, *Shakespeare in the Eighteenth Century*, pp. 82 ff.

been bound to acknowledge that Shakespeare's plays did not come up to the standard that they set up for him. Most of them, except a strict formalist like Rymer, had allowed him great genius, but at the same time they had expressed their regret that his works were sadly marred by his gross violations of decorum. Morgann on the other hand thinks that Shakespeare occupies a separate place in literary art, that he therefore cannot be examined by the same laws as other writers. He does not first and foremost appeal to the intellect, but to the feelings of the readers. 'Him we may profess rather to feel than to understand; and it is safer to say, on many occasions, that we are possessed by him than that we possess him. And no wonder; — He scatters the seeds of things, the principles of character and action, with so cunning a hand yet with so careless an air, and, master of our feelings, submits himself so little to our judgment, that every thing seems superior' [1]. It would therefore be absurd to measure his merits by intellectual tests. The logical connection of cause and effect that the critic looks for in the writings of other authors, and that his judgment enables him to trace, are often absent in Shakespeare, but he is 'rapt in ignorant admiration .... he commands every passage to our heads and to our hearts, and moulds us as he pleases' [2]. For a writer with such a strong emotional appeal a strict observance of the unities is of no consequence. So much is the audience impressed by the magic of his art that they 'are insensible to the shifting of place and the lapse of time, and till the curtain drops, never once wake to the truth of things, or recognize the laws of existence' [3]. Johnson had defended Shakespeare's neglect of the unities by an appeal to the reason of the spectators, who are conscious of the dramatic deception throughout the performance. Morgann thinks that the powerful spell under which the consummate art of the dramatist holds the audience, makes them unconscious of irregularities in time and place.

The passage that follows contains an open protest against Aristotelian formalism, an emphatic denial that the rules of the

---

[1] *Morgann's Essay on the Dramatic Character of Sir John Falstaff,* ed. by Gill. Oxford, 1912, p. 66.

[2] P. 67.

[3] P. 69.

Greek critic have any authority for the modern drama. Dryden
is reported to have said that, if Aristotle could have seen modern
plays, he would have changed his mind. Morgann goes much
further when he represents the Greek critic himself as the
denouncer of all the absurdities that have been said in his name by
the upholders of his dictatorship. After the curtain has dropped
at the end of one of Shakespeare's plays and the spectators have
come back to reality, a critic like Rymer is represented as awaking
from his trance; he lifts up his constable's staff and calls upon
'this great Magician, this daring *practicer of arts inhibited,* in the
name of *Aristotle,* to surrender; whilst *Aristotle* himself, disowning
his wretched Officer, would fall prostrate at his feet and acknowledge his supremacy. — O supreme of Dramatic excellence! (*might
he say,*) not to me be imputed the insolence of fools. The bards
of *Greece* were confined within the narrow circle of the Chorus,
and hence they found themselves constrained to practice, for the
most part, the precision, and copy the details of nature. I followed
them, and knew not that a larger circle might be drawn, and the
Drama extended to the whole reach of human genius' [1].

Morgann next considers the rationalistic conception of nature
which had so long been paramount. In the name of reason a close
observance of the unities of time and place had been insisted on
by the critics. But there is another kind of nature, which Morgann
calls 'the nature of *effects*' and for which a strict adherence to these
dramatic rules is not essential. Human life is subject to a chain of
visible causes and effects, but the effect of poetry is the result of
causes hidden or unknown: 'True Poesy is *magic,* not *nature*' and
for the magician in the domain of art the laws of Aristotle were
not meant. 'Poetry delights in surprise, conceals her steps, seizes
at once upon the heart, and obtains the Sublime of things without
betraying the rounds of her ascent'. Hurd had made a distinction
between nature in the generally accepted sense that the pseudo-
classical critics had attached to it, and that of the poetical world.
Morgann draws a contrast between 'nature' and 'magic'. As appears
from a long note to the passage, he defines nature as 'a felt
propriety, or truth of art, from an unseen, tho' supposed adequate

---

[1] P. 70.

cause'. A feeling of propriety and truth, for which no adequate cause can be given, is what he calls magic. In this remarkable passage the purely intellectual view of poetic art is exposed. Morgann does not look upon literary creation as a mechanical process, but as an inspiration; its means, whether apparent or hidden, are justified by *success* and their success will be all the greater, if the means by which it is attained are concealed.

The interesting *Essays Philosophical, Historical and Literary,* which appeared anonymously in 1789, were written by William Belsham, a supporter of the Whig party and a writer on political and historical subjects. As the title indicates, only some of these essays belong to literary criticism, but all of these show distinct traces of a reaction, and exhibit the author's dissatisfaction with common-sense standards. He stands up for emotion, the genuine expression of passion, 'a fine frenzy'. He is an enthusiastic admirer of Shakespeare's tragedies, which he ranks far higher than the masterpieces of the French theatre, than *Le Cid* or *Athalie* for example, or the regular and faultless English dramatic productions of his own time, which are all wanting in 'that first and greatest power of composition, the power of seizing, fascinating and enchanting the attention!' He appreciates tragedies like Addison's *Cato* and Johnson's *Irene* for their lofty and poetical diction, but he has read them with so little emotion and sympathy that he will never be induced to peruse them a second time. He endorses Lord Kames's distinction between 'imitation' and 'description', and agrees with him that only delineations of passion can awaken the spectator's attention.

The appeal to emotion is for Belsham the unmistakable evidence of true genius. Not *reason,* but *taste* is the ultimate test of literary merit. He does not consider *useless* all rules that are the result of a rational process of deduction, (he is even convinced that uniformity in our mental feelings and perceptions points to some rational foundation), but he realizes that there will always be something in art that is not reducible to the laws of common sense. This is the reason why he cannot admire the method Lord Kames followed in his elaborate *Elements of Criticism,* in spite of the many 'acute and sagacious' observations it contains. Its fundamental defect is,

19

according to Belsham, that it judges in matters of taste by *rules* and not by *feeling*. Where the rule had not yet been established by experience, he was compelled to draw on his own invention, and explain by reason that which could only be accounted for by taste.

'Is it not then better', he asks, 'without making an empty parade of knowledge, which we do not really possess, at once to confess our ignorance and inability to account for those sensations of pleasure which we derive from these sources, than vainly to attempt to reduce those feelings to the dominion of reason, which refuse to acknowledge any authority but that of taste?' [1].

This open rejection of rational criteria, this consciousness of the impossibility of finding the underlying principles of art by an analysis on scientific lines, justify Belsham's place among the eighteenth century precursors of the romantic conception in criticism. There is an echo of Joseph Warton's *Essay on Pope* in his comparison between the Augustan poet and the Elizabethans: 'Pope was, as an elegant critic justly stiles him, the Poet of Reason; and in perusing his productions, the understanding is improved, while the imagination is delighted. But still it must be allowed, that the sacred mantle which descended from Shakespeare to Milton, and which Dryden sometimes wore with dignity, hung loose upon Pope, "like a giant's robe upon a dwarfish thief!" '

William Hayley is best known as the friend of Blake and Cowper, and as the latter's biographer. His poetry is now almost entirely forgotten, though it enjoyed great popularity in the author's lifetime and went through several editions. Of his *Poetical Essays*, that on painting is addressed to Romney, that on history to Gibbon, and his *Essay on Epic poetry* (1782), consisting of five epistles, to his friend W. Mason. Several passages in this poem, and some of the notes appended by the poet himself, are directed against the pride and arrogance of the lawgivers who would like

---

[1]   P. 217. The passage about 'the affectation of judging in matters of taste by rule; and not by feeling' is quoted by J. Warton in his edition of *The Works of Pope*, I, p. 227. Warton adds: 'The turn and manner of many passages in our author are much like Dryden's prologues; and particularly the famous prologue and epilogue to *All for Love*.'

to bind the fancy of the poet by all sorts of absurd precepts. The author thinks that poetry addresses itself pre-eminently to the human heart and reason is therefore an inadequate judge:

> In vain would Reason those nice questions solve,
> Which the fine play of mental powers involve:
> In Bards of ancient time, with genius fraught,
> What mind can trace how thought engender'd thought, [1]

Hayley next ridicules the 'sober critics' who attribute thoughts to Homer that he never had [2], and makes fun of Le Bossu for his advice to the epic poet to choose the moral first and then invent the fable to illustrate it [3]. He agrees with J. Warton that there is a natural hostility between critical canons and the invention of the writer and that poetry cannot thrive in a time when criticism is at the height of its perfection. The young poet is advised

> To deem infallible no Critic's word;
> Not e'en the dictates of thy Attic *Hurd*:
> No! not the Stagyrite's unquestion'd page,
> The Sire of Critics, sanctified by age! [4]

He defends Pope against Warton and other detractors who had thought him wanting in imagination and sensibility. The *Rape of the Lock,* and *Eloisa to Abelard* are in Hayley's opinion sufficient proofs of his exquisite fancy and his tender enthusiasm, which the critic considers as 'the great constituents of the real Poet'.

---

[1] *Epistle I.*
[2] Cf. Note IV to the first epistle: 'Perhaps few individuals differ more from each other in their modes of thinking, by the force of education and of national manners, than a modern French Critic and an early Poet of Greece; yet the former will often pretend, with the most decisive air, to lay open the sensorium of an ancient Bard and to count every link in the chain of his ideas.'
[3] Of Le Bossu Hayley says in the same note: 'Though Bossu is called "the best explainer of Aristotle, and one of the most learned and judicious of modern critics", by a writer for whose opinions I have much esteem, I cannot help thinking that his celebrated *Essay on Epic Poetry* is very ill calculated either to guide or to inspirit a young Poet.'
[4] *Epistle I.* Cf. also *Epistle V*:
> False to themselves, and to their interest blind,
> Are those cold judges, of fastidious mind,
> Who with vain rules the suffering Arts would load,
> Who, ere they smile, consult the Critic's code;

John Aikin was a physician and a writer of miscellaneous essays. His *Letters from a Father to his Son* (1793) [1] contain some contributions to criticism.

The author is a firm believer in the highly cultivated taste of the Age of Enlightenment. He thinks the literature of his own day far superior to that of any previous period of literary history. Those of his contemporaries who believe that the Age of Queen Elizabeth offers the highest manifestation of literary art, are called 'very prejudiced readers'. It naturally follows from this conviction of the pre-eminence of his age that he disagrees with the critics who profess great reverence for the writers of antiquity. He regrets that in his day classical canons are still looked upon as never-failing standards and every transgression of them as equivalent to a deviation from 'truth and nature'. To the works of modern writers such a narrow code is not applicable, and the chief aim of Aikin's letters is to suggest some general principles to serve as 'a kind of counterpoise to the prepossessions usually entertained on these subjects'. They are not directed only against prejudices in favour of the classics but rather against authoritative precepts in general. He thinks for instance that the idolatry of Shakespeare has been carried to an equally ridiculous extreme.

Aikin's most important critical statements are contained in the letters dealing with Pope's *Essay on Criticism*, where he points out some contradictions in the poet's creed. He rightly blames him for his wavering attitude towards Aristotle's rules, which led to these inconsistencies in his dicta. Some of them are, in point of fact, the suggestions of Pope's natural good sense, whereas others are the result of his reading and education. On one hand the poet praises Virgil for following the rules very strictly 'As if the Stagirite o'erlook'd each line' and even goes so far as to say that 'To copy nature is to copy them'. But, if such were his belief, how could he blame Dennis for condemning any violation of these precepts [2], Aikin asks. If moreover every lucky licence is a rule —

---

[1] *Letters from a Father to his Son on Various Topics Relative to Literature and the Conduct of Life,* written in the years 1792 and 1793 by J. Aikin, M. D. London, 1793.

[2] Concluding all were desp'rate sots and fools,
Who durst depart from Aristotle's rules. (II. 271, 272).

and Aikin agrees with Pope that it is — how is it that the poet calls it 'a fault' a few lines further on [1]. Such successful deviations from common practice, far from being faults, only prove that the critic should enlarge his creed so as to comprehend this new licence. Aikin then rejects Pope's advice to the modern poet not to transgress the rules, if it is not necessary [2]. On the contrary, a liberal mode of reasoning would allow more freedom to the moderns, who possess such a store of new ideas that a rigid observance of classical canons cannot be expected from them.

There is another maxim in the *Essay* which Aikin thinks equally erroneous. It is the one contained in lines 390 and 391:

> Yet let not each gay Turn thy rapture move;
> For fools admire, but men of sense approve:

It is evident that the context qualifies the sense to such a degree that it cannot be accepted as a general statement, as is done by Aikin. He strongly disapproves of the rationalistic view it expresses. Cool approbation is in his eyes not sufficient for the critic; he should be capable of feeling enthusiasm. Proneness to admiration may sometimes be the characteristic of weak minds, it is also 'inseparable from that warmth of imagination which is requisite for the strong perception of what is excellent in art and nature' [3].

This passage like the one to the same effect in Belsham's *Essays Philosophical, Historical and Literary,* is quoted by J. Warton in his commentary on the lines in his edition of Pope. Both Aikin and Belsham are convinced that ultimately the imagination should decide literary merit, a conviction which fell in with the views of the editor.

Among the miscellaneous pieces, appended to the *Memoir of John Aikin,* published by his daughter Lucy in 1823, there are some dealing with critical subjects. The *Account of the Life and Works of Spenser* [4] offers little worthy of a discussion. Of course Aikin agrees with Hughes, Upton and others that want of unity

---

[1] Great wits sometimes may gloriously offend,
     And rise to faults true Critics dare not mend. (ll. 159, 160).
[2] ll. 162 ff.
[3] P. 170.
[4] Vol. II, pp. 3 ff.

is the chief demerit of the *Faerie Queene*. He follows Thomas
Warton in suggesting that no objection could be made to its plan,
if each book might be considered as a separate whole. Since,
however, Spenser avowedly aimed at connecting these parts by
their common hero, the epic cannot be defended on these grounds [1].

The *Essay on the Heroic Poem of Gondibert* was called forth
by some observations in Hurd's *Discourse of Poetical Imitation*.
Hurd had condemned Davenant's epic on three grounds: its narrow
compass, which prevented the introduction of digressive ornaments,
its rejection of supernatural machinery, and last of all the poet's
dread of imitation, which prompted him to choose far-fetched
sentiments and obscure imagery. Aikin does not think the first
objection valid, as Davenant disavowed the epic rules before
embarking on his task, and it would therefore be unjust to try
his poem by these arbitrary precepts. He founds his refutation
of the second objection on Hurd's own assertion that a poet should
be careful not to exceed the limits of popular belief. In the
Discourse of Poetical Imitation he had commended Davenant for
'not running into the wild fable of the Italian romancers', which
had no adequate foundation in the belief of his time. If, however,
this pseudo-classical criterion is adopted, Aikin is right when he
says that the religious opinions of the enlightened age in which
Gondibert was written, forbade the use of 'machinery' altogether,
even if allowance was made for popular superstition. Nor does
Aikin agree with Hurd, when he blames Davenant for retaining
'the fantastic notion of love and honour', derived from the field
of romance. These romantic ideas prevailed a long time after the
days of chivalry had come to an end, whereas the belief in supernatural interference with human events had already lost its hold
on the English people when the epic was written. Machinery would
therefore have been inconsistent with the dictates of good sense
and improved taste.

---

[1] Aikin is one of the few critics who are susceptible to the music of the
Spenserian stanza: '.... when well executed, it has a fulness of melody, and
sonorous majesty, scarcely equalled by any other English measure.' But he
too, like Warton, considered it as the *ottava rima* to which an alexandrine
had been added.

John Pinkerton is now chiefly known in connection with Ballad
Literature, especially for his forgery of the second part of *Hardy
Kanute,* which he published together with many other ballads in
the year 1783. He corresponded with Percy [1], Beattie, Horace
Walpole and others, and won the esteem of no less a person than
Gibbon for his antiquarian and historical research.

In 1785 he published his *Letters of Literature* under the pseudo-
nym of Robert Heron, Heron being the maiden name of his mother.
Though the author is not a man of great critical acumen and many
of his sweeping statements have no sufficient foundation, the letters
are an interesting illustration of the general tendency of the time
to get rid of the dead weight of neo-classicism. Authoritative laws
are Pinkerton's principal object of censure, Aristotle and Longinus
are denounced as incompetent judges [2], the only critics of antiquity
worthy of attention are Quintilian and Horace. The French
authorities are treated with no less contempt, Bouhours is called
'an ecclesiastic who debauches taste', 'a critic who prates much
by rote, like a parrot, of what he could not understand', Boileau
is according to Pinkerton a writer of the meanest talents, 'whose

---

[1]   See *The Literary Correspondence of John Pinkerton, Esq.,* 2 vols. London 1830.
[2]   Aristotle's *Poetics* is said to be 'full of gross improprieties and absurdities,
that could only proceed from an author's writing on a subject he knew
nothing of. The book of Longinus on the Sublime is the second ancient work
of criticism that hath reached us; and in it the Sublime is confounded with
the Beautiful and the Tender, qualities of writings, directly opposite. So that
little can be said of the perfection of ancient criticism'. (*Letters of Literature
by Robert Heron, Esq.,* London 1785, p. 231).
'Criticism, if I mistake not, originated with Aristotle, who was as fond of
subduing the mental world, as his pupil Alexander was of conquering the
habitable. After that this Aristotle by dint of many a base trick and cavil . . . .
had usurped a tyrannical power over almost every branch of science, he was,
like his mad disciple, weeping for other worlds to vanquish . . . . (then P.
makes him go in his air balloon to the planet of poetry) . . . . To drop the
allegory, ere it grows stale; to an impartial reader, who is able to judge for
himself, it must be matter of infinite surprise how the authority of Aristotle
should ever be anything in poetry. All he hath done is to give a parcel of
metaphysical names, his common trick, to different points of poetry; which
points he draws without any invention or addition from Homer and Sophocles.
He then sits down with as much satisfaction as that Indian chief; who gets
up every morning before sun-rise; steps to the door of his cabin, marks with
his finger the course the sun is to pursue in his day's journey, which he always
takes care shall be the usual one; and then returns in the glory of having
given his direction to the *sun his brother*' (pp. 508 ff.).

genius was imitation, and whose taste was envy'. L'Abbé du Bos finds somewhat more favour in his eyes and is called the most judicious of the French critics. Of his English contemporaries there are only two who can lay claim to genuine taste, namely the Wartons. Kames's *Elements of Criticism* has a good title, but is 'a woeful book', Blair is called a slavish imitator of the French writers.

Of the English poets Pinkerton praises Milton, and especially Gray; Pope's works are full of superfluous and unmeaning verbiage, but the most incorrect of them all is Thomson, whose *Seasons* has, according to the critic, found far too much appreciation [1]. Modern literature, at least modern dramatic literature, is considered far superior to that of the ancients, whose plots were barren, and whose choruses destroyed the moral effect of their drama by making it unnecessary for the audience to think for themselves.

Good sense is Pinkerton's slogan; it is the only safe guide in judging literary art; the capricious dictates of authority are far inferior to it. Criticism should never exceed the limits of its proper sphere, and not prescribe rules for that which only genius can perform. The author compares it to the pilot of a ship who knows only the shores that have already been explored, but as soon as the vessel sets out for undiscovered islands, the captain (genius) has to take the helm himself. Criticism is therefore always dependent on the flights of creative genius. It is a science, not an art, 'because there can be no art where there is no room for invention' [2]. Pinkerton grants that a general collection of critical observations based on the practice of eminent writers, may be of some value but he gives strong warning against the judging of an author by rules deduced from the work of others. He therefore condemns the method followed by Addison 'who instead of drawing new rules from Milton judged him by foreign laws' [3]. The author severely inveighs against the Royal Academy. The only service it does to art, he says, is 'to spoil many good taylors, by converting

---

[1] 'Any reader who understands grammar and classic composition, is disgusted in every page of that poem by faults.' (*Op. cit.*, p. 64).

[2] P. 507.

[3] Yet in letter III, containing an estimate of Tasso's *Gerusalemme Liberata*, Pinkerton proceeds on similar lines: he first considers the faults of the work, then examines the Fable, Persons and Language.

them into *artists,* as they call themselves. It is to be hoped some future prince will just have sense enough to dissolve this lump of regal folly and to say to art and science: "Be free" '.

In the thirtieth letter Pinkerton gives a lengthy analysis of Gravina's *Ragion Poetica.* Though he praises the author as a man of fine taste and great talents, he disagrees with the main idea that underlies the work of the great Italian critic: namely the comparison of the rules of architecture and poetry. As those of the former art have geometry for their *ragione* or *first cause,* as Pinkerton translates, so those of poetry must have a similar fundamental principle. This analogy between geometry, 'the coldest operation of the judgment', and poetry, 'the warmest exertion of the imagination', is the chief cause of Pinkerton's violent anim- adversion. 'Poetry knows no rules', he says, 'the code of laws which genius prescribes to his subjects, will ever rest in their own bosoms'. Nature is the poet's teacher, a far greater leader than Homer, Sophocles, or Pindar, and genius is 'the supreme arbiter and lord of Nature's whole domain, her superior, her king, her God' [1]. This open rejection of all external rules, the emphatic statement that a work of art is subject only to laws imposed by creative genius itself, makes up for the pages of trivial matter in which Pinkerton's essay abounds. Works like Gravina's *Ragion Poetica* are in the opinion of the critic the result of a pernicious tendency to reduce poetry to a scientific system of rules.

Poetry is not an art but a faculty of the mind, the term *art of poetry* is therefore a contradiction in terms. Attachment to system hampers the poet's invention. Only a soul 'free as the mountain winds and large as the universe' can produce something great.

In spite of Pinkerton's repeated insistence on good sense and its sway over the imagination, he does not expect rationalistic truth. He does not require strict conformity to actuality and distinguishes between 'the paltry truth of fact' and 'the grand truth of Nature' [2]. By the latter he means the universal truth that poetry is to depict, it consists in 'the propriety and consistence of event, of character, of sentiment, of language'. A dramatic character may therefore

---

[1]   P. 208.
[2]   P. 460.

lie outside the domain of common life and still have truth. As an example he mentions Shakespeare's Caliban, which is true to itself; 'it offends no idea of propriety, yet is not in nature'.

Some passages in the *Letters* show that Pinkerton accepts the historical method in criticism. 'In estimating the defects of a valuable author, we should make ourselves his cotemporaries', he says in Letter XII. If Homer is pardoned for the simplicity of manners he has painted in his *Iliad,* why should not allowance be made for Tasso's excessive love of adornment, which characterized the Italian style of his time. The term 'tinsel', which Boileau applied to this great poet, might with more justice be used of the French writer's own *Ode sur la prise de Namur,* for all his other works are only 'prose lace put in starch'.

Further passages from the *Letters* might be adduced to exemplify Pinkerton's critical outlook, but the foregoing sufficiently prove his dissatisfaction with the old creed and his desire to deliver criticism from the paralysing influence of the rules.

CHAPTER XXV

SUBLIMITY AND MINUTENESS

Reynolds's aesthetic views, embodied in the *Discourses* dominated the theory of the art of painting till far into the nineteenth century. Though in his last discourse the author had expressed his great admiration of Michelangelo, in whose works the general and the particular were most happily blended, it was chiefly through Reynolds's influence that minute particularization continued to be considered as incompatible with true sublimity. Hazlitt was the first critic to express his disagreement with Reynolds's speculations on the grand style and to oppose the view that the painter, by disregarding the doctrine of generalized nature would 'pollute his canvas with deformity' [1]. He was of opinion that individual attention to the minute should go hand in hand with general effects and universal truth and that the highest form of art represents a union of the two, that 'the greatest grandeur may coexist with the most perfect, nay with a microscopic accuracy of detail' [2].

For the two most important kinds of poetry, the epic and tragedy, which were pre-eminently concerned with the human mind, the old views were maintained till the end of the century: excessive detail was thought to be inconsistent with greatness and nobility of thought. In descriptive poetry, which occupied a lower place in the scale of the literary *genres* [3], the poet was allowed more freedom, though here, too, a minute specification of particulars was considered dangerous. Selection rather than enumeration of details was required to attain the desired effect.

Attention has been drawn to Johnson's admiration of Thomson, whom he praised for his descriptions of 'extended scenes and general effects', combined with enumerations of well-selected details: 'he looks round on Nature and on Life with the eye which Nature bestows only on a poet . . . . and with a mind that at once

---

[1] *Idler,* 82.
[2] *Table-Talk,* ed. World's Classics, p. 178. See *Hazlitt as a Critic of Art* by Stanley P. Chase (PMLA, XXXIX, 1924).
[3] See p. 95, supra.

comprehends the vast, and attends to the minute' [1]. Critics have seen a contradiction between this statement and Imlac's warning that the poet should neglect the minute discriminations 'which one may have remarked and another have neglected' [2]. It is evident, however, that Johnson, when he praised Thomson's 'circumstantial varieties', was not thinking of highly individualized descriptions, but only of such as would appeal to the majority of readers and would 'recal the original to every mind'. 'The reader of *The Seasons*', he says, 'wonders that he never saw before what Thomson shews him and that he never yet has felt what Thomson expresses'. It should not be forgotten that the descriptions Thomson gives and the feelings he expresses are much less coloured by the poet's own imagination than those of Cowper and Burns some sixty years later. They are 'generic' rather than individual, as Saintsbury puts it and are within the range of ordinary human experience [3].

Johnson's defence of picturesque details in *The Seasons* may have been prompted or at least influenced by J. Warton's high commendation of Thomson's poetry in the *Essay on Pope*. Though Warton dislikes its diction, which is sometimes 'harsh and un-harmonious', sometimes 'turgid and obscure', and though he thinks 'the numbers are not sufficiently diversified by different pauses', he praises the poem even more lavishly than Johnson for its descriptive beauties, which 'are not of a fugacious kind, as depending on particular customs and manners' [4]. Of these beauties Warton quotes copious examples and he contrasts Thomson's 'strokes of nature' based on actual observation, with the conventional remarks of the Augustan poets, who 'dwelt for years in the Strand' and introduced into their poetry 'a set of hereditary images without proper regard to the age, or climate, or occasion, in which they were formerly used' [5]. The long digression winds up with the

---

[1] *Lives,* III, pp. 298, 299.

[2] *Rasselas,* p. 63. See Scott Elledge, *The Background and Development in English Criticism of the Theories of Generality and Particularity* (PMLA, LXII, 1947). Cf. also W. R. Keast's comment. (PQ, XXVII, 1948).

[3] Cf. Jeffrey's review of Crabbe's poetry (*Ed. Rev.,* April 1808), where a parallel is drawn between Crabbe's descriptions and those of Wordsworth. (quoted and commented on in J. Sutherland, *op. cit.,* p. 22).

[4] *Essay on Pope,* p. 43.

[5] *Ibid.,* p. 42.

curious statement that 'A minute and particular enumeration of circumstances judiciously selected, is what chiefly discriminates poetry from history, and renders the former, for that reason, a more close and faithful representation of nature than the latter' [1]. The superiority of poetry over history is therefore proclaimed on grounds which are diametrically opposed to Aristotle's [2].

Warton criticizes Pope's stereotyped diction in *Windsor Forest,* where few images are used 'which are not applicable to any place whatsoever'. He thinks that Denham has been extolled far beyond his merits and compares the cold and prosaic descriptions of *Cooper's Hill* with those given by Thomson, 'the true son of Nature', who has delineated its most striking objects 'with a force and distinctness hitherto unparalleled' [3].

Johnson's laudatory remarks on Thomson's poetry are quoted and endorsed by Hugh Blair in a note to his fortieth lecture, which deals with didactic and descriptive poetry. He calls Thomson 'a strong and a beautiful describer; for he has a feeling heart and a strong imagination.... The impression which he felt, he transmutes to his readers'. Blair agrees with Johnson that a proper selection of circumstances is one of the great merits of *The Seasons.* He distinguishes between the sublime and pathetic kind of poetry in which 'anxious minuteness of laboured illustration' [4] should be carefully avoided, and descriptive poetry, where every object should be particularized: 'No description that rests in generals, can be good: for we can conceive nothing clearly in the abstract; all distinct ideas are formed upon particulars' [5]. In describing the beauties of nature the poet should be as particular as possible: 'A hill, a river, or a lake rises up more conspicuous to the fancy, when some particular lake, or river, or hill, is specified, than when the terms are left general' [6]. What Blair means by particularization becomes clear when Milton's *L'Allegro* and *Il Penseroso* are held up as the best English poems in the descriptive style. 'Here, there

---

1   *Essay on Pope,* p. 47.
2   Cf. Scott Elledge, PMLA, LXII, 1947.
3   *The Works of A. Pope.* London, 1797, vol. I, p. XXII.
4   *Op. cit.,* p. 552.
5   *Ibid.,* p. 549.
6   *Ibid.,* p. 553.

are no unmeaning general impressions; all is particular; all is picturesque; nothing forced or exaggerated', Blair observes. But Milton's descriptions in his two companion pieces are no more particular in the modern sense of the word than Thomson's. His pictures of the various aspects of English scenery which follow each other in rapid succession, are not the individualistic and particularized results of actual observation, but rather the idealized products of the poet's memory well-stored with sense-impressions [1].

The practice of avoiding circumstantial imagery, the mania for circumlocution, had led to a system of stereotyped convention-alities, a 'vague, glossy and unfeeling language', as Wordsworth called it [2], which at last began to pall on the ears of the majority of readers. The Preface to the *Lyrical Ballads* was not the first critical document directed against this Augustan phraseology: dissident opinions are to be found at a much earlier period. To my knowledge the first is that of Joseph Warton, who in his *Essay* denounces Pope's use of florid epithets and useless circumlocutions in the *Messiah* and in general attacks the vagueness of neo-classic descriptions. 'The judicious addition of circumstances and adjuncts is what renders poesy a more lively imitation of nature than prose', he says [3]. In the same essay he expresses his great admiration of Homer and Shakespeare; he thinks that they excel all other poets because they do not merely give general ideas. Every image is particular, it cannot be alienated from the person who uses it, and would not suit any other character [4].

In the second volume Warton praises Spenser highly for his detailed descriptions. His allegorical personages are so minutely drawn, he thinks, that we seem to behold them with our own

---

[1]　Cf. T. S. Eliot, *A Note on the Verse of John Milton*. (Essays and Studies of the English Association, XXI, 1936).

[2]　*Wordsworth's Literary Criticism*. Oxford, 1905, p. 189.

[3]　*Op. cit.*, p. 11.

[4]　P. 321. This very minuteness of Homer's descriptions had been considered by critics as a serious blemish in the works of the Greek poet. Wood in his *Essay on the Original Genius and Writings of Homer* (London, 1775), affords a good illustration of this. He mentions as one of Homer's faults that he is often minutely descriptive: 'He frequently introduces superfluous circumstances of mere precision, rather than leave his object vague and uncircumscribed; even where a general view of it would have done as well or perhaps better.' (p. 218).

eyes [1]. Only clear, complete, and circumstantial imagery will produce such vivid impressions that readers are turned into spectators. One of the favourable circumstances under which Homer wrote was in Warton's opinion that general and abstract terms had not yet been invented in his time. 'Hence his Muse (like his own Helen standing on the walls of Troy) points out every *person* and *thing, accurately* and *forcibly*' [2]. Warton quotes the opinion of a celebrated foreigner, Count Algarotti, who had contrasted Virgil's minuteness and the absence of detail in Milton's description of Eve. He adds, however, that the Puritan poet offers plenty of instances where he has drawn his figures with great accuracy and distinctness. The critic discusses this subject at some length, because of the many symptoms in the literature of his time 'of departing from these *true* and lively and *minute* representations of Nature, and of *dwelling in generalities*' [3]. He also defends the use of familiar words and protests against the mistaken notion that terms like market-place, alms-house, seats, spire and others should be excluded from poetry to save it from meanness and vulgarity [4].

In his commentary on lines 317 and 318 of Horace's *Epistola ad Pisones* Hurd expresses the ordinary neo-classic view that the writer of dramatic poetry should represent 'the general idea of the kind' and 'not confine himself too scrupulously to the exhibition of particulars'. He also censures the Flemish school of painters for taking their models from real nature and not 'from the contemplative idea of beauty', as the Italians did. He thinks it is the duty of the poet as well as of the painter to eliminate anything that characterizes the *individual : universal* truth ought to be their aim [5]. On the other hand Hurd praises Shakespeare for preferring the *specific* idea to the general in his metaphors and descriptions, 'an excellence in poetical expression which cannot be sufficiently

---

[1] *Op. cit.,* p. 32.

[2] P. 161.

[3] P. 168.

[4] P. 170. In the dedication to his translation of Virgil Joseph Warton had himself regretted the necessity of using such coarse and common words as plough, sow, wheat, dung, ashes, horse and cow, words which would disgust 'many a delicate reader'.

[5] *Op. cit.,* I, pp. 255, 256.

studied [1]. Addison's *Cato* is criticized for its general statements and uncharacteristic imagery.

Some passages in the *Discourse on Poetical Imitation* point even more distinctly to Hurd's dissatisfaction with the neo-classic conception of generalized diction. He compares descriptions of daybreak by three different poets: Homer, Virgil and Shakespeare and thinks that of the Elizabethan poet far superior to the others, because it is *particular,* those of Homer and Virgil *general.* The use of particular images is in Hurd's opinion one of the characteristics of real genius and one of the distinguishing marks of originality. Dull minds only catch a faint glimpse of the form before them, and see it as through a mist. To the true poet 'every object stands forth in bright sunshine . . . . Every minute mark and lineament of the contemplated form leaves a corresponding trace on his fancy. And having these bright and determinate conceptions of things in his own mind, he finds it no difficulty to convey the liveliest ideas of them to others. This is what we call *painting* in poetry; by which not only the general natures of things are described, and their more obvious appearances shadowed forth; but every single *property* marked, and the poet's own image set in distinct *relief* before the view of his reader'. The proper task of true genius is 'to give life and colour to the selected circumstance and imprint it on the imagination with distinctness and vivacity' [2].

Lord Kames deals with the subject of poetic imitation in the twenty-first chapter of his treatise. He lays down some rules for the poet's guidance in narrating events and giving descriptions. Those kinds of poetry which aim exclusively at entertainment, ought to describe things as they appear in reality, Kames observes. The objects should be painted so accurately that a distinct and lively image is formed in the mind of the reader. Every useless circumstance should therefore be avoided, but if a circumstance is necessary, however slight it may be, it cannot be described too minutely [3]. Every kind of literary performance requires the

---

[1] *Op. cit.,* p. 59.
[2] *Ibid.,* pp. 19, 20. Cf. K. L. F. Thielke, Literatur- und Kunstkritik in ihren Wechselbeziehungen (Studien zur englischen Philologie, LXXXIV). Halle, 1935, p. 45.
[3] *Elements of Criticism,* II, p. 329.

avoidance of abstract and general terms. Images, which Kames considers as the life of poetry, cannot conduce to true sublimity without the introduction of particular objects. The critic makes one curious restriction, namely for general terms that comprehend a number of individuals, like *our kindred, our clan, our country* etc.: 'tho they scarcely raise any image, (they) have however a wonderful power over our passions: the greatness of the complex object overbalances the obscurity of the image' [1].

Another critic who disapproves of the Augustan method of dealing in generalities is George Campbell. The subject of the third book of his essay is 'Vivacity as depending on the Choice of Words'. Here the author discusses the qualities of style which please the imagination and tend to awaken and fix the attention of the reader: 'proper terms', 'rhetorical tropes' and the 'relation between sound and sense'. The most important characteristic of proper terms is according to Campbell their speciality. The more general they are, the fainter the picture is. He quotes the passage from Luke, Ch. XII, 27, 28 [2], and adds: 'Let us here adopt a little of the tasteless manner of modern paraphrasts, by the substitution of more general terms, one of their many expedients of infrigidating, and let us observe the effect produced by this change.' The result is as follows: 'Consider the flowers, how they gradually increase in their size, they do no manner of work, and yet I declare to you, that no king whatever, in his most splendid habit, is dressed up like them. If then God in his providence doth so adorn the vegetable productions, which continue but a little time on the land, and are afterwards put into the fire, how much more will he provide clothing for you?' Campbell then compares the original with this spiritless paraphrase [3]. He says that many critics of his time would assert that in the first the beauty of one sort of flowers is described, in the latter the beauty of the whole kind, but he himself rejects the Augustan conception that the poet has to represent the type,

---

[1] *Elements of Criticism*, I, p. 239. Cf. II, p. 352. 'Abstract or general terms have no good effect in any composition for amusement; because it is only of particular objects that images can be formed'.

[2] 'Consider the lilies how they grow': etc.

[3] *The Philosophy of Rhetoric*. Edinburgh, 1816, II, pp. 166, 167. Cf. Wordsworth's comment on Johnson's paraphrase of Proverbs, Ch. VI, 6 ff. *Appendix to Lyrical Ballads* (1802), *Wordsworth's Lit. Crit.* 1905, pp. 44 ff.

not the individual. The effect will often be all the greater, not only if he particularizes but even if he individualizes the object presented to the mind. He draws a parallel between philosophy, which addresses the understanding and therefore abounds in general terms, and poetry, which directs itself to the fancy and consequently makes use of terms that are as particular as possible. Various examples are adduced from Dryden, Milton, and Thomson to illustrate the particular expressiveness of some of their images [1].

John Scott, the author of the *Critical Essays on some of the Poems of several English Poets* (1785), quotes Warton's words about the poet's task of turning readers into spectators. As an example where 'every epithet paints its object and paints it distinctly' he mentions the description of the inn in Goldsmith's *Deserted Village* [2]. He condemns the practice of some authors who, to avoid the repetition of an epithet, indulge in some florid and far-fetched circumlocution. 'Writers .... often have recourse to a kind of metonymical or rather catachrestical expressions, which are mostly either improper or inelegant' [3]. As an instance in point he adduces Thomson's various pompous appellations for rain: 'falling verdure', 'lucid moisture', 'promis'd sweetness', 'treasures of the clouds', 'heaven descending in universal bounty', and 'milky nutriment'. On the other hand he admires the poet's detailed account of the different places where the birds build their nests [4], and quotes it as a proof that it is erroneous to suppose, as some critics do, 'that poetry can only deal in generals; or in other words, that it cannot subsist with any very minute specification of particulars' [5].

The above references prove that a reaction in favour of minuteness manifested itself as the century progressed. The aversion to minute descriptions, which Johnson and Reynolds had professed, was by no means universal, even during their lifetime. A direct attack on Reynolds's conception of art is found in William Blake's marginal notes to the *Discourses* [6]. Though they belong to

---

[1] P. 166 ff.
[2] Near yonder thorn etc., ll. 137—236.
[3] P. 303.
[4] *Spring,* ll. 635 ff.
[5] *Critical Essays,* p. 315.
[6] *The Works of William Blake by E. J. Ellis and W. B. Yeats,* 3 vols. 1893, vol. II, pp. 318 ff.

the next century, they may receive a short notice here. Blake's remarks are chiefly concerned with painting, but many of them have a much wider scope. In opposition to the advocate of the grand style, who judged art by the general effect of the whole, Blake pleads the necessity of minute discriminations: 'Real effect is making out of Parts, and it is Nothing Else but That' [1]. Reynolds had expressed the belief that excessive attention to detail does not go with true sublimity. Blake's opinion is diametrically opposite, as appears from a note to the third Discourse. He thinks that without minuteness grandeur and sublimity can never be attained. 'Sacrifice the Parts: what becomes of the whole?' is his comment on Reynolds's statement that all smaller things are to be sacrificed to the greater because they are injurious to sublimity [2]. What the great portrait-painter considered as a serious defect, namely 'peculiar marks' [3], was to Blake the only merit of art.

---

[1] *Op. cit.,* vol II, p. 322.
[2] Discourse IV.
[3] Discourse VI. Some other notes to the same effect are:

Minute Discrimination is not accidental. All Sublimity is founded on Minute Discrimination. (Note to Discourse I).

Without minute neatness of execution the sublime cannot exist. Grandeur of ideas is founded on precision of ideas (Note to Discourse III).

To Reynolds's statement: 'and the whole beauty and grandeur of the art consists, in my opinion, in being able to get above all singular forms, local custom, particularities, details of every kind' (Discourse III): A folly; singular and particular detail is the foundation of the sublime!

Here he is for Determinate, and yet for Indeterminate. Distinct General Form Cannot Exist. Distinctness is Particular, Not General. (Note to Discourse III).

To the statement in the fifth Discourse that 'the ancients, when they employed their art to represent Jupiter, confined his character to majesty alone': False! The Ancients were chiefly attentive to Complicated and Minute Discrimination of Character. It is the whole of Art. Reynolds cannot bear Expression.

CHAPTER XXVI

CONCLUSION

In its essential form the conflict of which I have traced the development is not restricted to a particular period of literary history or to a particular country. It is a struggle between two schools of criticism which have always existed and will always exist. Each of the two has its own canons of judgment and is actuated by its own principles, principles which are intimately connected with those that underlie the processes of literary creation. To try and establish a fixed line of demarcation or give a definition of either of the two antagonistic tendencies, comprising its various manifestations at all times and in all places, would be as futile as the many attempts that have been made to define the exact nature of the antithesis between the Classic and the Romantic in art. This much may be said, however, that one of the types of criticism is always more or less judicial: it passes judgment on a work of art, appraises its merits and demerits from its own point of view and by a standard it has erected for itself. It compares what the author has achieved with that which he ought to have attained.

The second type is concerned mainly with the impression which the artistic production makes upon the critic's mind and with the idea that has guided the artist in his search for beauty. It tries to understand and interpret rather than to judge, and if it expresses a judgment, it grounds it exclusively on the organic laws of the work of art itself. Reason is the idol of the first school of critics, whereas the other group consider feeling and imagination as the supreme sources of knowledge. They do not deny that art ultimately addresses itself to the understanding, but believe that it always does so 'through affections of pleasure and sympathy', as De Quincey expressed it.

These two opposing critical tendencies manifest themselves at all times, and it is the spirit of the age, the general mental atmosphere, with which all the ruling intellectual conceptions are correlated, that determines which of the two is in the ascendant. It may be safely inferred that the judicial school of criticism reigned supreme in the latter part of the eighteenth century. In the eyes of Johnson

and the majority of his contemporaries the critic's task was still
exclusively to judge by principles which their scientific analysis
had proved to be essential. The Doctor himself called it his first
duty to accept only those means of pleasing which depend on known
causes, and he carefully distinguished them from the 'inexplicable
elegancies' which appeal only to the fancy, from 'which we feel
delight, but know not how they produce it' [1]. This antagonism
between feeling and the understanding was the natural consequence
of the application of purely rational tests to something which
is pre-eminently the expression of imaginative experience. Thomas
Warton, who repeatedly censures the Augustan Age for its
coldness and insensibility to genuine emotion, betrays the influence of his environment when he observes that 'in regarding
Spenser, if the critic is not satisfied, yet the reader is transported'.
He failed to recognize that a course of criticism which leads to such
preposterous results, stands condemned for that very reason. People
in the eighteenth century were taught to condemn what they could
not help admiring.

This explains their curiously half-hearted attitude towards the
great Elizabethan writers, in particular towards Shakespeare. As
long as his art was measured by 'good-sense' standards, his glaring
offences could not escape notice. From Dryden's days onward his
defects had been balanced against his excellencies, and Johnson,
the last representative of this sort of judicial Shakespearean
criticism, is less merciful than some of his predecessors [2].

However much the rationalistic method of criticism dominated
the Age of Johnson, it would be beside the mark to say that it
enjoyed undisturbed sway till the opening years of the next century.
The incompetency of reason as the only judge of literary merit
began at last to be recognized. Reynolds contrasted the rational

---

[1] *Rambler*, 92.
[2] Cf. his comment on *Cymbeline*: 'The Play has many just sentiments, some
     natural dialogues, and some pleasing scenes, but they are obtained at the
     expence of much incongruity.
     To remark the folly of the fiction, the absurdity of the conduct, the confusion
     of the names and manners of different times, and the impossibility of the
     events in any system of life, were to waste criticism upon unresisting im-
     becillity, upon faults too evident for detection, and too gross for aggravation'.
     (Raleigh, *Johnson on Shakespeare*, p. 183).

and the intuitive side of human nature, and stated that the latter
faculty, whose decisions outrun those of the deliberate understanding, is the ultimate source of truth. He accepted reason as an
interpreter, not as a law-giver and judge. Goldsmith, Beattie, and
Blair discredited its interpretative power in so far as they obeyed
a higher authority, namely 'taste', though at the same time they
granted that judgment was one of its chief constituent qualities.
Hurd made the important assertion that feeling or sentiment is the
sole arbiter of works of genius, and Belsham put his finger on the
spot when he condemned the practice of judging in matters of taste
by reason and not by feeling. His opinion was endorsed by Joseph
Warton in his edition of Pope [1]. What Hurd and Belsham said of
art in general, Morgann restricted to Shakespeare. He did not deny
that for other writers reason might be a competent judge. In
Shakespeare, however, everything seemed to him lifted above
human judgment: 'Him we may profess rather to feel than to
understand.'

The most important feature of English literary criticism in the
Age of Johnson was the establishment of a new conception of
poetry, based on the supremacy of the imagination. We have seen
that the old rationalistic outlook led a vigorous life; it not only continued to exist side by side with the new one, but in Johnson's
lifetime it was even the most generally accepted creed. To the
scientific critics imagination remained the handmaid of reason.
Its operations were determined by the mechanical processes that
empiric philosophy accepted, its sphere was restricted to that of
the aggregating faculty of the mind for which Coleridge chose
the name of *fancy* and which he carefully kept apart from the
'modifying and coadunating faculty' of the imagination [2]. With the
empiricists of the eighteenth century the imagination or fancy —
we saw that the two terms were used as equivalent or nearly
equivalent — continued to be the means of adornment to which
Hobbes had reduced it long before. Its combination of images,

---

[1] Cf. Cowper's statement: '.... persons of much sensibility are always persons
    of taste; a taste for poetry depends indeed upon that very article more than
    upon any other.' (*Works,* ed. Southey, II, p. 420).
[2] Letter to Sotheby, Sept. 1802.

apparently dissimilar, was a purely intellectual activity, in which the emotion of the artist had no share. As I have pointed out, however, there were indications of a growing dissatisfaction with the old neo-classic outlook. Reynolds recognized that ultimately the artist was led by intuition rather than by reason and Alison looked upon the imagination as the principal source of aesthetic emotions.

It was the great merit of the Wartons and Hurd that they attempted to reinstate the imagination in its rightful place. To these three critics it was a living force, a creative power, not satisfied with the limited sphere that the rationalists would allow it and contemptuous of continual control of reason. Its field of operation extended far beyond the narrow compass of the sensuous world. Joseph Warton distinguished between 'a Man of Wit, a Man of Sense' and the true poet, and called 'a creative and glowing Imagination' the first requisite of a genuinely poetic genius. Two years before, his brother had championed the cause of imagination and enthusiasm in his *Observations on the Faerie Queene*. Neither of these two critics, nor Richard Hurd makes an attempt to define the nature and functions of this creative faculty, but their strong insistence on complete abandonment to the poetic fury, to 'the fine frenzy', as Hurd, quoting from Shakespeare, calls it, makes it apparent that they meant something else than the cool automatic workings of the fancy. A warm imagination and a 'strong sensibility' are the two qualities on which these romantic writers laid chief stress; they were inseparably connected in their minds. Emotional fervour and unchecked spontaneity were considered by them as the necessary conditions under which the imaginative faculty must act.

As soon as the true nature of poetic art began to be understood, the attitude towards imitation was bound to change. The new conception of poetry engendered the conviction that all that comes to the poet's mind from the world outside is transformed there by the emotions that it rouses, that, as Hazlitt said, 'he holds the mirror up to nature, seen through the medium of passion and imagination'. Thomas Warton showed some consciousness of this imaginative experience, when he spoke of 'the chymical energy of true genius' and of the noble transmutation it can produce. Webb

exposed the fallacy of the pseudo-classical assertion that originality
is not always possible because nature is the same in all ages and in
all places. He at least, was aware that what the poet describes has
no real existence but is the product of his own creation. On the
other hand, however, Hurd's *Dissertation on Poetical Imitation,*
which is so typical of the age, betrays the old misconception, when
it reverts to Boileau's and Pope's distinction between originality
of manner and of matter. This assertion is based on the assumption
that the form of a literary composition can be separated from the
substance. Pope had called expression the *dress* of thought and we
find his statement reiterated by several eighteenth century critics.
Hurd, Burke, and others speak about the use of figures as if it was
a deliberate, mechanical means on the part of the poet to adorn
his style. None of them realized that the relation is of too subtle
a nature to justify this conception, that, if the form is original, the
idea of which the form is the imaginative embodiment must be
original as well. Wordsworth considered language as the *incarna-
tion* of thought and De Quincey, repeating this statement, explained
that the two are inseparable, that each co-exists 'not merely *with*
the other, but each *in* and through the other'. At this conviction
the eighteenth century critics had not yet arrived.

   When imagination and emotion had come into their own again,
the criteria of *truth* and *nature* in the pseudo-classical sense of
the words lost their influential positions. Critics began to see
how much harm had been done to poetry by the abuse of
rationalism, they felt that the mere understanding is an inadequate
test for the higher truth of art. Reynolds discriminated between
truth in art and mathematical truth, Hurd distinguished *poetical*
truth, which requires no external evidence, from that based on
rational belief. He thought it sufficient if the poet could bring
the reader to imagine the possibility of his fictions and thus
anticipated Coleridge, who called poetic faith 'a semblance of
truth sufficient to procure for these shadows of imagination that
willing suspension of disbelief for the moment'. Gray deemed that
by good management *verisimilitude* might be attained even in such
absurd stories as *The Tempest* and that Shakespeare has shown that
supernatural characters like the witches in *Macbeth* and the fairies

in *A Midsummer Night's Dream* can be made acceptable by the genius of the poet [1]. Hurd was also the first critic to recognize that nature, as the rationalists interpreted it, differed materially from that of the poetical world. In this world 'experience has less to do than consistent imagination', he said, and he made it clear that by artistic treatment even the wildest fancies may assume an air of probability. Both he and Twining were aware that the poet is free to go beyond the bounds of actuality provided that the poetic illusion is consistent with and does not violate the laws of generalized experience. Thus the much debated and misinterpreted Aristotelian doctrine was seen in a new light.

When the power of reason was on the wane and the conviction growing that the imagination is the dominating factor in poetic creation, it was inevitable that the reputation of the Augustan poets, in particular that of Pope, should lose some of its lustre. Joseph Warton called his supremacy in question, and though his brother's works and those of Richard Hurd do not contain any direct attack on the pseudo-classic poets, there are clear indications of a discontent with their cold intellectualism, which had required an adherence to solid fact, had held the poets down to earth and had expelled romance. They considered the 'mathematical and scientific spirit' which permeated the Age of Reason to be the chief cause of the decay of true poetic sentiment. The 'extravagances that are above propriety', 'the world of fine fabling', were to these romantic critics things of higher value than the gain of good sense which the rationalistic movement evolved. Judged by this new standard Pope's poetry was found to be lacking in imaginative power and emotional appeal. It was considered to be the fruit of incessant labour and indefatigable industry under the guidance of common sense, rather than of inspiration [2]. His translation of Homer's *Iliad*, which Johnson had called 'the noblest version of poetry which the world has ever seen' [3], and which was greatly admired by Gray and Gibbon, excited the anger and contempt of

---

[1] *The Letters of Thomas Gray,* ed. by Tovey, vol. II, p. 295.
[2] Cf. Cowper's verdict: Made poetry a mere mechanic art
                            And every warbler had his tune by heart.
[3] *Lives,* III, p. 119.

William Cowper. In the latter part of the century it was often censured for its false refinement; its artificial diction and tawdry ornaments were contrasted with the simple grandeur of the original.

As Pope's fame lessened, that of Milton and Spenser grew. The view that Milton's poetry fell into almost complete oblivion in the days of Augustanism until Addison made it popular, has long since been given up. As Professor R. D. Havens has shown, the great epic of the Puritan poet was far from being neglected during the last few decades of the seventeenth century and the beginning of the next. On the other hand I cannot agree with those who assert that its fame was equal to or even greater than that of Pope's poetry. Such statements prove how dangerous it is to measure the popularity of the epic exclusively by the number of editions it went through and the numerous blank verse poems that saw the light. Milton's minor poems found few admirers during the first half of the eighteenth century and it was not till a comparatively late period that they began to be appreciated as they deserved. In the Age of Johnson Milton attained his great vogue. Miltonic phraseology and metrical skill served as an antidote to the monotony of the heroic couplet. 'The school of Milton rose in emulation of the school of Pope', as Thomas Warton observed.

With Spenser it was different. We saw that the Augustans had not neglected the poet but in their own way had admired him. The qualities for which Spenser won the devotion of the Wartons, Hurd, and other romantic critics: 'the impetuosity of imagination', 'the exuberance of his fancy', had been greatly underestimated by Pope and his contemporaries. To the subtle beauty of the Spenserian stanza, the music and melody of Spenser's verse, even the precursors of romanticism were insensible. Such a genuine admirer of the poet as Thomas Warton was of opinion that the constraint which the use of the stanza entailed, led Spenser into many absurdities.

In the introduction to his *English Literary Criticism* (1903), Professor Vaughan observed that *correctness* remained the idol both of poets and critics throughout the eighteenth century and that 'nothing less than the furious onslaught of the *Lyrical Ballads* was needed to overthrow it'. This statement is of course only partially correct. As I have shown, Johnson and Goldsmith were in this respect, as in so many others, staunch upholders of the Augustan tradition, and besides these two there were a host of minor figures who remained true to it. But on the other hand there were indications from the beginning of the era that the tide was on the turn, and neither Johnson's nor Goldsmith's vituperations could prevent the 'innovators' steadily gaining ground. When emotion and imagination again became recognized as the basic qualities of art, when the renewed interest in the past, the study and consequent imitation of Elizabethan writers caused a reaction against the tyranny of the heroic couplet, and led to the common acceptance of other vehicles to express poetic thought, the old veneration for mechanical correctness began rapidly to lose its hold on the critics. The leaders of the revolt were again the Wartons and Hurd, but we have traced the same tendency in Twining and Shenstone. J. Warton's and Twining's remarks prove that prim regularity began to be associated in their minds with lack of emotion and imagination. Too great an attention to formal excellences was now thought incompatible with the lofty flights of true poetic genius: the correctness of the Augustans was identified with 'the labour and delay of the file'. Long before the *Lyrical Ballads*, long before Hazlitt declared that Pope's poetry was by no means faultless, and before De Quincey opposed the view that correctness was Pope's 'plume of distinction from preceding poets', there had at least been some among the eighteenth century critics who had asserted that these claims were not well founded.

Lastly, some critics had expressed their dissatisfaction with the doctrine of generalization. The conception that genuine grandeur was inconsistent with detailed descriptions had had its day. Pseudo-classical conventional vagueness and the artificial circumlocutory diction were no longer relished. The revival of emotionalism brought along with it a sudden and strong outburst of individualism, which required realistic touches instead of universal truths. Thus Johnson's theory of general properties and large appearances began to give way to a more individualistic conception of nature, characterized by a love of particular circumstances and by the use of excessive detail.

If we take the Johnsonian era as a whole, we may safely conclude that rationalism was the prevailing attitude; even the heralds of the new period of romantic criticism, were still trammelled by the old prejudices. Some students of this period of literary history are inclined to represent the Wartons, Hurd, and some others as thoroughgoing romanticists. This view is entirely erroneous. They were in advance of their age, it is true, their attacks were directed against the vital elements of the neo-classic creed. On the other hand their works offer several instances to prove that they had by no means emancipated themselves completely from its powerful influence.

The results of my investigation may be summed up as follows: Before the century drew towards its close, the validity of several of the old conventional dogmas had been seriously questioned. The mechanical standards that had satisfied the earlier generations of critics, had been renounced; the conception of absolute and unchanging literary perfection had given place to an historical outlook, a sense for relative values which recognized that every age has its own ideals of beauty and tried to find in its social conditions the explanation of its literary forms. The canonical value of Aristotle's *Poetics* and Horace's *Ars Poetica* had become discredited. French authority on aesthetic questions was completely at an end. Classical dogmatism, which after all had never gained a very strong hold on English critics, had been succeeded by an inductive form of criticism, which aimed at the establishment of rational principles of universal application. Side by side with these empiricists, however, there were the exponents of a wider outlook, who repudiated the strictly rationalistic view of art. They asserted the value of emotion in the attainment of knowledge, and exalted imaginative passion into a sphere far higher than that of good judgment.

APPENDIX

The low estimation of textual criticism in the Age of Dryden and that of Pope was the outcome of a general aversion to pedantry and eccentricity, which must be considered as a reaction against the excessive show of learning in the early part of the century. The English critics followed their French masters in their depreciation of mere erudition. The *honnête homme* of the seventeenth century in France was a man of the world, a person of good breeding and taste as well as 'good sense'. The French pseudo-classical writers laid particular stress on these urbane qualities, and all agreed in their disdain of narrow booklearning. 'Il faut qu'on n'en puisse dire, ni: il est mathématicien, ni prédicateur, ni éloquent, mais il est honnête homme; cette qualité universelle me plaît seule,' Pascal says in his *Pensées*. Bouhours (*Entretiens d'Ariste et d'Eugène: Le Bel Esprit*) carefully distinguishes between 'les savants' and 'les beaux esprits': 'La plus heureuse naissance a besoin d'une bonne éducation et de ce bel usage du monde qui raffine l'intelligence et qui subtilise le bon sens . . . . Comme ils (les savants) sont toujours ensevelis dans l'étude et qu'ils ont peu de commerce avec les honnêtes gens, ils n'ont pas dans l'esprit une certaine politesse et je ne sais quel agrément qu'il faut y avoir' etc. Boileau's advice to the poet in the fourth canto of *L'Art poétique* is equally illustrative:

> Que les vers ne soient pas votre éternel emploi;
> Cultivez vos amis, soyez homme de foi.
> C'est peu d'être agréable et charmant dans un livre,
> Il faut savoir encore et converser et vivre.

We find the statements of these two French critics re-echoed in the English essays of the period, for instance in Roscommon's *Essay on Translated Verse* (Spingarn, *Crit. Essays*, II, p. 299). Temple mentions as one of the causes of the inferiority of modern learning to that of the ancients the habit of going 'in quest of Books rather than men for their guides, though these are living and those in comparison but dead Instructors, ...' (*op. cit.*, p. 7). W. Wotton in his *Reflexions upon Ancient and Modern Learning* thinks that Temple's attack must be directed against Learning as it was fifty or sixty years before, for in their own time 'the New Philosophy has introduced so great a Correspondence between Men of Learning and Men of Business . . . . that that *Pedantry* which formerly was almost universal, is now in a great measure disused' (*op. cit.*, p. 416). The Boyle-Bentley controversy and especially Bentley's *Horace* naturally tended to increase the contempt for ponderous learning among the opponents of the great classical scholar. The pedant was identified with one who spent all his time on mere trifles, with a diligent plodder, devoid of that supreme quality of a critic, *taste*. Thus Bentley and Theobald became the targets at which the arrows of the men of the world were aimed. Pedantry and textual criticism were closely associated in their minds. The great English Augustans: Swift, Addison, Pope, Bolingbroke and Shaftesbury are all equally severe in their censures. Swift's *Battle of the Books* (1697) was one of the author's earliest expressions of his hostility towards scholastic minuteness. The attack was renewed in the third section of the *Tale of a Tub* (1704), where Dennis, Rymer, Wotton and Perrault shared Bentley's fate and were all grouped among the descendants of Momus and Hybris. The principal aim of the *Scriblerus Club*, which was never definitely organized but would have counted as members Pope, Swift, Arbuthnot and Gay, was to write a satire on the abuse of learning by the pedants. Pope's line in the *Essay on Criticism*: 'Tho' learned, well-bred; and tho' well-bred, sincere', was probably suggested by Boileau. The best-known attack is of course Pope's *Dunciad*, where Bentley and Theobald are represented as the exponents of dullness and indefatigable plodding. The latter figures as the original hero of the poem, whereas Bentley is satirized in the fourth book, published in 1742, where he is dubbed:

> Thy mighty scholiast, whose unweary'd pains
> Made Horace dull, and humbled Milton's strains.

In ll. 190—194 of the third book there is moreover the following remark on verbal criticism in general:

> "There, dim in clouds, the poring Scholiasts mark,
> Wits, who like owls, see only in the dark,
> A Lumberhouse of books in ev'ry head,
> For ever reading, never to be read!

Shaftesbury, the champion of taste, is no less severe in his denunciations. He distinguishes between true knowledge and pedantry in the following passage: 'A good Poet and an honest Historian, may afford Learning enough to a *Gentleman*. And such a one, whilst he reads these Authors as his Diversion, will have a truer relish of their sense and understand 'em better than a *Pedant* with all his Labours, and the assistance of his Volumes of Commentators' (*op. cit.*, I, p. 122). One of the most vehement animadversions on the abuse of textual criticism is David Mallet's poem *Of Verbal Criticism* (Chalmers, XIV), written, as the author says in the 'Advertisement', as 'a testimony of his inviolable esteem for Mr. Pope.' The learning of the verbal critic is designated as the result of 'much hard study, without sense or breeding,' and Bentley is styled the 'prime pattern of the captious art' who, 'Out-tibbalding poor Tibbald', 'holds high the scourge o'er each fam'd author's head'. J. Armstrong's *Essay on Taste*, meant as an advice to a young critic, speaks of the

> .... thousands of scholastic merit.
Who worm their sense (i. e. of the classics) out but ne'er taste their spirit'.

In one of the notes to the *Vernoniad*, a political pamphlet cast in the form of an epic, Fielding parodies the manner of commentating adopted by Bentley and his school. In his *Covent Garden Journal* the author mentions as the objects of his satire the 'petty scholars employed in the pedantry of etymology and text-editing and in vain scientific pursuits and men with knowledge but no wisdom.' In number 24 he ridicules the 'many industrious Critics' who 'have spent their Lives in *all such Reading as was never read*, as Mr. Pope hath it.'

Johnson did not attach much value to philological inquiry. He failed to grasp the importance of the new method which Bentley had inaugurated and Theobald had applied to Shakespeare. In the *Preface* he calls him 'a man of narrow comprehensions and small acquisitions, with no native and intrinsick splendour of genius' (Raleigh, p. 45). In one of his *Ramblers* he had long before censured the writers who 'read with the microscope of criticism', and in the same number of the periodical he speaks of those 'who are furnished by criticism with a telescope', who indulge in all kinds of far-fetched explanations and have no eye for the obvious. It was perhaps partly from personal reasons that he ranked Warburton much higher than Theobald. Boswell tells us that the answer to Burney's question which of the two he thought the greatest critic, was that Warburton would 'make two-and-fifty Theobalds cut into slices.' Johnson was a great admirer of the criticism of a poet like Dryden, which was 'exact without minuteness and lofty without exaggeration' (*Lives*, I, p. 412).

Goldsmith's opinion resembles that of his friend. In the *Inquiry into the Present State of Polite Learning* (1759) he expresses his dissatisfaction with the pursuits of the scholars who 'exhaust their natural sagacity in exploring the intricacies of another man's thoughts and thus never to have leisure to think for themselves . . . . By the industry of such, the sciences, which in themselves are easy of access, affright the learner with the severity of their appearance.' This work of misapplied genius is in Goldsmith's opinion the cause of the mutual contempt between the scholar and the man of the world. He thinks that the best guide for the reading public is the man of taste who 'stands neutral in the controversy' and holds a middle station, between the world and the cell (Gibbs, III, p. 499).

J. Warton's *Essay on Pope* shows signs of the new attitude that was to become general in the last few decades of the century. He calls the dread of pedantry 'a characteristic folly of the present age' and thinks that the English adopted it from the French, 'without considering the reasons that gave rise to it among that people' (vol. II, p. 123). To the men of the world who cry: 'Study life' he answers that the world cannot become known merely by the study of mankind. In his comment on Pope's couplet in the *Epistle to Dr. Arbuthnot* (ll. 163, 164), he defends Bentley and Theobald against Pope's attack. 'Bentley's works' he says, 'exhibit the most striking marks of accurate and extensive erudition, and a vigorous and acute understanding.' The author of *Shakespeare Restored* is called the first editor of the dramatist 'that hit upon the true and rational method of correcting and illustrating his author, that is, by reading such books (whatever trash Pope might call them) as Shakespeare read and by attending to the genius, learning, and notions of his times' (vol. II, pp. 228, 229). Mallet's poem on verbal criticism is called a very feeble and flimsy poem, 'stuffed with illiberal cant about pedantry' (note to vol. II, p. 231). Warton praises the indefatigable researches of Dutch and German editors and thinks it very easy, but ungrateful 'to laugh at collectors of various readings and adjusters of texts.'

From J. Warton's remarks we see clearly that at the time when the second volume of his *Essay* appeared, the reaction against neo-classicism had also affected the attitude towards verbal criticism. The critical literature of the last part of the century offers more illustrations of this remarkable reversal of opinion (Cf. V. Knox, *Essays, Moral and Literary*, 1824, pp. 169 ff.), but there is no need to trace the development of the new conception any further.

BIBLIOGRAPHY

A. TEXTS.

ADDISON JOSEPH, ed. R. Hurd (Bohn's Standard Library). London, 1854—56.

AIKIN, JOHN, Letters from a Father to his Son. London, 2 vols., 1792-1800.
Essays Literary and Miscellaneous. London, 1811.
Memoir of John Aikin by Lucy Aikin, with a Selection of his Miscellaneous Pieces, 2 vols. London, 1823.

ALISON, ARCHIBALD, Essays on the Nature and Principles of Taste. Edinburgh, 1790.

ANON.: An Essay on the New Species of Writing founded by Mr. Fielding: with a Word or two upon the Modern State of Criticism. London, 1751.
Cursory Remarks on Tragedy, on Shakespeare and on certain French and Italian Poets, principally Tragedians. London, 1774.

ARMSTRONG, JOHN, Taste, an Epistle to a young Critic. London, 1753.
[L. Temple] Sketches or Essays on various Subjects. London, 1758.

BACON, FRANCIS, The Advancement of Learning, and The New Atlantis, ed. World's Classics. Oxford, 1906.

BEATTIE, JAMES, Essays (On the Nature and Immutability of Truth, On Poetry and Music, On Laughter, On the Utility of Classical Learning). Edinburgh, 1776.
Dissertations Moral and Critical. London, 1783.

BELSHAM, WILLIAM, Essays Philosophical, Historical and Literary. 2 vols. London, 1789.

BLACKWELL, ANTHONY, The Sacred Classics Defended and Illustrated, 1725.

BLACKWELL, THOMAS, An Enquiry into the Life and Writings of Homer. London, 1735.

BLAIR, HUGH, A Critical Dissertation on the Poems of Ossian. London, 1763.
Lectures on Rhetoric and Belles Lettres. Edinburgh, 1783. (Ed. London, 1833).

BLAKE, WILLIAM, Works, ed. by E. J. Ellis and W. Butler Yeats, 3 vols. London, 1893.

BOILEAU-DESPRÉAUX, NICOLAS, Oeuvres poétiques, ed. Brunetière, 9th ed. 1912.
L'Art poétique (A. S. Cook, The Art of Poetry). Boston, 1892.

BOSWELL, JAMES, Life of Johnson, including Boswell's Journal of a Tour to the Hebrides and Johnson's Diary of a Journey into North Wales, ed. by G. Birkbeck Hill, 6 vols. Oxford, 1887.

BOUHOURS, DOMINIQUE, Entretiens d'Ariste et d'Eugène. Paris, 1671. (Ed. René Radouant. Paris, 1920).
La Manière de bien penser dans les ouvrages d'esprit. Paris, 1687.
Pensées ingénieuses des anciens et des modernes. Paris, 1693.
The Arts of Logick and Rhetorick, interpreted and explained by Father Bouhours, translated by J. Oldmixon. London, 1728.

BROWN, JOHN, Essay on the Characteristics of the Earl of Shaftesbury. London, 1751.
An Estimate of the Manners and Principles of the Times. London, 1757.
An Explanatory Defence of the Estimate of the Manners and Principles of the Times. London, 1758.
The History of the Rise and Progress of Poetry through its several Species. Newcastle, 1764.

BRUMOY, PIERRE, Théâtre des Grecs, 4 vols. Paris, 1730.

BUCKINGHAM, GEORGE VILLIERS, DUKE OF, The Rehearsal, 1671. (Arber's Reprints).

BURKE, EDMUND, A Philosophical Enquiry into the Origin of our Ideas of the Sublime and Beautiful, 1757. (The Works of E. Burke. London, 1826).

BURNEY FRANCES, Diary and Letters, ed. C. Barrett and A. Dobson, 6 vols. London, 1904, 1905.

BYROM, JOHN, The Private Journal and Literary Remains (Remarks Historical and Literary connected with the Palatine Counties of Lancaster and Chester, published by The Chetham Society, vol. XXXII, 1854).

BYSSCHE, EDWARD, The Art of English Poetry. London, 1702; 7th ed., 1724.

CAMPBELL, GEORGE, The Philosophy of Rhetoric. London, 2 vols., 1776. (Ed. Edinburgh, 1816).

CAPELL, EDWARD, Reflections on Originality in Authors; being Remarks on a Letter to Mr. Mason on the Marks of Imitation. London, 1766.

CAWTHORN, JAMES, Poems (Chalmers, The Works of the English Poets, vol. XIV).

CHURCHILL, CHARLES, Poems (Chalmers, The Works of the English Poets, vol. XIV).

COLERIDGE, SAMUEL T., Biographia Literaria, ed. J. Shawcross, 2 vols. Oxford, 1907.
Table Talk, ed. London, 1835.
Coleridge's Literary Criticism, ed. J. W. Mackail. Oxford, 1908.

COOKE, WILLIAM, The Elements of Dramatic Criticism. London, 1775.

COOPER, JOHN GILBERT, Letters concerning Taste. London, 1755; 3rd ed., 1757.

CORNEILLE, PIERRE, Oeuvres (Grands Écrivains de la France), 12 vols., 1862—68.

COWPER, WILLIAM, Works, ed. R. Southey (Bohn's Standard Library), 8 vols. London, 1853.

DACIER, ANDRÉ, La Poétique d'Aristote, traduite en français avec des remarques. Paris, 1692.

DE QUINCEY, THOMAS, Literary Criticism. Oxford, 1909.

DOUGLAS, JOHN, Milton vindicated from the Charge of Plagiarism. London, 1751.

DRYDEN, JOHN, Works, ed. Scott-Saintsbury, 18 vols. Edinburgh, 1882—1893.
Essays, ed. W. P. Ker, 2 vols. Oxford, 1899; 2nd impr. 1926.

DUBOS, JEAN BAPTISTE, Réflexions critiques sur la poésie et sur la peinture. Paris, 1719.

DUFF, WILLIAM, An Essay on Original Genius. London, 1767.

DURHAM, W. H., Critical Essays of the XVIIIth Century. New Haven, 1915.

EDWARDS, THOMAS, The Canons of Criticism, and a Glossary being a Supplement to Mr. Warburton's Edition of Shakespear, 4th ed. London, 1750.

FIELDING, HENRY, Works, with an Essay on his Life and Genius by A. Murphy, 14 vols. London, 1808.
The Covent-Garden Journal, ed. G. E. Jensen. New Haven, 1915.

GERARD, ALEXANDER, An Essay on Taste. London, 1759; 2nd ed., Edinburgh, 1764.
An Essay on Genius. London, 1774.

GIBBON, EDWARD, Miscellaneous Works. With Memoirs of his Life. London, 1796; new ed. with additions, 5 vols. London, 1814.
The Memoirs of The Life of Edward Gibbon, ed. G. Birkbeck Hill. London, 1900.

GOLDSMITH, OLIVER, Works, ed. J. W. M. Gibbs (Bohn's Standard Library), 5 vols. London, 1884—86.
The Miscellaneous Works, ed. D. Masson. London, 1869.

GRAY, THOMAS, The Poems, to which are prefixed Memoirs of the Life and Writings by W. Mason. York, 1775.
The Letters of Thomas Gray, ed. D. C. Tovey, 3 vols. London, 1900—1912.
The Works in Prose and Verse, ed. E. Gosse, 4 vols. London, 1884.
The Correspondence of Gray, Walpole, West and Ashton, 2 vols., ed. by Paget Toynbee. Oxford, 1915.

HARRIS, JAMES, Works, with an Account of his Life etc. by his Son the Earl of Malmesbury, 5 vols. London, 1803.

HARTE, WALTER, Poems (Chalmers, The Works of the English Poets, vol. XVI).

HAYLEY, WILLIAM, Poetical Epistles on Epic Poetry. London, 1782.

Poems and Plays, 6 vols. London, 1785.

HAZLITT, WILLIAM, Lectures on English Poets. London, 1818.

Lectures on the English Comic Writers. London, 1819.

Table Talk, 1821, 22 (Ed. World's Classics. Oxford, 1901).

HISTOIRE de l'Académie des inscriptions et belles lettres, vol. XX.

HOBBES, THOMAS, The English Works, ed. Molesworth, 11 vols. London, 1841.

HOGARTH, WILLIAM, The Analysis of Beauty. London, 1753.

HOOLE, JOHN, Translations of Tasso's Gerusalemme Liberata (1763) and Ariosto's Orlando Furioso (1773). (Chalmers, The Works of the English Poets, vol. XXI).

HUGHES, JOHN, The Works of Mr. Edmund Spenser in six Volumes, with a Glossary. London, 1715.

HUME, DAVID, The Philosophical Works, 4 vols. Boston, 1854.

Essays, Moral, Political and Literary, ed. Green and Grose, 2 vols. London, 1875.

Letters to William Strahan, ed. G. Birkbeck Hill. Oxford, 1888.

HUNT, J. H. LEIGH, Imagination and Fancy. London, 1844.

HURD, RICHARD, Epistolae ad Pisones et Augustum, with an English Commentary and Notes: To which are added Critical Dissertations, 5th ed. London, 1776.

The Works in Prose and Verse of Mr. A. Cowley, with Notes. London 1809.

Works. London, 1811.

Letters from a Late Eminent Prelate to one of his Friends. London, 1808.

Letters on Chivalry and Romance, ed. E. J. Morley. Oxford, 1911.

The Correspondence of Richard Hurd and William Mason. And Letters of Richard Hurd to Thomas Gray, ed. by L. Whibley. Cambridge, 1932.

HUTCHESON, FRANCIS, An Inquiry into the Original of our Ideas of Beauty and Virtue, in two Treatises. London, 1725.

JEFFREY, FRANCIS, Literary Criticism, ed. D. Nichol Smith. Oxford, 1910.

JOHNSON, SAMUEL, A Dictionary of the English Language in which the Words are deduced from their Originals etc., 2 vols. London, 1755.

Works, ed. Robert Lynam, 6 vols. London, 1825.

Works, Literary Club Edition, 16 vols. New York, 1903.

Johnsonian Miscellanies, ed. G. Birkbeck Hill, 2 vols. Oxford, 1897.

Lives of the English Poets, ed. G. Birkbeck Hill, 3 vols. Oxford, 1905.

Johnson on Shakespeare, Essays and Notes Selected, ed. W. Raleigh, 5th impr. Oxford, 1925.

KAMES, HENRY HOME, LORD, Elements of Criticism, 3 vols. Edinburgh, 1762; 6th ed. in two vols., 1785.

KNOX, VICESIMUS, Works, in seven vols. London, 1824.

LANGBAINE, GERARD, Momus Triumphans: or the Plagiaries of the English Stage exposed. London, 1681.

LAUDER, WILLIAM, An Essay on Milton's Use and Imitation of the Moderns in his Paradise Lost. London, 1750.

LE BOSSU, RENÉ, Traité du poème épique. Paris, 1675; 6 ième ed. La Haye, 1714.

LLOYD, ROBERT, Poems (Chalmers, The Works of the English Poets, vol. XV).

LOWTH, ROBERT, Lectures on the Sacred Poetry of the Hebrews, translated into English by G. Gregory. London, 1787.

LYTTELTON, GEORGE, first Baron, Dialogues of the Dead. London, 1760.

MALLET, DAVID, Poems (Chalmers, The Works of the English Poets, vol. XIV).

MASON, JOHN, An Essay on the Powers of Numbers and the Principles of Harmony in Poetical Composition. London, 1749.
An Essay on the Power and Harmony of Prosaic Numbers. London, 1749.
MASON, WILLIAM, Elfrida, A Dramatic Poem written on the Model of the Ancient Greek Tragedy. London, 1752.
Works, 4 vols. London, 1811.
MITFORD, WILLIAM, An Essay upon the Harmony of Language etc. London, 1774.
NICHOLS, JOHN, Illustrations of the Literary History of the Eighteenth Century, etc. intended as a Sequel to the 'Literary Anecdotes', 8 vols. London, 1817—58.
OGILVIE, JOHN, Philosophical and Critical Observations on the Nature, Characters and Various Species of Composition, 2 vols. London, 1774.
PARR, SAMUEL, Tracts by Warburton and a Warburtonian, not admitted into the Collections of their respective Works. London, 1789.
PERCY, THOMAS, Reliques of Ancient English Poetry, 3 vols. London, 1765; 2nd ed., 1767.
Northern Antiquities or a description of the manners, customs, religion, and laws of the ancient Danes, 2 vols. London, 1770.
Letters from Thomas Percy, John Callander, David Herd and others to George Paton. Edinburgh, 1830.
Bishop Percy's Folio Manuscript, ed. J. W. Hales and F. J. Furnivall, 3 vols., 1867—8.
PILES, ROGER DE, The Art of Painting and the Lives of the Painters. London, 1706.
PINKERTON, JOHN, [R. Heron], Letters of Literature. London, 1785.
Literary Correspondence, 2 vols. London, 1830.
POPE, ALEXANDER, Works, ed. Elwin and Courthope, 10 vols., 1871—89.
The Twickenham Edition of the Poems of Alexander Pope (general ed. John Butt), vols. II, IV, V. London, 1939, 1940, 1943.
PYE, HENRY JAMES, A Commentary illustrating the Poetic of Aristotle, by Examples taken chiefly from the Modern Poets. London, 1792.
RAPIN, RENÉ, Oeuvres. Amsterdam, 1693 (Ed. La Haye, 1725).
REYNOLDS, SIR JOSHUA, The Works, ed. by E. Malone, 2 vols. London, 1797.
Discourses, ed. Austin Dobson. Oxford, 1907.
RUFFHEAD, OWEN, The Works of Alexander Pope, 6 vols. London, 1769.
SAINT-ÉVREMOND, CHARLES DE MARGUETEL DE SAINT-DENIS, SEIGNEUR DE, Oeuvres mêlées, ed. Giraud, 3 vols. Paris, 1865.
Critique littéraire, ed. Bossard (Collection des chefs-d'oeuvre méconnus), 1921.
SAINTE-PALAYE, JEAN-BAPTISTE DE LA CURNE DE, Mémoires sur l'ancienne chevalerie. Paris, 1759.
Memoirs of Ancient Chivalry, translated by Mrs. Dobson, 1784.
SAINTSBURY, G., Loci Critici. Boston, 1903.
SCOTT, JOHN, OF AMWELL, Critical Essays on some of the Poems of several English Poets. London, 1785.
SHAFTESBURY, ANTHONY ASHLEY COOPER, EARL OF, Characteristicks of Men, Manners, Opinions, Times. 3 vols. London, 1711.
SHELLEY, PERCY BYSSHE, Literary and Philosophical Criticism, ed. J. Shawcross. Oxford, 1909.
SHENSTONE, WILLIAM, The Works in Verse and Prose, 2 vols. London 1764; 3 vols., 1765.
Select Letters between the Late Duchess of Somerset, Lady Luxborough, Miss Dolman, Mr. Whistler, Mr. R. Dodsley, William Shenstone Esq. And others, ed. by T. Hull, 2 vols. London, 1778.

SIDNEY, SIR PHILIP, The Defense of Poesy, ed. Cook. New York, 1890.

SMART, CHRISTOPHER, The Poems, to which is prefixed an Account of his Life and Writings, 2 vols. Reading, 1791.

SMITH, D. NICHOL, Eighteenth Century Essays on Shakespeare. Glasgow, 1903.

SMITH, G. GREGORY, Elizabethan Critical Essays, 2 vols. Oxford, 1904.

SOAME (or SOAMES), SIR WILLIAM, Translation of Boileau's Art poétique, 1683. (Ed. Cook, The Art of Poetry).

SPENCE, JOSEPH, Polymetis: or an Enquiry concerning the Agreement between the Works of the Roman Poets and the Remains of the Antient Artists. London, 1747.
Anecdotes, Observations and Characters of Books and Men, ed. by S. W. Singer, 1820; 2nd ed., London, 1858.

SPINGARN, J. E., Critical Essays of the Seventeenth Century, 3 vols. Oxford, 1908, 1909.

STERNE, LAURENCE, Tristram Shandy (Works, ed. W. L. Cross, 12 vols. New York, 1904).

STOCKDALE, PERCIVAL, An Inquiry into the Nature and Genuine Laws of Poetry including a particular Defence of the Writings and Genius of Mr. Pope. London, 1778.
Lectures on the truly Eminent English Poets, 2 vols. London, 1807.

TEMPLE, SIR WILLIAM, Essays on Ancient and Modern Learning and on Poetry, ed. J. E. Spingarn. Oxford, 1909.

TWINING, THOMAS, Aristotle's Treatise on Poetry, translated; with Notes on the Translation and on the Original, and Two Dissertations on Poetical and Musical Imitation, 2 vols., 1789; 2nd ed. 1812.
Recreations and Studies of a Country Clergyman of the Eighteenth Century. London, 1882.

TYRWHITT, THOMAS, Observations and Conjectures upon some Passages of Shakespeare. London, 1766.
Poems supposed to have been written at Bristol by Thomas Rowley and others in the Fifteenth Century, 1777.
The Canterbury Tales of Chaucer with an Essay upon his Language and Versification etc., 4 vols., 1775; 5th vol., 1778.

TYTLER, A. FRASER, Essay on the Principles of Translation. London, 1791.

VIAL ET DENISE, Idées et doctrines littéraires du XVIIe siècle, troisième ed. Paris, 1922.
Idées et doctrines littéraires du XVIIIe siècle, quatrième ed. Paris, 1926.

UPTON, JAMES, Spenser's Faerie Queene, 2 vols. London, 1758.

WAKEFIELD, GILBERT, The Works of Alexander Pope, Esq., with Remarks and Illustrations. Warrington, 1794.
The Poems of Mr. Gray. London, 1786.

WARBURTON, WILLIAM, The Works of Alexander Pope, Esq. In Nine Volumes Complete with his last Corrections, Additions and Improvements together with the Commentaries and Notes. London, 1751.

WARTON, JOSEPH, Odes on Various Subjects. London, 1746.
The Works of Virgil in Latin and English, 4 vols. London, 1753.
An Essay on the Writings and Genius of Pope. London, 1756; vol. II, 1782; 5th ed. in 2 vols., 1806.
The Works of Alexander Pope, 9 vols. London, 1797.

WARTON, THOMAS, Observations on the Faerie Queene of Spenser. London, 1754; 2nd ed., 1762.
The History of English Poetry, vol. I, 1774; vol. II, 1778; vol. III, 1781.

Poems upon Several Occasions, English, Italian, and Latin with translations by J. Milton. London, 1785.

WEEKES, NATHANIEL, On the Abuse of Poetry, a Satire. 1752; 2nd ed., 1754.

WILKIE, WILLIAM, Preface to The Epigoniad. (Chalmers, The Works of the English Poets, vol. XVI).

WOOD, ROBERT, An Essay on the Original Genius and Writings of Homer with a comparative View of the Ancient and Present State of the Troade. London, 1769, 1775.

WORDSWORTH, WILLIAM, Literary Criticism, ed. Nowell C. Smith. Oxford, 1905.

WOTTON, WILLIAM, Reflections upon Ancient and Modern Learning. London, 1694; 2nd ed., 1697.

YOUNG, EDWARD, Ocean, An Ode. London, 1728.

Conjectures on Original Composition, ed. E. J. Morley. London, 1918.

PERIODICALS

The British Essayists, ed. by J. Ferguson, 45 vols. London, 1819.

The Critical Review, 1756—1817, vols. 1—144.

Common Sense; Or, The Englishman's Journal, 1737—1739.

Dodsley's Museum, 1746—47.

The Gray's Inn Journal, 1752—1754.

The Gentleman's Magazine; Or, Monthly Intelligencer, 1731—1826.

The Monthly Review, 1749—1845.

The Universal Visiter And Monthly Memorialist for April 1756.

B. HISTORICAL AND CRITICAL STUDIES

ABBREVIATIONS

ELH	A Journal of English Literary History. Baltimore, 1934—
ES	Englische Studien. Leipzig, 1877—
JEGP	The Journal of English and Germanic Philology. Bloomington (later Urbana), 1903—
MLN	Modern Language Notes. Baltimore, 1886—
MLR	The Modern Language Review. Cambridge, 1905—
MP	Modern Philology. Chicago, 1903—
PMLA	The Publications of the Modern Language Association of America. New York, 1886—
PQ	Philological Quarterly. Iowa City, 1922—
RAA	La Revue Anglo-Américaine. Paris, 1923—
SP	Studies in Philology, Chapel Hill, 1904—

ABERCROMBIE, L., Poetry and Contemporary Speech (The English Association Pamphlets). Oxford, 1914.

The Theory of Poetry. London, 1924.

ALDERMAN, W. E., Shaftesbury and the Doctrine of Benevolence in the Eighteenth

Century (Transactions of the Wisconsin Academy of Sciences, Arts and Letters, 1931).

ALDRIDGE, A. O., "Akenside and Imagination" (SP, XLII, 1945).

ATKINS, J. W. H., English Literary Criticism: 17th and 18th Centuries. London, 1951.

AUDRA, E., L'Influence française dans l'oeuvre de Pope. Paris, 1931.
(Bibliothèque de la Revue de littérature comparée, tome 72).

AULT, Norman, New Light on Pope. London, 1949.

BABCOCK, R. W., The Genesis of Shakespeare Idolatry 1766—1799: A Study in English Criticism of the late Eighteenth Century. Univ. of North Car. Press, 1931.

BASIL WILLEY, The Eighteenth Century Background. New York, 1941.

BATE, W. J., Imagination in English Criticism (ELH, 12, 1945).
From Classic to Romantic. Premises of Taste in Eighteenth-Century England. Cambridge (Mass), 1946.

BEERS, H. A., A History of English Romanticism in the Eighteenth Century. London, 1899.

BELL, C. F., Thomas Gray and the Fine Arts (Essays and Studies of the English Association, XXX, 1945).

BENN, A. W., The History of English Rationalism in the 19th Century, 2 vols. London, 1906.

BERGER, P., William Blake; mysticisme et poésie. Paris, 1907.

BLACK, J. B., The Art of History. London, 1926.

BOHN, W. E., John Dryden's Literary Criticism (PMLA, XXII, 1907).

BOND, D. F., 'Distrust' of Imagination in English Neo-classicism (PQ, XIV, 1935).
The Neo-classical Psychology of the Imagination (ELH, 4, 1937).

BREDVOLD, L. I., Dryden, Hobbes and the Royal Society (MP, XXV, 1928).
The Intellectual Milieu of John Dryden: Studies in some Aspects of Seventeenth Century Thought (Univ. of Michigan Publ. — Language and Literature, XII).

BRETT, R. L., Coleridge's Theory of the Imagination (Essays and Studies of the English Association, XXXIV, 1949).

BROWN, J. E., The Critical Opinions of Samuel Johnson. Princeton Univ. Press, 1926.

BRUNETIÈRE, T., L'Esthétique de Boileau. (Études critiques, 6ième série, 1899).

BULLITT, JOHN and BATE, W. J., Distinctions between Fancy and Imagination in Eighteenth Century English Criticism (MLN, LX, 1945).

BURY, J. B., The Idea of Progress. London, 1920.

BUTCHER, S. H., Aristotle's Theory of Poetry and Fine Art. London, 1895; 4th ed., 1923.

CATLIN, S. E. G., Thomas Hobbes as Philosopher, Publicist and Man of Letters: An Introduction. Oxford, 1922.

CHARLANNE, L., L'influence française en Angleterre au XVIIe siècle. Le theâtre et la critique. Paris, 1906.

CHASE, S. P., Hazlitt as a Critic of Art (PMLA, XXXIX, 1924).

CLARK, A. F. B., Boileau and the French Classical Critics in England (1660—1830) [Bibliothèque de la revue de littérature comparée]. Paris, 1925.

CLARK, H. H., The Romanticism of Edward Young. Transactions of the Wisconsin Academy of Sciences, Arts and Letters, vol. XXIV, 1929).

CLUTTON-BROCK, A., Description in Poetry (Essays and Studies by Members of the Eng. Association, vol. II). Oxford, 1911.
Essays on Literature and Life. London, 1926.

COLLINS, J. CHURTON, Studies in Poetry and Criticism. London, 1905.

COOK, A. S., The Art of Poetry, The Poetical Treatises of Horace, Vida and Boileau with the Translations. Boston, 1892.

COOPER, L., Methods and Aims in the Study of Literature. Boston, 1915.
CORY, H. E., Spenser, Thomson and Romanticism (PMLA, XXVI, 1911).
The Critics of Edmund Spenser (University of California Publications in Modern Philology, vol. II, 1911).
Edmund Spenser; A Critical Study (ibid., vol. V, 1917).
COURTHOPE, W. J., Addison (English Men of Letters). London, 1884.
The Liberal Movement in English Literature. London, 1885.
Life in Poetry: Law in Taste. London, 1901.
A History of English Poetry, 6 vols. London, 1895—1910.
Ancient and Modern Romance (The British Academy). Oxford, 1911.
COURTNEY, W. and SMITH, D. N., A Bibliography of S. Johnson. Oxford, 1915; 2nd ed. 1925.
CRANE, R. S., BREDVOLD, L. I. and others, English Literature of the Restoration and Eighteenth Century: A current Bibliography (PQ, V, 1926 and ff.). This is being reprinted in book-form. The title is 'English Literature 1660—1800, A Bibliography of Modern Studies compiled for the Philological Quarterly'. Vol. I (1926—1938) appeared in Princetown, 1950.
Imitation of Spenser and Milton in the Early Eighteenth Century: A New Document (SP, XV, 1918).
A Neglected Mid-eighteenth Century Plea for Originality and its Authors (PQ, XIII, 1934).
CROSS, W. L., The Life and Times of Laurence Sterne, 2 vols. New Haven, 1925.
CRUICKSHANK, A. H., Thomas Parnell, What was wrong with the Eighteenth Century (Essays and Studies by Members of the English Association, vol. VII). Oxford, 1921.
DANIELS, W. M., Saint-Évremond en Angleterre. Versailles, 1907.
DE MAAR, H. G., Elizabethan Romance in the Eighteenth Century. Diss. Amsterdam, 1924.
DENNIS, J., Studies in English Literature. London, 1876.
The Age of Pope. London, 1894.
Dr. Johnson (Bell's Miniature Series of Great Writers). London, 1905.
DOBSON, A., Eighteenth Century Vignettes, 3 vols. London, 1892—96.
DONCIEUX, G., Un Jésuite homme de lettres: le Père Bouhours. Paris, 1886.
DOUGHTY, O., English Lyric in the Age of Reason. London, 1922.
Forgotten Lyrics of the 18th Century. London, 1924.
DRAPER, J. W., Aristotelian 'Mimesis' in Eighteenth Century England (PMLA, XXXVI, 1921).
William Mason, A Study in Eighteenth Century Culture. New York, 1924.
The Funeral Elegy and the Rise of English Romanticism. New York, 1929.
Eighteenth Century English Aesthetics, a Bibliography. Heidelberg, 1931 (Anglistische Forschungen, 71).
Poetry and Music in Eighteenth Century Aesthetics (ES, LXVII, 1932).
The Rise of English Neo-classicism (RAA, X, 1933).
DRENNON, H., Scientific Rationalism and James Thomson's Poetic Art (SP, XXXI, 1934).
DUTTON, S. B., The French Aristotelian Formalists and Thomas Rymer (PMLA, XXIX, 1914).
ELIOT, T. S., The Use of Poetry and the Use of Criticism. London, 1933.
A Note on the Verse of John Milton (Essays and Studies of the English Association, XXI, 1936).
ELLIS, A. M., Horace's Influence on Dryden (PQ, IV, 1925).

ELTON, O., The Augustan Ages (Periods of European Literature, ed. by Saintsbury, VIII). Edinburgh, 1899.
A Survey of English Literature (1780—1830), 2 vols., 1912.
Reason and Enthusiasm in the Eighteenth Century (Essays and Studies by Members of the Eng. Association, vol. X). Oxford, 1924.
ESSAYS on the Eighteenth Century, presented to D. N. Smith. Oxford, 1945.
FAIRCHILD, H. N., The Noble Savage: A Study in Romantic Naturalism. New York, 1928.
The Romantic Quest. New York, 1931.
Protestantism and the Cult of Sentiment 1700—1740. New York, 1939. (Vol. I of his 'Religions Trends in English Poetry').
FLASDIECK, H. M., John Brown (1715—1766) und seine Dissertation On Poetry and Music (Studien zur englischen Philologie, LXVIII). Halle, 1924.
FLINT, R., History of the Philosophy of History. Edinburgh, 1893.
FOERSTER, D. M., Homer in English Criticism: the Historical Approach in the Eighteenth Century (Yale Studies in English, vol. CV. New Haven, 1947).
FOWLER, T., Shaftesbury and Hutcheson. London, 1882.
Locke (English Men of Letters). London, 1909.
GARNETT, R., The Age of Dryden. London, 1895.
GAUSSEN, A. C. C., Percy: Prelate and Poet. London, 1908.
GAYLEY, C. M. and KURTZ, B. P., Methods and Materials of Literary Criticism: Lyric, Epic and Allied Forms of Poetry. Boston, 1919.
GAYLEY, C. M. and SCOTT, F. N., A Guide to the Literature of Aesthetics. Berkeley (California), 1890.
An Introduction to the Methods and Materials of Literary Criticism. Boston, 1899.
GILBERT, A. H., Literary Criticism: Plato to Dryden. New York, 1940.
GILBERT, A. H. and SNUGGS, H. L., On the Relation of Horace to Aristotle in Lit. Crit. (JEGP, XLVI, 1947).
GOAD, C., Horace in the English Literature of the Eighteenth Century (Yale Studies in English, vol. LVIII). New Haven, 1918.
GOLDRING, D., Reputations, Essays in Criticism. London, 1920.
GOLLANCZ, SIR I., The Middle Ages in the Lineage of English Poetry. London, 1921.
GOOCH, G. P., History and Historians in the 19th Century. London, 1913.
GORDON, G. S., English Literature and the Classics. Oxford, 1912.
GOSSE, E., Two Pioneers of Romanticism, Joseph and Thomas Warton (Warton Lectures on English Poetry). Oxford, 1915.
GRAHAM, H. G., Scottish Men of Letters in the Eighteenth Century. London, 1901.
GRANT, A. J., English Historians. London, 1906.
GRANT, F. R. C., Life and Writings of S. Johnson (Great Writers Series). London, 1887.
GRAVES, R., Recollection of some Particulars in the Life of the late W. Shenstone, 1788.
GREEN, C. C., Neo-classic Theory of Tragedy in England during the Eighteenth Century (Harvard Studies in English, XI, 1934).
HAGSTRUM, J. H., Johnson's Conception of the Beautiful, the Pathetic, and the Sublime (PMLA, LXIV, 1949).
HALE, E. E., The Influence of Salvator Rosa in English Literature of the Eighteenth Century (PMLA, XXIV, 1909).
HALES, J. W., Introduction to Johnson's Lives of the Poets, ed. Mrs. Napier. London, 1890.
HAMELIUS, P., Die Kritik in der englischen Literatur des 17. und 18. Jahrhunderts

(Bibliothèque de la faculté de philosophie et lettres de l'univ. de Liège). Bruxelles, 1897.

HAMM, V. M., A Seventeenth Century French Source for Hurd's Letters on Chivalry and Romance (PMLA, LII, 1937).

The Imagination in English Neo-classical Thought and Literature (1650—1780) [Harvard Univ. Summaries of Theses, 1932].

Addison and the Pleasures of the Imagination (MLN, LII, 1937).

HAVENS, R. D., Seventeenth Century Notices of Milton (ES, XL).

Romantic Aspects of the Age of Pope (PMLA, XXVII, 1912).

The Influence of Milton on English Poetry. Cambridge (Mass.), 1922.

Changing Taste in the Eighteenth Century. A Study of Dryden's and Dodsley's Miscellanies (PMLA, XLIV, 1929).

Johnson's Distrust of the Imagination (ELH, 10, 1943).

HAZELTINE, A. I., A Study of W. Shenstone and of his Critics. Menasha, Wisconsin, 1918.

HECHT, H., Thomas Percy and William Shenstone, Ein Briefwechsel aus der Entstehungszeit der Reliques of Ancient English Poetry (Quellen und Forschungen, Heft 103). Strassburg, 1909.

Daniel Webb, Ein Beitrag zur englischen Ästhetik des achtzehnten Jahrhunderts. Mit einem Abdruck der Remarks on the Beauties of Poetry (1762). Hamburg, 1920.

HIBBEN. J. G., The Philosophy of the Enlightenment (Epochs of Philosophy, vol. I). London, 1910.

HILL, G. BIRKBECK, Dr. Johnson, his Friends and Critics. London, 1878.

HOOKER, E. N., The Discussion of Taste, from 1750 to 1770, and the New Trends in Literary Criticism (PMLA, XLIX, 1934).

The Critical Works of John Dennis, 2 vols. Baltimore, 1939, 1943.

HOSTE, J. W., Johnson and his Circle. London, 1900.

HOUSTON, P. H., Doctor Johnson, A Study in Eighteenth Century Humanism. Cambridge (Mass.), 1923.

HUDSON, W. H., Johnson and Goldsmith and their Poetry (Poetry and Life Series, vol. II). London, 1918; repr. 1922.

HUXLEY, T. H., Hume (English Men of Letters). London, 1878.

HYETT and BAZELEY, Chattertoniana. Gloucester, 1914.

JEBB, R. C., Bentley (English Men of Letters). London, 1882.

JONES, R. F., Lewis Theobald: A Contribution to English Scholarship with some Unpublished Letters. New York, 1919.

Science and English Prose Style in the third quarter of the Seventeenth Century (PMLA, XLV, 1930).

Ancients and Moderns, A Study of the Background of the Battle of the Books (Washington Univ. Studies — New Series. Language and Literature. — no. 6. St. Louis, 1936).

KALLICH, M., The Association of Ideas and Critical Theory in XVIII-century England. Baltimore 1945 (reprinted in ELH, 12, 1945).

The Association of Ideas and Akenside's Pleasures of Imagination (MLN, LXII, 1947).

KENNEDY, W. L., The English Heritage of Coleridge of Bristol, 1798: the Basis in Eighteenth-Century English Thought for his distinction between Imagination and Fancy (Yale Studies in English, CIV. New Haven, 1947).

KER, W. P., Collected Essays, ed. Whibley, 2 vols. London, 1925.

KILVERT, Memoirs of the Life and Writings of the Right. Rev. Richard Hurd. London, 1860.

KING, R. W., Italian Influence on English Scholarship and Literature (MLR, XX, Jan. 1925).

KRANTZ, E., Essai sur l'esthétique de Descartes. Paris, 1882.

LAMPRECHT, S. P., The Role of Descartes in Seventeenth Century England (Studies in the History of Ideas, vol. III. Columbia Univ. Press 1935).

LANGDON, I., Milton's Theory of Poetry and Fine Art (Cornell Studies in English). New Haven, 1924.

LEAVIS, F. R., Revaluation. London, 1936.

LECKY, W. E. H., A History of England in the 18th Century. London, 1878—90.

LEEDY, P. F., Genres Criticism and the Significance of Warton's Essay on Pope (JEGP, XLV, 1946).

LOMBARD, A., La querelle des anciens et des modernes, L'Abbé du Bos. Neuchâtel, 1908.
L'Abbé du Bos, un initiateur de la pensée moderne. Paris, 1913.

LOUNSBURY, T. R., Shakespeare as a Dramatic Artist. New York, 1911.

LOVEJOY, A. O., On the Discrimination of Romanticisms (PMLA, XXXIX, 1924).
"Nature" as Aesthetic Form (MLN, XLII, 1927).
Optimism and Romanticism (PMLA, XLII, 1927).
The Parallel of Deism and Classicism (MP, XXIX, 1932).
The Chinese Origin of a Romanticism (JEGP, XXXII, 1933).

MACAULAY, T. B., Critical and Historical Essays, ed. Leipzig 1850, 5 vols.

MAC CLINTOCK, W. D., Joseph Warton's Essay on Pope, A History of the Five Editions. Univ. of North Car. Press, 1933.

MAC LEAN, K., John Locke and English Literature of the 18th Century. New Haven, 1936.

MAINZER, P., Die schöne Literatur Englands und die literarische Kritik in einigen der kleineren englischen Zeitschriften des 18. Jahrhunderts. Strassburg, 1911.

MANWARING, E. WHEELER, Italian Landscape in Eighteenth Century England. New York, 1925.

MARGRAF, E., Einfluss der deutschen Literatur auf die englische am Ende des achtzehnten und ersten Drittel des neunzehnten Jahrhunderts. Diss. Leipzig, 1901.

MARTIN, L. C., Thomas Warton and the early Poems of Milton (Proceedings of the British Academy, XX, 1936).

MILLAR, J. H., The Mid Eighteenth Century (Periods of European Literature, ed. by Saintsbury). Edinburgh, 1902.

MILLER, G. M., The Historical Point of View in English Literary Criticism from 1570—1770 (Anglistische Forschungen, 35). Heidelberg, 1913.

MONK, S. H., The Sublime: A Study of Critical Theories in XVIII-Century England. New York, Mod. L. A. of Am. (General Series), 1935.

MOORE, C. A., Shaftesbury and the Ethical Poets in England, 1700—1760 (PMLA, XXXI, 1916).

MORLEY, E. J., Joseph Warton, a Comparison of the Essay on the Genius of Pope with his Edition of Pope's Works (Essays and Studies by Members of the Eng. Association, vol. IX). Oxford, 1924.

MOULTON, C. W., The Library of Literary Criticism of English and American Authors. Buffalo, 1901—05.

NETHERCOT, A. H., The term 'Metaphysical Poets' before Johnson (MLN, XXXVII, 1922).
The Reputation of the 'Metaphysical Poets' during the 17th Century (JEGP, XXIII, 1924).
The Reputation of the 'Metaphysical Poets' during the Age of Pope (PQ, IV, 1925).

The Reputation of the 'Metaphysical Poets' during the Age of Johnson and the Romantic Revival (SP, XXII, 1925).

NEUMANN, W., Die Bedeutung Home's für die Ästhetik und sein Einfluss auf die deutschen Ästhetiker. Halle, 1894.

NORTHRUP, C. S., A Bibliography of Thomas Gray, Oxford. 1917.

PATTISON, M. Essays, collected by H. Nettleship. Oxford, 1889.

PAUL, H. G., John Dennis: his Life and Criticism. New York, 1911.

PERRY, T. S., English Literature in the 18th Century. New York, 1883.

PHELPS, W. L., The Beginning of the English Romantic Movement. New York, 1893.

PYLES, T., The Romantic Side of Dr Johnson (ELH, 11, 1944).

RADTKE, B., Henry Fielding als Kritiker. Berlin, 1926.

RALEIGH, SIR WALTER, Six Essays on Johnson. Oxford, 1910.

RIGAULT, M. H., Histoire de la querelle des anciens et des modernes. Paris, 1856.

RINAKER, C., Thomas Warton: A Biographical and Critical Study (Univ. of Illinois Studies in Lang. and Lit., vol. II, 1916).

ROBERTS, W. R., Longinus and the Sublime. Cambridge, 1907.

ROBERTSON, J. G., Studies in the Genesis of Romantic Theory in the Eighteenth Century. Cambridge, 1923.

ROBERTSON, J. M., Essays towards a Critical Mood. London, 1889.

New Essays towards a Critical Mood. London, 1897.

Shaftesbury's Characteristics. London, 1900.

Pioneer Humanists. London, 1907.

Gibbon (Life Stories of Famous Men). London, 1925.

ROSENBERG, A., Longinus in England bis zum Ende des 18. Jahrhunderts. Berlin, 1917.

ROUTH, J., The Rise of Classical English Criticism. New Orleans, 1915.

SAINTSBURY, G., Essays in English Literature (1780—1860). London, 1891; 2nd series, 1895.

History of Criticism and Literary Taste in Europe, 3 vols. Edinburgh, 1900—04.

A History of English Criticism. Edinburgh, 1911.

The Peace of the Augustans. London, 1916.

SANDYS, SIR J. E., A History of Classical Scholarship. Cambridge, 1906—08.

SAUDÉ, E., Die Grundlagen der literarischen Kritik bei Joseph Addison. Weimar, 1906.

SCHÖFFLER, H., Protestantismus und Literatur. Leipzig, 1922.

SCOTT ELLEDGE, The Background and Development in English Criticism of the Theories of Generality and Particularity (PMLA, LXII, 1947).

(discussed by W. R. Keast in English Lit. 1660—1800: A current Bibliography, PQ, XXVII, 1949).

SECCOMBE, T., The Age of Johnson. London, 1909; reprinted 1923.

SHELLEY, H. C., Life and Letters of Edward Young. London, 1914.

SHOFIELD, W. H., Chivalry in English Literature (Harvard Studies in Comparative Literature, vol. II, 1912).

SMITH, A. L., Richard Hurd's Letters on Chivalry and Romance (ELH, 6, 1939).

SMITH, D. NICHOL, Shakespeare in the Eighteenth Century. Oxford, 1928.

SPINGARN, J. E., A History of Literary Criticism in the Renaissance. New York, 1899; 5th ed. 1925.

Creative Criticism. New York, 1917.

SPITTAL, J. K., Contemporary Criticisms of Dr. Johnson. London, 1923.

SPURGEON, C. F. E., Five Hundred Years of Chaucer Criticism and Allusion. Cambridge, 1925.

STEDMAN, E. C., The Nature and Elements of Poetry. Boston and New York, 1892.

STEEVES, H. ROSS, Learned Societies and English Literary Scholarship in Great Britain and the United States. New York, 1913.

STEEVES, G. W., Francis Bacon: A Sketch of his Life, Works and Literary Friends, 1910.

STEINKE, M. W., Edward Young's 'Conjectures on Original Composition' in England and Germany. New York, 1917.

STEPHEN, L., History of English Thought in the Eighteenth Century, 2 vols. London, 1876.

Johnson (English Men of Letters). London, 1878.

Pope (English Men of Letters). London, 1880.

English Literature and Society in the 18th Century. London, 1904.

Hobbes (English Men of Letters). London, 1904.

STOKOE, T. W., German Influence in the English Romantic Period. Cambridge. 1926.

STUART, D. M., Landscape in Augustan Verse (Essays and Studies of the Eng. Ass., XXVI, 1941).

STUART TEGGART, Dr. Johnson as a Literary Critic (The Westminster Review, Sept. 1913).

SWEDENBORG, H. T., The Theory of the Epic in England, 1650—1800 (Univ. of Col. Publ. in Eng., XV, 1944).

SWINBURNE, A. C., William Blake, 1868 (Ed. Heinemann, 1925).

SYMONDS, J. A., Essays Speculative and Suggestive, 2 vols. London, 1890.

THIELKE, K. L. F., Literatur und Kunstkritik in ihren Wechselbeziehungen. Ein Beitrag zur englischen Ästhetik des 18. Jahrhunderts (Studien zur englischen Philologie, LXXXIV). Halle, 1935.

THOMPSON, D. W., Montani, Saint Évremond, and Longinus (MLN, LI, 1936).

THORPE, CL. D., Addison and Hutcheson on the Imagination (ELH, 2, 1935).

The Imagination: Coleridge versus Wordsworth (PQ, 1939).

The Aesthetic Theory of Thomas Hobbes (Univ. of Michigan Publ. - Language and Literature, XVIII, 1940).

TILLOTSON, S., Eighteenth-Century Poetic Diction (Essays and Studies of the Eng. Ass., XXV, 1940).

'Warton' on the Rowley Papers (MLR, XXXV, 1940).

TROWBRIDGE, H., Joseph Warton's Classification of English Poets (MLN, LI, 1936).

Bishop Hurd: A Reinterpretation (PMLA, LVIII, 1943).

TUCKER, F. G., The Foreign Debt of English Literature. London, 1907.

TUPPER, C. E., Essays erroneously attributed to Goldsmith (PMLA, XXXIX, 1924).

UPHAM, A. H., The French Influence in English Literature. New York, 1908.

VAUGHAN, C. E., English Literary Criticism. London, 1903.

WARD, W. S., Some Aspects of the Conservative Attitude toward Poetry in English Criticism, 1798—1820 (PMLA, LX, 1945).

WARNER, J. H., The Basis of J. J. Rousseau's Contemporaneous Reputation in England (MLN, LV, 1940).

Émile in Eighteenth-Century England (PMLA, LIX, 1944).

WASSERMAN, E. R., Another Eighteenth-Century Distinction between Fancy and Imagination (MLN, LXIV, 1949).

WHIPPLE, E. P., Essays and Reviews, 2 vols. Boston. 1861.

WHITNEY, L., Thomas Blackwell, A Disciple of Shaftesbury (PQ, V, 1926).

WILLIAMS, I. A., Dr. Johnson in Poetry (The Cornhill Magazine, May, 1923).

Seven Eighteenth-Century Bibliographies. 1924.

WILLIAMSON, G., The Restoration Revolt against Enthusiasm (SP, XXX, 1933).

WOOD, P. S., The Opposition to Neo-classicism in England between 1660 and 1700 (PMLA, XLIII, 1928).

WOODHOUSE, A. S. P., Collins and the Creative Imagination: A Study in the Critical Background of his Odes (1746) [Studies in Eng. by Members of Univ. College, Toronto. Univ. of Toronto Press, 1931].

WOOLL, J., Biographical Memoirs of the late Rev^d. J. Warton. London, 1806.

WORSFOLD, W. BASIL, The Principles of Criticism. London, 1897. New ed. 1923. On the Exercise of Judgment in Literature. London, 1900; reprinted 1925.

WRIGHT, C. H. C., French Classicism. Cambridge (Mass.), 1920.

WYLIE, L. J., Studies in the Evolution of English Criticism. Boston, 1894.

INDEX